The Mutual Fund Portfolio Planner

The Mutual Fund Portfolio Planner

A Guide for Selecting the Best Funds for You in Today's Market

Richard C. Dorf

Probus Publishing
Chicago, Illinois

© RICHARD C. DORF, 1988

ALL RIGHTS RESERVED. No part of this publication may be reproduced, stored in a retrieval system, or transmitted, in any form or by any means, electronic, mechanical, photocopying, recording or otherwise, without the prior written permission of the publisher and the copyright holder.

This publication is designed to provide accurate and authoritative information in regard to the subject matter covered. It is sold with the understanding that the publisher is not engaged in rendering legal, accounting or other professional service. If legal advice or other expert assistance is required, the services of a competent professional person should be sought.

FROM A DECLARATION OF PRINCIPLES JOINTLY ADOPTED BY A COMMITTEE OF THE AMERICAN BAR ASSOCIATION AND A COMMITTEE OF PUBLISHERS.

Library of Congress Cataloging in Publication Data Available

ISBN: 0-917253-94-9

Printed in the United States of America

1 2 3 4 5 6 7 8 9 0

Preface

Even the casual reader of the financial news clearly sees the growth in the number and types of mutual funds. Advances in fund management and distribution offer the investor an enviable opportunity to own a broadly diversified portfolio of mutual funds and achieve above-average returns.

The goal of this book is to provide you with a tool for selecting and rearranging your portfolio of funds. *The Mutual Fund Portfolio Planner* will take you on the path to successful investing through difficult times. Addressing 19 classifications of funds, we cut right to the characteristics of these funds and show how they may fit into the portfolio of all investors, be they young professional, middle-aged family person, or retired.

You will see how to construct a portfolio of leading funds and learn what factors to look for in order to succeed in up or down markets. In short, *The Mutual Fund Portfolio Planner* will help you to profit continually from the vast array of mutual funds while avoiding the crush of news and overwhelming numbers of funds.

A debt of gratitude is owed to many, with a special note of thanks to Reg Green of Mutual Fund News Service and the people at Probus Publishing. Thanks also to Maren Murphy, who typed the manuscript.

Richard C. Dorf

Contents

PART I: TYPES OF FUNDS

Chapter 1: Introduction 1
  More on the Matter of Risk 2
  Risk Tolerance 2
    Establishing a Portfolio of Mutual Funds 4
    Market Timing 5
    The Family of Funds Approach to Market Timing 6
    Selecting Mutual Funds 6
  The Plan of the Book 7

Chapter 2: Mutual Fund Basics 9
  What Are Mutual Funds? 9
  The Advantages and Disadvantages of Mutual Funds 9
    Advantages 9
    Load Charges 10
  Classifications of Mutual Funds 12
    By Investment Goal 12
    By Risk 13

Chapter 3: Investment-Grade Corporate Bond Funds 15
  Background Information 15
    Type of Security 15
    Risk/Stability 15
  Special Benefits and Exposures 15
    Investment Quality 16
    Interest-Rate Risk 16
    Determining Yields of Bond Funds 17
  Portfolio Fit 17
  Six Representative Investment Grade Bond Funds 18
    Capital Preservation Treasury Note Trust 18
    Nicholas Income Fund 19
    Northeast Investors Trust 20
    T. Rowe Price New Income Fund 20

T. Rowe Price Short-Term Bond Fund *21*
Vanguard Qualified Dividend Portfolio II Fund *21*

Chapter 4: High-Yield Corporate Bond Funds **29**

Background Information *29*
   Type of Security *29*
   Risk/Stability *29*
Special Benefits and Exposures *30*
   Default of Junk Bonds *30*
   Junk Bonds Defaults and Total Returns *31*
Portfolio Fit *31*
Six Representative High-Yield Corporate Bond Funds *32*
   Bull and Bear High Yield Fund *32*
   Financial High Yield Bond Fund *33*
   Pacific Horizon High Yield Bond Fund *33*
   T. Rowe Price High Yield Fund *33*
   Strong Income Fund *35*
   Vanguard Fixed Income High Yield Fund *35*

Chapter 5: GNMA and Government Bond Funds **43**

Background Information *43*
   Type of Security *43*
   Risk/Stability *43*
Special Benefits and Exposures *44*
   Interest Rates and Prepayments *44*
   Income Vulnerability *44*
   Face Value Vulnerability *44*
Portfolio Fit *44*
Seven Representative GNMA and Government Bond Funds *45*
   Amev U.S. Government Securities Fund *46*
   Benham GNMA Fund *46*
   Dreyfus GNMA Fund *46*
   Fidelity Government Securities Fund *46*
   Lexington GNMA Fund *47*
   T. Rowe Price GNMA Fund *47*
   Vanguard GNMA Fund *47*

Chapter 6: Convertible Securities Funds **57**

Background Information *57*
   Type of Security *57*
Recent Performance of Convertible Securities *58*
Special Benefits and Exposures *58*

Contents

      Limited Downward Risk   *58*
      Market Opportunity   *58*
      Bears on Both Sides   *58*
   Portfolio Fit   *59*
   Five Representative Convertible Securities Funds   *59*
      Dreyfus Convertible Securities Fund   *59*
      Calamos Convertible Income Fund   *60*
      Phoenix Convertible Fund   *62*
      Putnam Convertible Income-Growth Trust   *62*
      Value Line Convertible Fund   *62*

Chapter 7: Short- and Intermediate-Term Tax-Exempt Funds   71

   Background Information   *71*
      Type of Security   *71*
      Risk/Stability   *71*
   Portfolio Fit   *72*
   Five Representative Short- and Intermediate-Term Tax-Exempt Funds   *72*
      Fidelity Limited Term Municipals   *72*
      T. Rowe Price Tax Free Short-Intermediate Fund   *73*
      Stein Roe Intermediate Municipals   *74*
      USAA Tax Exempt Intermediate Term Fund   *74*
      Vanguard Municipals—Intermediate Term Fund   *74*

Chapter 8: Long-Term Tax-Exempt Bond Funds   81

   Background Information   *81*
      Type of Security   *81*
      Risk/Stability   *81*
   Special Benefits and Exposures   *81*
      Price (NAV)   *82*
      State and Municipal Tax Exemptions   *82*
   Ten Representative Long-Term Tax-Exempt Bond Funds   *83*
      Dreyfus Tax Exempt Bond Fund   *83*
      Fidelity Aggressive Tax Free Fund   *84*
      Fidelity High Yield Municipals Fund   *84*
      Financial Tax Free Income Shares   *85*
      T. Rowe Price Tax Free Income Fund   *85*
      Putnam Tax Exempt Income Fund   *86*
      Scudder Managed Municipal Bond Fund   *86*
      Shearson Managed Municipal Bond Fund   *87*
      Stein Roe Managed Municipal Bond Fund   *87*
      Vanguard Municipal High Yield Fund   *88*

Chapter 9: Balanced Funds 99
Background Information *99*
   Type of Security *99*
   Risk/Stability *99*
Portfolio Fit *99*
Six Representative Balanced Funds *100*
   Axe-Houghton Fund B *100*
   Dodge & Cox Balanced Fund *101*
   Loomis Sayles Mutual Fund *101*
   Strong Investment Fund *102*
   Wellesley Fund *103*
   Wellington Fund *105*

Chapter 10: Equity Income Funds 113
Background Information *113*
   Type of Security *113*
   Risk/Stability *113*
Special Benefits and Exposures *113*
   Increasing Income *113*
   Downside Protection *113*
   Improvements under New Tax Laws *114*
Portfolio Fit *114*
Six Representative Equity Income Funds *115*
   Fidelity Equity Income Fund *115*
   Fidelity Industrial Income Fund *116*
   GIT Equity Income Fund *116*
   Lindner Dividend Fund *116*
   T. Rowe Price Equity Income Fund *117*
   Safeco Income Fund *118*

Chapter 11: Growth and Income Funds 127
Background Information *127*
   Type of Security *127*
   Methods *127*
   Risk/Stability *127*
Portfolio Fit *128*
Eight Representative Growth and Income Funds *128*
   Copley Fund *129*
   Eaton Vance Total Return Trust *129*
   Evergreen Total Return Fund *130*

Contents   XI

    Mutual Qualified Income Fund   *131*
    Mutual Shares Fund   *132*
    Selected American Shares Fund   *132*
    Strong Total Return Fund   *133*
    Windsor II Fund   *135*

Chapter 12: Growth Funds   145
  Background Information   *145*
    Type of Security   *145*
    Risk/Stability   *145*
  Special Benefits and Exposures   *145*
    Market Effects   *146*
  Portfolio Fit   *146*
  Nine Representative Growth Funds   *146*
    Acorn Fund   *146*
    Boston Company Capital Appreciation Fund   *148*
    Dodge & Cox Stock Fund   *148*
    The Evergreen Fund   *150*
    Ivy Growth Fund   *150*
    Nicholas Fund   *151*
    Partners Fund   *152*
    T. Rowe Price Growth Stock Fund   *152*
    Quest for Value Fund   *153*

Chapter 13: Aggressive Growth Funds   165
  Background Information   *165*
    Type of Security   *165*
    Risk/Stability   *165*
  Special Benefits and Exposures   *165*
    Speculative Strategies   *165*
    Volatility   *165*
    Specialty Funds   *166*
  Portfolio Fit   *166*
  Eight Representative Aggressive Growth Funds   *166*
    Bruce Fund   *166*
    Fidelity Magellan Fund   *167*
    Lehman Capital Fund   *168*
    Loomis Sayles Capital Development Fund   *168*
    Manhattan Fund   *170*
    Pacific Horizon Aggressive Growth Fund   *170*

    Tudor Fund   *170*
    Twentieth Century Select Fund   *171*

Chapter 14: International Funds   181
    Background Information   *181*
        Type of Security   *181*
        Risk/Stability   *181*
    Special Benefits and Exposures   *182*
        Volatility   *182*
        Regional Funds   *184*
        The Falling Dollar Factor in 1986   *184*
    Portfolio Fit   *184*
    Ten Representative International Funds   *184*
        Fidelity Overseas Fund   *185*
        G. T. Pacific Growth Fund   *186*
        Kemper International Fund   *186*
        T. Rowe Price International Fund   *187*
        Putnam International Equities Fund   *188*
        Scudder International Fund   *188*
        SoGen International Fund   *188*
        Templeton World Fund   *190*
        Transatlantic Fund   *190*
        Vanguard World-International Fund   *191*

Chapter 15: Technology Funds   203
    Background Information   *203*
        Type of Security   *203*
        Risk/Stability   *203*
    Portfolio Fit   *203*
    Six Representative Technology Funds   *204*
        Alliance Technology Fund   *204*
        Fidelity Select Technology Fund   *205*
        Financial Strategic Technology Fund   *206*
        Nova Fund   *206*
        Vanguard Technology Fund   *208*
        Medical Technology Fund   *209*

Chapter 16: Energy and Utility Funds   217
    Energy and Natural Resource Funds   *217*
        Background Information   *217*
            Type of Security   *217*

Contents XIII

      Risk/Stability *217*
    Special Benefits and Exposures *217*
      Price and Supply *217*
      Inflation *217*
  Utility Funds *218*
    Background Information *218*
      Type of Security *218*
      Risk/Stability *218*
    Special Benefits and Exposures *219*
      The Nature of the Business *219*
      Nuclear Power Issues *219*
      The Future *219*
  Portfolio Fit *219*
    Energy and Natural Resource Funds *219*
    Utility Funds *220*
  Seven Representative Energy and Utility Funds *220*
    Fidelity Select Energy Fund *220*
    Fidelity Select Utilities Fund *221*
    Neuberger & Berman Energy Fund *222*
    T. Rowe Price New Era Fund *223*
    Prudential-Bache Utility Fund *224*
    Stratton Monthly Dividend Shares *224*
    Vanguard Energy Fund *226*

Chapter 17: Small-Company Growth Funds *235*
  Background Information *235*
    Type of Security *235*
    Risk/Stability *235*
  Special Benefits and Exposures *236*
    Volatility *236*
    Price/Earnings Ratio *236*
    Continuing Effects of the 1986–87 Bull Market *237*
  Portfolio Fit *237*
  Seven Representative Small-Company Growth Funds *237*
    Babson Enterprise Fund *237*
    Fidelity OTC Fund *238*
    Janus Venture Fund *239*
    Mathers Fund *239*
    Nicholas II Fund *239*
    Over-the-Counter Securities Fund *241*
    Twentieth Century Vista Fund *242*

Chapter 18: Gold and Precious Metal Funds 251
Background Information *251*
  Type of Security *251*
  Risk/Stability *251*
Special Benefits and Exposures *252*
  Short Response Time *252*
  Gold as Anxiety Hedge *253*
  South Africa and the Supply Question *253*
  Marginal Producers *253*
Portfolio Fit *253*
Five Representative Gold and Precious Metal Funds *254*
  Fidelity Precious Metals *255*
  Golconda Investors Fund *255*
  Lexington Goldfund *256*
  United Services Gold Shares *256*
  Vanguard Specialized Gold and Precious Metals Fund *256*

Chapter 19: Specialized and Sector Funds 263
Background Information *263*
  Type of Security *263*
  Risk/Stability *264*
Special Benefits and Exposures *264*
  Control *264*
  Downside Risk *265*
  Timing Expertise *265*
Portfolio Fit *265*
Eight Representative Specialized and Sector Funds *266*
  Century Shares Trust *266*
  Note on the Fidelity Sector Family *267*
    Hourly Pricing *267*
    Short Selling *267*
    Zero Net Income *268*
  Fidelity Select Financial Services Portfolio *268*
  Fidelity Select Health Care Portfolio Fund *269*
  Fidelity Select Leisure Fund *270*
  IAI North Star Regional Fund *271*
  Vanguard Index Trust Fund *272*
  Vanguard Specialized Health Care Portfolio *273*
  Vanguard Specialized Service Economy Portfolio *274*

Chapter 20: Money-Market Funds 285
Background Information *285*

Contents   XV

        Type of Security   *285*
        Risk/Stability   *285*
    Special Benefits and Exposures   *286*
        Liquidity   *286*
        Check-Writing Access   *286*
        Cash Management   *286*
    Portfolio Fit   *286*
    Eight Representative Money-Market Funds   *287*
        Dreyfus Liquid Assets   *289*
        Fidelity Cash Reserves   *289*
        Kemper Money Market   *290*
        T. Rowe Price Prime Reserve   *290*
        Scudder Cash Investment Trust   *291*
        Stein Roe Cash Reserves   *291*
        Value Line Cash Fund   *292*
        Vanguard Money Market Reserves   *292*

Chapter 21: Tax-Exempt Money-Market Funds   293
    Background Information   *293*
        Type of Security   *293*
        Risk/Stability   *293*
    Special Benefits and Exposures   *293*
    Portfolio Fit   *294*
    Seven Representative Tax-Exempt Money-Market Funds   *294*
        Calvert Tax-Free Reserves   *296*
        Dreyfus Tax-Exempt Money Market Fund   *296*
        Fidelity Tax-Exempt Money Market Fund   *297*
        Neuberger & Berman Tax-Free Money Fund   *297*
        T. Rowe Price Tax-Exempt Money Market Fund   *298*
        USAA Tax-Exempt Money Market Fund   *298*
        Vanguard Municipal Bond Money Market   *299*

PART II: FUND SELECTION AND TIMING

Chapter 22: Mutual Funds: More Choices Than Ever Before   301
by Reg Green, Green Communications

Chapter 23: Choosing an Aggressive Growth Fund   305
by Sheldon Jacobs, No-Load Fund Investor Inc.
Cash Inflow   *305*
    How to Determine Cash Inflow   *307*
Net Redemptions Hurt Performance   *308*

Sell Aggressive Growth Funds in Bear Markets   *308*

Chapter 24: Selecting Mutual Funds and Market Timers   *311*
by Paul A. Merriman, Paul A. Merriman & Assoc., Inc.

Chapter 25: Market Timing and Selecting Growth Funds   *319*
by William E. Donoghue and Mary C. Driscoll, The Donoghue Organization, Inc.
The Risks of the Buy-Hold Approach   *319*
The Donoghue Alternative   *320*
  Timing Indicators   *323*
  Fund Selection   *324*

Chapter 26: The Upgrading Strategy   *327*
by Burton Berry, DAL Investment Company

Chapter 27: Using Moving Averages   *331*
by John Waggoner, Personal Investing
How They Work   *331*
Time Span   *333*
Market Timing with Moving Averages   *333*
  Variations on a Theme   *336*
  The Joys of the Average   *338*
Moving Average Newsletters   *338*

Chapter 28: Switch Strategies   *339*
by James McKeever, The Mutual Fund Advantage
The Discount Rate   *340*
  The Swiss Franc   *345*
  London P.M. Gold Fixing   *346*
  Dow Jones Industrial Average   *351*
Selecting a System   *355*

Chapter 29: Sector Funds Investing on Margin through a Broker   *357*
by Cato Ohrn, Sector Funds Newsletter
The Advantages of Sector Funds   *357*
The Advantages of Trading Through a Discount Broker   *358*
  Saving Legwork   *358*
  Saving Time When Switching   *358*
  No "Fund Family" Restrictions   *358*
  Simplified Bookkeeping   *359*
  The Ability to Hedge Your Portfolio   *359*
  Leverage   *359*

Time Sectors   *359*
The Need for a Strategy   *360*
Some Chart Illustrations   *360*
Sell Signals   *364*
Conclusion   *364*

Chapter 30: Building an All-Weather Portfolio   365
by Gerald Perritt, Mutual Fund Letter

Glossary   369

Appendix   373

About the Author   375

PART I: TYPES OF FUNDS

Chapter 1
Introduction

Today's investor is faced with a huge array of investment choices. New products compete with older, established investment vehicles for the investor's interest and dollars. Not surprisingly, one of the most well established investment systems—mutual funds—also has undergone substantial changes and tremendous growth. If today's investors were able to look back and view the evolution of the mutual funds's industry over the last twenty-five years, they would see an industry that has introduced a bewildering number of new funds and services to investors.

Evolution and change in the mutual funds industry offer both opportunities and a serious dilemma. How does the investor go about making choices? What funds are the right choices for me at my time in life? Is it possible to compare the various kinds of funds and gain a reasonable understanding of each fund type's advantages and disadvantages? Finally, how does a particular type of fund fit into my current portfolio? Of course, these questions and many more are what this book is all about.

Information is key to solving this dilemma. Sound information and a rational understanding of mutual funds, by category, is the first step in improving overall investment performance via mutual funds.

Second, investors need to realize that while the characteristics of individual investments stay relatively the same over time, the needs of individuals change dramatically over time. The mutual fund investments that made sense for a single individual at age 25 may not make sense for a married couple in the their 40's with children and a mortgage.

Third, mutual fund investment choices must be made within the overall context of a portfolio, that is the combination of all investments and savings available to an investor at any one time. A choice of a high-risk mutual fund, for example, may make a great deal of sense if the investor's overall portfolio will protect him in the case of default or a loss of principal. The assumption is that the investor has other resources on which to depend. Hence, a portfolio of investments serves to "protect" the investor in the event that any one component looses value.[1]

Fourth, investors must pay special attention to the degree of risk they are willing to tolerate. Investors will find that any choice of mutual fund will have some degree of risk,

---

[1]On many of the concepts discussed here, investors will find *The Investor's Desktop Portfolio Planner*, by Hirt, Block and Jury (Probus Publishing, Chicago, IL) to be an excellent companion to this book.

either from the economy as a whole, the particular industry group that dominates the mutual fund or the securities contained in the fund's portfolio. The investor needs to compare the degree of risk with the expected rate of return. Basically, the fundamental question should be: "Will the return on this mutual fund be worth the degree of risk (chance of default, loss of value, loss of principal) that I am willing to tolerate?"

MORE ON THE MATTER OF RISK

The overall relationship between investment risk and rate of return is very simple: the greater the degree of risk, the greater the potential reward to the investor. Investment experts generally accept the notion that groups of funds can be compared and therefore ranked on a continuum of risk and reward. Figure 1-1 does just that. The lowest risk, therefore, the lowest expected return on a fund is one which is dominated by Treasury Bills; the assumption is that the U. S. Government will never default. (If worse comes to worse, it can print more money to cover its obligations!). Historically, gold funds are one of the riskiest of mutual funds, and therefore have one of the highest expected rates of returns.

While Figure 1-1 is theoretically correct, investors must recognize that in actuality, the choices of securities by investment managers for a particular fund will determine the actual degree of risk. Figure 1-1 will serve as a general guideline for investors considering a particular fund. Investors must remember that some groups of funds are tax-advantaged, thus the investor's marginal tax rate will have a significant impact on the after-tax return that the investor receives. The obvious example, of course, is a fund dominated by municipal bonds. In all cases, investors must examine a particular fund carefully, understand its investment goals and objectives fully and only then invest!

How is it possible, then, that the subject of risk, so very important to mutual fund investors, can be ignored or downplayed? But in fact it is ignored. The popular press often fails to report risk when ranking mutual funds. For example, most annual mutual fund rankings ignore the overall risk of portfolios when they list the fund's performance for the past year. Without knowing anything about the degree of risk that a fund is willing to assume, investors might believe that the fund's success was based on a willingness to hold investments that are risky, perhaps more so than the actual expected return. A mutual fund's success in not measured just by the return it provides investors.

RISK TOLERANCE

The level of risk acceptable to an investor is referred to as *Risk Tolerance* and can be derived by a very simple procedure. Assume that an investor has both risk-free treasury bills that return 8 percent a year and a growth stock fund that has an annual return of 14 percent a year, but carries a correlative level of risk equal to that of the market as a whole. What percentage of the total available funds would that investor be comfortable

Chapter 1

Figure 1-1: Risk versus Reward for Types of Mutual Funds

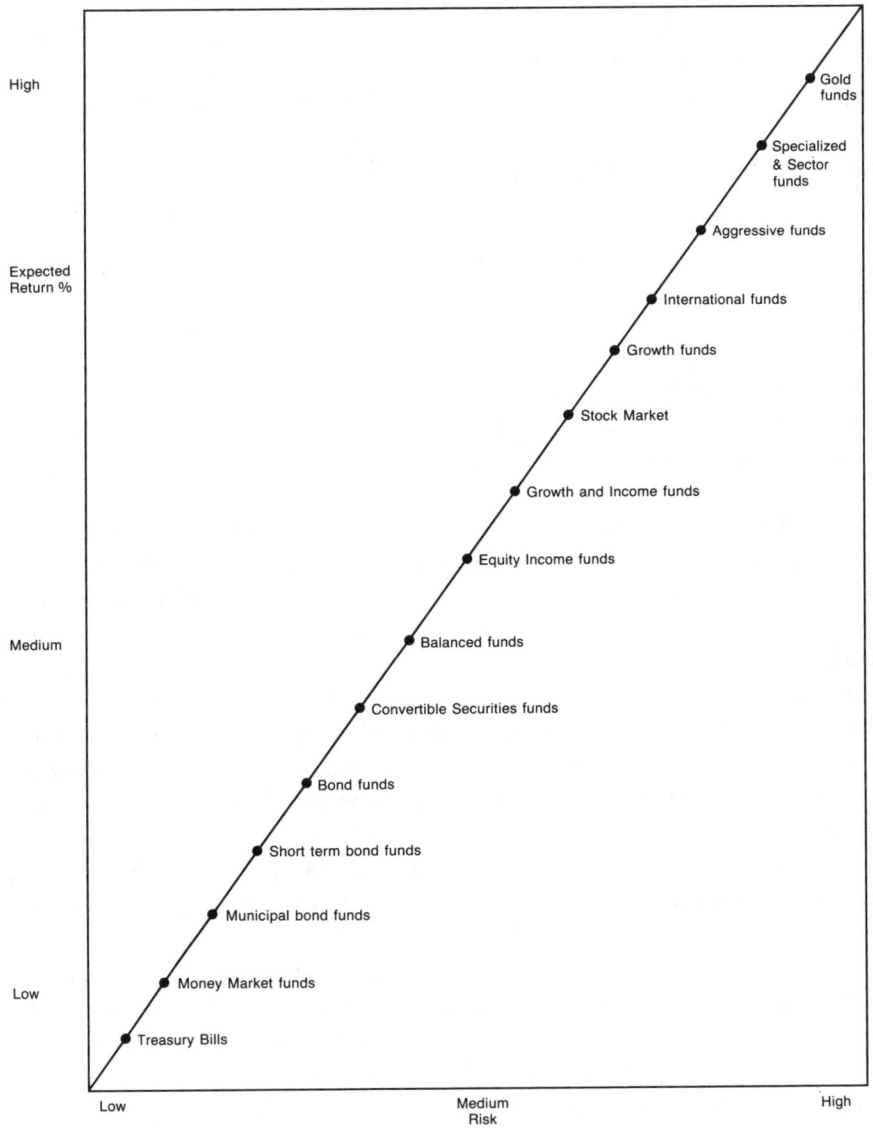

investing in the growth fund? If the answer is 50 percent, the risk tolerance is said to be 50. Therefore, the greater the risk tolerance of this investor, the greater his investment in growth funds. If his risk tolerance is equal to 100, his portfolio might contain only growth stock funds.

Risk tolerance is neither quantifiable nor static. Much will be determined by an individual's current economic circumstances, perceived future needs and overall personality makeup. Probably, the best measure of risk tolerance is the so-called "sleep quotient"—at what point do I find the risk I am assuming disturbing? If you worry about those high risk investments, start selling them and move into lower risk mutual funds.[2]

Establishing a Portfolio of Mutual Funds

As mentioned briefly above, the concept of a portfolio is extremely important; it allows investors to diversify their holdings, and thereby reduce risk.

A portfolio of mutual funds, for example, should allow investors to meet three investment objectives:

1. Liquidity to handle financial emergencies.
2. Preservation and enhancement of capital.
3. Current income (typically for retired investors).

In order to achieve these three goals, sometimes simultaneously, investors may have to hold five to ten different mutual funds selected from a variety of fund classifications. Some funds will provide defensive protection (in declining markets or uncertain economic conditions) while others will seek appreciation of capital (to take advantages of upward movement in the markets).

Diversification (establishing a portfolio of funds) is not just for investors who have a large capital base. Even small investors can diversify through mutual funds. As an investor's assets increase over time and income increases, even greater diversification is possible, and the investor may be willing to assume more risk in order to achieve even greater return.

Savvy investors know that they cannot escape risk, but risk can be managed. Detailed knowledge about classifications of mutual funds and individual funds is the best strategy to manage risk.

By way of example, consider a portfolio of mutual funds held by a married couple with two teen-aged children. (See Table 1-1.) The family has an annual income of $50,000. This portfolio assumes that the family has sufficient cash held in bank accounts or money market certificates for emergency needs. These investors have used an asset allocation procedure to determine how much of their assets would be allocated to each type of mutual fund in the portfolio.

---

[2] My earlier book, *The New Mutual Fund Investment Advisor* (Probus, Chicago) discusses the issues of risk and return more fully.

Table 1–1: A Portfolio for a Middle-Aged Couple

Type of Fund	Percentage of Total Portfolio
Growth	20%
Growth and Income	20%
Equity Income	25%
Corporate Bond	25%
International	10%

While this may be an ideal portfolio of mutual funds at this particular time, successful investors know that the composition of a portoflio will and should change over time. Changes in a portfolio should not be made based on the current investment fads or what is "hot." Fads and hot stocks fade quickly, only to produce permanent losses. Investing for the long-term is always preferable. Every year or two, investors should examine their investment goals, income level, risk tolerance and current investment portfolio. Once these factors are considered, they can determine new goals and adjust their mutual fund portfolios accordingly.

Market Timing

Whether investors take a conservative "five year" approach to their investment portfolios or are more active in the markets, many investors "time" their moves in and out of markets via mutual funds in order to take advantage of market rallies or to avoid major market declines.

The essence of market time is to buy low and sell high—the age-old dream of every investor! There, of course, is no foolproof way to achieve this goal every time. Fluctuations in the investment markets and their corresponding reflections in mutual fund price changes are difficult to discern. Hunches about future market changes are correct only about 50% of the time. Not particularly good odds.

Some investors, however, are successful in timing the market. There is every reason to believe that investors can time their movement into and out of mutual funds just like investors have timed their movement into and out of individual stock positions. In fact, forecasting general market returns is more valuable and has a better success rate than forecasting the movement of individual stocks. One reason that this is so is due to the fact that a market forecaster's investment strategies and his buy and sell actions resulting from that strategy will have less of an effect on the price of stocks (or bonds) in the aggregate than it would on any individual stock.

Market timing is, in practice, a hybrid of fundamental and technical methodologies, blending business analysis with technical projections. Market timing tracks such economic conditions as the trend and level of interest rates, the degree and direction of business activity, corporate profits and industrial production.

Successful market timers strive to position their portfolios of funds to achieve higher risk values prior to market rises and lower risk protection before market declines. IF THAT CAN BE DONE AND IF THE RESULTING BENEFITS ARE NOT OUTWEIGHED BY ADDED TRANSACTION AND TAX COSTS, OVERALL PERFORMANCE WILL BE SUPERIOR TO THAT OF A PORTFOLIO THAT MAINTAINS CONSTANT RISK VALUE IRRESPECTIVE OF MARKET MOVEMENTS. Unsuccessful market timers, on the other hand, tend to alter their portfolios' risk levels in ways unrelated to market moves, adding costs, but not benefits.

Unfortunately, in the real world, market movements give dozens of signals, flashing buy, sell and hold actions all at once. To further complicate the situation, institutional holders of stocks and bonds track each other's buy and sell actions as well as closely following the same leading economic indicators.

The Family of Funds Approach to Market Timing

To take advantage of this approach, mutual fund investors can use a family of funds to quickly and easily switch between high risk and low risk funds as the markets indicate. When the stock market is bullish, they would reallocate fund investments to concentrate on those high risk funds within the family of funds that are geared toward equity appreciation through investment in common stocks with a high growth potential. In contrast, when the market becomes bearish, investors would switch to funds within the family that seek preservation of capital and high current income such as those offered by a short term fund. By switching to a near cash fund they can still maintain decent earnings during bear markets.

In a recent study, the volatility of return versus the length of the holding period was examined for stocks and bonds. The study showed that risk, as represented by variability of return, declines with increasing holding periods. The study clearly illustrates that a long-term holding period helps to reduce the variability of return. Investors should note also that if they plan to hold investments for ten years or more, investors are better off holding stocks rather than bonds. While market timing can be useful, especially in the short run, in general it has been demonstrated that investors with longer holding periods generally enjoy better investment returns that those with shorter investment horizons. Patience really can be a virtue! Part II of this book is devoted exclusively to the discussion of market timing and mutual funds. Investors will find a series of essays by the experts on many aspects of successful market timing of mutual funds.

Selecting Mutual Funds

Investors often use historical mutual fund performance as our basis for selecting funds for superior future performance potential. Numerous academic studies have attempted to show that very few funds can consistently perform in the top ranks year after year. The evidence from these studies indicated that observations of historical fund returns alone contain limited predictive content with regard to future perfomance. Throughout this book, investors are reminded that PAST PERFORMANCE IS NOT AN INDICATOR OF FUTURE PERFORMANCE. Let the buyer beware!

In some periods, specific mutual funds outperform the market, while in others they underperform. It also has been found that fund performance is not necessarily tied to the mutual fund's risk level. Some high risk funds outperform the market and some underperform the market. The same is true of low risk funds.

Because we are interested in evaluating the performance of mutual funds, one factor we should take into account is the asset size of the fund. How important is a fund's size when assessing potential performance? A small, emerging mutual fund may promise better future returns, but may also carry greater than expected risk. On the other hand, an established, larger fund may be stable in performance, but also be less nimble and slower to react in market changes. Large funds generally provide diversification and stability whereas small funds offer flexibility and higher volatility of performance. The optimum range would seem to be funds with no less than $10 million and no more than $800 million in assets.

THE PLAN OF THE BOOK

This book is organized as a ready reference to help investors understand the major groupings of mutual funds and their overall investment objectives and philosophies.

Chapter 2 reviews some of the essentials of mutual funds. The next 19 chapters, 3 through 21, present detailed information about specific classifications of funds, e.g., Investment-Grade Corporate Bonds, Gold and Precious Metals, Money Market Funds, and so forth. (See Table 2-1 for Classification of Mutual Funds and corresponding chapter numbers.)

Throughout the book, investors are provided with general Background Information for each classification of fund (types of securities in the fund, risk and stability of the fund); Special Benefits and Exposures (investment quality, interest rate risk); Portfolio Fit; and Representative Funds for each classification.

Investors are reminded that Representative Funds are provided by way of example. They are not recommended necessarily and should not be construed as an endorsement of a particular fund. They were chosen because they are representative the qualities and features for a particular classification of mutual funds.

Every effort has been made to represent these funds accurately; investors are reminded to obtain a copy of the current prospectus and to research the current status of a particular fund before investing.

Finally, Part II, chapters 22 to 30, provide investors with insights and strategies about market timing of mutual funds. Each chapter was written by an expert in the mtual fund field and the opinions expressed are those of the individual authors.

Reg Green tells investors how to select mutual funds in light of the fact that there are so many choices available. Sheldon Jacobs shows investors how to pick an agrressive growth fund. Paul Merriman discusses the selection of a market timing service. William Donoghue and Mary Driscoll discuss market timing using interest rates as an indicator. Bert Berry shows investors the value of the upgrading methods of market timing—a form of momentum timing. John Waggoner illustrates market timing using moving averages and, James McKeever shows how he approaches market timing. Finally Cato Ohrn presents his appraoch on sector funds while Gerald Perritt offers strategies on building the "all weather" portfolio.

Chapter 2
Mutual Fund Basics

WHAT ARE MUTUAL FUNDS?

Mutual funds are investment companies that issue and sell redeemable securities, each of which represents an undivided interest in the assets held by the fund. These companies typically manage fund investments in a broad number of investment areas—including stocks, bonds, and government securities, providing fund shareholders with varying levels of risk and return.

Most commonly, mutual funds are classified as *open-end investment companies.* That is, they continuously offer new shares to investors and guarantee to redeem shares at net asset value (NAV) per share any time an investor wishes to liquidate his or her position.

A fund's per share NAV is determined by dividing the fund's total asset value at any given time by the number of shares it has outstanding at that time. For instance, if the fund's total assets are $10,000,000 and the fund's shares outstanding are 79,000, its NAV is $12.65—$10,000,000/79,000 shares = $12.65.

The concept of mutuality stems from the fact there is only one class of owner, who shares proportionally the gains or losses of the fund with all other owners.

THE ADVANTAGES AND DISADVANTAGES OF MUTUAL FUNDS

Mutual funds are convenient and flexible investment alternatives. They offer desirable levels of liquidity and can be a highly efficient—and often inexpensive—way to receive the benefits of portfolio diversification and professional money management. Below is a discussion of the more important reasons for investing in mutual funds, each of which will be more or less significant depending on individual investor goals and needs.

Advantages

The most important benefit of purchasing a mutual fund is *diversification,* that is, the reduction of portfolio risk by spreading one's holdings to include a variety of industries and companies. The assumption is that if the quality of the fund's investment in one company or industry group should deteriorate, the loss to each fund shareholder would be at least partly offset by increases in the fund's investments in other companies or industry groups.

Professional *management*, another important mutual fund benefit, relieves the individual investor from the extensive effort required to track various stocks or bonds and stay informed of changes in economic and investment conditions. Many investors choose mutual funds because mutual funds have a large and knowledgeable staff of investment professionals to track changes in the economy and accumulate information about the performance of companies or industry groups.

Fund investors also choose mutual funds because of the more manageable *selection process*. The investor is faced with the prospect of choosing stocks and bonds from many thousands of individual issues. For each issue, the investor in stocks or bonds (as opposed to mutual funds) may have to evaluate many factors, some of them requiring a great deal of detailed and specialized knowledge about the issuer that changes frequently.

To give a partial picture: for corporate stocks, the investor would want to know the level of capitalization needed in the industry compared to the individual firm's capital position, the quality of the firm's management and of their investment and marketing decisions; for municipal bonds, the city's revenue projections and changes in requirements for city services that might affect the city's ability to repay.

Mutual funds make this selection process more manageable, since the investor need only select a fund that meets his or her objectives. The total number of mutual funds is about 1000, considerably less than the number of individual securities issues. Since mutual fund prospectuses state quite clearly the risk and return philosophy under which the fund is managed, the number of factors to consider is much reduced, and the information needed to make the selection is much more readily available.

Finally, mutual funds are relatively *easy to buy and sell*. In many cases, assets can be bought or sold through the mail or with a simple phone call.

More and more investors are discovering the advantages of mutual funds. In 1986, net sales of mutual funds were $190 million. (See Figure 2-1.) Sales are expected to continue to increase yearly. In addition, the number of new funds is expected to grow. While such a broad range of choices offers more opportunities than ever, it also means that investors must be more disciplined than ever when selecting a fund.

Load Charges

Of course, all this convenience and expertise is not made available to investors without a cost. Many funds—especially those sponsored by insurance companies and brokerage houses—collect a sales charge (load) when investors buy shares; still others charge a fee when shares are sold. All funds, including "no load" funds, charge investors a yearly management fee.

Load charges typically range from 4 to 8.5 percent of the fund's share price at the time of purchase. Most load funds offer a quantity discount. For example, a fund may charge 8.5 percent for a purchase under $10,000 and, as the purchase amount increases, reduce the charge in steps down to 4 percent for purchases over $100,000. Currently, less than one-half of all funds are load funds.

Chapter 2

Figure 2-1: The Sales of Mutual Funds by Category for 1986

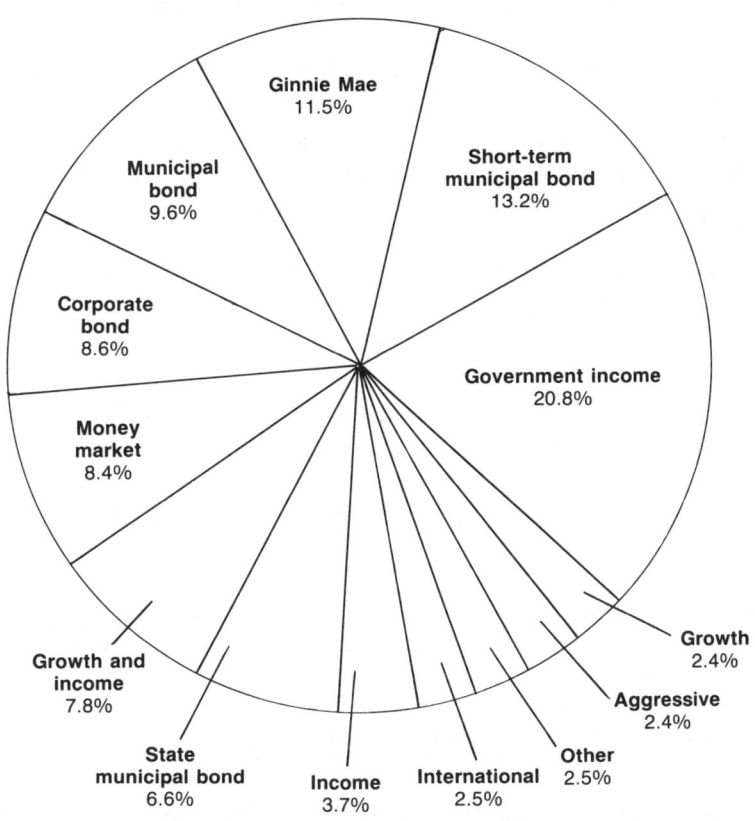

One generally can determine whether a fund is a load or a no-load fund by comparing its offer price to its net asset value in the newspaper's mutual fund listings. When the two values are listed and they are different, it is a load fund. In contrast, the use of the letters "N.L." in the offer price column indicates that it is a no-load fund and, as a result, the shares are bought and sold at the net asset value. Occasionally, a no-load fund will have a small back-end load amounting to a 1 or 2 percent commission on the value of shares redeemed. There are a number of low-load funds that charge a modest sales commission of 1 or 2 percent.

Although most load funds charge their sales commissions up front when the investor makes a purchase, there is a growing trend on the part of some brokerage sponsored funds to disguise the load charge in the form of redemption fees (which could be as high as 5 percent) and hidden annual distribution fees that run from 1 to 1.5 percent of the average assets.

When comparing load and no-load funds, investors usually consider only the up-front sales charge. They do not examine the prospectus to compare yearly management fees and other charges. All factors must be assessed when determining the true cost of fund shares. For example, consider a load fund with a 5 percent sales charge and an annual management fee of 0.5 percent. Compare this to a no-load fund with a yearly management fee of 1.0 percent. Assume that the performance of the two is the same over a ten-year period. Redemption results in the same net return. In fact, if they are held beyond the tenth year, the load fund will start yielding a higher net return. In effect, after ten years, the lower (by 0.5 percent) annual fee of the load fund has paid back the initial sales charge ($10 \times 0.5\% = 5\%$).

As a rule, no-load funds are the recommended course of action for the investor actively managing a portfolio of investments in mutual funds. There are, of course, some very good reasons for buying load funds, especially broker-sponsored load funds:

1. Ability to direct the purchase and redemption of shares through a broker/dealer.
2. Review of individual investment objectives with a broker in order to select the appropriate funds.
3. Continuing contact with a broker in order to review changing conditions and investment needs.

If a load fund is purchased, select a fund that reinvests your dividends at the net asset value without assessing additional sales charges.

CLASSIFICATIONS OF MUTUAL FUNDS

The three principal types of mutual funds are classified according to the type of security making up the bulk of the fund's assets:

1. Common Stock Funds
2. Bond Funds
3. Money Market Funds

By Investment Goal

Funds can also be classified according to the investment philosophy of the fund's management. There are funds that strive to maximize current *income*, those that try to maximize *growth* of principal or equity, and those that try to combine the two objectives.

A growth fund, for example, has as its primary objective the growth of capital, which it achieves by investing in common stocks and securities convertible into common stocks. An income fund concentrates on the generation of current income, which it achieves by investing in bonds or other securities with high yields (e.g., utility stocks).

By Risk

Funds also differ in their aggressiveness, that is, in the amount of risk they will accept in an investment. An aggressive growth stock fund strives for maximum capital gains, using such higher-risk strategies as buying securities on margin (leverage), trading stock or index options, and selecting the high-potential but thinly capitalized stocks of small companies. An aggressive income fund, for example, would invest in higher-risk bonds that are below investment grade ("junk" bonds) but that offer a correspondingly higher return (or premium) to the investor. A conservative fund would concentrate on investment-grade securities and attempt to include in its portfolio securities that will fluctuate less in value and provide a more predictable total return.

We can also differentiate homogeneous groups of funds by the characteristics relevant to the group.

For stock funds, risk is relevant. By risk, the categories would be charted thus, from low to high:

1. Equity Income
2. Growth & Income
3. Growth
4. Aggressive Growth
5. Small-Company Growth

Bond funds are best differentiated by the type of security held:

- GNMA
- Convertible
- Government
- Short-Term Tax-Exempt
- Long-Term Tax-Exempt
- Municipal
- Investment-Grade
- High-Yield Corporate

Specialized funds are best grouped by the area of specialization:

- Gold & Precious Metals
- International
- Technology
- Energy & Utility
- Other

And then money-market funds are divided simply into tax-exempt and taxable.

Building on these basic classifications, we have selected nineteen categories of funds for analysis and discussion. Each of the nineteen categories includes primarily either common stock funds, bond funds, or money market funds. A chapter is devoted to each fund category. Table 2–1 lists the chapter number and the symbol for each fund. The symbols will be used throughout the text when abbreviated reference is required.

Table 2–1: Classifications of Mutual Funds

Category	Chapter	Category	Abbreviation
Investment-Grade Corporate Bonds	3	Bond & Preferred	BP
High-Yield Corporate Bond	4	High-Yield Bond	HYB
GNMA and Government Bonds	5	Government Bond	GB
Convertible Bonds	6	Convertible Bond	CB
Short- and Intermediate-Term Tax-Exempt	7	Municipal Bond	MB
Long-Term and High-Yield Tax-Exempt	8	Municipal Bond Long-Term	MBLT
Balanced	9	Balanced	B
Equity Income	10	Equity Income	EI
Growth and Income	11	Growth and Income	GI
Growth	12	Growth	G
Aggressive Growth	13	Aggressive Growth	AG
International	14	International	IN
Technology	15	Technology	T
Energy and Utility	16	Energy & Utility	EU
Small-Company Growth	17	Small-Company Growth	SCG
Gold and Precious Metals	18	Metals	ME
Specialized and Sector	19	Specialized	S
Money-Market	20	Money-Market	MM
Tax-Exempt Money-Market	21	Money-Market Tax-Free	MMTF

Chapter 3
Investment-Grade Corporate Bond Funds

BACKGROUND INFORMATION

Type of Security

As would be expected, these funds invest primarily in corporate bonds. The goal is to provide investors with high current income; therefore, growth of capital is of secondary importance.

Risk/Stability

Investment-grade corporate bond funds traditionally are held by investors who are less tolerant of risk and require higher current yields to maintain a desired standard of living. As the name suggests, a majority of these funds' assets consist of high-quality corporate paper (bonds). If such funds are compared to stock or money-market funds, investors will find that investment-grade corporate bond funds offer more stability of principal than equity income funds (generally because bond prices fluctuate less than stock prices) but less stability than money-market or government bond funds. The current income provided by these funds generally is superior to both stock and money-market funds. (See Chapter 5 for government bond funds, Chapter 10 for a discussion of equity income funds, and Chapter 20 for a treatment of money-market funds.)

SPECIAL BENEFITS AND EXPOSURES

Investors must understand that within the investment-grade corporate bond fund category, individual funds vary greatly in principal stability and dividend yields. In other words, not all bond funds contain the same highquality level of investments that most investors would expect from an "investment-grade" fund. This variation is a function of the differences in credit rating and maturities of the securities in which the fund's risk versus yield is the relevant tradeoff. The higher the credit rating (Standard & Poor's or Moody's) and the shorter the maturity, the more stable the investment is expected to be. Stability results in lower risk, but also lower yields.

Investment Quality

Investment-grade corporate bonds are bonds that are classified as BB or higher by Standard and Poor's. A rating below BB indicates concern by the independent rating agencies about the ability of the bond issuer to meet payments of interest or principal. An investment-grade corporate bond fund with investments rated less than BB would have less stability of principal—which might result in higher yields, but the corresponding risk would be inconsistent with the usual goals of an investment-grade corporate bond fund. Nevertheless, there remains a range of choice for fund managers; some will choose a slightly higher emphasis on yield, some slightly higher emphasis on stability.

Interest-Rate Risk

The quality of investments is not the only concern for investors of investment-grade corporate bond funds. Such holdings are subject as well to risk resulting from interest rate changes.

Consider an example of a bond with a current yield of 10 percent with ten years to maturity. If interest rates rise by 40 percent, the bond price would drop 21 percent. If interest rates fall by 40 percent, the bond's value would increase by 29 percent. It is fluctuations in interest rates that most often are the primary cause of dramatic rises and falls in bond fund prices—especially during volatile economic conditions.

Investors can approximate the change in bond prices from a change in interest rates by using the following formula:

$$\Delta P = \frac{-M \times \Delta I \times CY}{150}$$

Where:
ΔP = percentage change in the bond price
M = years to maturity
ΔI = percentage change in interest rates (up or down)
CY = current yield in percent

In using the example of a bond maturing in ten years with a yield of 10 percent and interest rates dropping 40 percent, we can calculate the approximate equivalent value of the bond as follows:

$$P = \frac{-10 \times -40 \times 10}{150}$$

Note that the formula yields only approximate results. The formula does not yield the more precise estimates of -21 percent and +29 percent cited for this same example in the text above.

Determining Yields of Bond Funds

Because many investors hold some bond funds in their portfolios, they should understand how to determine the yield. The yield of a particular fund, as it often is advertised in the newspaper for example, refers to the fund's past or current yield only and says nothing about future yields. A truer picture of a bond fund's yield is to calculate its quarterly annualized yield. This is done by dividing the fund's most recent quarterly distribution (income) by its net asset value (NAV) at the end of the quarter and annualizing it—multiplying by four. For example, if the distribution is $0.50 and the NAV is $20.00, the annualized return is:

$$\text{yield} = \frac{.50}{20} \times 4 \times 100\% = 10\%$$

With the advent of relatively high real (inflation-adjusted) interest rates since 1982, many bond and income funds have become increasingly attractive to investors. They will continue to remain attractive as long as inflation stays at or below 5 percent and real interest rates for longer-term bonds exceed 6 percent.

Whether interest rates will remain stable is another important concern for buyers of investment-grade corporate bond funds. Investors who can anticipate changes in interest rates hold a substantial advantage over passive investors who are inclined to buy and hold. Some common indicators of interest-rate changes are shown in Table 3-1.

Table 3-1: Indicators Of Interest Rate Changes

The Case For Lower Rates:	*The Case For Higher Rates:*
Decline in oil prices	Federal budget deficits
Low inflation	Economic rebound expected
Loose monetary policy	Growth of the money supply
Slow growth in the economy	Revival of inflationary expectations

PORTFOLIO FIT

Bond funds are usually favored by investors who seek reasonably high current income and have a low risk tolerance. Investment-grade corporate bonds will have a low risk of default; they are still, however, subject to the effects of general interest-rate change. An investor should hold a bond fund for income and expect a reasonably stable price.

If an investor seeks high stability in the fund's NAV, it would be wise to select a fund composed of short-term bonds. If the need to liquidate is unlikely to arise, a long-term fund is a good choice. Any short-term liquidity needs suggest choosing a short-term bond fund.

Every investor should hold one or two bond funds. The young, aggressive investor will typically restrict bond fund holdings to 20 percent of the portfolio; a retired person will usually prefer concentrating more than 50 percent of the portfolio in bond funds.

In times when the investor believes interest rates will decline in the future, bond funds should be purchased to take advantage of the expected rise in NAV. When the investor believes interest rates will be rising, a portion of the portfolio should be moved to short-term bond funds.

SIX REPRESENTATIVE INVESTMENT-GRADE BOND FUNDS

To illustrate, we have chosen six investment-grade bond funds that show the qualities that investors seek when purchasing shares of investment-grade bond funds. Note that all of these examples are no-load funds. Table 3-2 contains a summary listing of the six funds. It is followed by a more detailed description of each fund's objectives and investment philosophy and practice, as well as capsule Profiles of their recent performance. (Profiles will be found grouped at the end of the chapters.)

Investors are reminded that past performance is no indicator of future performance.

Capital Preservation Treasury Note Trust

Capital Preservation Treasury Note Trust's investment objectives are to earn and distribute the highest level of current income consistent with the conservation of assets and the safety provided by the U.S. Treasury notes, U.S. Treasury bills, and repurchase agreements consisting of U.S. Treasury securities.

The Trust invests at least 90 percent of its portfolio in U.S. Treasury notes, which carry the "full faith and credit" pledge of the U.S. government. The interest on these notes, when paid to the Trust, is exempt from state and local taxes. The Trust may also invest up to 10 percent of its assets in U.S. Treasury bills.

Since the Trust's portfolio of securities carries the full backing of the U.S. government, the Trust's portfolio presents virtually no credit risk to investors. (As we mentioned before, however, the NAV of a Trust share will vary as interest rates change.)

Again, the longer the maturity of a debt security, the greater the fluctuation in its market value due to interest rate changes. The Trust attempts to maximize its expected total return by purchasing, selling, or swapping securities in its portfolio to take advantage of anticipated interest rate changes, including changes resulting from cyclical market conditions and temporary yield disparities. The average maturity of the Fund as of December 31, 1986, for example, was eight years, with a yield of 6.64 percent.

Table 3-2: Six Representative Investment-Grade Bond Funds

Fund	Annual Return (%) for 3 Years	Load
Capital Preservation Treasury Note Trust	15.2	NL
Nicholas Income Fund	15.1	NL
Northeast Investors Trust	19.0	NL
T. Rowe Price New Income	14.4	NL
T. Rowe Price Short-Term Bond	10.9*	NL
Vanguard Qualified Dividend Portfolio II Fund	20.9	NL

*Annual return based on only two years.

Capital Preservation Treasury Note Trust is a vehicle designed for those who want a low-risk portfolio of U.S. government securities. This Fund has done well in times of interest rate decline, such as the period from 1984–86. Some investors may find that as interest rates stabilize, the lower yield is less attractive. For example, in 1986 and 1987, the price of the Fund changed only by 0.4 percent—reflecting the then current pattern of interest rate stabilization. In some respects, the Trust acts like a money-market fund, but with a somewhat higher yield (because the Fund holds securities with a longer term to maturity—8 years versus 40 days).

Nicholas Income Fund

The primary investment objective of the Nicholas Income Fund is to obtain high current income, consistent with the preservation and conservation of capital values. While current income is primary, the Fund's management believes that there also should be a reasonable opportunity for long-term improvement in both capital and income.

The Fund is required to concentrate at least 25 percent but not more than 50 percent of its total assets in securities of electric companies or systems. The Fund provides investors with diversification by also investing in the securities of many different companies in a variety of industries outside of the utility group.

Nicholas Income Fund seeks high current income with minimal downside risk. This is accomplished by having a broad diversification in intermediate-term bonds with an average maturity of eight years. The average rating of all bonds in the portfolio is BB.

The Fund is able to generate high current income by concentrating its holdings in lower-rated investment-grade bonds. Albert Nicholas states that the Fund "maintains a balancing act" between providing a good return and holding shorter-term securities for lower price risk. As a result, he believes the Fund is best suited to "conservative investors who seek high income and lower volatility of total return than stocks or long-term bonds."

Northeast Investors Trust

The primary objective of Northeast Investors Trust is the production of income with capital appreciation as a secondary goal.

Over the past several years, the Trust has concentrated not less than 10 percent and not more than 50 percent of its assets in electric utility securities. The Fund, begun in 1950, provided an excellent return to investors over the last ten years. Yields of 12 to 14 percent were common since 1981, placing the Fund's performance on a level compatible with that of an income fund.

With the exception of some new preferred stocks in utilities (1 percent of assets), Northeast is a pure bond fund. The Trust typically holds about 171 different corporate and utility bonds in its portfolio, diversified among some two dozen industry sectors, including major positions in the bonds of Philadelphia Electric, Occidental Petroleum, Tenneco, Beatrice Foods, and Coastal Corp. Total assets are approximately $343 million, 12 percent of which are electric utility bonds.

The Trust purchases bonds rated Ba or Baa with the expectation of some upgrading over time. The average maturity is 12 years. The turnover averaged 40 percent from 1985 to 1987. The risk on this well-diversified Fund is moderate.

The Trust uses leverage to buy debt securities with yields that are greater than the interest rate on the loan. When loan rates exceed the yields available, leveraged buying is terminated. This use of leverage has assisted the Fund in building up an undistributed income account to be used as protection against unforeseen economic problems. It also has increased the Fund's capacity for income payouts. Since its inception in 1950, Northeast has paid a continuous and growing dividend.

Ernest E. Monrad, Chairman of the trustees, explained the Fund this way: "What I am trying to find is improving situations with the chance of an upgrade in ratings." Because Monrad or his pension plan holds a total of 4 percent of the Trust, he runs the money as if it is his own—since it is his own.

The Trust is ideal for investors who want higher yields than those provided by money-market funds and less price volatility than usually is associated with longer-term bonds.

T. Rowe Price New Income Fund

T. Rowe Price New Income Fund seeks the highest income over the long term that is consistent with the preservation of principal.

The Fund invests in a diversified portfolio of long-, intermediate-, and short-term corporate debt securities. Market conditions (such as interest and inflation rates) determine the percentage of assets held by the Fund in debt securities of various maturities.

The Fund's management has responded to recent market conditions by holding bonds with an average maturity of 10.6 years. The Fund consists of about 59 bonds with an average rating of AA. U.S. government bonds make up about 44 percent of the holdings, with telephone and financial services each accounting for an additional 9 percent of the portfolio.

The T. Rowe Price New Income Fund is suitable for investors seeking reasonable returns with little risk. The volatility of this Fund is quite low; its standard deviation is 1.12.

T. Rowe Price Short-Term Bond Fund

The T. Rowe Price Short-Term Bond Fund seeks minimal fluctuation in principal value, liquidity, and, consistent with these two investment objectives, the highest level of income.

To achieve these goals, the Fund invests primarily in a diversified portfolio of short- and intermediate-term debt securities. The Fund seeks to reduce the volatility normally associated with long-term bonds by limiting the Fund's maximum weighted maturity to three years.

As a result of the Fund's strategy, its risk is the lowest of the six investment-grade bond funds described here (volatility = 1.0). Shorter maturities generally provide lower yields but greater stability of principal. In 1987, for example, the average maturity of the bonds held in the portfolio was 2.18 years. (A typical bond fund has a weighted maturity of about ten years.) The average quality rating of the bonds in the portfolio is A+.

The Fund favors corporate securities over U.S. government obligations because of higher yields. The Fund may hold up to 5 percent of its portfolio in foreign currency debt instruments, providing additional value to the Fund. Edward Taber, portfolio manager, expects to maintain the current portfolio mix for the foreseeable future. "We will continue to look for opportunities to switch among sectors to enhance the income or yield. Purchase of foreign (nondollar-denominated) securities is also being implemented as a way to provide greater diversification and a higher return to shareholders. shareholders."

The Fund makes an excellent selection for the investor who seeks a low-risk way to benefit from the returns of the bond market. The Fund is, particularly, a good compromise for the investor torn between the stability of a money-market fund and the returns of a long-term bond fund.

Vanguard Qualified Dividend Portfolio II Fund

Qualified Dividend Portfolio II's investment objectives are to maximize dividend income from investments in securities of domestic corporations and to preserve capital.

Investments are made in corporations that qualify for the 85 percent dividend deduction (as allowed by federal tax code.) The Fund expects to have 80 percent of its assets invested in dividend-paying securities. Seventy-five percent of these dividend-paying investments are investment-grade cumulative preferred stocks. The remainder of the Fund's assets are invested in preferred stocks of other kinds, fixed-income securities, and cash equivalents. The Fund typically does not make investments in common stocks.

The Fund's holdings in preferred stocks perform much like bonds, in that their values rise and fall with changes in interest rates and changes in the creditworthiness of the issuing companies. The Fund is diversified by both issuer and rating quality. As the Profile illustrates, the most recent three-year performance of Vanguard Qualified Dividend Portfolio II has been exceptionally good.

While the Fund provides a higher yield than other investment-grade bond funds, its risk (standard deviation = 2.54) is higher than that of other such funds. Nevertheless, with its modest turnover and expense ratio, the Fund has a good return/risk ratio.

The Fund suits the objectives of the investor seeking higher yields within the limits of the comparatively low risk of investment-grade bond funds.

Chapter 3

PROFILE 3-1

CAPITAL PRESERVATION TREASURY NOTE TRUST
755 Page Mill Road
Palo Alto, CA 94304
1-800-227-8380 or 1-800-472-3389
415-858-3600

Fund Classification:	BP	
Total Assets:	$39 million	
Fund Manager:	Paul Single	
Year of Inception:	1980	
Minimum Investment:	$1000	
Sales Charge:	No load	
12b-1 Charge:	No	
Expense Ratio:	0.68	
Portfolio Mix:	*%*	*Issues*
Bonds	0	0
Common Stock	0	0
Preferred Stock	0	0
U. S. Government Securities	99	11
Certificates of Deposit	0	
Commercial Paper	0	
Estimated Annual		
Portfolio Turnover	53%	
Estimates of Fund Performance:		
Annual Return for Three Years:	15.2%	
Annual Return for Five Years:	NA	
Annual Return in Bull Markets:		
1985	18.1%	
1986	15.5%	
Annual Return in Bear Markets:		
Mid 1983-84	7.10%	
Representative Current Yield (1/31/87):	6.7%	
Measures of Risk and Reward:		
Alpha	5.3	
Beta	0.17	
R square	21	
Standard deviation	1.51	
Reward/risk ratio	10.1	
Net Asset Value:		
9/25/87	9.84	
10/28/87	10.08	

PROFILE 3-2

NICHOLAS INCOME FUND
700 N. Water Suite 1010
Milwaukee, WI 53202
414-272-6133
1-800-227-5987

Fund Classification:	BP	
Total Assets:	$65 million	
Fund Manager:	Albert Nicholas	
Year of Inception:	1929	
Minimum Investment:	$500	
Sales Charge:	No load	
12b-1 Charge:	No	
Expense Ratio:	0.96	
Portfolio Mix:	%	*Issues*
Bonds	82	76
Common Stock	3	3
Preferred Stock	4	2
U. S. Government Securities	0	0
Cash	11	NA
Commercial Paper	0	0
Estimated Annual Portfolio Turnover	20%	
Estimates of Fund Performance:		
Annual Return for Three Years:	15.1%	
Annual Return for Five Years:	17.8%	
Annual Return in Bull Markets:		
1985	21.2%	
1986	11.5%	
Annual Return in Bear Markets:		
6/30/86–9/30/86	2.21%	
Representative Current Yield (1/31/87):	9.3%	
Measures of Risk and Reward:		
Alpha	5.3	
Beta	0.16	
R square	18	
Standard deviation	1.52	
Reward/risk ratio	9.9	
Net Asset Value:		
9/25/87	3.70	
10/28/87	3.63	

PROFILE 3-3

NORTHEAST INVESTORS TRUST
50 Congress Street
Boston, MA 02109
1-800-225-6704
617-523-3588

Fund Classification:	BP
Total Assets:	$343 million
Fund Manager:	Ernest Monrad
Year of Inception:	1950
Minimum Investment:	$500
Sales Charge:	No load
12b-1 Charge:	No
Expense Ratio:	0.72

Portfolio Mix:	%	Issues
Bonds	99	171
Common Stock	0	0
Preferred Stock	0	0
U. S. Government Securities	0	0
Certificates of Deposit	0	0
Commercial Paper	0	0
Estimated Annual Portfolio Turnover	43%	

Estimates of Fund Performance:	
Annual Return for Three Years:	19.0%
Annual Return for Five Years:	21.2%
Annual Return in Bull Markets:	
1985	25.6%
1986	20.4%
Annual Return in Bear Markets:	
Mid 1983-84	-2.99%
Representative Current Yield (1/31/87):	10.5%

Measures of Risk and Reward:	
Alpha	9.1
Beta	0.19
R square	22
Standard deviation	1.67
Reward/risk ratio	11.4
Net Asset Value:	
9/25/87	13.01
10/28/87	12.38

PROFILE 3-4

(T. ROWE) PRICE NEW INCOME FUND
100 E. Pratt Street
Baltimore, MD 21202
1-800-638-5660
301-547-2000

Fund Classification:	BP	
Total Assets:	$969 million	
Fund Manager:	Charles P. Smith	
Year of Inception:	1973	
Minimum Investment:	$1000	
Sales Charge:	No load	
12b-1 Charge:	No	
Expense Ratio:	0.66	
Portfolio Mix:	*%*	*Issues*
Bonds	NA	NA
Common Stock	NA	NA
Preferred Stock	NA	NA
U. S. Government Securities	NA	NA
Certificates of Deposit	NA	NA
Commercial Paper	NA	NA
Estimated Annual		
Portfolio Turnover	185%	
Estimates of Fund Performance:		
Annual Return for Three Years:	14.4%	
Annual Return for Five Years:	15.6%	
Annual Return in Bull Markets:		
1985	17.6%	
1986	13.9%	
Annual Return in Bear Markets:		
Mid 1983-84	6.14%	
Representative Current Yield (1/31/87):	8.2%	
Measures of Risk and Reward:		
Alpha	4.7	
Beta	0.16	
R square	32	
Standard deviation	1.12	
Reward/risk ratio	12.9	
Net Asset Value:		
9/25/87	8.28	
10/28/87	8.42	

PROFILE 3-5

(T. ROWE) PRICE SHORT-TERM BOND FUND
100 E. Pratt Street
Baltimore, MD 21202
1-800-638-5660
301-547-2308

Fund Classification:	BP	
Total Assets:	$126 million	
Fund Manager:	Edward A. Taber III	
Year of Inception:	1984	
Minimum Investment:	$1000	
Sales Charge:	No load	
12b-1 Charge:	No	
Expense Ratio:	1.31	
Portfolio Mix:	%	*Issues*
Bonds	50.9	29
Common Stock	0	0
Preferred Stock	0	0
U. S. Government Securities	13.4	6
Certificates of Deposit	14.6	6
Commercial Paper	20.6	6
Estimated Annual Portfolio Turnover	21%	
Estimates of Fund Performance:		
Annual Return for Three Years:	NA	
Annual Return for Five Years:	NA	
Annual Return in Bull Markets:		
1985	13.0%	
1986	8.82%	
Annual Return in Bear Markets:		
Mid 1983-84	NA	
Representative Current Yield (1/31/87):	7.08%	
Measures of Risk and Reward:		
Alpha	NA	
Beta	20.10	
R square	20	
Standard deviation	1.0	
Reward/risk ratio	10.9	
Net Asset Value:		
9/25/87	5.00	
10/28/87	5.03	

PROFILE 3-6

VANGUARD QUALIFIED DIVIDEND PORTFOLIO II FUND
P.O. Box 2600
Valley Forge, PA 19482
1-800-662-7447
215-648-6000

Fund Classification:	BP	
Total Assets:	$170 million	
Fund Manager:	Earl McEvoy	
Year of Inception:	1975	
Minimum Investment:	$3000	
Sales Charge:	No load	
12b-1 Charge:	No	
Expense Ratio:	0.53	
Portfolio Mix:	%	*Issues*
Bonds	0	0
Common Stock	0	0
Preferred Stock	96.0	90
U. S. Government Securities	3.9	1
Certificates of Deposit	0	0
Commercial Paper	NA	NA
Estimated Annual Portfolio Turnover	34%	
Estimates of Fund Performance:		
Annual Return for Three Years:	20.9%	
Annual Return for Five Years:	21.6%	
Annual Return in Bull Markets:		
1985	29.7%	
1986	24.7%	
Annual Return in Bear Markets:		
Mid 1983-84	-6.10%	
Representative Current Yield (1/31/87):	8.7%	
Measures of Risk and Reward:		
Alpha	9.2	
Beta	0.33	
R square	28	
Standard deviation	2.54	
Reward/risk ratio	8.2	
Net Asset Value:		
9/25/87	8.17	
10/28/87	8.02	

Chapter 4
High-Yield Corporate Bond Funds

BACKGROUND INFORMATION

Type of Security

What differentiates high-yield corporate bond funds from investment-grade corporate bond funds (see Chapter 3) is the quality of the bonds held by the fund. High-yield corporate bond funds invest primarily in low-rated or nonrated corporate bonds (often called "junk bonds").

In this chapter we will frequently refer to the *rating* of a bond. The rating will be either Moody's or Standard & Poor's, whichever is available. So the reader may make comparisons, Table 4-1 shows the two rating systems side by side.

Risk/Stability

It is important for investors to understand that a fund portfolio of junk bonds may include a variety of issues, many of which are deemed to be quite acceptable for investments and not merely for speculation. In other words, investors must distinguish between issues that are not rated by outside agencies from issues that have been rated below investment grade (Bb rating or lower—Standard & Poors). Issues that are rated below investment grade certainly *are* considered speculative investments.

Many nonrated issues are from new companies or smaller companies that are growing rapidly but with low capitalization. Prospects for the future may be quite good, but the current condition of their balance sheets disallows conventional ratings agencies from commenting on the quality of their debt.

An investor's assets are protected in a bond fund made up of nonrated or lower-rated securities by the diversification within the portfolio—many companies in many industries—which spreads the risk. Issues are chosen for such funds when the yield prospects seem good to the fund managers and the risk seems equivalent to that in a conventionally rated security.

Under present economic conditions, investors can feel relatively comfortable with lower-quality corporate bond funds because of stable or declining interest rates and continued economic expansion. If today's economic conditions were to change—higher interest rates, recession, trade wars, or higher commodity prices—investors would be advised to and reassess their high-yield corporate bond fund positions.

Table 4-1: Comparison of Moody's And S&P's Bond Ratings

Quality	Moody's	S&P's
High Grade		
	Aaa	AAA
	Aa	AA
	A	A
Medium Grade		
	Baa	BBB
	Ba	BB
Speculative		
	B	B

SPECIAL BENEFITS AND EXPOSURES

High-yield corporate bond funds hold slightly lower average quality issues in their portfolios than do investment-grade corporate bond funds because of the additional income they generate (primarily from dividends) for shareholders. The spread between the yield of a high-yield fund and an investment-grade (high-quality) bond fund is typically 3.5 percentage points. For example, compare the T. Rowe Price High Yield Fund (see page 39), yielding 11.83 percent, with the T. Rowe Price New Income Fund (see page 26), yielding 7.6 percent—the 4.23-point difference can be a tremendous advantage to an investor over time!

Over the past few years, more than $25 billion has been invested in high-yield corporate bond funds; since 1984, these funds have consistently rewarded investors with attractive returns. An interesting fact is that, despite lower ratings, the default rate on high-yield corporate bond funds has been relatively low. One reason for the low default rate is that many of the factors that result in downgrading by the ratings agencies often have little to do with a company's ability to service its debt—i.e., meet payments of interest and principal in a timely fashion.

Default of Junk Bonds

High-yield bonds are issued to finance corporate growth and are particularly popular among smaller, emerging growth companies. Monies raised from the sale of these bonds are generally used to build new plants, finance research and development, or establish distribution and marketing systems. As mentioned previously, this type of junk bond is vastly different from a purely speculative issue.

The primary risk to high-yield bond fund investors is the possibility of rising defaults. During 1986, for example, more than $3 billion worth of junk bonds defaulted, representing some 3 percent of the issues on the market—and this figure omits the issues that narrowly escaped default. This 1986 average default rate of 3 percent, by the way, was three times as high as the annual averages for 1983 to 1985.

As a rule of thumb, investors should assume that about 5 percent of all junk bonds are at risk of default at any time; this means that 95 percent are of reasonably good quality. This, therefore, would put high-yield corporate bond funds somewhere between investment-grade corporate bond funds and common stocks with respect to yield versus risk.

Junk Bond Defaults and Total Returns

According to First Boston Corporation, 1986 defaults reduced the total return (interest payments and price changes) by 2.5 percent to an average of 15.63 percent. These figures are based on an index composed of 159 junk bond issues. In contrast, safer investment-grade issues, as measured by a Salomon Brothers corporate index, showed a total return of 17.03 percent, indicating that investors were not being rewarded for their greater risk in junk-bond portfolios. "The fact that there were over 3 percent defaults in a good growth year does not bode well for what the defaults would be in a bad year," says New York University researcher Edward I. Altman.

Richard S. Swingle, Manager of the T. Rowe Price High Yield Fund, however, is "bullish" on the high-yield bond market, despite the 1986 increase in the default rate and recent allegations of insider trading: "First, the economic environment should favor this sector. Our forecasts call for moderate economic growth, continued low inflation, and steady interest rates. When prices on high-yield bonds recover recent losses and resume a more usual relationship to Treasuries and high-grade corporates, demand for these bonds should strengthen. In addition, we expect tax reform to benefit high-yield bonds because the elimination of favorable tax rates for capital gains enhances the appeal of current income, and lower marginal tax brackets reduce the tax bite."

Swingle notes that over long periods of time, non-investment-grade bonds have outperformed high-rated corporate and government securities on a total return basis. Total return for high-yield bond mutual funds, on average, was 202 percent; for a comparable ten-year period, high-grade corporate bond funds yielded 164 percent on average.

Because of the long-term objectives of high-yield bond funds, the primary risk to shareholders is rising interest rates, which would result in a decline in the NAV of a fund. Investors are advised to watch interest rates carefully. If they do rise, the effects can be mitigated by switching to a short-term bond fund for increased safety.

PORTFOLIO FIT

High-yield bond funds are riskier than investment-grade bond funds due to the lower quality of the bonds. They are, of course, affected by interest-rate changes as are all bond funds. They are, in addition, affected by economic downturns that decrease the ability of the issuers to make interest payments—leading in the worst case to defaults.

High-yield bond funds offer good yields and may be safely held by those who can accommodate moderate risk. Retired persons might hold half their bond investments in investment-grade funds and half in high-yield funds. A younger, more aggressive investor might hold a 60-40 percent split between the two.

High-yield bond funds are an excellent choice for the investor who seeks higher yields and can accommodate the somewhat higher risk resulting from the potential default of some of the bonds within a fund's portfolio.

SIX REPRESENTATIVE HIGH-YIELD CORPORATE BOND FUNDS

To illustrate, we have chosen six high-yield corporate bond funds that show the qualities that investors seek when purchasing shares of high-yield bond funds. Note that all of these examples are no-load funds. Table 4-2 contains a summary listing of the six funds. It is followed by a more detailed description of each fund's objectives and investment philosophy and practice, as well as capsule Profiles of their recent performance.

Investors are reminded that past performance is no indicator of future performance.

Table 4-2: Six Representative High-Yield Corporate Bond Funds

Fund	Annual Return (%) for 3 Years	Load
Bull and Bear High Yield Fund	13.5	NL
Financial High Yield Bond Fund	20.45	NL
Pacific Horizon High Yield Bond Fund	19.95	NL
T. Rowe Price High Yield Fund	14.00	NL
Strong Income Fund	22.90*	NL
Vanguard Fixed Income High Yield Fund	19.00	NL

*Return based on only one year's performance.

Bull and Bear High Yield Fund

The investment objective of Bull and Bear High Yield Fund is to obtain for its shareholders the highest income over the long term. As a secondary objective, the Fund seeks capital growth, but only when consistent with its goal of providing shareholders with high income.

To accomplish its goals, the Fund invests in a diversified portfolio of high-yield fixed-income debt securities, securities without undue risk. The Fund will buy securities with long, short or intermediate maturities, depending upon management's evaluation of current and anticipated market trends.

The Fund's assets have grown considerably over the past several years, and now consists of 50 or more bonds, diversified over many industry groups. As might be expected from a fund of this type, performance can vary from one quarter to the next. The Fund has had a moderate risk and turnover and has provided reasonable returns for much of its life. While yields have remained high, total return was less spectacular in 1986, primarily because of loss of principal due to a drop in value of several of the Fund's holdings.

Financial High Yield Bond Fund

Financial High Yield Bond Fund invests almost all of its assets in bonds, other debt securities, and preferred stocks. The Fund typically holds lower-rated securities (as determined by established rating services). The Fund also may invest in nonrated securities if management believes that the financial conditions of the issuer and/or the protection afforded by the terms of the securities adequately limit risk.

The Fund holds approximately 51 bonds, of which the largest group held are utilities (7.6 percent). The largest individual companies held by the Fund are Carlton, Price Communications, Comdisco, Koor Industries, American Financial, and Mueller Co.

The Fund has a moderate turnover and volatility, resulting in an excellent return/risk ratio of 11.6. It should serve the investor seeking higher yields.

Pacific Horizon High Yield Bond Fund

Pacific Horizon High Yield Bond Fund holds a diversified portfolio of lower-rated and nonrated corporate bonds. Currently, the Fund holds about 60 securities. Harte-Hanks, Wickes Co., Dairy Mart Stores, Navistar, and Golden Nugget Finance are the largest individual securities held by the Fund.

The Fund's management actively trades bonds, so that the portfolio turnover exceeds 100 percent annually.

The Fund provides a high yield, and is suited to the investor who can accommodate moderate risk in the quest for a higher return.

T. Rowe Price High Yield Fund

The T. Rowe Price High Yield Fund is designed as a high-yield bond fund.

In order to deliver higher yields, the Fund invests in a select but diversified portfolio of long-term unrated bonds or bonds with low- to medium-quality ratings. T. Rowe Price conducts its own credit analysis, widely considered to be the most stringent in the industry. The average quality rating is B+. The Fund holds 110 different corporate bonds representing some 25 different industries.

The average maturity of the securities held by the Fund is 12.5 years, with some 80 percent of the assets having a maturity of 10 years. Its turnover rate is moderate. The Fund has grown tremendously since its inception in December 1984—it now has total assets of approximately $703 million.

The Fund offers an excellent reward/risk ratio with a moderate expense ratio.

Half of the investors bought the Fund for their IRA accounts.

Richard S. Swingle, formerly the manager of the T. Rowe Price New Income Fund, is the current Manager; Swingle is "optimistic about the market. . . ." and suggests the T. Rowe Price High Yield Fund for IRAs, tax-sheltered accounts or for retired individuals.

The Fund is an excellent choice for an investor seeking higher yields who can also accommodate moderate risk. (See Figure 4-1.)

Figure 4-1: The Net Asset Value of the Price High Yield Bond Fund for the Year Ending 5/1/87. (Courtesy of Telescan.)

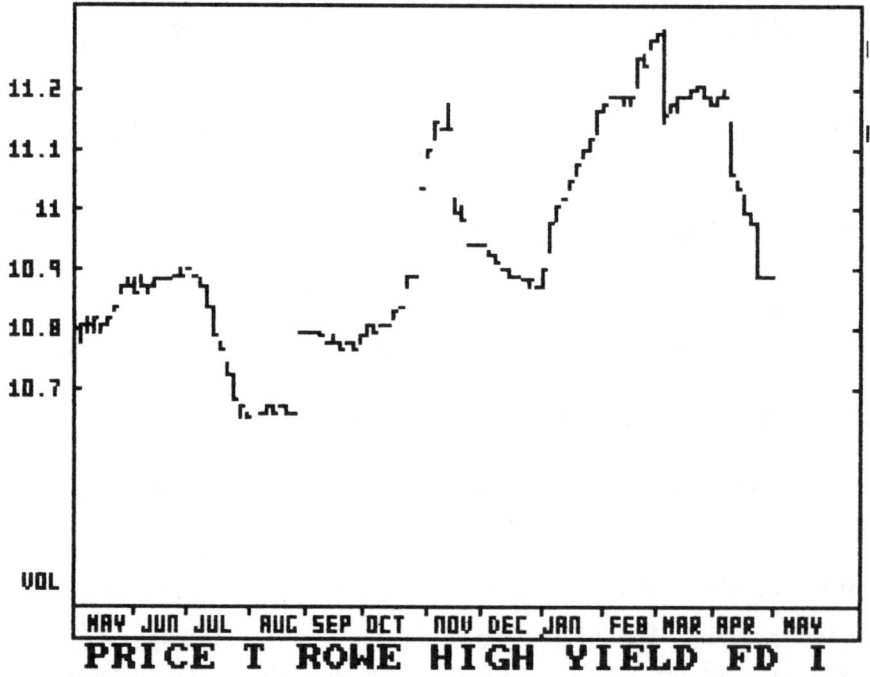

Strong Income Fund

The Strong Income Fund's investment objective is to obtain a high level of current income from its investments.

The Fund holds a diversified portfolio of fixed-income securities and dividend-paying common stocks. It holds unrated bonds of corporations in a diversified portfolio. The Fund has no restrictions on the percentage of its assets that it may invest in nonrated fixed-income securities, or securities rated as low as Ca (Moody's—see Table 4-1).

The Fund uses a wide range of investment vehicles to meet its investment goals. In addition to corporate stocks and bonds (of any quality rating), its other fixed-income securities investments are government securities, certificates of deposit, commercial paper, and preferred stocks.

Strong Income Fund controls portfolio risk by actively managing the length of the maturities of its securities.

Strong Income Fund has performed in its first year of operation (1986) with a total return of 30 percent. To quote Richard Strong: "We like to go wherever the action is, but to do it in a way that keeps our shareholders out of trouble."

Strong Income Fund is a well-managed high-yield fund with moderate risk and excellent return.

Vanguard Fixed Income High Yield Fund

The Vanguard Fixed Income High Yield Fund seeks to provide the highest level of current income available through investment in a diversified portfolio of higher-yielding medium- and lower-quality bonds. Growth of capital is also considered important, but only when consistent with the primary objective of high current income.

Management seeks to achieve these objectives by investing at least 89 percent of the Fund's assets in high-yielding, income-producing debt issues, with the balance made up of other debt securities that at the time of purchase are rated B or better. (Of all its assets, 80 percent are rated B or better.) The turnover is modest.

A survey of the most recent five years has shown the Vanguard Fixed Income High Yield Fund to have a risk rating somewhat better than the average high-yield fund. Its return/risk ratio makes it an excellent choice for the investor who seeks higher yields and can accommodate risks higher than those attendant on investment-grade bond funds.

PROFILE 4-1

BULL AND BEAR HIGH YIELD FUND
11 Hanovere Square
New York, NY 10005
1-800-847-4200
212-785-0900

Fund Classification:	HYB	
Total Assets:	$151 million	
Fund Manager:	John Schmucker	
Year of Inception:	1983	
Minimum Investment:	$1000	
Sales Charge:	No load	
12b-1 Charge:	Yes (.26%)	
Expense Ratio:	1.37	

Portfolio Mix:	%	*Issues*
Bonds	NA	50
Common Stock	0	0
Preferred Stock	0	0
U. S. Government Securities	0	0
Certificates of Deposit	0	0
Commercial Paper	0	0
Estimated Annual Portfolio Turnover	77%	

Estimates of Fund Performance:	
Annual Return for Three Years:	11.0%
Annual Return for Five Years:	NA
Annual Return in Bull Markets:	
1985	21.0%
1986	6.0%
Annual Return in Bear Markets:	
6/30/86–9/30/86	-2.9%

Representative Current Yield (12/31/86):	13.6%

Measures of Risk and Reward:	
Alpha	1.0
Beta	0.22
R square	30
Standard deviation	1.68
Reward/risk ratio	6.5

Net Asset Value:	
9/25/87	12.47
10/28/87	11.65

PROFILE 4-2

FINANCIAL HIGH YIELD BOND FUND
Box 2040
Denver, CO 80201
1-800-525-8085
303-779-1233

Fund Classification:	HYB	
Total Assets:	$44 million	
Fund Manager:	William Veronda	
Year of Inception:	1984	
Minimum Investment:	$1000	
Sales Charge:	No load	
12b-1 Charge:	No	
Expense Ratio:	0.76	
Portfolio Mix:	*%*	*Issues*
Bonds	NA	51
Common Stock	0	0
Preferred Stock	0	0
U. S. Government Securities	0	0
Certificates of Deposit	0	0
Commercial Paper	0	0
Estimated Annual Portfolio Turnover	96%	
Estimates of Fund Performance:		
Annual Return for Three Years:	NA	
Annual Return for Five Years:	NA	
Annual Return in Bull Markets:		
1985	26.4%	
1986	14.5%	
Annual Return in Bear Markets:		
6/30/86–9/30/86	2.6%	
Representative Current Yield (12/31/86):	11.8%	
Measures of Risk and Reward:		
Alpha	NA	
Beta	0.25	
R square	NA	
Standard deviation	1.75	
Reward/risk ratio	11.6	
Net Asset Value:		
9/25/87	8.11	
10/28/87	7.62	

PROFILE 4-3

PACIFIC HORIZON HIGH YIELD BOND FUND
3550 Wilshire Blvd.
Los Angeles, CA 90010
1-800-645-3515

Fund Classification:	HYB	
Total Assets:	$27 million	
Fund Manager:	James Caywood	
Year of Inception:	1984	
Minimum Investment:	$1000	
Sales Charge:	4.5%	
12b-1 Charge:	No	
Expense Ratio:	1.05	
Portfolio Mix:	%	*Issues*
Bonds	0	0
Convertible Bonds	4.4	3
Common Stock	0	0
Preferred Stock	0	0
U. S. Government Securities	91.2	57
Cash	0	0
Commercial Paper	0	0
Estimated Annual Portfolio Turnover	389%	
Estimates of Fund Performance:		
Annual Return for Three Years:	NA	
Annual Return for Five Years:	NA	
Annual Return in Bull Markets:		
1985	24.8%	
1986	15.1%	
Annual Return in Bear Markets:		
6/30/86–9/30/86	2.2%	
Representative Current Yield (12/31/86):	11.1%	
Measures of Risk and Reward:		
Alpha	NA	
Beta	0.25	
R square	NA	
Standard deviation	1.75	
Reward/risk ratio	11.3	
Net Asset Value:		
9/25/87	15.34	
10/28/87	14.67	

PROFILE 4-4

(T. ROWE) PRICE HIGH YIELD FUND
100 East Pratt Stree
Baltimore, MD 21202
1-800-638-5660
In Baltimore 301-547-2308

Fund Classification:	HYB	
Total Assets:	$703 million	
Fund Manager:	Richard Swingle	
Year of Inception:	1984	
Minimum Investment:	$1000	
Sales Charge:	No load	
12b-1 Charge:	No	
Expense Ratio:	1.00	
Portfolio Mix:	%	*Issues*
Bonds	NA	NA
Convertible Bonds	NA	NA
Common Stock	NA	NA
Preferred Stock	NA	NA
U. S. Government Securities	NA	NA
Certificates of Deposit	NA	NA
Estimated Annual		
Portfolio Turnover	164%	
Estimates of Fund Performance:		
Annual Return for Three Years:	NA	
Annual Return for Five Years:	NA	
Annual Return in Bull Markets:		
1985	13.10%	
1986	14.9%	
Annual Return in Bear Markets:		
6/30/86–9/30/86	-0.3%	
Representative Current Yield (12/31/86):	11.8%	
Measures of Risk and Reward:		
Alpha	NA	
Beta	0.28	
R square	NA	
Standard deviation	1.78	
Risk/reward ratio	7.8	
Net Asset Value:		
9/25/87	10.28	
10/28/87	9.75	

PROFILE 4-5

STRONG INCOME FUND
815 E. Mason Street
Milwaukee, WI 53202
1-800-368-3863

Fund Classification:	HYB	
Total Assets:	$72 million	
Fund Manager:	Richard Strong	
	William Corneliuson	
Year of Inception:	1985	
Minimum Investment:	$1000	
Sales Charge:	No load	
12b-1 Charge:	No	
Expense Ratio:	1.0	
Portfolio Mix:	*%*	*Issues*
Bonds	NA	41
Convertible Bonds	0	0
Common Stock	0	0
Preferred Stock	0	0
U. S. Government Securities	0	0
Certificates of Deposit	0	0
Estimated Annual		
Portfolio Turnover	205%	
Estimates of Fund Performance:		
Annual Return for Three Years:	NA	
Annual Return for Five Years:	NA	
Annual Return in Bull Markets:		
1985	NA	
1986	29.9%	
Annual Return in Bear Markets:		
Mid 1983-84	2.8%	
Representative Current Yield (2/5/86):	12.0%	
Measures of Risk and Reward:		
Alpha	NA	
Beta	NA	
R square	NA	
Standard deviation	1.80	
Reward/risk ratio	13.9	
Net Asset Value:		
9/25/87	11.90	
10/28/87	11.56	

PROFILE 4-6

VANGUARD FIXED INCOME HIGH YIELD FUND
P.O. Box 2600
Valley Forge, PA 19482
1-800-662-7447
215-648-6000

Fund Classification:	HYB	
Total Assets:	$1,158 million	
Fund Manager:	Earl McEvoy	
Year of Inception:	1979	
Minimum Investment:	$3000	
Sales Charge:	No load	
12b-1 Charge:	No	
Expense Ratio:	0.60	
Portfolio Mix:	%	*Issues*
Bonds	NA	114
Convertible Bonds		
Common Stock	0	0
Preferred Stock	0	0
U. S. Government Securities	0	0
Certificates of Deposit	0	0
Estimated Annual		
Portfolio Turnover	50%	
Estimates of Fund Performance:		
Annual Return for Three Years:	15.0%	
Annual Return for Five Years:	17.7%	
Annual Return in Bull Markets:		
1985	21.9%	
1986	16.1%	
Annual Return in Bear Markets:		
6/30/86–9/30/86	2.0%	
Representative Current Yield (12/31/86):	11.2%	
Measures of Risk and Reward:		
Alpha	4.7	
Beta	.22	
R square	27	
Standard deviation	1.70	
Reward/risk ratio	8.8	
Net Asset Value:		
9/25/87	8.42	
10/28/87	8.06	

Chapter 5
GNMA and Government Bond Funds

BACKGROUND INFORMATION

Type of Security

Government securities include those offered by various agencies of the U.S. government, including the Federal Farm Credit Bank, the Government National Mortgage Association, and the Federal Housing Administration, among others.

The Government National Mortgage Association (GNMA) purchases mortgages from private lenders, such as banks and savings and loans, packages them into pooled securities (in denominations of at least $25,000) called Ginnie Maes, and then sells them to investors.

GNMAs are, in effect, self-liquidating securities, combining the best features of both bonds and mortgages. Like bonds, GNMAs move up and down with changes in interest rates and other determinants of bond market values. Like mortgages, GNMAs provide investors with monthly payments of both principal and interest.

Risk/Stability

GNMA certificates are backed by the full faith and credit of the federal government. They are in general low-risk investments of the fixed-income type.

Over the last three years, mutual funds have been created for the purpose of investing in Ginnie Maes. They are the fastest-growing sector of the fixed-income sector of mutual funds. They are good investments for the conservative investor seeking income with safety of principal. These funds have yielded one full percentage point more than ten-year Treasury notes. As a group, GNMA funds have produced yields of 13 percent in 1985, 10 percent by the end of 1986, and about 8 percent through the first quarter of 1987. Many of these funds balance their investment positions in Ginnie Maes by purchasing other fixed-income government securities, such as Treasury notes, Treasury bills, Treasury bonds, and often securities of other government agencies, such as the Federal Farm Credit Bank, Federal Housing Administration and the Federal Home Loan Bank.

SPECIAL BENEFITS AND EXPOSURES

Interest Rates and Prepayments

GNMA funds, like bonds and other fixed-income investments, are subject to interest-rate fluctuations. As rates go up, the value and subsequent total yield of GNMA securities go down.

Prepayments on Ginnie Maes resemble calls on corporate bonds. Issuers tend to repay early when a savings on interest will result. Homeowners tend to hold low-cost mortgages, limiting the size of the opportunity for new Ginnie Maes at higher rates. When interest rates fall, GNMA funds tend to increase in value, because they would be paying a return that is higher than what was currently available. However, homeowners may decide to refinance to take advantage of lower rates, which would accelerate the maturity (life) of the funds and thus reduce total yield.

James Benham, Chairman of the Benham GNMA Fund, says: "At today's [relatively low mortgage] rates, Ginnie Maes issued at 12 percent prior to 1985 are vulnerable to refinancing. But often it is forgotten that some Ginnie Maes were issued at 12 percent as recently as August, 1985—before rates fell. Because they are relatively new, they are less likely to be refinanced in the near future, even if interest rates go much lower."

Currently, the average life of a Ginnie Mae mortgage is about 12 years.

Income Vulnerability

Because of interest-rate declines, most investors found that GNMA funds did not keep pace with other fixed-income funds in 1986. But if interest rates stabilize or advance modestly (as they are expected to do in the next couple of years), fewer households will refinance their mortgages, and GNMA certificates (and funds) should regain some of their lost value.

Face Value Vulnerability

When considering GNMA funds, investors must recognize the risk—and it is a real one—that any rise in interest rates will chip away at the quality of the original investment. Prices drop when interest rates go up—investors may find the face value dropping below their original purchase price at times. If shareholders need to cash in during times of rising interest rates, they could be in for a painful introduction to the trade-offs inherent in investing.

PORTFOLIO FIT

U.S. government bonds are without credit risk, since the government will not default on payment of interest and principal. They are, however, subject to risks from interest-rate changes.

GNMA and government bond funds are suitable for retired persons and others seeking reasonably high yields free from credit risk. GNMA funds will yield about 10 percent less than investment-grade bond funds and about 20 percent less than high-yield corporate bond funds. They are primarily for the risk-averse investor.

SEVEN REPRESENTATIVE GNMA AND GOVERNMENT BOND FUNDS

Below are funds that have been chosen because each is representative of the qualities that investors seek when purchasing shares of GNMA and government bond funds. Note that six of the seven examples are no-load funds.

To illustrate, we have chosen seven GNMA and government bond funds that show the qualities that investors seek when purchasing shares of GNMA and government bond funds. Note that six of these examples are no-load funds. Table 5-1 contains a summary listing of the seven funds. It is followed by a more detailed description of each fund's objectives and investment philosophy and practice, as well as capsule Profiles of their recent performance.

These seven have equivalent average maturities (about 10 years) and similar risk levels because of the inevitable similarity in their portfolios (there is only one GNMA and only one federal government).

Investors are reminded that past performance is no indicator of future performance.

Table 5-1: Seven Representative GNMA and Government Securities Funds

Fund	Annual Return (%) for 2 Years	Load
Amev U.S. Government Securities Fund	16.60	L
Benham GNMA Fund	11.50*	NL
Dreyfus GNMA Fund	9.60*	NL
Fidelity Government Securities Fund	16.20	NL
Lexington GNMA Fund	14.60	NL
T. Rowe Price GNMA Fund	10.40*	NL
Vanguard GNMA Fund	16.25	NL

*Annual return based on only one year.

Amev U.S. Government Securities Fund

Amev U.S. Government Securities has as its goal a high level of current income.

The Fund invests at least 65 percent of its assets in U.S. Government securities. This Fund, which was begun in 1972, typically holds Ginnie Maes as well as the securities of U.S. Government agencies such as the Federal Farm Credit Bank.

The Fund has averaged a 15 percent annual return for the last five years, an attractive yield for a low-risk investment.

Benham GNMA Fund

The investment objective of the Benham GNMA Fund is to provide a high level of current income consistent with safety of principal and the maintenance of liquidity.

The Fund invests almost exclusively in GNMA certificates. Other investments, when there are others, consist of short-term notes.

According to Randall Merk, the Fund's Portfolio Manager, "The focus of our fund is to maximize total return—which includes current yield and changes in share price. That's why we consider a number of factors, including prepayment risk, market risk, and diversification."

The advantages of the Benham Fund, according to Chairman James Benham are: "Yields are high, income is distributed monthly, and the portfolio consists of government guaranteed mortgages. If I decide I don't need the monthly income, I can choose to have the dividends automatically reinvested for monthly compounding."

Dreyfus GNMA Fund

The goal of the Dreyfus GNMA Fund is to provide investors with as high a level of current income as is consistent with the preservation of capital.

It is fundamental to the Fund's philosophy to invest at least 65 percent of its assets in GNMA certificates. (The rest would be held in short-term notes and cash.) Exceptions are made to this rule when management decides it must take a temporary defensive position, for example when interest rates are rising or falling dramatically.

The portfolio manager, Ina Goodman, recently stated that the "focus of the fund is on highest income possible with preservation of capital."

Investors have only one full year on which to judge management's performance; in 1986, total return was 9.6 percent.

Fidelity Government Securities Fund

Fidelity Government Securities Fund seeks a high level of current income consistent with preserving principal.

The Fund invests only in those obligations of the U.S. Government, its agencies, or its instrumentalities that provide interest income exempt from state and local taxes.

The Fund typically holds U.S. Treasury bills, notes, and bonds as well as securities issued by agencies such as the Federal Housing Administration and the Federal Home Loan Bank.

The Fund is organized as a limited partnership in order to pass on the special tax benefits that result from the direct ownership of U.S. Government obligations.

As Figure 5-1 shows, the Fund has achieved excellent returns for investors—particularly during years when interest rates were declining.

The Fidelity Government Securities Fund is considered to be a well-managed fund suitable for investors who require income without risk of default.

Lexington GNMA Fund

The Lexington GNMA Fund's investment objective is to seek a high level of current income, consistent with liquidity and safety of principal.

The Fund invests primarily in GNMA certificates. Fund Manager Robert DeMichele typically holds about 88 GNMA certificates in the Fund's portfolio.

The Fund has provided investors with a compounded five-year annual return of 15 percent.

The Lexington GNMA Fund is worth holding for that portion of an investment portfolio devoted to current income, especially in light of the Fund's low-risk feature (as measured by a beta of 0.13).

T. Rowe Price GNMA Fund

The T. Rowe Price GNMA Fund seeks to provide the highest level of current income, consistent with preservation of capital and maximum credit protection by purchase of GNMA certificates.

The Fund invests exclusively in securities backed by the full faith and credit of the U.S. government. 90 percent of the Fund's investments must be high-quality GNMA securities.

In order to provide the highest level of current income consistent with preservation of capital, the Fund tends to concentrate its investments in current-coupon issues rather than older, high-coupon issues that are more volatile in price and more likely to be prepaid if mortgage rates fall.

Vanguard GNMA Fund

The Vanguard GNMA Fund seeks to provide a high level of current income, consistent with safety of principal and maintenance of liquidity.

The Fund invests primarily in GNMA securities, which compose approximately 80 percent of the Fund's total assets. Most of the securities owned by the Fund are insured either by the Federal Housing Administration (FHA) or the Veterans Administration (VA).

According to the Vanguard management, the Fund's major concern in 1986 has been call (prepayment) protection. In response, management lowered the average coupon of the portfolio to 10.9 percent from 11.8 percent. (Compare this to the average coupon for the entire GNMA market of 10.6 percent.)

Figure 5-1: The Performance of the Fidelity Government Securities Fund Shown with its 26 Week Moving Average. (Courtesy of Telescan.)

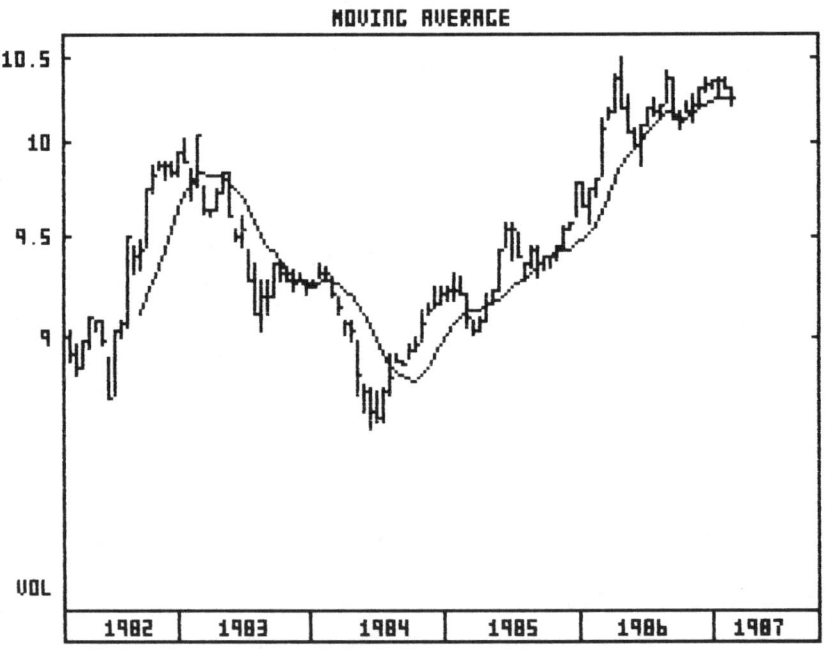

When investors have fears about prepayments, they tend to look for those funds that are paying better yields. While fears of prepayments and a large supply of new issues have caused the Fund's yields to be only 2.2 percent higher than that of U.S. Treasury notes, the Vanguard GNMA Fund is well-managed and has been one of the excellent performers, as illustrated in the Fund Profile. Investors will note in Figure 5-2 that the Fund has maintained a level or increasing price, despite the fact that yields have declined.

Chapter 5

Figure 5-2: The Price and Yield of the Vanguard GNMA Fund for 83 Weeks. Note How the Price Steadily Rose as the Yield Declined.

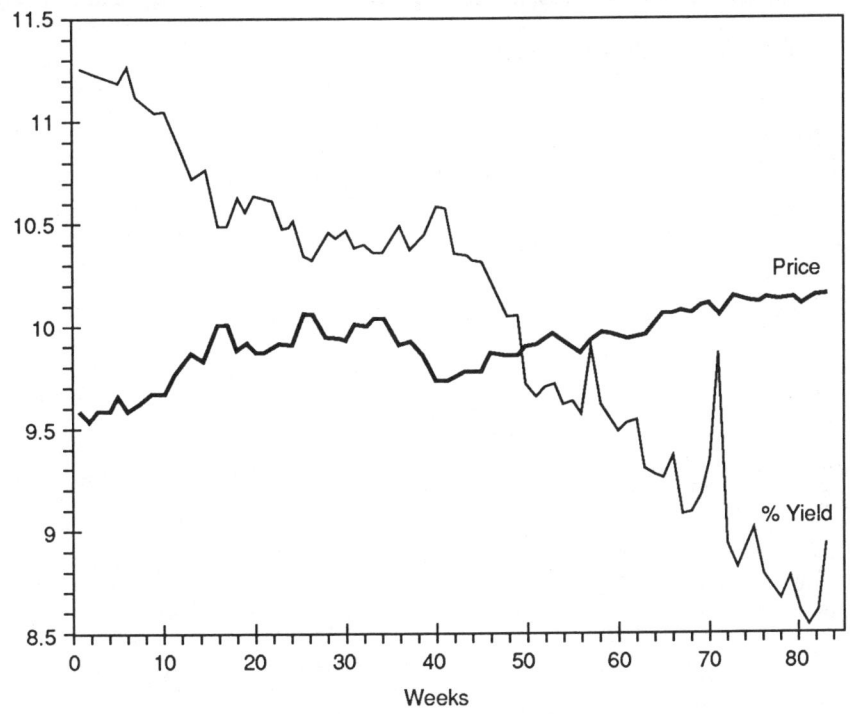

PROFILE 5-1

AMEV U.S. GOVERNMENT SECURITIES FUND
P.O. Box 64284
St. Paul, MN 55164
1-800-872-2638
612-738-4276

Fund Classification:	GB	
Total Assets:	$63 million	
Fund Manager:	Dennis Ott	
Year of Inception:	1972	
Minimum Investment:	$500	
Sales Charge:	4.50%	
12b-1 Charge:	No	
Expense Ratio:	1.13	
Portfolio Mix:	%	*Issues*
Bonds	0	0
Common Stock	0	0
U. S. Government Securities	0	0
Fed. Farm Credits	9	NA
Fannie Mae	55	NA
Ginnie Mae	30	NA
Cash	6	NA
Estimated Annual		
Portfolio Turnover	210%	
Estimates of Fund Performance:		
Annual Return for Three Years:	14.3%	
Annual Return for Five Years:	15.4%	
Annual Return in Bull Markets:		
1985	20.9%	
1986	12.3%	
Annual Return in Bear Markets:		
Mid 1983-84	5.0%	
Representative Current Yield (12/31/86):	9.2%	
Measures of Risk and Reward:		
Alpha	4.7	
Beta	.15	
R square	16	
Standard deviation	1.58	
Reward/risk ratio	9.1	
Net Asset Value:		
9/25/87	9.47	
10/28/87	9.60	

PROFILE 5-2

BENHAM GNMA INCOME FUND
755 Page Mill Road
Palo Alto, CA 94304
1-800-227-8380
415-858-2400

Fund Classification:	GB	
Total Assets:	$256 million	
Fund Manager:	Randy Merk	
Year of Inception:	1985	
Minimum Investment:	$1000	
Sales Charge:	No Load	
12b-1 Charge:	No	
Expense Ratio:	0.75	
Portfolio Mix:	%	*Issues*
Bonds	0	0
Common Stock	0	0
U. S. Government Securities	35	NA
Fed. Farm Credits	0	0
Ginnie Mae	65	NA
Estimated Annual Portfolio Turnover	NA	
Estimates of Fund Performance:		
Annual Return for Three Years:	NA	
Annual Return for Five Years:	NA	
Annual Return in Bull Markets:		
1985	NA	
1986	11.5%	
Annual Return in Bear Markets:		
Mid 1983-84	NA	
Representative Current Yield (12/31/86):	9.80%	
Measures of Risk and Reward:		
Alpha	NA	
Beta	.19	
R square	NA	
Standard deviation	1.75	
Reward/risk ratio	6.6	
Net Asset Value:		
9/25/87	9.51	
10/28/87	9.71	

PROFILE 5-3

DREYFUS GNMA FUND
767 Fifth Avenue
New York, NY 10022
1-800-645-6561
718-895-1206

Fund Classification:	GB	
Total Assets:	$1,963 million	
Fund Manager:	Ina G. Goodman	
Year of Inception:	1985	
Minimum Investment:	$2500	
Sales Charge:	No load	
12b-1 Charge:	Yes (0.2%)	
Expense Ratio:	0.96	
Portfolio Mix:	%	*Issues*
Bonds	0	0
Convertible Bonds	0	0
Common Stock	0	0
Preferred Stock	0	0
U. S. Government Securities	NA	42
Cash	0	0
Estimated Annual		
Portfolio Turnover	245	
Estimates of Fund Performance:		
Annual Return for Three Years:	NA	
Annual Return for Five Years:	NA	
Annual Return in Bull Markets:		
1985	NA	
1986	9.6%	
Annual Return in Bear Markets:		
Mid 1983-84	NA	
Representative Current Yield (2/28/87):	9.3%	
Measures of Risk and Reward:		
Alpha	NA	
Beta	0.19	
R square	NA	
Standard deviation	1.75	
Reward/risk ratio	5.5	
Net Asset Value:		
9/25/87	14.41	
10/28/87	14.55	

PROFILE 5-4

FIDELITY GOVERNMENT SECURITIES FUND
82 Devonshire
Boston, MA 02109
1-800-544-6666
617-523-1919

Fund Classification:	BP	
Total Assets:	$573 million	
Fund Manager:	John Todd	
Year of Inception:	1979	
Minimum Investment:	$1000	
Sales Charge:	No load	
12b-1 Charge:	No	
Expense Ratio:	0.81	
Portfolio Mix:	%	*Issues*
Bonds	0	0
Common Stock	0	0
U. S. Government Securities	55.5	20
U. S. Government Agencies	42.6	20
Certificates of Deposit	0	0
Estimated Annual Portfolio Turnover	NA	
Estimates of Fund Performance:		
Annual Return for Three Years:	14.6%	
Annual Return for Five Years:	15.0%	
Annual Return in Bull Markets:		
1985	17.7%	
1986	14.7%	
Annual Return in Bear Markets:		
Mid 1983-84	0.47%	
Representative Current Yield (12/31/86):	8.9%	
Measures of Risk and Reward:		
Alpha	4.5	
Beta	0.19	
R square	20	
Standard deviation	1.64	
Reward/risk ratio	8.9	
Net Asset Value:		
9/25/87	9.39	
10/28/87	9.50	

PROFILE 5-5

LEXINGTON GNMA FUND
Park 80 West Plaza Two
P.O. Box 1515
Saddle Brook, NJ 07632
1-800-526-0057
201-845-7300

Fund Classification:	GB	
Total Assets:	$129 million	
Fund Manager:	Robert DeMichele	
Year of Inception:	1973	
Minimum Investment:	$1000	
Sales Charge:	No load	
12b-1 Charge:	Yes (0.25%)	
Expense Ratio:	1.01	
Portfolio Mix:	*%*	*Issues*
Bonds	0	0
Common Stock	0	0
U. S. Government Securities	0	0
U. S. Government Agencies	0	0
Ginnie Mae	91.6	88
Estimated Annual Portfolio Turnover	167.76	
Estimates of Fund Performance:		
Annual Return for Three Years:	13.6%	
Annual Return for Five Years:	14.8%	
Annual Return in Bull Markets:		
1985	17.2%	
1986	11.9%	
Annual Return in Bear Markets:		
Mid 1983-84	-0.16%	
Representative Current Yield (12/31/86):	9.1%	
Measures of Risk and Reward:		
Alpha	4.3	
Beta	0.13	
R square	12	
Standard deviation	1.97	
Reward/risk ratio	6.9	
Net Asset Value:		
9/25/87	7.38	
10/28/87	7.55	

PROFILE 5-6

(T. ROWE) PRICE GNMA FUND
100 E. Pratt Street
Baltimore, MD 21202
1-800-638-5660
301-547-2308

Fund Classification:	GB	
Total Assets:	$345 million	
Fund Manager:	Edward Taber	
Year of Inception:	1985	
Minimum Investment:	$1000	
Sales Charge:	No load	
12b-1 Charge:	No	
Expense Ratio:	1.00	
Portfolio Mix:	%	*Issues*
Bonds	NA	NA
Common Stock	NA	NA
U. S. Government Securities	NA	NA
U. S. Government Agencies	NA	NA
Certificates of Deposit	NA	NA
Estimated Annual Portfolio Turnover	51.2%	
Estimates of Fund Performance:		
Annual Return for Three Years:	NA	
Annual Return for Five Years:	NA	
Annual Return in Bull Markets:		
1985	NA	
1986	10.4%	
Annual Return in Bear Markets:		
Mid 1983-84	NA	
Representative Current Yield (12/31/86):	8.69%	
Measures of Risk and Reward:		
Alpha	NA	
Beta	0.19	
R square	NA	
Standard deviation	1.75	
Reward/risk ratio	5.9	
Net Asset Value:		
9/25/87	9.34	
10/28/87	9.34	

PROFILE 5-7

VANGUARD GNMA FUND
P. O. Box 2600
Valley Forge, PA 19482
1-800-662-7447
215-648-6000

Fund Classification:	GB	
Total Assets:	$1,853 million	
Fund Manager:	Paul Sullivan	
Year of Inception:	1980	
Minimum Investment:	$3000	
Sales Charge:	No load	
12b-1 Charge:	No	
Expense Ratio:	0.38	
Portfolio Mix:	%	*Issues*
Bonds	0	0
Common Stock	0	0
Preferred Stock	0	0
U. S. Government Securities	0	0
U. S. Government Agencies	0	0
Ginnie Mae	100%	19
Estimated Annual Portfolio Turnover	32%	
Estimates of Fund Performance:		
Annual Return for Three Years:	15.4%	
Annual Return for Five Years:	17.3%	
Annual Return in Bull Markets:		
1985	20.7%	
1986	11.8%	
Annual Return in Bear Markets:		
6/30/86–9/30/86	2.01%	
Representative Current Yield (12/31/86):	10.0%	
Measures of Risk and Reward:		
Alpha	5.9	
Beta	0.14	
R square	11	
Standard deviation	1.72	
Reward/risk ratio	9.0	
Net Asset Value:		
9/25/87	9.05	
10/28/87	9.24	

Chapter 6
Convertible Securities Funds

BACKGROUND INFORMATION

Type of Security

Convertibles (bonds and preferred stock) are hybrid securities possessing the features of both stocks and bonds. (Since convertible bonds and preferred stocks have similar fixed-income and equity characteristics, they are often considered interchangeable for investment purposes.)

Most investors invest in to these securities not because of the attractive yields they offer (their fixed-income characteristics), but rather because of the potential run-up in price the equity side that such securities offer. They usually are viewed as a form of deferred equity because they are intended to be converted eventually into shares of the company's common stock. Therefore, it is not surprising that whenever the stock market is strong, convertible securities also are strong performers.

Convertible bonds are more common than convertible preferreds. They are issued as debentures (long-term unsecured corporate debt), but carry the provision of being converted into a certain number of shares of the issuing company's common stock.

When issued, every convertible bond is assigned a conversion ratio: the number of common stock shares for which it can be exchanged. If a bond were issued at $1000 and had a conversion ratio of 40, it would be exchangeable into 40 shares of common stock. The conversion price for this exchange would be $25 per share of common stock ($1000 / 40 = $25). Each convertible bond issue stipulates the time period within which this conversion may take place. (At the time of conversion, generally no cash is involved in the transaction; the holder/investor merely trades in the convertible bond for the stipulated number of shares of common stock.)

Because convertibles are fixed-income securities linked to the equity position of the issuing company, they normally are valued by reference to both the bond and the stock dimensions of the issue. Convertible securities trade much like common stock whenever the market price of the stock is equal to or greater than the stated conversion price.

On the other hand, if the price of the common stock is depressed (the trading price of the common is well below the conversion price) the convertible will loosen its ties to the underlying common stock and begin to trade as through it were a pure bond.

RECENT PERFORMANCE OF CONVERTIBLE SECURITIES

Convertible securities are one of the fastest-growing segments of the securities industry. A record $12 billion in convertibles, representing some 180 issues, was offered in 1985. In 1986, new issues surpassed the $20 billion mark. The market for convertible securities totals some $80 billion, representing slightly more than 1000 issues.

Convertible securities have been strong recent performers. From 1980 through 1985, convertible bonds as a group returned 17.4 percent annually, compared with 14.7 percent for the S&P 500 Index and 16.2 percent for the Shearson Lehman Government/Corporate Bond Index. Not unexpectedly, similar performance levels were recorded by mutual funds specializing in convertible securities. For the 10-year period ending December 31, 1985, convertible securities funds averaged a 17.9 percent annual return, compared to 14.3 percent for the S&P 500.

SPECIAL BENEFITS AND EXPOSURES

Limited Downward Risk

The major advantage of a convertible to the investor is that it reduces downward risk (because of its value or price floor as a bond) while providing an upward price potential comparable to the common stock of the issuing company. Neither straight stock nor straight bonds can match this critical double-sided feature. An additional benefit is that investors in convertibles receive current income in the form of bond interest payments; this income—although usually less than that of straight bond issues—normally exceeds the dividend income that might be available from comparable investments in the common stock.

Convertibles are a sound way to achieve attractive risk/return tradeoffs. Although the potential return provided by a convertible might not be the highest available in absolute terms, neither is the risk. Convertibles are particularly useful for prudent investors in volatile markets who seek long-term returns.

Market Opportunity

Because of the rather limited number of convertible issues available and the relatively small size of each issue, the convertible securities market has not attracted a large institutional following. As a result, the market tends to be undermanaged and somewhat inefficient, providing a unique opportunity for investors who place money with astute fund managers.

Bears on Both Sides

Convertible securities and the funds that are composed of them provide investors with a hedge in one-sided investment markets, that is, when there is either a bull stock market

Chapter 6

and a bear bond market or when there is a bear stock market and a bull bond market. Unfortunately, convertibles provide no hedge for investors if the stock and bond markets are simultaneously bearish. Conversely, convertible securities funds have been helped tremendously in the last four years by the bull market in both stocks and bonds.

PORTFOLIO FIT

Convertible securities are a hybrid with the features of both bond and equity securities. They are riskier than a corporate bond fund but less risky than a common stock fund.

These funds provide a balance between income and capital gains and limit the downside risk on the value of them original investment. They typically provide high current income that is substantially greater than the dividend return of the S&P 500 and competitive with money-market fund yields (see Chapter 20). They also have significant potential for capital appreciation, which generally provides about one-half of their total return. (The other half, of course, is provided by their income yield.) At the same time, these funds tend to be less volatile than either stocks or bonds, providing investors with some downside protection when bond values are affected by interest-rate changes.

These are important concerns for investors seeking a well-balanced portfolio strategy using mutual funds. Convertible securities funds are attractive to long-term investors who seek excellent returns with limited risk. Investors who find these features attractive should hold 5 to 10 percent of their portfolios in convertible securities funds.

FIVE REPRESENTATIVE CONVERTIBLE SECURITIES FUNDS

To illustrate, we have chosen five convertible securities funds that show the qualities that investors seek when purchasing shares of convertible securities funds. Note that three of these examples are no-load funds. Table 6-1 contains a summary listing of the six funds. It is followed by a more detailed description of each fund's objectives and investment philosophy and practice, as well as capsule Profiles of their recent performance.

Investors are reminded that past performance is no indicator of future performance.

Dreyfus Convertible Securities Fund

The Dreyfus Convertible Securities Fund seeks high current income, with capital appreciation a secondary goal.

The Fund was formerly called the Dreyfus Special Income Fund. It was modestly reorganized and renamed in May 1986 to reflect the fact that its investment goal is to hold at least 65 percent of its assets in convertible securities. Barbara Kenworth, one of the Fund Managers, offered these comments on the repositioning of the Fund: "The new fund is a more visible, understandable product. There is a broader range of investment-grade issuers of convertibles available now." The Fund holds approximately $172 million worth

Table 6-1: Five Representative Convertible Securities Funds

Fund	Annual Return (%) for 3 Years	Load
Dreyfus Convertible Securities Fund	18.30	NL
Calamos Convertible Income Fund	16.10*	NL
Phoenix Convertible Fund	14.50	L
Putnam Convertible Income-Growth Trust	15.80	L
Value Line Convertible Fund	16.10*	NL

*Annual return for one year only.

of convertible securities and other assets, with an annual yield of 64 percent. Fund Managers Jeffrey Friedman and Ms. Kenworth maintain a portfolio of nearly 100 securities in the fund, including major positions in the convertible securities of Cray Research, Sun Electric, Hazelton Labs, Arkansas Best, and USX. Management invests in both rated and nonrated securities. Currently the Fund holds approximately 175 million in convertibles and other assets with an annual yield of 6.4 percent.

As Figure 6-1 illustrates, the Fund has been a good participant in recent market developments, outperforming the S&P 500.

Calamos Convertible Income Fund

The Calamos Convertible Income Fund seeks high current income as its primary goal. Capital appreciation is a secondary goal but is only sought when this is consistent with its first.

To accomplish its objectives, the Fund invests at least 65 percent of its total assets in a diversified portfolio of convertible securities. This portion of the investment portfolio is made up of securities with higher-than-average ratings as determined by independent ratings agencies. Management, however, allows itself the flexibility to invest up to 30 percent of the fund in lesser-rated securities or nonrated convertible securities.

The Fund Managers, John Calamos and Thomas Noddings, employ a risk-reward investment approach that uses options to hedge its positions in convertible preferreds and bonds. "Our goal is to outperform the market over a cycle with low risk," says Calamos. "In good market environments, our convertible preferred stocks and bonds give us a good 'equity play,' while during market declines they cushion the loss. When we buy a convertible security, we want one that has the proper balance of upside potential and downside safety."

Chapter 6   61

Figure 6-1: The Performance of Dreyfus Convertible Securities Fund Shown with Its 26-Week Moving Average. (Courtesy of Telescan.)

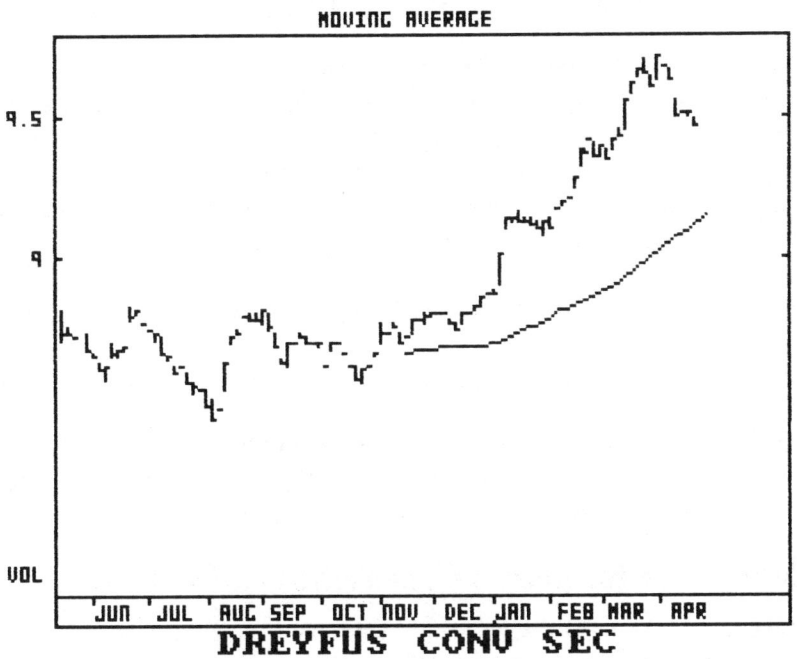

An interesting feature of the Fund is that it tends to underperform the stock market when the market is rising; it usually more than makes up for lost ground during declines. The net effect is that from 1981 to 1986 the annual compounded growth rate of private accounts managed by Noddings-Calamos averaged 19.2 percent. (The Fund first offered its shares to the public in 1985.) The Noddings-Calamos Convertible Income Fund uses a mathematical method to evaluate convertibles that figures in each issue's conversion premium, yield, quality, and price. "Looking at all those factors, we come up with a risk-reward relationship for each issue. Out of twelve hundred actively traded convertibles, we might be interested in 40 or 50 that our evaluation shows us are situated just right," says Calamos.

Before making a final buy decision, the Fund also looks at the fundamentals of the issues, but only if it qualifies mathematically first. Also, management would sell a convertible when its mathematical evaluation showed that it had the same risk as the company's common stock (again, regardless of the fundamentals).

The Noddings-Calamos Convertible Income Fund is a well-managed defensive fund that offers investors ample opportunity to protect their investments during declining markets while enabling them to participate to a great extent in bull markets.

Phoenix Convertible Fund

The Phoenix Convertible Fund seeks both income and the potential for capital appreciation as its investment objectives. In the mind of management, the two goals are weighted equally.

The Fund invests at least 80 percent of its noncash assets (about 63 percent of total assets) in convertible debt securities and preferred stocks and the remainder in common stocks and bonds (about 14 percent of total assets). The Fund maintains about 20 to 23 percent of total assets in cash and short-term investments.

Although the portfolio usually consists primarily of convertible securities and other debt and equity securities, there can be circumstances in which the Phoenix Convertible Fund would invest a significant portion of its assets in cash or cash equivalents. These measures would be temporary and are defensive transition maneuvers to cope with changing markets.

The Fund has taken significant positions in the convertible securities of Data Corp, Westinghouse, and IBM.

The Phoenix Fund is managed by Phoenix Investment Counsel, Inc., an affiliate of the highly respected insurance company, Phoenix Mutual Life Insurance Co. Jack Martin, a long-time fund manager, has been the Fund's Director since 1981.

Putnam Convertible Income-Growth Trust

Putnam Convertible Income-Growth Trust's primary investment goal is to seek, with equal emphasis, current income and capital appreciation. The Trust's secondary goal is the conservation of capital.

To accomplish its ends, the Trust invests primarily in convertible bonds and preferreds. While the Trust normally invests at least 65 percent of its total assets in convertible securities (excluding cash, cash equivalents, and government securities), Putnam's management seeks to maintain a portfolio that will be responsive to changes in economic trends and developments while providing relative stability of principal. Management actively makes portfolio adjustments that reflect this investment strategy, but does not trade securities for short-term profits.

As George Putnam states: "Convertibles continue to be popular with institutional and individual investors alike, so demand has been high. At the same time, many companies have been calling in their high-coupon convertible bonds in order to refinance at lower interest rates, just as homeowners have been refinancing their mortgages. Nevertheless, plenty of new issues have been coming out, so availability has not been a problem."

The Trust began operations in 1972 and has a solid long-term record of providing investors with an enviable average annual return of 16 percent.

Value Line Convertible Fund

The Value Line Convertible Fund's investment goals are high current income together with capital appreciation.

Chapter 6

The Fund has a policy of investing at least 70 percent of its assets in convertible securities. The rest is kept in cash. Normally, the Fund is 90 percent invested. The Fund has approximately 30 holdings, including convertible securities from Anheuser-Busch, Arkansas Best, Caterpillar Tractor, Compaq Computer, and Dreyers Ice Cream. The portfolio turnover is expected to be about 100 percent annually. Figure 6-2 tracks the exceptional performance of the Value Line Convertible Fund since its inception in 1985.

Figure 6-2: The Performance of Value Line Convertible Securities Fund Shown with Its 26-Week Moving Average. (Courtesy of Telescan.)

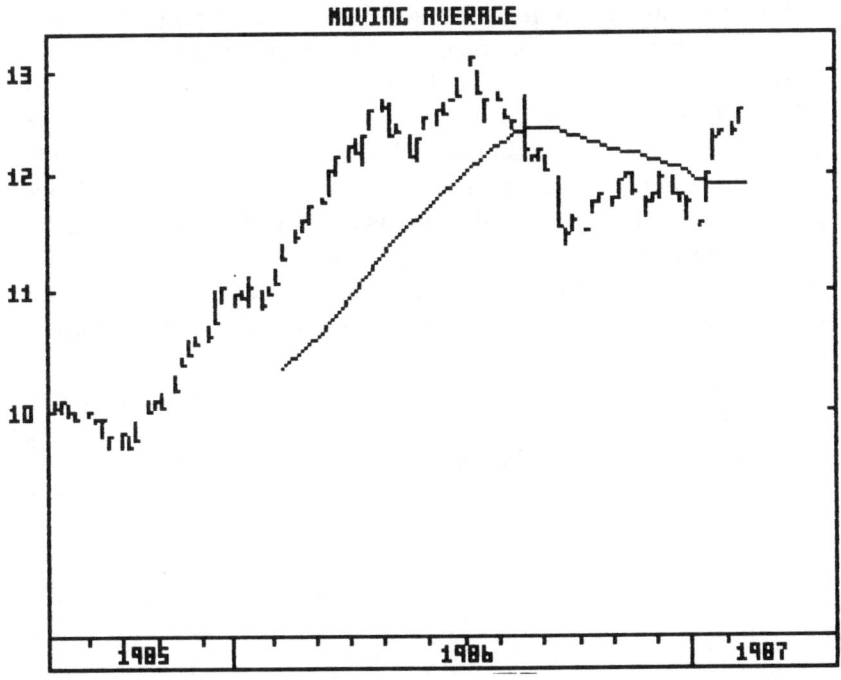

Allan Lyons, Value Line Convertible Fund's Portfolio Manager, sums up the outlook for convertibles as follows: "Market conditions are highly favorable to convertibles as a whole right now. If the market continues to go up, but less rapidly than of late, investors will participate fully; if it goes down, the convertible will hold up much better than the market; if it (the market) stays flat investors will get a much higher yield than from most stocks."

The Fund's adviser is Value Line, the publisher of one of the nation's major investment advisory services, *The Value Line Investment Survey* (as well as *The Value Line Convertibles Report*). Value Line also furnishes investment counseling services to private and institutional accounts that have combined assets in excess of $2 billion. The company employs a staff of approximately 100 investment research specialists, security analysts, economists, statisticians, and librarians. The Value Line Convertible Fund has direct access to the research and analytical work of the entire organization. Allan S. Lyons, the President of the Fund, has also been the Director of the company's *Value Line Convertibles Report* since 1972.

When selecting securities for purchase or sale, the Fund relies on the Value Line ranking system for convertible securities. The return of a convertible security depends largely on the performance of the common stock for which it can be exchanged. Value Line's evaluation of the convertible therefore begins with a ranking of the security's underlying common stock.

The Value Line ranking system for common stock is based on its historical prices and reported earnings, as well as its most recent earnings and price momentum; in addition, Value Line considers the degree to which the latest reported earnings have deviated from its previously estimated earnings. Value Line's evaluation of the convertible side uses a statistical evaluation model that ranks the 585 convertibles and 95 warrants it tracks. By making a comparison of the historical price relationship of the convertible with that of its underlying common stock (making adjustments for any changes in conditions that may affect the comparison), Value Line arrives at an estimate of the degree to which the convertible may be under- or overpriced. Each convertible security then is ranked on a scale of 1 (highest) to 5 (lowest), based on its total expected return (from income or dividends plus any appreciation).

Using this system, Value Line has provided its clients with an annual average increase of 22 percent over the last 14 years. It is no wonder that the Fund's management uses Value Line's approach when selecting issues for the Fund's portfolio.

PROFILE 6-1

DREYFUS CONVERTIBLE SECURITIES FUND
767 Fifth Avenue
New York, NY 10022
1-800-645-6561
718-895-1206

Fund Classification:	GB	
Total Assets:	$172 million	
Fund Manager:	Jeff Friedman	
	Barbara Kenworthy	
Year of Inception:	1970	
Minimum Investment:	$2500	
Sales Charge:	No load	
12b-1 Charge:	No	
Expense Ratio:	0.85	
Portfolio Mix:	*%*	*Issues*
Bonds	0	0
Convertible Bonds	0	0
Common Stock	48.6	43
Preferred Stock	0	0
U. S. Government Securities	25.9	35
Cash	25.3	2
Estimated Annual		
Portfolio Turnover	38%	
Estimates of Fund Performance:		
Annual Return for Three Years:	20.5%	
Annual Return for Five Years:	21.3%	
Annual Return in Bull Markets:		
1985	23.7%	
1986	24.3%	
Annual Return in Bear Markets:		
6/30/86–9/30/86	0.2%	
Representative Current Yield (2/28/87):	5.3%	
Measures of Risk and Reward:		
Alpha	5.5	
Beta	0.44	
R square	59	
Standard deviation	2.33	
Reward/risk ratio	8.8	
Net Asset Value:		
9/25/87	14.41	
10/28/87	14.55	

PROFILE 6-2

CALAMOS CONVERTIBLE INCOME
2001 Spring Road, Ste 750
Oak Brook, IL 60521
1-800-323-9943
312-789-8444

Fund Classification:	CB	
Total Assets:	$16 million	
Fund Manager:	John Calamos	
	Thomas Noddings	
Year of Inception:	1985	
Minimum Investment:	$5000	
Sales Charge:	No load	
12b-1 Charge:	No	
Expense Ratio:	2.0	
Portfolio Mix:	%	*Issues*
Bonds	0	0
Convertible Bonds	90	NA
Common Stock	0	0
Preferred Stock	0	0
U. S. Government Securities	0	0
Certificates of Deposit	0	0
Estimated Annual Portfolio Turnover	26%	
Estimates of Fund Performance:		
Annual Return for 18 Months:	21.8%	
Annual Return for Five Years:	NA	
Annual Return in Bull Markets:		
8/23/85–8/22/86	25.0%	
1986	16.1%	
Annual Return in Bear Markets:		
6/30/86–9/30/86	-3.9%	
Representative Current Yield (2/28/87):	4.2%	
Measures of Risk and Reward:		
Alpha	NA	
Beta	0.70	
R square	NA	
Standard deviation	2.50	
Reward/risk ratio	8.7	
Net Asset Value:		
9/25/87	12.24	
10/28/87	10.02	

PROFILE 6-3

PHOENIX CONVERTIBLE FUND
1 American Row
Hartford, CT 06115
1-800-243-1574
203-275-5749

Fund Classification:	CB	
Total Assets:	$100 million	
Fund Manager:	Jack Martin	
Year of Inception:	1975	
Minimum Investment:	$500	
Sales Charge:	7.0	
12b-1 Charge:	No	
Expense Ratio:	.80	

Portfolio Mix:	%	Issues
Bonds	0	0
Convertible Bonds	47	NA
Common Stock	13	NA
Preferred Stock	16	NA
U. S. Government Securities	0	0
Short term Obligation	22	NA
Estimated Annual Portfolio Turnover	121%	

Estimates of Fund Performance:	
Annual Return for Three Years:	19.7%
Annual Return for Five Years:	23.3%
Annual Return in Bull Markets:	
1985	21.6%
1986	17.3%
Annual Return in Bear Markets:	
Mid 1983-84	0.53%
Representative Current Yield (2/28/87):	3.7%

Measures of Risk and Reward:	
Alpha	0.5
Beta	0.62
R square	88
Standard deviation	2.65
Reward/risk ratio	7.5

Net Asset Value:	
9/25/87	19.96
10/28/87	16.83

PROFILE 6-4

PUTNAM CONVERTIBLE GROWTH-INCOME TRUST

One Post Office Square
Boston, MA 02109
1-800-225-1581
617-423-4960
617-292-1000

Fund Classification:	CB	
Total Assets:	$755 million	
Fund Manager:	Lawrence Haverty	
	Ronald Clark	
Year of Inception:	1972	
Minimum Investment:	$500	
Sales Charge:	8.50	
12b-1 Charge:	No	
Expense Ratio:	1.01	
Portfolio Mix:	%	*Issues*
Bonds	0	0
Convertible Bonds	78.5	NA
Common Stock	18	NA
Preferred Stock	0	0
U. S. Government Securities	0	0
Cash	3.5	NA
Estimated Annual		
Portfolio Turnover	119.78%	
Estimates of Fund Performance:		
Annual Return for Three Years:	21.8%	
Annual Return for Five Years:	20.7%	
Annual Return in Bull Markets:		
1985	27.0%	
1986	15.7%	
Annual Return in Bear Markets:		
Mid 1983-84	-5.1%	
Representative Current Yield (2/28/87):	5.0%	
Measures of Risk and Reward:		
Alpha	0.8	
Beta	0.74	
R square	92	
Standard deviation	2.98	
Reward/risk ratio	7.3	
Net Asset Value:		
9/25/87	17.90	
10/28/87	13.61	

PROFILE 6-5

VALUE LINE CONVERTIBLE
711 Third Avenue
New York, NY 10017
1-800-223-0818
212-687-3965

Fund Classification:	CB	
Total Assets:	$68 million	
Fund Manager:	Allan Lyons	
Year of Inception:	1985	
Minimum Investment:	$1000	
Sales Charge:	No load	
12b-1 Charge:	No	
Expense Ratio:	1.10	
Portfolio Mix:	%	*Issues*
Bonds	NA	NA
Convertible Bonds	NA	NA
Common Stock	NA	NA
Preferred Stock	NA	NA
U. S. Government Securities	NA	NA
Cash	NA	NA
Estimated Annual Portfolio Turnover	104.%	
Estimates of Fund Performance:		
Annual Return for Three Years:	NA	
Annual Return for Five Years:	NA	
Annual Return in Bull Markets:		
6/1/85–7/31/86	29.2%	
1986	16.1%	
Annual Return in Bear Markets:		
6/30/86–9/30/86	-6.4%	
Representative Current Yield (12/31/86):	4.4%	
Measures of Risk and Reward:		
Alpha	NA	
Beta	0.75	
R square	NA	
Standard deviation	2.50	
Reward/risk ratio	7.9	
Net Asset Value:		
9/25/87	12.19	
10/28/87	8.82	

Chapter 7
Short- and Intermediate-Term Tax-Exempt Bond Funds

BACKGROUND INFORMATION

Type of Security

Current tax-free income is the primary investment objective of short- and intermediate-term tax-exempt bond funds. To achieve this goal, these funds invest in a broad range of tax-exempt bonds issued by federal, state, city, and local governments. The funds are tax-exempt in that the interest paid on these bonds is passed through to shareholders free of federal income tax. Bonds issued by state governments may be free also of state tax, if they are held by investors living within the state of origin.

Short- and intermediate-term tax-exempt bond funds are distinct from their long-term counterparts in their goal of maintaining a more constant NAV during periods of fluctuating interest rates than the latter.

Risk/Stability

There are tradeoffs in bond funds between yield and per-share price stability.

The yield of a short- or intermediate-term bond fund responds more quickly to the market—the yield goes up and down with interest rates because the bonds in the fund are maturing more often. The maturing funds are regularly replaced with new bonds at the current market rate. Long-term bond funds naturally preserve earlier interest rates longer, since the fund holds the bonds longer.

The other side of this picture is that long-term bond funds have greater price volatility. The market is not willing to pay full face value on a bond locked into a below-market yield, but is willing to pay above face value on a bond locked into a yield higher than the current market. Short- and intermediate-term bonds, since the yield will be closer to market value, are less subject to this mechanism.

This all boils down to: longer-term bond funds for relatively better yield (income) stability but more price risk (i.e., capital risk); shorter-term bond funds for relatively better capital preservation but more income risk.

PORTFOLIO FIT

Short- and intermediate-term tax-exempt bond funds are suitable particularly for investors in high tax brackets. While recent tax changes have made these funds less attractive than they once were, they remain one of the few ways to lessen the impact of federal taxes. If marginal tax rates are increased in the future, these funds may become even more popular with investors. Many investors have found such funds to be an attractive alternative to corporate bond funds (see Chapter 3). In addition, they compare very favorably to tax-exempt money-market funds (see Chapter 21) in that the return often is 20 percent higher.

In addition to tax exemptions, these funds are ideal for investors who are concerned about stability of principal. Investors also find that the yields of these funds respond more quickly to interest rate changes. If interest rates are moving up, the yields of the bonds in short- and intermediate-term tax-exempt bond funds tend to move up as well. (On the other hand, if interest rates are falling, investors may wish to lock in higher yields by investing in longer-term bond funds—see Chapter 8).

Investors who are concerned about rising inflation are advised to invest in short- and intermediate-term tax-exempt bond funds rather than funds with longer maturities. Once again, yields of shorter-term maturities respond more quickly to market changes and economic conditions.

FIVE REPRESENTATIVE SHORT- AND INTERMEDIATE-TERM TAX-EXEMPT BOND FUNDS

To illustrate, we have chosen short- and intermediate-term tax-exempt bond funds that show the qualities that investors seek when purchasing shares of short- and intermediate-term tax-exempt bond funds. Note that all of these examples are no-load funds. Table 7-1 contains a summary listing of the six funds. Average maturity in years is also shown. It is followed by a more detailed description of each fund's objectives and investment philosophy and practice, as well as capsule Profiles of their recent performance.

Investors are reminded that past performance is no indicator of future performance.

Fidelity Limited Term Municipals

Fidelity Limited Term Municipals seeks the highest level of current income consistent with the reservation of capital.

The Fund strives to achieve this goal by investing primarily in high-quality municipal obligations (those bonds in the top three ratings categories—see Table 4-1) and by maintaining an average portfolio maturity of 12 years or less.

As the Profile shows, the Fidelity Limited Term Municipals Fund has performed quite well over time. With low risk and a solid yield, it provides an attractive return to the investor seeking a lower risk tax-exempt bond fund. Of course, in exchange for more

Table 7-1: Five Representative Short- And Intermediate-Term Tax-Exempt Bond Funds

Fund	Annual Return (%) for Three Years	Load	Average Maturity (years)
Fidelity Limited Term Municipals	14.2	NL	12
T. Rowe Price Tax Free Short–Intermediate Fund	9.6*	NL	4
Stein Roe Intermediate Municipal Fund	NA	NL	5
USAA Tax Exempt Intermediate Term Fund	12.9	NL	10
Vanguard Municipals–Intermediate Term	14.6	NL	10

*Return based on two years performance.

limited price fluctuations, the yield of the Fund is lower than other, longer-term municipal funds.

The Fund's strategy insures investors of relative price stability, which is important for investors concerned about security of investment capital.

T. Rowe Price Tax Free Short–Intermediate Fund

T. Rowe Price Tax Free Short–Intermediate Fund is a municipal bond fund that holds primarily short- and intermediate-term securities. Not surprisingly, the Fund has an average maturity for its bond holdings of five years or less. The Fund's primary goal is to provide investors with short-term tax-free yields.

Unlike tax-free money-market funds, the T. Rowe Price Tax Free Short–Intermediate Fund's price per share will fluctuate with changes in interest rates. True to the nature of all short- and intermediate-term tax-exempt bond funds, price changes of the Fund's shares should be more moderate than the per-share fluctuations of funds holding longer-term bonds. This contention is supported by data collected since 1977 by T. Rowe Price. Accordingly, price volatility of five-year municipal bonds is less than half of comparable 30-year municipal bonds.

The average maturity of the Fund, as of the end of 1986, was four years. Accordingly, share prices have remained relatively stable. Its low volatility and consistent tax-free yields make the Fund attractive to investors seeking a safe alternative to money-market funds. Because of the overall stability of the Fund, investors are provided with check-writing privileges.

Stein Roe Intermediate Municipal Fund

The investment philosophy of the Stein Roe Intermediate Municipal Fund is high current yield exempt from federal income tax, consistent with the preservation of capital.

The Fund primarily invests in a diversified portfolio of intermediate-term municipal securities.

The average maturity of the bonds in the Fund is 5.5 years. Because the Fund is so new, performance data are limited. The Fund offers check-writing privileges.

USAA Tax Exempt Intermediate Term Fund

The USAA Tax Exempt Intermediate Term Fund invests primarily in investment-grade tax-exempt securities having an average maturity of 12 years or less. The Fund maintains an average weighted maturity of ten years or less.

Currently, the Fund holds about 104 bonds from 34 states. As a result of its conservative strategy, the Fund has provided investors with an attractive tax-exempt return.

Vanguard Municipals—Intermediate Term Fund

The Vanguard Municipals—Intermediate Term Fund's primary objective is to provide investors with the highest available level of interest income exempt from federal income tax.

The Fund also strives for the preservation of investors' capital and standards of maturity and quality as prescribed by the Fund's charter.

The Vanguard Municipal—Intermediate Term Fund has an expected average weighted maturity between 7 and 12 years. Currently, the maximum maturity of any individual security is 15 years. Bonds held by the Fund must be rated at the time of purchase within the three highest ratings grades assigned by Moody's or S&P. (See Table 4-1.)

As Figure 7-1 illustrates, the Vanguard Municipals—Intermediate Term Fund has provided investors with a consistently excellent tax-free return. Low volatility and steady yields are hallmarks of the Fund. With the convenience of check-writing privileges, it is an excellent fund for investors interested in shorter-term tax-free funds.

Figure 7-1: The Performance of the Vanguard Municipals–Intermediate Term Fund Shown with Its 26-Week Moving Average (Courtesy of Telescan.)

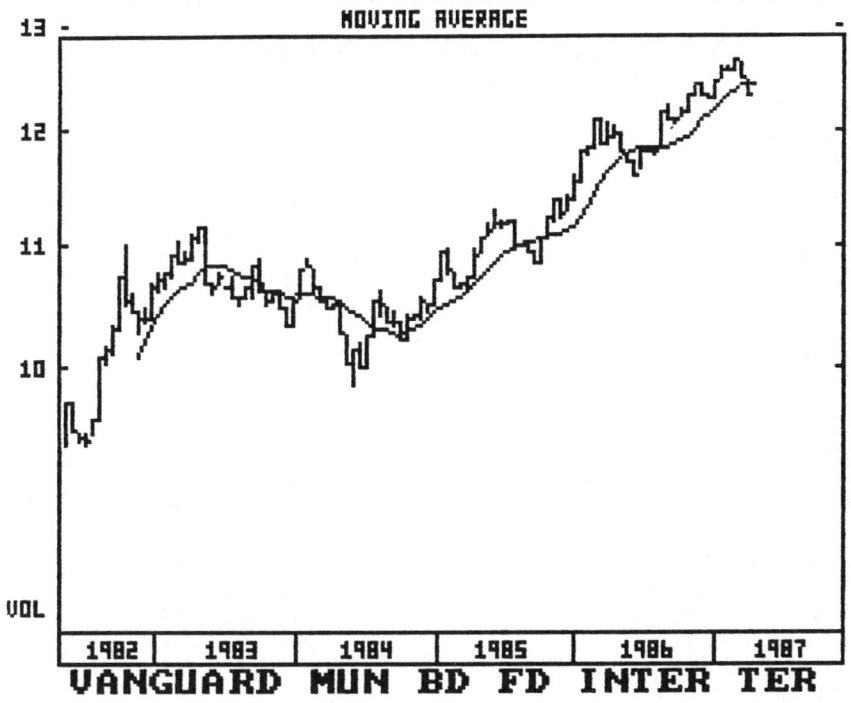

PROFILE 7-1

FIDELITY LIMITED TERM MUNICIPALS
82 Devonshire Street
Boston, MA 02109
1-800-544-6666
617-523-1919

Fund Classification:	MB	
Total Assets:	$579 million	
Fund Manager:	Jack Haley	
Year of Inception:	1977	
Minimum Investment:	$2500	
Sales Charge:	No load	
12b-1 Charge:	No	
Expense Ratio:	0.71	
Portfolio Mix:	%	*Issues*
Bonds	NA	NA
Municipal Bonds	NA	NA
Common Stock	NA	NA
Preferred Stock	NA	NA
U. S. Government Securities	NA	NA
Cash	NA	NA
Commercial Paper	NA	NA
Estimated Annual Portfolio Turnover	124%	
Estimates of Fund Performance:		
Annual Return for Three Years:	14.2%	
Annual Return for Five Years:	15.1%	
Annual Return in Bull Markets:		
1985	17.3%	
1986	15.2%	
Annual Return in Bear Markets:		
3/30/86–6/30/86	-0.1%	
Representative Current Yield (1/28/87):	6.2%	
Measures of Risk and Reward:		
Alpha	3.9	
Beta	0.21	
R square	23	
Standard deviation	1.81	
Reward/risk ratio	7.8	
Net Asset Value:		
9/25/87	8.99	
10/28/87	8.67	

PROFILE 7-2

(T. ROWE) PRICE TAX-FREE SHORT-INTERMEDIATE BONDS
100 E. Pratt Street
Baltimore, MD 21202
1-800-638-5660
301-547-2000

Fund Classification:	MB	
Total Assets:	$307 million	
Fund Manager:	Peter J. D. Gordon	
Year of Inception:	1983	
Minimum Investment:	$1000	
Sales Charge:	No load	
12b-1 Charge:	No	
Expense Ratio:	0.79	
Portfolio Mix:	%	*Issues*
Bonds	NA	NA
Municipal Bonds	NA	NA
Common Stock	NA	NA
Preferred Stock	NA	NA
U. S. Government Securities	NA	NA
Cash	NA	NA
Commercial Paper	NA	NA
Estimated Annual Portfolio Turnover	129%	
Estimates of Fund Performance:		
Annual Return for Two Years, Two Months:	9.6%	
Annual Return for Five Years:	NA	
Annual Return in Bull Markets:		
1985	8.9%	
1986	9.7%	
Annual Return in Bear Markets:		
3/30/86–6/30/86	1.1%	
Representative Current Yield (2/28/87):	5.5%	
Measures of Risk and Reward:		
Alpha	0.1	
Beta	0.09	
R square	23	
Standard deviation	.77	
Reward/risk ratio	12.1	
Net Asset Value:		
9/25/87	5.07	
10/28/87	5.05	

PROFILE 7-3

STEIN ROE INTERMEDIATE MUNICIPAL FUND
Box 1143
Chicago, IL 60690
1-800-621-0320
312-368-7826

Fund Classification:	MB	
Total Assets:	$105 million	
Fund Manager:	Timothy Schlindwein	
Year of Inception:	1985	
Minimum Investment:	$2500	
Sales Charge:	No load	
12b-1 Charge:	No	
Expense Ratio:	0.90	
Portfolio Mix:	%	*Issues*
Bonds	0	0
Municipal Bonds	NA	115
Common Stock	0	0
Preferred Stock	0	0
U. S. Government Securities	0	0
Cash	0	0
Commercial Paper	0	0
Estimated Annual Portfolio Turnover	10%	
Estimates of Fund Performance:		
Annual Return for Three Years:	NA	
Annual Return for Five Years:	NA	
Annual Return in Bull Markets:		
1985	NA	
1986	13.1%	
Annual Return in Bear Markets:		
3/30/86–6/30/86	NA	
Representative Current Yield (2/28/87):	5.7%	
Measures of Risk and Reward:		
Alpha	NA	
Beta	.28	
R square	NA	
Standard deviation	2.0	
Reward/risk ratio	6.5	
Net Asset Value:		
9/25/87	10.26	
10/28/87	10.10	

PROFILE 7-4

USAA TAX EXEMPT INTERMEDIATE TERM FUND
P.O. Box 33338
San Antonio, TX 78265
1-800-531-8000 or 531-8448
512-498-8000

Fund Classification:	MB	
Total Assets:	$338 million	
Fund Manager:	Ken Willman	
Year of Inception:	1982	
Minimum Investment:	$1000	
Sales Charge:	No load	
12b-1 Charge:	No	
Expense Ratio:	0.57	
Portfolio Mix:	*%*	*Issues*
Bonds	NA	NA
Municipal Bonds	NA	NA
Common Stock	NA	NA
Preferred Stock	NA	NA
U. S. Government Securities	NA	NA
Cash	NA	NA
Commercial Paper	NA	NA
Estimated Annual Portfolio Turnover	85%	
Estimates of Fund Performance:		
Annual Return for Three Years:	12.9%	
Annual Return for Five Years:	NA	
Annual Return in Bull Markets:		
1985	16.3%	
1986	13.4%	
Annual Return in Bear Markets:		
3/30/86–6/30/86	-0.3%	
Representative Current Yield (2/28/87):	7.4%	
Measures of Risk and Reward:		
Alpha	3.1	
Beta	.17	
R square	16	
Standard deviation	1.76	
Reward/risk ratio	7.3	
Net Asset Value:		
9/25/87	11.32	
10/28/87	11.25	

PROFILE 7-5

VANGUARD MUNICIPALS—
INTERMEDIATE-TERM BOND
P.O. Box 2600
Valley Forge, PA 19482
1-800-662-7447
215-648-6000

Fund Classification:	MB	
Total Assets:	$998 million	
Fund Manager:	Ian MacKinnon	
Year of Inception:	1977	
Minimum Investment:	$3000	
Sales Charge:	No load	
12b-1 Charge:	No	
Expense Ratio:	0.33	
Portfolio Mix:	%	*Issues*
Bonds	NA	NA
Municipal Bonds	NA	NA
Common Stock	NA	NA
Preferred Stock	NA	NA
U. S. Government Securities	NA	NA
Cash	NA	NA
Commercial Paper	NA	NA
Estimated Annual Portfolio Turnover	26%	
Estimates of Fund Performance:		
Annual Return for Three Years:	14.6%	
Annual Return for Five Years:	15.4%	
Annual Return in Bull Markets:		
1985	17.4%	
1986	16.2%	
Annual Return in Bear Markets:		
3/30/86–6/30/86	-0.3%	
Representative Current Yield (2/28/87):	6.9%	
Measures of Risk and Reward:		
Alpha	4.1	
Beta	0.21	
R square	20	
Standard deviation	1.91	
Reward/risk ratio	7.6	
Net Asset Value:		
9/25/87	11.35	
10/28/87	11.22	

Chapter 8
Long-Term Tax-Exempt Bond Funds

BACKGROUND INFORMATION

Type of Security

Long-term tax-exempt bond funds are designed to provide investors with tax-exempt income. Long-term municipal bonds are promissory notes of a state, city, county, town, or some other special taxation district. By investing in municipal securities with longer maturities, these funds offer higher tax-exempt income than tax-exempt money-market funds (see Chapter 21) or short- and intermediate-term tax-exempt bond funds (see Chapter 7). Because long-term tax-exempt bond funds invest in securities with longer maturities, the ratings (quality) of the holdings within the funds are poorer than funds with shorter maturities.

Risk/Stability

Investors must be aware that funds in this group vary greatly in the quality and maturity of the municipal bonds in which they invest. The longer the maturity, the higher the interest rate. Remember also that though the yield is greater when the rating of the issuer is lower the risk also is greater. (Investors may want to inspect a listing of the state and local government securities held by a particular fund. The creditworthiness of some issuers is substantially better than others.)

SPECIAL BENEFITS AND EXPOSURES

When compared with income funds (see Chapter 10) of debt obligations that are not tax-exempt, long-term tax-exempt bond funds offer lower yields (assuming similar maturities and ratings). On the other hand, after-tax yields for high-income individuals may be higher because of the tax exemption.

Price (NAV)

Overall, investors in long-term tax-exempt bond funds will find that the price and yield of the municipal bonds that compose the majority of the funds' holdings will fluctuate moderately with interest rates. As interest rates decline, the value of the principal tends to increase while yield decreases. On the other hand, as interest rates increase, bond prices decline but yields increase. Other economic and financial conditions may also affect the overall strength of these funds. For example, the net asset value of most long-term tax-exempt bond funds declined in the second quarter of 1986 due to uncertainty regarding the tax reform bill. Table 8-1 illustrates the changes of net asset value of long-term tax-exempt bond funds over a two-year period.

Table 8-1: Changes In Net Asset Value Of Long-Term Tax-Exempt Bond Funds

Date	Yield
November 1985	9%
February 1986	7%
June 1986	8%
January 1987	7%
June 1987	8%

Periods of uncertainty about interest rates such as 1987–88 require caution when investing in long-term bond funds. At such times, the effects of price fluctuations can be minimized by adding a short-term fund to one's portfolio.

State and Municipal Tax Exemptions

Some long-term tax-exempt bond funds provide investors with an even greater tax advantage by concentrating investments in the municipal bonds issued by a specific state or city. This allows the investor to select a fund whose interest qualifies for an exemption not only from federal income tax, but from the investor's city and state income taxes as well. For example, if an investor lived in New York City and invested in Fidelity New York Tax Free Fund, the return on this fund would be exempt from federal, New York State, and New York City income taxes.

Chapter 8

TEN REPRESENTATIVE LONG-TERM TAX-EXEMPT BOND FUNDS

To illustrate, we have chosen ten long-term tax-exempt bond funds that show the qualities that investors seek when purchasing shares of long-term tax-exempt bond funds. Note that all but one of these examples are no-load funds. Table 8-2 contains a summary listing of the ten funds. It is followed by a more detailed description of each fund's objectives and investment philosophy and practice, as well as capsule Profiles of their recent performance.

Investors are reminded that past performance is no indicator of future performance.

While we anticipate continued positive results from long-term tax-exempt bond funds, the new tax law environment increases the complexity of this market and places a premium on experienced, professional management. The climate for municipal bonds should become less volatile than in the recent past as the pressure of strong demand on the available supply of bonds dampens trading fervor.

Table 8-2: Ten Representative Long-Term Tax Exempt Bond Funds

Fund	Annual Return (%) for Three Years	Load
Dreyfus Tax Exempt Bond Fund	15.0	NL
Fidelity Aggressive Tax Free Fund	NA	NL
Fidelity High Yield Municipals	16.7	NL
Financial Tax Free Income Shares	17.9	NL
T. Rowe Price Tax Free Income Fund	14.5	NL
Putnam Tax Exempt Income Fund	16.3	NL
Scudder Managed Municipal Bond Fund	14.8	NL
Shearson Managed Municipal Bond Fund	16.6	L
Stein Roe Managed Municipal Bond Fund	17.1	NL
Vanguard Municipal High Yield Fund	16.9	NL

Dreyfus Tax Exempt Bond Fund

The investment objective of this Fund is to provide investors with tax-free income by investing primarily in municipal bonds.

The Dreyfus Tax Exempt Bond Fund has some $3.5 billion in assets, spread over 350 municipal bonds. This extensive diversification is important to investors concerned about the creditworthiness of individual municipal bonds.

Fidelity Aggressive Tax Free Fund

Fidelity Aggressive Tax Free Fund seeks a high current yield by investing primarily in a portfolio of lower-quality municipal bonds.

The Fund purchases municipal securities with maturities of 20 years or more. The Fund's average maturity may vary because of anticipated market conditions. Management purchases bonds with an eye toward income rather than stability of the Fund's share price.

The Fund uses both its own extensive research facilities and the ratings agencies when deciding on the appropriateness of investments. (For example, the Fund may purchase bonds that are nonrated by either of the major agencies, when, in the judgment of management, the bonds are suitable for the Fund.) When purchasing bonds, whether rated or nonrated, the Fidelity Aggressive Tax Free Fund performs its own credit analysis. Investors should be aware of the fact that nonrated bonds may be less marketable than rated bonds.

While this Fund may provide an enhanced yield, it also may result in more volatility in the price of the Fund. Thus, buyers should plan to hold this Fund through some price swings. Despite its occasional volatility, this Fund is an excellent investment for those seeking higher tax-free yields.

Fidelity High Yield Municipals Fund

Fidelity High Yield Municipals Fund seeks a high current yield primarily by investing in long-term, medium-quality (Moody's A or S&P A—see Table 4-1) municipal bonds.

When purchasing bonds for the portfolio, management is not restricted to specific ratings categories. Thus, management may chose to purchase bonds that are nonrated or rated below medium quality if it judges that the bonds have the same characteristics as the bonds of medium quality (i.e., an adequate but not outstanding capacity to service debt).

The Fund purchases long-term obligations with maturities of 20 years or more because they generally produce higher yields than short-term obligations. However, such bonds tend to be more exposed to market fluctuations in NAV when interest rates change. During periods of economic difficulty or rising interest rates, the Fund attempts to adjust its portfolio by shortening the average maturity and/or by upgrading the quality of bonds held by the Fund.

The Fund has provided excellent returns to investors for the last five years. And it will continue to produce quality returns for investors seeking tax-free income as long as interest rates are reasonably stable. It is best suited to the investor who seeks higher tax-free income and can accommodate fluctuations in the NAV per share.

Chapter 8

Financial Tax Free Income Shares

The investment objective of Financial Tax Free Income Shares is to seek as high a level of current income exempt from federal income taxes as is consistent with the preservation of investor capital.

Figure 8-1 illustrates the exceptional performance of this Fund; of particular note are the 23 percent and 22 percent returns in 1985 and 1986 respectively!

The Fund performs well in both down and up markets because it is actively managed.

The Fund has a low beta and a high alpha. These statistics, when combined with its exceptional yields and total annual returns, makes it one of the best-performing funds in this classification.

Figure 8-1: The Performance of the Financial Tax Free Income Fund Shown with Its 26-Week Moving Average. (Courtesy of Telescan.)

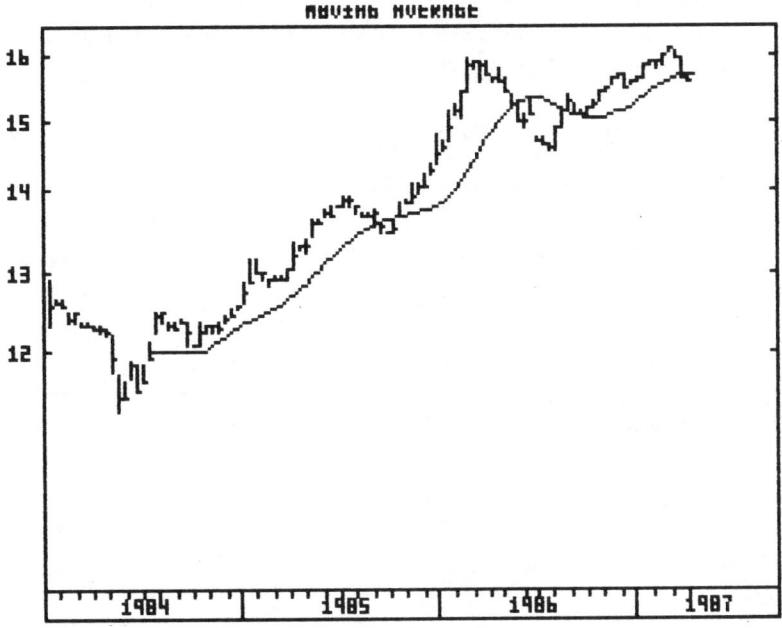

T. Rowe Price Tax Free Income Fund

T. Rowe Price Tax Free Income Fund seeks to provide investors with a high level of income exempt from federal income taxes and a positive total return.

The Fund primarily invests in longer-term bonds. The Fund's holdings tend to be highly diversified, affording additional protection to investors.

In order to achieve the Fund's primary goal, T. Rowe Price actively manages the Fund with constant buying and selling. The Fund typically holds 150 municipal bonds significantly diversified by geography and type.

While the Fund has no restriction on portfolio maturity, in actuality the average maturity is expected to be greater than five years. (A recent analysis showed that the average maturity was 22 years, yielding 7 percent.)

Putnam Tax Exempt Income Fund

The Putnam Tax Exempt Income Fund's objective is high current tax-free income and, secondarily, a good total return.

The strategy of the Fund is to hold a diversified portfolio of municipal bonds exempt from federal taxes. The Fund currently holds about 150 bonds in its portfolio and is well diversified.

Most industry experts consider the Putnam Tax Exempt Income Fund to be well managed and a good investment for those investors seeking tax-exempt income. The Fund has provided exemplary returns since 1982, and ranks number 1 among its competitors with a total return of 170.2 percent for the five years ended December 31, 1986.

Scudder Managed Municipal Bond Fund

Scudder Managed Municipal Bond Fund seeks to provide income exempt from federal income taxes.

The Fund invests primarily in municipal bonds. Management attempts to take advantage of price changes of bonds in the market to achieve a higher total return for investors. This is in contrast to the management of other funds, which often are more passive in management style—holding their bonds longer and buying and selling less frequently.

Fund Manager Donald Carleton recently said (personal communication) "Our policy now is to be fully invested (85–100 percent) in long-term bonds. Our prospectus requires that half of the portfolio be rated Aa [Moody's—see Table 4-1] or better. At present we have about 65 percent in this category, so we are still a high quality fund and will . . . remain so."

Scudder Managed Municipal Bond Fund has flexible investment policies regarding maturity; however, typical holdings are long-term municipal bonds.

Scudder, Stevens & Clark is the investment advisor for the Scudder Family of Funds. (Scudder Managed Municipal Bond Fund historically has had the highest yields of all the funds in this family.) Scudder was a pioneer in the investment counseling profession since opening its doors in 1919. In 1928 it introduced the first no-load mutual fund to the public. Assets under management currently exceed $15 billion.

At least 50 percent of all investments are rated within the top two quality ratings, with at least 80 percent within the top three ratings categories (see Table 4-1). For example, by late 1986 the Fund had 90 percent of the bonds in its portfolio rated (S&P) AA or AAA, 5 percent rated A, and no holdings below A.

Carleton's strategy is to "take care of the principal and let the income take care of itself." Carleton manages the maturity of the holdings within this Fund carefully. Average maturities were reduced from a high of 31 years in January 1985 to 14 years in early 1986.

Dividends are declared daily and paid monthly. The average compounded rate of return for a recent five-year period was 19 percent.

With assets of over $630 million, this Fund is conservatively managed. The portfolio consists of some 100 securities, spread over 30 states. Furthermore, 60 percent of the Fund's holdings are backed by T-bills held in escrow accounts by the issuing agencies or municipalities. The Fund has low volatility as measured by an estimated standard deviation of 2.55.

Annual yields peaked at 10 percent in early 1984, and since then have settled in the 6.5 percent range. However, when investors consider the increases in net asset value, the Fund provided a representative total return of 16.8 percent for 1986. Clearly, this Fund is ideal for conservative investors seeking tax-free income from a conservatively managed source.

Shearson Managed Municipal Bond Fund

Shearson Managed Municipal Bond Fund holds long-term higher-quality municipal bonds. The investment goal is income exempt from federal income tax.

The Fund is characterized as "low-risk," having a beta of 0.29 for a representative three-year period. It is an ideal investment for those seeking a combination of good returns, low risk, and exemption from federal taxes.

Stein Roe Managed Municipal Bond Fund

Stein Roe Managed Municipal Bond Fund seeks a high level of current income consistent with the preservation of capital.

By investing primarily in a portfolio of municipal bonds, the income is exempt from federal taxes. (While management invests so that at least 80 percent of the income received will be exempt from federal taxes, it does reserve the right to alter this position at times when it believes that a temporary defensive position is advisable.)

The Fund invests primarily in long-term municipal securities (ten-year maturities or more); however, shorter-term securities may be added as temporary defensive measures. At least 75 percent of the Fund's investments in municipal securities will be rated (at the time of purchase) in the three highest ratings assigned by Moody's or S&P.

Because interest rates have been steady or declining, the Fund has continued to achieve good results for investors. Anthony Zulfer, the Fund's Portfolio Manager, sees a "temporary firming in yield levels as higher economic activity unfolds [and] interest rates should turn down again as the positive effects of tax reform begin to take hold."

Vanguard Municipal High Yield Fund

As the name implies, the Vanguard Municipal High Yield Fund's objective is income exempt from federal taxes. The Fund concentrates on generating a high yield while maintaining a reasonable volatility in share price.

The Fund invests primarily in medium- to lower-quality municipal bonds with average maturities of more than 20 years. (A recent sampling found the Fund holding a portfolio with an average maturity of 26 years.)

Figure 8-2 illustrates the Fund's performance from 1985 through 1987. Total return (yields plus increases in the net asset value of the Fund) were 22 and 20 percent for 1985 and 1986, respectively. Industry experts feel that the Vanguard Municipal High Yield Fund bested 80 percent of all municipal bond funds in total return from 1982 to 1986.

Figure 8-2: The Performance of Vanguard Municipal Bond High Yield Fund Shown with Its 26-Week Moving Average. (Courtesy of Telescan.)

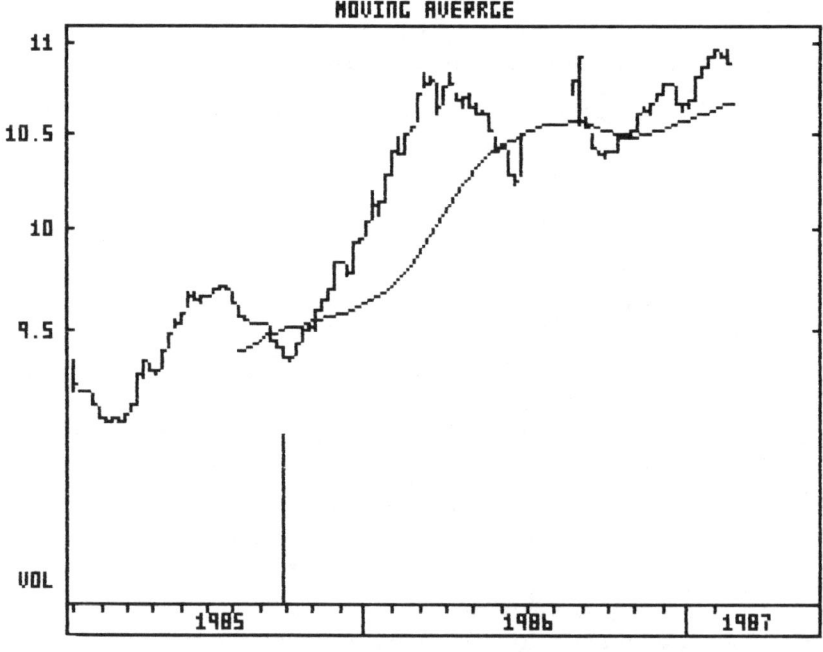

PROFILE 8-1

DREYFUS TAX-EXEMPT BOND FUND
767 Fifth Avenue
New York, NY 10022
1-800-645-6561
718-895-1206

Fund Classification:	MB	
Total Assets:	$3540 million	
Fund Manager:	Richard J. Moynihan	
Year of Inception:	1976	
Minimum Investment:	$2500	
Sales Charge:	No load	
12b-1 Charge:	No	
Expense Ratio:	0.68	
Portfolio Mix:	%	*Issues*
Bonds	0	0
Municipal Bonds	NA	350
Common Stock	0	0
Preferred Stock	0	0
U. S. Government Securities	0	0
Cash	0	0
Commercial Paper	0	0
Estimated Annual Portfolio Turnover	56%	
Estimates of Fund Performance:		
Annual Return for Three Years:	15.0%	
Annual Return for Five Years:	18.8%	
Annual Return in Bull Markets:		
1985	19.5%	
1986	17.3%	
Annual Return in Bear Markets:		
3/30/86–6/30/86	-0.1%	
Representative Current Yield (12/31/86):	7.4%	
Measures of Risk and Reward:		
Alpha	4.2	
Beta	0.29	
R square	30	
Standard deviation	1.96	
Reward/risk ratio	7.7	
Net Asset Value:		
9/25/87	11.63	
10/28/87	11.42	

PROFILE 8-2

FIDELITY AGGRESSIVE TAX FREE FUND
82 Devonshire Street
Boston, MA 02109
1-800-544-6666
617-523-1919

Fund Classification:	MB	
Total Assets:	$308 million	
Fund Manager:	Guy Wickwire	
Year of Inception:	1985	
Minimum Investment:	$2500	
Sales Charge:	No load	
12b-1 Charge:	No	
Expense Ratio:	0.65	
Portfolio Mix:	%	*Issues*
Bonds	0	0
Municipal Bonds	NA	125
Common Stock	0	0
Preferred Stock	0	0
U. S. Government Securities	0	0
Cash	0	0
Commercial Paper	0	0
Estimated Annual Portfolio Turnover	22%	
Estimates of Fund Performance:		
Annual Return for Three Years:	NA	
Annual Return for Five Years:	NA	
Annual Return in Bull Markets:		
1985	NA	
1986	17.5%	
Annual Return in Bear Markets:		
3/30/86–6/30/86	-0.6%	
Representative Current Yield (12/31/86):	8.1%	
Measures of Risk and Reward:		
Alpha	NA	
Beta	0.35	
R square	NA	
Standard deviation	2.2	
Reward/risk ratio	8.0	
Net Asset Value:		
9/25/87	10.97	
10/28/87	10.61	

PROFILE 8-3

FIDELITY HIGH YIELD MUNICIPALS
82 Devonshire Street
Boston, MA 02109
1-800-544-6666
617-523-1919

Fund Classification:	MB	
Total Assets:	$2065 million	
Fund Manager:	Guy Wickwire	
Year of Inception:	1977	
Minimum Investment:	$2500	
Sales Charge:	No load	
12b-1 Charge:	No	
Expense Ratio:	0.56	
Portfolio Mix:	%	*Issues*
Bonds	93	NA
Municipal Bonds	0	0
Common Stock	0	0
Preferred Stock	0	0
U. S. Government Securities	0	0
Cash	0	0
Commercial Paper	0	0
Estimated Annual Portfolio Turnover	70%	
Estimates of Fund Performance:		
Annual Return for Three Years:	16.7%	
Annual Return for Five Years:	19.5%	
Annual Return in Bull Markets:		
1985	21.4%	
1986	19.0%	
Annual Return in Bear Markets:		
3/30/86–6/30/86	-0.6%	
Representative Current Yield (12/30/86):	7.3%	
Measures of Risk and Reward:		
Alpha	5.6	
Beta	0.27	
R square	27	
Standard deviation	2.16	
Reward/risk ratio	7.7	
Net Asset Value:		
9/25/87	11.88	
10/28/87	11.48	

PROFILE 8-4

FINANCIAL TAX FREE INCOME SHARES
P.O. Box 2040
Denver, CO 80201
1-800-525-8085
303-779-1233

Fund Classification:	MB	
Total Assets:	$117 million	
Fund Manager:	William Veronda	
Year of Inception:	1981	
Minimum Investment:	$250	
Sales Charge:	No load	
12b-1 Charge:	No	
Expense Ratio:	0.68	
Portfolio Mix:	%	*Issues*
Bonds	NA	NA
Municipal Bonds	NA	NA
Common Stock	NA	NA
Preferred Stock	NA	NA
U. S. Government Securities	NA	NA
Cash	NA	NA
Commercial Paper	NA	NA
Estimated Annual Portfolio Turnover	NA	
Estimates of Fund Performance:		
Annual Return for Three Years:	17.9%	
Annual Return for Five Years:	NA	
Annual Return in Bull Markets:		
1985	22.9%	
1986	22.1%	
Annual Return in Bear Markets:		
3/30/86–6/30/86	-1.2%	
Representative Current Yield (12/31/86):	7.1%	
Measures of Risk and Reward:		
Alpha	6.5	
Beta	0.29	
R square	17	
Standard deviation	2.92	
Reward/risk ratio	6.1	
Net Asset Value:		
9/25/87	13.22	
10/28/87	12.93	

PROFILE 8-5

(T. ROWE) PRICE TAX FREE INCOME FUND
100 E. Pratt Street
Baltimore, MD 21202
1-800-638-5660
301-547-2000

Fund Classification:	MB	
Total Assets:	$1411 million	
Fund Manager:	Peter Gordon	
Year of Inception:	1976	
Minimum Investment:	$1000	
Sales Charge:	No load	
12b-1 Charge:	No	
Expense Ratio:	0.62	

Portfolio Mix:	%	*Issues*
Bonds	0	0
Municipal Bonds	NA	125
Common Stock	0	0
Preferred Stock	0	0
U. S. Government Securities	0	0
Cash	0	0
Commercial Paper	0	0
Estimated Annual Portfolio Turnover	187%	

Estimates of Fund Performance:	
Annual Return for Three Years:	14.5%
Annual Return for Five Years:	16.0%
Annual Return in Bull Markets:	
1985	16.9%
1986	19.8%
Annual Return in Bear Markets:	
3/30/86–6/30/86	-1.1%
Representative Current Yield (12/31/86):	7.0%

Measures of Risk and Reward:	
Alpha	4.1
Beta	20.23
R square	29
Standard deviation	1.77
Reward/risk ratio	8.2

Net Asset Value:	
9/25/87	8.45
10/28/87	8.33

PROFILE 8-6

PUTNAM TAX EXEMPT INCOME FUND
One Post Office Square
Boston, MA 02109
1-800-225-1581
617-423-4960
617-292-1000

Fund Classification:	MB	
Total Assets:	$624 million	
Fund Manager:	David Eurkus	
Year of Inception:	1976	
Minimum Investment:	$500	
Sales Charge:	4.75	
12b-1 Charge:	No	
Expense Ratio:	0.68	

Portfolio Mix:	%	Issues
Bonds	0	0
Municipal Bonds	NA	150
Common Stock	0	0
Preferred Stock	0	0
U. S. Government Securities	0	0
Cash	0	0
Commercial Paper	0	0
Estimated Annual Portfolio Turnover	123.27%	

Estimates of Fund Performance:	
Annual Return for Three Years:	16.3%
Annual Return for Five Years:	21.9%
Annual Return in Bull Markets:	
1985	23.6%
1986	21.9%
Annual Return in Bear Markets:	
3/30/86–6/30/86	0.8%
Representative Current Yield (12/31/86):	7.37%
Measures of Risk and Reward:	
Alpha	4.7
Beta	0.34
R square	32
Standard deviation	2.29
Reward/risk ratio	7.1
Net Asset Value:	
9/25/87	13.34
10/28/87	13.13

PROFILE 8-7

SCUDDER MANAGED MUNICIPAL BOND FUND
175 Federal Street
Boston, MA 02110
1-800 453-3305 or 1-800-225-2470
617-482-3990

Fund Classification:	MB	
Total Assets:	$630 million	
Fund Manager:	Donald Carleton	
Year of Inception:	1976	
Minimum Investment:	$1000	
Sales Charge:	No load	
12b-1 Charge:	No	
Expense Ratio:	0.58	
Portfolio Mix:	*%*	*Issues*
Bonds	0	0
Municipal Bonds	NA	125
Common Stock	0	0
Preferred Stock	0	0
U. S. Government Securities	0	0
Cash	0	0
Commercial Paper	0	0
Estimated Annual Portfolio Turnover	78%	
Estimates of Fund Performance:		
Annual Return for Three Years:	14.8%	
Annual Return for Five Years:	19.0%	
Annual Return in Bull Markets:		
1985	17.5%	
1986	16.8%	
Annual Return in Bear Markets:		
3/30/86–6/30/86	1.1%	
Representative Current Yield (1/31/87):	6.7%	
Measures of Risk and Reward:		
Alpha	3.5	
Beta	0.32	
R square	27	
Standard deviation	2.55	
Reward/risk ratio	5.8	
Net Asset Value:		
9/25/87	8.11	
10/28/87	7.98	

PROFILE 8-8

SHEARSON MANAGED MUNICIPAL BOND FUND
31 St. James Ave. 5th Floor
Boston, MA 02116
1-800-221-3636
817-335-3051

Fund Classification:	MB	
Total Assets:	$628 million	
Fund Manager:	D. Lee Hayes	
Year of Inception:	1981	
Minimum Investment:	$2500	
Sales Charge:	5.00	
12b-1 Charge:	No	
Expense Ratio:	0.66	
Portfolio Mix:	%	*Issues*
Bonds	0	0
Municipal Bonds	NA	247
Common Stock	0	0
Preferred Stock	0	0
U. S. Government Securities	0	0
Cash	0	0
Commercial Paper	0	0
Estimated Annual Portfolio Turnover	27%	
Estimates of Fund Performance:		
Annual Return for Three Years:	16.6%	
Annual Return for Five Years:	NA	
Annual Return in Bull Markets:		
1985	20.9%	
1986	18.7%	
Annual Return in Bear Markets:		
3/30/86–6/30/86	-0.6%	
Representative Current Yield (12/31/87):	7.0%	
Measures of Risk and Reward:		
Alpha	5.3	
Beta	0.29	
R square	24	
Standard deviation	2.48	
Reward/risk ratio	6.7	
Net Asset Value:		
9/25/87	14.27	
10/28/87	13.99	

PROFILE 8-9

STEIN ROE MANAGED MUNICIPAL BOND FUND
Box 1143
Chicago, IL 60690
1-800-621-0320
312-368-7826

Fund Classification:	MB	
Total Assets:	$542 million	
Fund Manager:	Anthony Zulfer	
	David Snowbeck	
Year of Inception:	1977	
Minimum Investment:	$2500	
Sales Charge:	No load	
12b-1 Charge:	No	
Expense Ratio:	0.65	
Portfolio Mix:	%	*Issues*
Bonds	0	0
Municipal Bonds	NA	196
Common Stock	0	0
Preferred Stock	0	0
U. S. Government Securities	0	0
Cash	0	0
Commercial Paper	0	0
Estimated Annual		
Portfolio Turnover	92%	
Estimates of Fund Performance:		
Annual Return for Three Years:	17.1%	
Annual Return for Five Years:	21.0%	
Annual Return in Bull Markets:		
1985	22.6%	
1986	17.4%	
Annual Return in Bear Markets:		
6/30/86–9/30/86	-5.1%	
Representative Current Yield (1/31/87):	6.9%	
Measures of Risk and Reward:		
Alpha	5.3	
Beta	0.34	
R square	20	
Standard deviation	3.11	
Reward/risk ratio	5.5	
Net Asset Value:		
9/25/87	8.31	
10/28/87	8.18	

PROFILE 8-10

VANGUARD MUNICIPAL HIGH YIELD FUND
P.O. Box 2600
Valley Forge, PA 19482
215-648-6000

Fund Classification:	MB	
Total Assets:	$782 million	
Fund Manager:	Ian MacKinnon	
Year of Inception:	1978	
Minimum Investment:	$3000	
Sales Charge:	No load	
12b-1 Charge:	No	
Expense Ratio:	0.33	
Portfolio Mix:	%	*Issues*
Bonds	0	0
Municipal Bonds	NA	173
Common Stock	0	0
Preferred Stock	0	0
U. S. Government Securities	0	0
Cash	0	0
Commercial Paper	0	0
Estimated Annual Portfolio Turnover	41%	
Estimates of Fund Performance:		
Annual Return for Three Years:	15.9%	
Annual Return for Five Years:	19.1%	
Annual Return in Bull Markets:		
1985	21.7%	
1986	19.7%	
Annual Return in Bear Markets:		
3/30/86–6/30/86	0.5%	
Representative Current Yield (12/31/86):	7.7%	
Measures of Risk and Reward:		
Alpha	5.2	
Beta	0.33	
R square	30	
Standard deviation	2.52	
Reward/risk ratio	6.3	
Net Asset Value:		
9/25/87	9.45	
10/28/87	9.34	

Chapter 9
Balanced Funds

BACKGROUND INFORMATION

Type of Security

A balanced fund strives for income while maintaining a stable net asset value through a balanced portfolio of stocks and bonds. Typically, the ratio of stocks to bonds is around 60:40.

Risk/Stability

Balanced funds were designed with the express purpose of allowing shareholder investments to grow in bull stock markets while protecting principal with a substantial position in bonds when stock markets are falling. This strategy, and balanced funds in general, have been extremely popular with investors in the last five years. Bruce Behling, Vice President of Strong Investment Fund, expresses investor confidence in balanced funds this way: "These funds have never seen demand on this scale before. Yet some of them are 40 or 50 years old. After years of being overshadowed by other types of funds, the features that attract risk-averse investors suddenly are being discovered."

In the last five years, balanced funds have outperformed all other categories of stock funds. This is a surprising turn of events, in that a generally rising market would seem to favor more aggressive stock market funds, such as aggressive growth funds and growth and income funds (see Chapters 11 and 13). One advantage these funds have over other stock funds is the ability to move freely from stocks to bonds and back to stocks. While generally required to keep a percentage of the portfolio in fixed-income securities (most keep 30 to 50 percent in bonds at all times), balanced funds can take advantage of changing conditions to enhance investors' yields.

PORTFOLIO FIT

Balanced funds are essentially income funds; as important is their goal to maintain a stable or increasing net asset value. These funds, in other words, are essentially for conservative investors, who are risk-averse but want to maintain a good income with some chance for capital appreciation.

Most investors might have as much as 10 percent of their assets invested in balanced funds. A retired individual, fittingly concerned about risk but needing income, might put as much as 20 percent of invested assets into one or two balanced funds.

If an investor plans to use balanced funds to take advantage of both the stock and bond markets, he or she will have to pay attention to the direction of interest rates. In general, balanced funds are a good play if interest rates are declining or stable.

The current high level of attention to these funds is coming from those investors who want the stock–bond balance decision made for them. Although exchanges between funds are at record levels, millions of investors prefer to leave judgments on interest rates and stock market trends to professional money managers.

SIX REPRESENTATIVE BALANCED FUNDS

To illustrate, we have chosen six balanced funds that show the qualities that investors seek when purchasing shares of balanced funds. Note that five of the six examples are no-load funds. Table 9-1 contains a summary listing of the six funds. It is followed by a more detailed description of each fund's objectives and investment philosophy and practice, as well as capsule Profiles of their recent performance.

Investors are reminded that past performance is no indicator of future performance.

Table 9-1: Six Representative Balanced Funds

Fund	Annual Return (%) for Three Years	Load
Axe-Houghton Fund B	20.8	NL
Dodge & Cox Balanced Fund	18.3	NL
Loomis-Sayles Mutual Fund	21.3	NL
Strong Investment Fund	15.5	L
Wellesley Fund	20.7	NL
Wellington Fund	20.9	NL

Axe-Houghton Fund B

Investment objectives of the Axe-Houghton Fund B are the conservation of investment capital, reasonable income, and long-term capital growth. (Remarkably, the Fund has paid continuous quarterly dividends for over 47 years.)

To achieve its goals, the Fund invests in bonds, preferred stocks, and common stocks in such proportions and types as to match the current economic outlook. The Fund values securities offering income security and attractive yields. Common stock investments are limited to a maximum of 75 percent of the value of the Fund's total assets at any one time.

A recent sampling showed that the Fund held one-half of its portfolio in stocks and one half in bonds and short-term notes. The five largest holdings of common stock were Con-Agra, Digital Equipment, Battle Mt. Gold Co., Federal Paper Board, and Carter-Wallace. Portfolio Manager William McElroy recently reported that long-term financial assets (common stocks and long-maturity bonds) dominate the Fund's portfolio. Not surprisingly, these are the securities that performed best for the Fund.

In McElroy's view, an increased rate of economic growth is likely over the next year or so. He further expects some increase in inflation. This outlook implies improved growth of corporate earnings, thus warranting a portfolio holding a significant amount of common stock. The common stocks selected by McElroy must be industries and companies likely to show rapid growth in earnings, despite increased inflation. In response to this challenge, McElroy has reduced the percentage of the Fund's holdings in longer-term bonds; cash assets correspondingly have increased, thus reducing the average maturity and price sensitivity of the total portfolio.

Dodge & Cox Balanced Fund

The Dodge & Cox Balanced Fund strives to provide investors with regular income, conservation of principal, and the opportunity for long-term growth of both principal and income.

The Fund hopes to achieve these objectives by investing in a diversified portfolio of common stocks, preferred stocks, and bonds. The Fund maintains no more than 75 percent of total assets in common stocks and convertible securities (that portion of the convertible that is attributable to the conversion right).

Since 1931 Dodge & Cox (San Francisco) have been both Fund Managers and Investment Advisers for the Fund. The Fund's managers take a conservative approach, looking for value in long-term stocks and bonds. (Bonds held in the portfolio are all investment-grade corporate or government securities.) A recent sampling of the Fund's stock holdings showed positions in International Paper, Procter and Gamble, General Electric, Eli Lilly, and IBM. The largest corporate bond holding was Pacific Telesis.

The Fund may be purchased only by residents of Hawaii, California, Oregon, Utah, Nevada, New York, and the District of Columbia.

Loomis-Sayles Mutual Fund

The Loomis-Sayles Mutual Fund is a flexibly managed mutual fund seeking reasonable long-term capital appreciation while protecting capital from unnecessary risks. Although current income is important when selecting securities for its investment portfolio, it is not a controlling factor.

Loomis-Sayles, founded in 1926, is one of the nation's oldest and largest investment counseling firms. The firm has 45 people on its research staff. The ability to research and judge securities independently of the ratings agencies and others is an important selling point for the Fund.

A portion of the Fund, between 20 and 50 percent, historically has been invested in bonds. A recent review of the Fund's holdings found that 75 percent of its assets were in stocks and 25 percent in bonds. Among the largest stock holdings are Marsh and Mc-Lennan, Phillip Morris, Marion Laboratories, UpJohn, and Ford Motor. A three-year tracking of the Fund's performance is shown in Figure 9-1.

The Loomis-Sayles Mutual Fund is less conservative than Axe-Houghton B or Dodge & Cox and is more suitable for the investor who seeks greater total return in a balanced fund with the attendant increased risk.

Figure 9-1: The Performance of the Loomis Sayles Mutual Fund Shown with Its 26-Week Moving Average. (Courtesy of Telescan.)

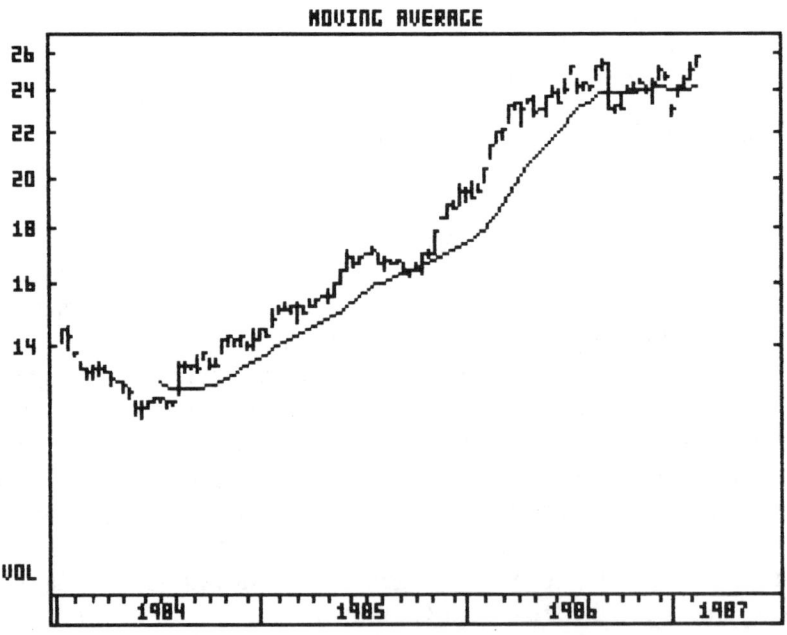

Strong Investment Fund

The investment objectives of the Strong Investment Fund is both income and capital appreciation (the highest total return consistent with the conservation of capital).

The Fund uses a diversified portfolio of common stocks (both growth and income stocks), preferred stocks, and debt securities (including convertible preferred stocks and convertible debentures). The Fund's investment in common stock (including convertible bonds, preferred stocks, and convertible preferreds) may not exceed 65 percent of the value of the Fund's total assets.

If economic conditions change, the Strong Investment Fund readily can change the balance and portfolio mix—especially if a defensive stance is needed in order to preserve capital.

In fact, the Strong Investment Fund is known for its ability to adjust the portfolio mix in times of change. For example, one year ago the Fund contained 30 percent stocks, 30 percent in bonds and 40 percent in cash. Recently, the Fund's managers found opportunities in bonds. The Fund's holdings were adjusted to almost 50 percent stocks and 50 percent bonds. The balance could change back again at any time.

The five largest stock holdings were General Mills, GAF, Ralston Purina, General RE, and CNA Financial. This portfolio (and any future changes) are designed for one purpose: "Our objectives are to generate a 3 percent real rate of return above the rate of inflation, avoid serious market declines if at all possible, and participate in a reasonable manner during those intermittent periods when the financial markets offer opportunities for appreciation."

Investors find the risk of holding Strong Investment Fund to be low, primarily because the Fund holds bonds as well as high-quality stocks. In fact, the beta of the Strong Investment Fund is a mere 0.4, meaning that its value will fluctuate less than one-half as much as the stock market as a whole.

Strong Investment Fund is less aggressive than Loomis-Sayles or Wellington since it will readily move to a significant holding in cash when it anticipates higher risk conditions.

The Wellesley Fund

The objective of the Wellesley Fund is to seek as much current income as is consistent with reasonable risk. The Fund secondarily seeks possibilities for moderate growth of capital.

The Fund balances its portfolio with stocks for growth and bonds for income. The Fund invests in both fixed-income securities (corporate bonds and preferred stocks) and common stocks. The common stock portion of the Fund consists of dividend-paying issues listed on the New York Stock Exchange. The bond holdings consist primarily of investment-grade securities. The Fund currently has assets of approximately $339 million (current yield on these holdings is about 7.9 percent). Typically, 35 percent of the Fund's assets will be in stocks and 65 percent in bonds.

The Wellington Management Co. serves as investment advisor; the management fee is 0.25 percent of assets. The Vanguard Group provides all shareholder services. (Total expense ratio is only 0.60 percent.)

Fund Managers Earl McEvoy and John Nyheem explained their philosophy: "We seek low price/earnings, high-yield stocks and try to grow the dividend and total return in that order." They also look for attractive growth prospects. More particularly, according to McEvoy "Wellesley's common stocks sell at an average price/earnings ratio of 10.0 times our 1987 earnings estimates, substantially below the market average. Our major tenets in managing the fixed-income portion of the Fund are diversification, call protection, and low turnover. We seek issuers of fixed-rate obligations whose ability to pay sustainable income is high. The Fund currently has 93 issuers of debt, with an average quality rating of A [see Table 4-1]."

With excellent holdings in solid corporate bonds and stocks, the Fund should serve those who seek dividend enhancement. The Fund is well-suited for retired individuals or for tax-sheltered accounts. The Fund's performance is tracked in Figure 9-2.

Finally, investors should be aware of the low-risk nature of the Fund (beta = .46). The conservative nature of the Fund is best illustrated by how it performed during the bear market of 1981–82. While the S&P dropped 16.6 percent, the Fund's total return was a positive 4.5 percent for the same period.

Figure 9-2: The Performance of the Wellesley Income Fund Shown with Its 26-Week Moving Average. (Courtesy of Telescan.)

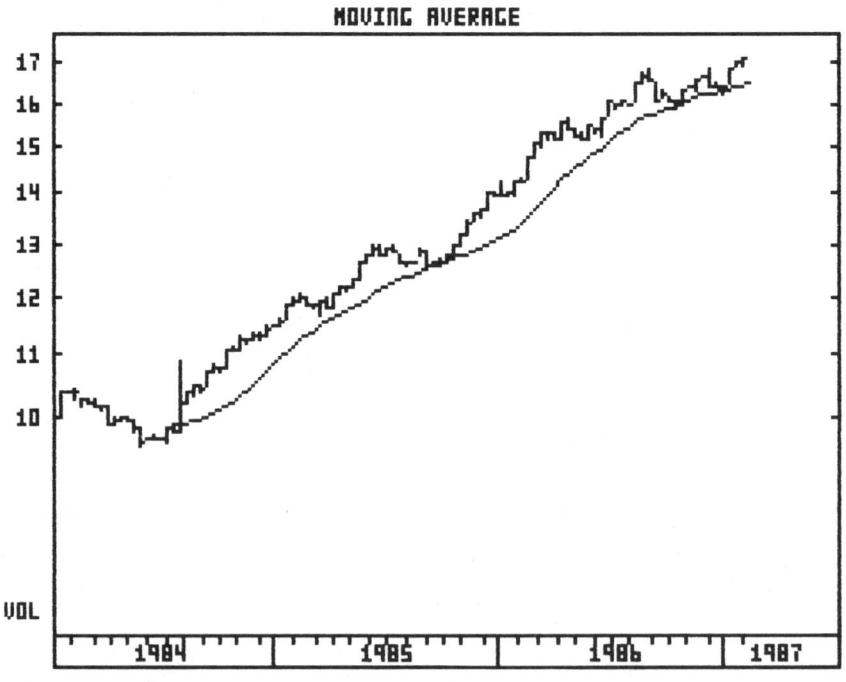

Wellington Fund

The Wellington Fund strives for a balance of stocks and bonds, income and preservation of capital.

A recent sampling of the Fund's holdings showed that from 60 to 70 percent of the portfolio was in stocks. The Fund holds large blocks of Ethyl, Bank of Boston, IBM, Mobil, and RJR–Nabisco. The bond holdings had an average maturity of 20 years and were protected from calls to 16 years (the current yield of the fixed-income portion is approximately 10.2 percent).

Vincent Bajakian, the Portfolio Manager, believes that the Fund is well-positioned to accommodate a range of business and market developments. When the economy picks up momentum and some stability is restored, he expects investors to continue to enjoy satisfactory returns on their stock and bond investments. But, he cautions, the path may not be entirely smooth, and a balanced investment approach remains an appropriate one.

The Fund's excellent long-term performance makes it suitable for the conservative investor who at the same time seeks participation in stock market gains balanced with approximately 35 percent in bonds.

PROFILE 9-1

AXE-HOUGHTON FUND B
400 Benedict Avenue
Tarrytown, NY 10591
1-800-431-1030
914-631-8131

Fund Classification:	B
Total Assets:	$182 million
Fund Manager:	William McElroy
Year of Inception:	1973
Minimum Investment:	$1000
Sales Charge:	No load
12b-1 Charge:	Yes (.45%)
Expense Ratio:	1.19

Portfolio Mix:	%	*Issues*
Bonds	38	NA
Convertible Bonds	0	0
Common Stock	44	NA
Preferred Stock	0	0
U. S. Government Securities	0	0
Cash	18	NA
Commercial Paper	0	0
Estimated Annual Portfolio Turnover	97%	

Estimates of Fund Performance:	
Annual Return for Three Years:	20.8%
Annual Return for Five Years:	19.8%
Annual Return in Bull Markets:	
1985	32.9%
1986	24.7%
Annual Return in Bear Markets:	
6/30/83–6/30/84	-11.2%
Representative Current Yield (12/31/86):	5.0%
Measures of Risk and Reward:	
Alpha	4.8
Beta	0.72
R square	77
Standard deviation	3.40
Reward/risk ratio	6.1
Net Asset Value:	
9/25/87	11.62
10/28/87	8.95

PROFILE 9-2

DODGE AND COX BALANCED FUND
One Post St., 35th Floor
San Francisco, CA 94104
415-981-1710

Fund Classification:	B
Total Assets:	$27 million
Fund Manager:	Harry Hagey
Year of Inception:	1931
Minimum Investment:	$250
Sales Charge:	No load
12b-1 Charge:	No
Expense Ratio:	0.75

Portfolio Mix:	%	*Issues*
Bonds	27.1	23
Convertible Bonds	0	0
Common Stock	67.2	39
Preferred Stock	0	0
U. S. Government Securities	0	0
Cash	4.8	1
Commercial Paper	0	0
Estimated Annual Portfolio Turnover	26%	

Estimates of Fund Performance:	
Annual Return for Three Years:	19.9%
Annual Return for Five Years:	21.7%
Annual Return in Bull Markets:	
1985	32.5%
1986	19.1%
Annual Return in Bear Markets:	
6/30/83–6/30/84	-3.66%
Representative Current Yield (12/31/86):	4.7%

Measures of Risk and Reward:	
Alpha	2.7
Beta	0.70
R square	93
Standard deviation	3.03
Reward/risk ratio	6.6

Net Asset Value:	
9/25/87	38.51
10/28/87	32.11

PROFILE 9-3

LOOMIS-SAYLES MUTUAL FUND
P.O. Box 449 Back Bay Annex
Boston, MA 02117
617-578-6262

Fund Classification:	B	
Total Assets:	$174 million	
Fund Manager:	G. Kenneth Heebner	
Year of Inception:	1929	
Minimum Investment:	$250	
Sales Charge:	No load	
12b-1 Charge:	No	
Expense Ratio:	0.86	
Portfolio Mix:	*%*	*Issues*
Bonds	24	NA
Convertible Bonds	0	0
Common Stock	63	NA
Preferred Stock	24	NA
U. S. Government Securities	0	0
Cash	3	NA
Commercial Paper	0	0
Estimated Annual		
Portfolio Turnover	175%	
Estimates of Fund Performance:		
Annual Return for Three Years:	21.3%	
Annual Return for Five Years:	22.6%	
Annual Return in Bull Markets:		
1985	34.4%	
1986	24.8%	
Annual Return in Bear Markets:		
6/30/83–6/30/84	-8.18%	
Representative Current Yield (12/31/86):	3.9%	
Measures of Risk and Reward:		
Alpha	4.1	
Beta	0.84	
R square	79	
Standard deviation	3.90	
Reward/risk ratio	5.5	
Net Asset Value:		
9/25/87	28.93	
10/28/87	19.99	

PROFILE 9-4

STRONG INVESTMENT FUND
815 E. Mason St.
Milwaukee, WI 53202
1-800-368-3863
414-765-0620

Fund Classification:	B	
Total Assets:	$319 million	
Fund Manager:	William Corneliuson	
	Richard Strong	
Year of Inception:	1981	
Minimum Investment:	$250	
Sales Charge:	1.0%	
12b-1 Charge:	No	
Expense Ratio:	1.10	
Portfolio Mix:	*%*	*Issues*
Bonds	30	NA
Convertible Bonds	0	0
Common Stock	30	35
Preferred Stock	0	0
U. S. Government Securities	0	0
Cash	40	NA
Commercial Paper	0	0
Estimated Annual Portfolio Turnover	93%	
Estimates of Fund Performance:		
Annual Return for Three Years:	15.5%	
Annual Return for Five Years:	24.4%	
Annual Return in Bull Markets:		
1985	19.4%	
1986	17.5%	
Annual Return in Bear Markets:		
6/30/83–6/30/84	5.6%	
Representative Current Yield (12/31/86):	5.4%	
Measures of Risk and Reward:		
Alpha	3.2	
Beta	0.41	
R square	59	
Standard deviation	2.20	
Reward/risk ratio	7.0	
Net Asset Value:		
9/25/87	20.07	
10/28/87	18.38	

PROFILE 9-5

WELLESLEY FUND
Vanguard Financial Ctr.
Valley Forge, PA 19482
1-800-662-7447
1-800-662-2739
In PA: 1-800-362-0530

Fund Classification:	B	
Total Assets:	$399 million	
Fund Manager:	Earl McEvoy	
	John Nyheim	
Year of Inception:	1966	
Minimum Investment:	$1500	
Sales Charge:	No load	
12b-1 Charge:	No	
Expense Ratio:	0.60	
Portfolio Mix:	%	*Issues*
Bonds	0	0
Corporate Bonds	49.9	96
Common Stock	37.73	39
Preferred Stock	0	0
U. S. Government Securities	10.3	15
Cash	0	0
Commercial Paper	0	0
Estimated Annual Portfolio Turnover	20%	
Estimates of Fund Performance:		
Annual Return for Three Years:	20.7%	
Annual Return for Five Years:	20.8%	
Annual Return in Bull Markets:		
1985	27.4%	
1986	18.4%	
Annual Return in Bear Markets:		
6/30/83–6/30/84	2.50%	
Representative Current Yield (12/31/86):	7.9%	
Measures of Risk and Reward:		
Alpha	7.3	
Beta	0.46	
R square	58	
Standard deviation	2.42	
Reward/risk ratio	8.6	
Net Asset Value:		
9/25/87	15.44	
10/28/87	14.79	

PROFILE 9-6

WELLINGTON FUND
Vanguard Financial Ctr.
Valley Forge, PA 19482
1-800-662-7447
1-800-662-2739
In PA: 1-800-362-0530

Fund Classification:	B	
Total Assets:	$1025 million	
Fund Manager:	Vincent Bajakian	
Year of Inception:	1928	
Minimum Investment:	$1500	
Sales Charge:	No load	
12b-1 Charge:	No	
Expense Ratio:	0.55	
Portfolio Mix:	%	*Issues*
Bonds	19.5	37
Common Stock	64.30	64
Preferred Stock	0	0
U. S. Government Securities	13.9	15
Cash	0	0
Commercial Paper	0	0
Estimated Annual Portfolio Turnover	27%	
Estimates of Fund Performance:		
Annual Return for Three Years:	18.9%	
Annual Return for Five Years:	20.9%	
Annual Return in Bull Markets:		
1985	28.5%	
1986	18.9%	
Annual Return in Bear Markets:		
6/30/83–6/30/84	-0.20%	
Representative Current Yield (12/31/86):	5.8%	
Measures of Risk and Reward:		
Alpha	3.4	
Beta	0.70	
R square	92	
Standard deviation	2.99	
Reward/risk ratio	6.3	
Net Asset Value:		
9/25/87	17.73	
10/28/87	14.85	

Chapter 10
Equity Income Funds

BACKGROUND INFORMATION

Type of Security

As the name suggests, the investment goal of equity income funds is to provide investors with current income from securities under management by the fund. An equity income fund normally has about 60 percent of its assets in common stocks and seeks an above-average yield (when compared to the S&P or some other measure of stock market performance).

Risk/Stability

Equity income funds are differentiated from growth and income funds (see Chapter 11) in that growth of principal, or other investment goals, are secondary.

Unlike fixed-income funds (see Chapters 3, 4, and 5), where income is derived from interest payments on bonds, equity income funds can raise or lower their dividends based on the performance of the companies held by the funds. Further, since yield-oriented stocks are more volatile than comparably rated fixed-income securities, equity income funds offer less stability of principal.

SPECIAL BENEFITS AND EXPOSURES

Increasing Income

Having read this, some investors might conclude that fixed-income funds offer investors a better return on their money than equity income funds. However, there is one very important advantage of equity income funds. Like any investment in equities, equity income funds offer investors the potential of greater income over time than their fixed-income counterparts. Yields remain constant for the life of the bond; dividends from equity income funds may increase—in some cases dramatically—thus producing greater income.

Downside Protection

Equity income funds also are an attractive alternative for individuals who invest in the stock market. They offer some downside protection, relative to other types of stock funds or the market in general, while still allowing for the benefits of subsequent upward moves in stock prices. The downside protection comes about because the stocks that have high levels of current income tend to have less price volatility than stocks that pay below-average dividends. Further, dividends normally are a more stable and predictable component of return than capital appreciation. This dividend yield helps cushion the decline in a stock's price during market downturns.

Consider, for example, the volatile stock market environment in the third quarter of 1986. Equity income funds on average declined 2.8 percent while the S&P 500 stock index dropped 7 percent.

Improvements under New Tax Laws

A final advantage of these funds may result from the recent revision of the federal income tax code. Lower tax rates make high-yielding investments more attractive relative to other investments. Further, because capital gains are no longer afforded preferential treatment, investors need not be concerned whether stocks held in an equity income fund are subject to long- or short-term capital gains.

Many investors underestimate the potential of the income component of the total return provided by common stock. Over a long period of time, reinvested dividend income compounds and can account for a very substantial part of the total return. The longer the time for which the proceeds of these funds are allowed to compound, the more meaningful the return over time. For example, reinvested dividends accounted for more than half the total return from the S&P 500 stock index for the ten-year period ended December 31, 1986. Or consider the investor that placed $10,000 investment in the Lipper Equity Income index fund in December 1976; that same investor, reinvesting all dividends, would have realized $43,028 by the end of December 1986. (By comparison, the same amount invested in stocks performing at the S&P index level would have netted the investor $36,580.)

PORTFOLIO FIT

Equity income funds are ideal for individuals who are conservative and willing to tolerate only a modest amount of risk. Because they offer investors both income and potential for capital appreciation, they are useful for investors who normally would not hold stocks of any kind.

An important feature of equity income funds is the protection offered during declining markets. Although there is of course no guarantee that the value of the original investment won't deteriorate during a bear market, there is a reasonable expectation that equity income fund investors will be less affected than other equity investors.

Equity income funds are most suitable for the long-term investor who seeks income and capital preservation with some participation in market gains. Conservative investors might hold as much as 10 to 20 percent of their capital in equity income funds.

SIX REPRESENTATIVE EQUITY INCOME FUNDS

To illustrate, we have chosen six equity income funds that show the qualities that investors seek when purchasing shares of equity income funds. Note that five of the six examples are no-load funds. Table 10-1 contains a summary listing of the six funds. It is followed by a more detailed description of each fund's objectives and investment philosophy and practice, as well as capsule Profiles of their recent performance.

Investors are reminded that past performance is no indicator of future performance.

Table 10-1: Six Representative Equity Income Funds

Fund	Annual Return (%) for Three Years	Load
Fidelity Equity Income Fund	17.3	L
Financial Industrial Income Fund	17.6	NL
GIT Equity Income Fund	18.8	NL
Lindner Dividend Fund	17.5	NL
T. Rowe Price Equity Income Fund	26.6*	NL
Safeco Income Fund	19.8	NL

*One year return.

Fidelity Equity Income Fund

The managers of the Fidelity Equity Income Fund search for securities that offer high levels of current income. Having found these securities, the managers go one step further: They select stocks that have the potential for substantial longer-term growth. (At minimum, the Fund seeks to surpass the composite yield of the S&P 500 index.)

Portfolio manager Bruce Johnstone (a fifteen-year veteran with Fidelity) has over $3 billion under management. He has allocated this influx of investors' dollars into an increasingly diverse number of holdings—434 different securities—representing some 30 industrial sectors. Common stocks compose some 76 percent of the portfolio, while preferred stock and bonds round out the investment program (representing some 10 percent each). The cash position of the Fund is less than 4 percent.

A recent review of the Fund's portfolio showed that the four largest holdings were Ford, American Electric Power, General Motors, and Eastman Kodak. Each of the four represented about 2.5 percent of the Fund's total assets. The three largest industrial sectors are utilities (11 percent), banking and finance (8 percent), and automotive (6.5 percent).

One strategy that the Fund has used effectively is to find companies that are undergoing temporary financial or operating problems and buy when the stock is depressed. This approach, and others like it, resulted in better-than-average performance (outperforming the S&P 500 index) for the last three, five, and ten years respectively.

The Fund, initiated in 1966, demonstrated excellent returns from 1976 to 1986. (There was not a negative return during that decade.)

Although the Fund is large (over $4 billion in assets), it is suitable for the investor seeking consistent long-term total returns.

Financial Industrial Income Fund

The investment objective of the Financial Industrial Income Fund is to earn the highest possible current income. Capital growth potential is an additional, but secondary, consideration in the selection of securities. The Fund invests in securities that will provide a relatively high yield and offer a stable return; in addition, over time, these securities may also provide substantial capital appreciation.

The Fund primarily invests in common stocks (68 percent) convertible bonds (25 percent), preferred stocks (4 percent) with the remainder of the portfolio in cash. A recent analysis showed that the Fund's five largest holdings were Squibb, Medtronic, Super Value Stores, Arvin Industries, and Union Carbide.

Portfolio manager John Kaweske has been making the investment decisions since 1985. He describes his investment philosophy as follows: "Some of the economic assumptions under which we are managing the Fund include declining interest rates, a gradually weakening dollar, low inflation, and slow economic growth. All of these elements should cause money to continue to flow into financial assets such as stocks and bonds, pushing the stock market higher. We think that this environment is going to favor companies that benefit from low interest rates, new product innovation, and high operating rates."

GIT Equity Income Fund

The GIT Equity Income Fund is designed for current dividend income from equity investments. Secondarily, the Fund tries for capital appreciation. Management strives for high income while seeking to preserve capital against erosion by inflation.

The Fund seemingly is well-positioned, with a diversified portfolio of common stocks, including Bank America Realty Trust, General Electric, Merck, NyNex, and IBM. While the Fund is small in total assets ($2.4 million), it does offer investors a good performance record and low risk (beta = 0.5).

This Fund is ideal for investors willing to take on reasonable levels of risk while seeking current income and preservation of capital.

Lindner Dividend Fund

The primary objective of the Lindner Dividend Fund is current income; capital appreciation is secondary.

Typically, management seeks stocks for their income-producing value; thus, the Lindner Dividend Fund is a stable investment, offering good yields and capital growth.

A recent analysis of the Fund's holdings showed the portfolio mix to be 40 percent stocks, 25 percent bonds, 17 percent preferred securities, and the remaining 18 percent in cash. The relatively high cash position was due to a rapid flow of investments into the Fund. The influx was too rapid to place the cash in investments suitable to the Fund managers according to Fund rules, and this situation caused a temporary closing of the Fund to new investments.

The Fund's largest holdings are Illinois Power, Energas Co, Penn Enterprises, and Queensland Coal Trust. Kurt Lindner has managed the Fund since its inception in 1976.

At the time of this writing, the Fund was still closed to new investment. Investors are urged to call to see whether the Fund is accepting new money before choosing this Fund.

T. Rowe Price Equity Income Fund

The T. Rowe Price Equity Income Fund seeks high current income by investing in dividend-paying common stocks of established companies. The Fund specifically looks for companies with favorable prospects for ever-increasing dividend income. The underlying philosophy of the Fund is that over time, dividend income can account for a significant component of the total return from equity investments.

To illustrate, consider the ten-year period ended December 31, 1985. Reinvested dividend income accounted for more than one-half of the total return of the S&P 500 index. This is the same program that the Fund managers, Tom Broadus and Brian Rogers, use when making investment decisions. In addition, they feel that dividends normally are a more stable and predictable source of return than capital appreciation. Therefore, an investment strategy that emphasizes dividend income actually may provide superior long-term investment returns.

The Fund is relatively new, having begun in October of 1985. Nevertheless, the Fund had assets of over $94 million by mid 1987. Of the total dollars under management, 60 percent is in stocks, 18 percent in convertible securities, and 12 percent is preferred stocks and bonds. About 10 percent of assets is in cash.

A recent analysis of the Fund's portfolio showed 70 different securities. The ten largest holdings are General Motors, U.S.F.&G., Xerox, G.T.E., Kodak, 3M, Ogden Corporation, Monsanto, Southwestern Bell, and Chesebrough Ponds. Bond holdings are equally diversified. Some 28 percent of the Fund is invested in telephone, electric, and gas utilities. Figure 10-1 shows the Fund's performance since its inception.

All the stocks held by the Fund are yielding more than the S&P 500 index. Brian Rogers, a four-year veteran with T. Rowe Price, says that the Fund is as "conservative as we are likely to get. We want safe yields and good cash flow." Broadus, a 20-year veteran with T. Rowe Price, stated that "if we get a bear market we will decrease equity holdings; the Equity Income Fund is the best T. Rowe Price fund for risk and return balance. This is a fund for all seasons."

Figure 10-1: The Performance of Price Equity Income Fund Shown with Its 26-Week Moving Average. (Courtesy of Telescan.)

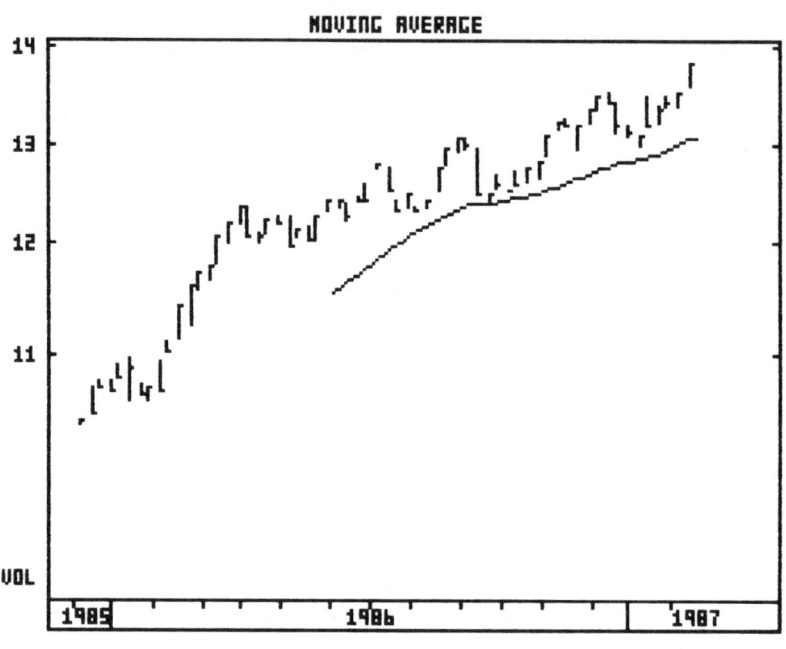

Safeco Income Fund

The investment objective of Safeco Income Fund (Safeco Income) is to provide investors with high current income and long-term growth of capital.

In pursuit of these objectives, the Fund invests in common stocks and in convertible and preferred securities. A typical allocation of the Fund's resources is 60 percent in common stocks, 36 percent in convertible bonds and preferred stocks, and 4 percent in cash.

Begun in mid-1968, the Fund has grown to over $102 million in assets under management. The five largest holdings, according to a recent survey of the Fund's portfolio, were IBM Convertible, Lucky Stores, Southwestern Bell, Washington Water Power, and Transamerica Corp. The Fund holds a total of 120 securities, and thus is well-diversified.

The Fund is heavily invested in high-yielding utility, financial, and real estate management company stocks. The Fund maintains an interest in high-technology growth companies through the use of convertible bonds. (Convertible bonds offer higher yields and less downside risk than their common stock counterparts.) The health care industry is an increasingly important component of this Fund; pharmaceuticals, nursing homes, and hospital management companies are typical investments.

Chapter 10   119

The Fund is well-managed, as illustrated by its performance record. Yield is in the range of 4.8 percent, with low volatility (beta is 0.77). Total return from January 1982 to August 1986 was 163.1 percent (an annual compounded return of 23.3 percent.) Shareholders will see increased emphasis on dividend production in this Fund as well as a possibility of increased portfolio turnover since tax reform removed the tax advantages of long-term capital gains. The Fund's performance is shown in Figure 10-2.

Figure 10-2: The Performance of the Safeco Income Fund Shown with Its 26-Week Moving Average. (Courtesy of Telescan.)

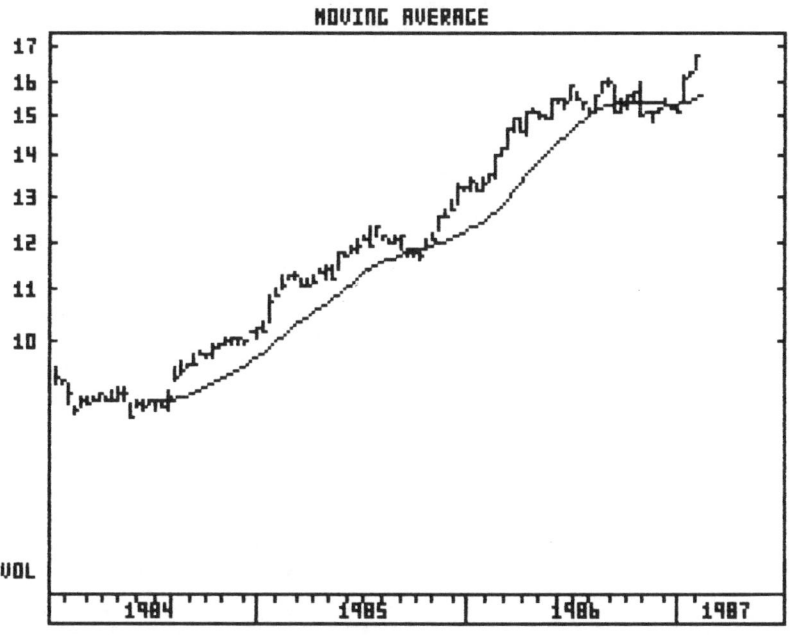

The Fund's portfolio manager for the last 7 years is Arley N. Hudson. He states his investment philosophy thus: "I try to build in as much growth potential as I can while also providing income. I keep the Fund fully invested at all times in the best ideas I can find. Our portfolio selections are designed to give the shareholder who is leery of the stock market's volatility a more conservative way to invest in the market. We hope to continue to achieve better overall performance than the general stock market averages while offering our shareholders higher current income and less downside exposure."

Hudson takes a two- to three-year view of the markets. He likes to buy out-of-favor stocks. He likes stocks that fall in price due to a poor earnings report. He finds the increased dividend, and the profit from the eventual price recovery, attractive and consistent with the Fund's purpose.

During a recent interview, Hudson stated: "In managing this steadily expanding Fund, we have maintained the portfolio's diversified and fully invested character. As new investments flowed into the Fund, we first added to holdings where the individual circumstances justified a larger position and then branched into new names for the portfolio. In both cases, our decisions were based on each stock's potential for gain versus loss, rather than characteristics of certain industry groups or other fixed criteria."

Since the Fund has a relatively heavy concentration in common stocks and convertible bonds, it is somewhat more aggressive than others in this group. Safeco has demonstrated excellent long-term performance, with an annual return of 17.5 percent from 1976 to 1986.

PROFILE 10-1

FIDELITY EQUITY INCOME FUND
82 Devonshire
Boston, MA 02109
1-800-544-6666
617-523-1919

Fund Classification:	EI
Total Assets:	$3,100 million
Fund Manager:	Bruce Johnston
Year of Inception:	1965
Minimum Investment:	$1000
Sales Charge:	2.0%
12b-1 Charge:	No
Expense Ratio:	0.66

Portfolio Mix:	%	Issues
Bonds	0	0
Corporate Bonds	15.7	113
Common Stock	52.7	224
Preferred Stock	22.4	86
U. S. Government Securities	0	0
Cash	0	0
Commercial Paper	0	0
Estimated Annual Portfolio Turnover	118%	

Estimates of Fund Performance:	
Annual Return for Three Years:	17.3%
Annual Return for Five Years:	22.8%
Annual Return in Bull Markets:	
1985	25.0%
1986	16.8%
Annual Return in Bear Markets:	
6/30/83–6/30/84	-2.89%
Representative Current Yield (12/31/86):	5.8%

Measures of Risk and Reward:	
Alpha	1.7
Beta	0.73
R square	84
Standard deviation	2.77
Reward/risk ratio	6.2

Net Asset Value:	
9/25/87	29.77
10/28/87	23.41

PROFILE 10-2

FINANCIAL INDUSTRIAL INCOME FUND
P.O. Box 2040
Denver, CO 80201
1-800-525-8085
303-779-1233

Fund Classification:	EI	
Total Assets:	$339 million	
Fund Manager:	John Kaweske	
Year of Inception:	1959	
Minimum Investment:	$250	
Sales Charge:	No load	
12b-1 Charge:	No	
Expense Ratio:	0.71	
Portfolio Mix:	%	*Issues*
Bonds	20	34
Corporate Bonds	19.1	NA
Common Stock	76.78	59
Preferred Stock	0	0
U. S. Government Securities	3.4	NA
Corporate Short Notes	12.7	NA
Commercial Paper	0	0
Estimated Annual Portfolio Turnover	117%	
Estimates of Fund Performance:		
Annual Return for Three Years:	17.6%	
Annual Return for Five Years:	21.3%	
Annual Return in Bull Markets:		
1985	30.7%	
1986	13.3%	
Annual Return in Bear Markets:		
6/30/83–6/30/84	-1.99%	
Representative Current Yield (12/31/86):	3.5%	
Measures of Risk and Reward:		
Alpha	1.1	
Beta	0.81	
R square	95	
Standard deviation	3.50	
Reward/risk ratio	5.0	
Net Asset Value:		
9/25/87	9.14	
10/28/87	7.02	

PROFILE 10-3

GIT EQUITY INCOME FUND
1655 No. Ft. Meyer Dr.
Arlington, VA 22209
1-800-336-3063
703-528-6500

Fund Classification:	EI	
Total Assets:	$2.4 million	
Fund Manager:	Thomas Miller	
Year of Inception:	1983	
Minimum Investment:	$1000	
Sales Charge:	No load	
12b-1 Charge:	No	
Expense Ratio:	0.93	
Portfolio Mix:	%	*Issues*
Bonds	NA	NA
Corporate Bonds	NA	NA
Common Stock	NA	NA
Preferred Stock	NA	NA
U. S. Government Securities	NA	NA
Corporate Short Notes	NA	NA
Commercial Paper	NA	NA
Estimated Annual Portfolio Turnover	19%	
Estimates of Fund Performance:		
Annual Return for Three Years:	18.8%	
Annual Return for Five Years:	NA	
Annual Return in Bull Markets:		
1985	26.3%	
1986	19.2%	
Annual Return in Bear Markets:		
6/30/86–9/30/86	0.0%	
Representative Current Yield (12/31/86):	5.1%	
Measures of Risk and Reward:		
Alpha	NA	
Beta	0.53	
R square	NA	
Standard deviation	2.64	
Reward/risk ratio	7.1	
Net Asset Value:		
9/25/87	13.78	
10/28/87	11.83	

PROFILE 10-4

LINDNER DIVIDEND FUND
P.O. Box 11208
St. Louis, MO 63105
314-727-5305

Fund Classification:	EI	
Total Assets:	$62 million	
Fund Manager:	Kurt Lindner	
Year of Inception:	1976	
Minimum Investment:	$2000	
Sales Charge:	No load	
12b-1 Charge:	No	
Expense Ratio:	0.95	

Portfolio Mix:	%	*Issues*
Bonds	0	0
Corporate Bonds	0	0
Common Stock	NA	14
Preferred Stock	0	0
U. S. Government Securities	0	0
Corporate Short Notes	0	0
Commercial Paper	0	0
Estimated Annual Portfolio Turnover	26%	

Estimates of Fund Performance:	
Annual Return for Three Years:	17.5%
Annual Return for Five Years:	25.0%
Annual Return in Bull Markets:	
1985	17.0%
1986	20.8%
Annual Return in Bear Markets:	
6/30/83–6/30/84	12.2%
Representative Current Yield (12/31/86):	7.4%

Measures of Risk and Reward:	
Alpha	6.2
Beta	0.29
R square	46
Standard deviation	1.79
Reward/risk ratio	9.8

Net Asset Value:	
9/25/87	22.36
10/28/87	20.41

PROFILE 10-5

T. ROWE PRICE EQUITY INCOME FUND
100 E. Pratt St.
Baltimore, MD 21202
1-800-638-5660
301-547-2308

Fund Classification:	EI
Total Assets:	$94 million
Fund Manager:	Thomas Broadus
	Brian Rogers
Year of Inception:	1985
Minimum Investment:	$1000
Sales Charge:	No load
12b-1 Charge:	No
Expense Ratio:	1.0

Portfolio Mix:	%	*Issues*
Bonds	0	0
Corporate Bonds	0	0
Common Stock	60	35
Preferred Stock	0	0
U. S. Government Securities	0	0
Cash	0	0
Commercial Paper	0	0
Estimated Annual Portfolio Turnover	73%	

Estimates of Fund Performance:	
Annual Return for Three Years:	NA
Annual Return for Five Years:	NA
Annual Return in Bull Markets:	
1985	NA
1986	26.6%
Annual Return in Bear Markets:	
6/30/83–6/30/84	-1.5%
Representative Current Yield (12/31/86):	4.9%

Measures of Risk and Reward:	
Alpha	NA
Beta	0.75
R square	86
Standard deviation	2.85
Reward/risk ratio	9.3

Net Asset Value:	
9/25/87	14.76
10/28/87	11.95

PROFILE 10-6

SAFECO INCOME FUND
Safeco Plaza
Seattle, WA 98185
1-800-426-6730
1-800-562-6810
206-545-5530

Fund Classification:	EI	
Total Assets:	$144 million	
Fund Manager:	Arley Hudson	
Year of Inception:	1968	
Minimum Investment:	$1000	
Sales Charge:	No load	
12b-1 Charge:	No	
Expense Ratio:	0.95	

Portfolio Mix:	%	*Issues*
Bonds	27.3	41
Corporate Bonds	0	0
Common Stock	61.2	64
Preferred Stock	7.9	NA
U. S. Government Securities	0	0
Corporate Short Notes	0	0
Commercial Paper	0	0
Estimated Annual Portfolio Turnover	29%	

Estimates of Fund Performance:	
Annual Return for Three Years:	19.8%
Annual Return for Five Years:	21.9%
Annual Return in Bull Markets:	
1985	31.4%
1986	19.9%
Annual Return in Bear Markets:	
6/30/83–6/30/84	2.76%
Representative Current Yield (12/31/86):	4.8%

Measures of Risk and Reward:	
Alpha	4.5
Beta	0.77
R square	90
Standard deviation	2.80
Reward/risk ratio	7.1

Net Asset Value:	
9/25/87	17.14
10/28/87	13.23

Chapter 11
Growth and Income Funds

BACKGROUND INFORMATION

Type of Security

Growth and income funds provide investors with both income and long-term growth of capital. Growth and income funds usually invest in high-yielding common and preferred stocks of seasoned, well-established firms. Companies are chosen because they pay relatively high cash dividends. Growth and income funds are positioned in such a way as to provide long-term growth without excessive volatility in share price. Portfolios include a significant number of public utilities, both common stocks, and convertible preferred stocks.

Methods

The methods used by growth and income funds to achieve these general goals will vary. Funds may invest in dual portfolios of growth stocks and income stocks; they may combine growth stocks with stocks paying high dividends, preferreds, convertibles, or fixed-income securities (bonds and money-market instruments). Still again, they may invest in growth stocks and earn current income by selling covered call options. Most funds will change from one strategy to another as conditions warrant. Investors are urged to research growth and income funds carefully to match fund strategy with individual investment preferences.

Risk/Stability

Growth and income funds have low to moderate stability of principal and moderate potential for current income and growth. As a result of the Tax Reform Act of 1986, growth and income funds will continue to be attractive investments. Fund managers will pay more attention to companies that provide significant income. (These companies have the added advantage that they tend to fluctuate far less than those whose attraction is future growth.)

PORTFOLIO FIT

Growth and income funds are suitable for investors who can assume some risk to achieve growth of capital, but who wish to maintain a moderate level of current income. They tend to have greater risk than equity income funds (see Chapter 10) and less risk than growth funds (see Chapter 12).

Investors with a three- to five-year timeframe are ideal candidates for growth and income funds. They are well-suited for almost any portfolio, but the percentage of total holdings will vary greatly. A young married couple, for example, might hold as much as 20 percent of their assets in growth and income funds. Conversely, a retired individual may hold 10 percent or less.

EIGHT REPRESENTATIVE GROWTH AND INCOME FUNDS

To illustrate, we have chosen eight growth and income funds that show the qualities that investors seek when purchasing shares of growth and income funds. Note that five of the eight examples are no-load funds. Table 11-1 contains a summary listing of the eight funds. It is followed by a more detailed description of each fund's objectives and investment philosophy and practice, as well as capsule Profiles of their recent performance.

Investors are reminded that past performance is no indicator of future performance.

Table 11-1: Eight Representative Growth and Income Funds

Fund	Annual Return (%) Three Years	Load
Copley Fund	22.1	NL
Eaton Vance Total Return Trust	28.9	L
Evergreen Total Return Fund	21.8	NL
Mutual Qualified Income Fund	18.6	NL
Mutual Shares Fund	19.0	NL
Selected American Shares	21.4	12b-1[*]
Strong Total Return Fund	18.4	L
Windsor II Fund	21.4[**]	NL

[*]A 12b-1 plan allows a fund to use assets for marketing and distribution purposes. A fund's maximum charge (in percent) is listed in its Profile.

[**]Annual return for one year.

Copley Fund

The Copley Fund seeks tax-advantaged accumulations of dividend income and long-term capital growth.

The Fund was set up to take advantage of the equity market while providing investors with the opportunity to reduce or postpone federal income tax liability. The Fund is taxed like a corporation, thus receiving an 85-percent exemption from federal income taxes on the dividends it receives. The structure protects the Fund from having to make annual distributions. (Under the old tax law, it also protected shareholders from short-term capital gains taxes; since tax reform, however, this advantage has been eliminated.)

Irving Levine, the president and portfolio manager, does not expect tax reform to adversely affect the Fund: "We have the size and flexibility to make changes and not hurt shareholders." Levine expects that the stocks held by the Fund will increase dividends, thus mitigating any negative impact of tax reform.

The Fund holds stocks of companies with strong balance sheets and a history of increasing dividends. The Fund has a portfolio of $31 million, of which more than $1 million belongs to Levine and his associates. A majority of the stocks in the portfolio are electric, gas, and telecommunications utilities that pay handsome dividends. The Fund has significant holdings in Ohio Edison, Rochester Gas and Electric, Contel, and Pacific Telesis, all companies that pay handsome dividends.

The Fund consistently provides investors with attractive returns, yet it has only one-half the volatility of the market in general (beta = .49) and an alpha of 7.8 percent. The Fund has a low portfolio turnover—about 11 percent annually. The expense ratio is an excellent 1.35 percent.

Since the Fund does little marketing, if any, it is relatively unknown. The Copley Fund exhibits excellent performance at a lower-than-market risk. The Fund is a good choice for the relatively conservative investor.

Eaton Vance Total Return Trust

The primary investment objective of Eaton Vance Total Return Trust is to seek a high level of total return, a predictable income stream, and capital appreciation. In addition, the Trust seeks the preservation of capital.

The Trust invests primarily in utilities and other high-yield common stocks, as well as fixed-income securities with above-average returns. Of the total amount under management, about 88 percent is invested in electrical utilities and telephone stocks. Four of the largest holdings are Consolidated Edison, Southern California Edison, Northern States Power, and Pacific Telesis. (The Trust holds six electrical utility stocks for every phone stock.) Management maintains such large positions in utilities because they are more predictable in their performance. While there are some short-term problems with utilities (flat earnings), cash flows remain strong and the industry is expected to rebound from a rather staid earnings picture.

Edwin Bragdon is the portfolio manager for the Eaton Vance Total Return Trust and has been with the company since 1975.

The Eaton Vance Total Return Trust has relatively little volatility (beta = 0.70) and has provided investors an excellent return over the past five years.

Evergreen Total Return Fund

The investment objective of the Evergreen Total Return Fund is current income and capital appreciation. The strategy was summarized by President Nola Maddox Falcone: "The Evergreen Total Return Fund is for a person seeking high income with capital appreciation and in addition is looking for lower volatility of annual return. The goal is to achieve a return of 20 percent annually over the long term."

The Fund invests primarily in common stock (66 percent of holdings), convertible preferred stocks (8 percent of holdings), convertible debentures (16 percent of holdings) and fixed-income securities (10 percent of holdings). This portfolio mix is designed to maximize the "total return" on the capital invested by the Fund.

Total assets under management are about $794 million, representing some 209 different securities. The five largest holdings are Southwestern Bell, Barton Edison, Louisville Gas & Electric, So. New England Telephone, and Eastman Kodak. The Fund also holds banks and thrifts, gas distributors, and REITs (real estate investment trusts).

Even though the majority of holdings are in common stock, the Fund does not limit the amount of assets that can be held in cash or short-term notes; this is especially important when the market turns down and a defensive position is required.

The Fund's strategy is inherently defensive. The cash equivalent position remains large enough to take advantage of the shifts in the market, while the balance of the portfolio is, to a substantial extent, immunized from market-related fluctuations (because of their relatively high yields). The Fund's performance is summarized in Figure 11-1.

Falcone expresses her views of the current economic climate this way: "We expect that in 1987 and 1988, the boards of directors of American companies regularly will consider sizable increases in dividend payout rates. They will recognize that investors will benefit more from higher dividend payments under the new tax law than at any time in decades. They also will note that the previous advantages of running companies exclusively to achieve capital gains in the price of their shares will no longer be paramount. A balanced approach between providing rising income and capital gains should be of broad benefit to shareholders generally and should also benefit this Fund."

The Evergreen Total Return Fund is a diversified lower-risk fund (beta = 0.60) that provides excellent risk-adjusted returns. The Fund offers investors excellent defensive characteristics against future downturns while equaling or beating the S&P 500 in rising markets. The Fund is a good match for the portfolio of the slightly less conservative investor.

Chapter 11

Figure 11-1: The Performance of the Evergreen Total Return Fund Shown with Its 26-Week Moving Average. (Courtesy of Telescan.)

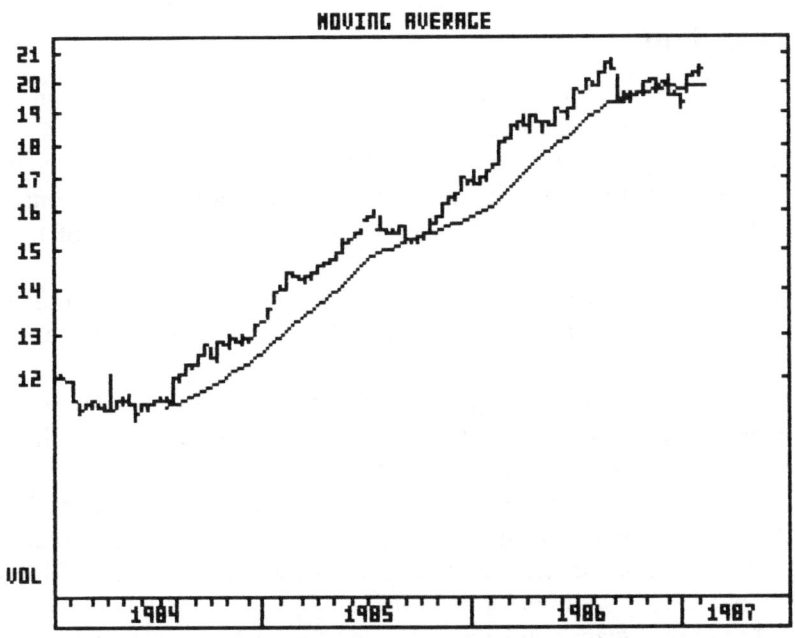

Mutual Qualified Income Fund

The Mutual Qualified Income Fund seeks capital appreciation with income as a secondary goal.

The Fund invests in common and preferred stock as well as debt securities. One strategy employed by the Fund is to search for companies that are selling for less than book value. The Fund will also seek out companies involved in mergers, consolidations, liquidations, or other special situations—as long as such investments do not total more than 50 percent of the Fund's holdings.

Investors will find that Mutual Qualified Income Fund is very similar to its sister fund, Mutual Shares Fund, in that equity holdings are almost identical. While the betas of the two funds are not significantly different, 0.41 for Mutual Qualified versus 0.42 for Mutual Shares, the former has a higher yield.

Examples of the Fund's strategy are illustrated by its participation in the leveraged buyout of R. H. Macy's and investment in the turnaround of Storage Technology. The Fund also participated in special situations involving City Investing, CBS, Inc., and Sperry (now part of Unisys).

Mutual Qualified Income Fund is managed by Max Heine and Michael Price. The Fund has a low volatility and an excellent record over the past five years. Therefore, on a risk-adjusted basis, this Fund is an outstanding performer.

Mutual Shares Fund

The primary investment goal of Mutual Shares Fund is capital appreciation (often short-term). A secondary objective is current income.

Both objectives are achieved through investing in common stock, preferred stock, and debt securities. Management particularly seeks investments below intrinsic value. (Management is sensitive to earnings multiples and the relationship of book value to market value.)

Max Heine (chairman) and Michael Price (president) serve as portfolio managers of this Fund and its sister fund, Mutual Qualified Income Fund (see above). The Fund managers, with their staff of eight analysts, search for companies selling at large discounts to net asset value and companies undergoing reorganization or involved in other special situations, such as mergers, acquisitions, and liquidations. Using this strategy, Mutual Shares Fund earned a ten-year compounded annual return of 21 percent.

Many investors are uncertain when they first review the Fund's holdings. For example, it is not unusual to find bonds from at least a half dozen companies that are in bankruptcy proceedings, shares of stock in more than a dozen corporations that are being liquidated, and stocks that are selling well below book value.

What may seem at first glance to be a junkyard of mistakes is actually a treasure trove of hidden values. For 35 years, Max Heine and his associates have been searching for stocks and bonds whose prices are a scant reflection of their worth. By sticking doggedly to this contrarian point of view, Heine has put together one of the best records in the mutual fund industry.

Heine's success is borne out by the fact that Mutual Shares Fund has never experienced a down year in 38 years. Over the last three years, annual returns are in the 19 percent range. The Fund has a relatively low beta of 0.42. The performance of the Fund as compared to that of the Strong Total Return Fund (see below), is shown in Figure 11-2.

For those investors who buy and hold for the long term, Mutual Share Fund has an outstanding performance record.

Selected American Shares

The investment objective of Selected American Shares is to provide both growth of capital and income.

To achieve these goals, the Fund invests in both common stocks (growth and income) and fixed-income securities (income). The overall philosophy of the Fund is conservative. Management seeks to minimize the magnitude and rapidity of short-term movements in the net asset value of the Fund's shares.

Figure 11-2: The Comparative Performance of Mutual Shares and Strong Total Return for the Period Aug. 5, 1983 to May 1, 1987. Note that Mutual Shares Provides a Higher Return with Lower Volatility. (Courtesy of American River Software.)

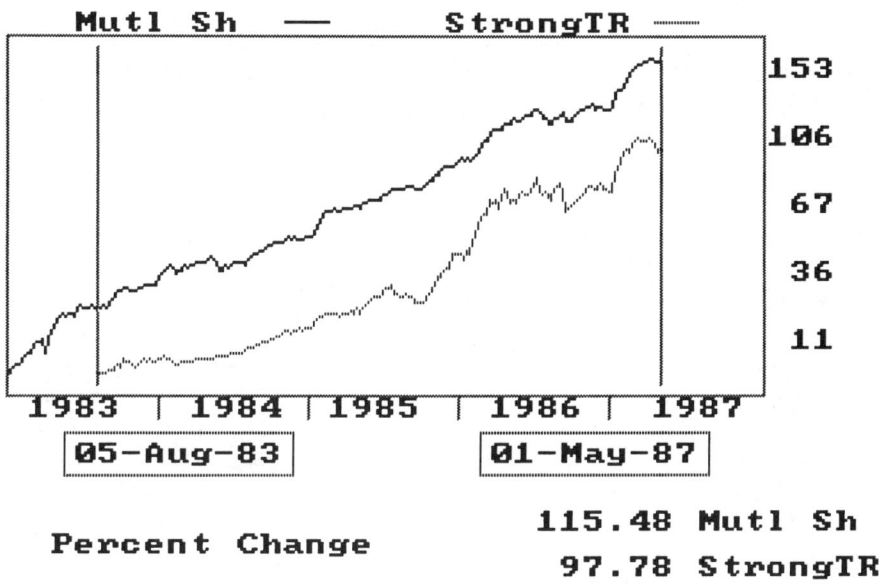

An important consideration is the Fund's strategy in times of adverse economic or market conditions. Under these circumstances, Management invests substantial portions of the Fund's assets in bonds, preferred stocks, cash, and cash equivalents—a defensive strategy designed to protect investors' capital. Donald Yacktman has been the Fund portfolio manager since 1982 (after ten years with Stein Roe). Yacktman selects strong, profitable companies selling at or near book value. For example, the Fund has major holdings in Philip Morris, RJR–Nabisco, Armentech, Wisconsin Electric, and Columbia Gas.

While overall performance for a selected five-year period has been excellent, investors should note that the Fund has an annual 12b-1 charge of 1 percent. (See the note on Table 11-1.)

Strong Total Return Fund

The Strong Total Return Fund strives for a combination of income and capital appreciation, resulting in the highest total return with a reasonable level of risk.

While the Fund invests primarily in common stocks (growth and income), corporate bonds and debentures, and short-term money-market instruments, the Fund's charter gives management unparalleled freedom in selecting securities for the Fund. The Fund's managers, Richard Strong and William Corneliuson, will select just about any security that will meet the stated goals. Unprecedented in the mutual fund industry is the freedom to move in and out of whole categories of securities as perceptions of the financial markets change.

Representative holdings within the Fund are GAF, Celanese, General Re, Home Shopping Network, and Cigna. However, investors are reminded to inspect the most current prospectus of the Fund before buying to ensure that current holdings are in line with individual preferences. Figure 11-3 shows the Fund's three-year performance.

Figure 11-3: The Performance of the Strong Total Return Fund Shown with Its 26-Week Moving Average. (Courtesy of Telescan.)

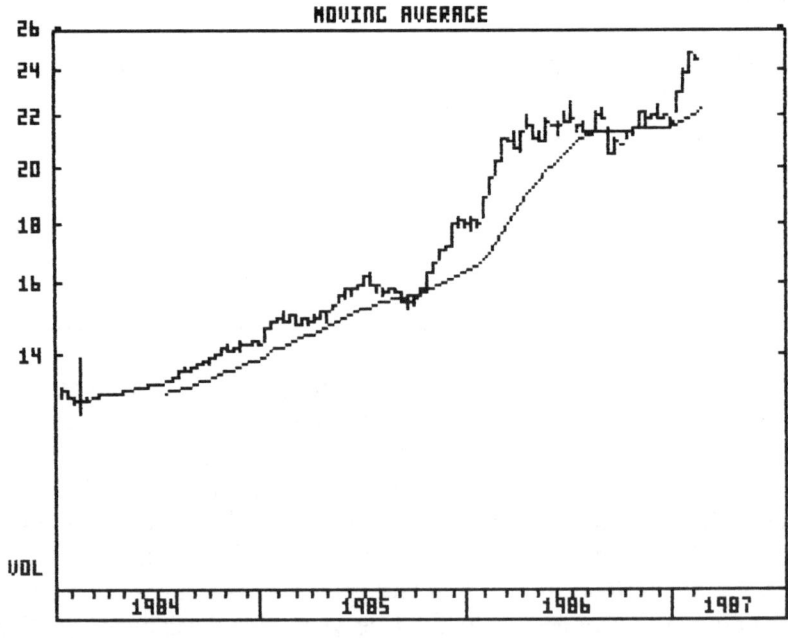

When selecting securities for the portfolio, Management relies on personal visits to companies. Strong has visited as many as 350 companies in one calendar year. "Personal contact with those who run the company gives us an insight we feel we can't get in any other way."

"When inflation is low, cash is king," says Strong. In this environment, the Fund favors high-yield bonds and stocks in companies that generate large cash flows. Management anticipates the environment for stocks and bonds to be favorable in the near term. "But if we are wrong, it has the ability to go where the action is—and be fully defensive if necessary."

Windsor II Fund

Windsor II Fund follows a value-oriented investment strategy, seeking long-term growth of capital and income through an investment program of income-producing common stocks. Three criteria are used by the Fund when selecting securities: (1) a price/earnings ratio lower than the market, (2) price-to-book values lower than the market; and (3) dividend yields higher than the market.

The Windsor II Fund is a relatively new member of the Vanguard family of funds. Introduced in June of 1985, the Fund is a so-called clone fund, in that it replaces the original Windsor Fund, which was closed to new investments in May 1985. (The original Windsor Fund had grown too popular, with $3.4 billion in assets.) Windsor II shows signs of being as popular as its predecessor, having in excess of $730 million under management in one and one-half years of operation.

Several factors account for the popularity of the Fund. The Windsor name is well established. In addition, total return for the Windsor II Fund hovers around the 20 percent range. Security selections are made by the Dallas-based firm of Barrow, Hanley, Mewhinney & Strauss, portfolio managers steeped in the value-oriented tradition that Windsor itself represents to consumers. Finally, Windsor II has grown not only because of the 63,000 individual investors (of which 26,000 are IRA accounts) but also because Windsor II is one of the Vanguard funds composing the STAR Fund (STAR is a Vanguard Fund that invests in a balanced portfolio of Vanguard stock, bond, and money-market funds.) The Fund holds approximately 40 common stocks (all of which are traded on the New York Stock Exchange). Jim Barrow, portfolio manager, patterns this Fund after the Windsor Fund. "Our style has been very much like the Windsor Fund for a long time." Portfolio turnover is expected to be about 50 percent, with a price/earnings ratio (P/E) of about 25 percent below the market and a price-to-book value ratio of 65 percent of the market. Barrow expects the Fund to have a yield of about 1.5 times the anticipated market yield.

Assuming an environment of relatively low inflation and low earnings, Barrow likes utilities, banks, and regional telephone companies characterized by earnings momentum, low price/earnings ratios, and good yields. Barrow likes utilities because "they are an area of the economy with the highest yields."

Windsor II is a good candidate for investors seeking long-term holdings. With above-average yields, it can provide protection during down markets while offering excellent participation in up markets.

PROFILE 11-1

COPLEY FUND
109 Howe Street
P.O. Box 66
Fall River, MA 02724
617-674-8459

Fund Classification:	GI
Total Assets:	$31 million
Fund Manager:	Irving Levine
Year of Inception:	1978
Minimum Investment:	$1000
Sales Charge:	No load
12b-1 Charge:	No
Expense Ratio:	1.35

Portfolio Mix:	%	*Issues*
Bonds	14	3
Corporate Bonds	0	0
Common Stock	86	47
Preferred Stock	0	0
U. S. Government Securities	0	0
Cash	0	0
Commercial Paper	0	0
Estimated Annual Portfolio Turnover	11%	

Estimates of Fund Performance:	
Annual Return for Three Years:	22.1%
Annual Return for Five Years:	19.5%
Annual Return in Bull Markets:	
1985	24.6%
1986	17.7%
Annual Return in Bear Markets:	
6/30/83–6/30/84	3.70%
Representative Current Yield (12/31/86):	0.0%

Measures of Risk and Reward:	
Alpha	7.8
Beta	0.49
R square	50
Standard deviation	3.09
Reward/risk ratio	7.2

Net Asset Value:	
9/25/87	11.50
10/28/87	10.23

PROFILE 11-2

EATON VANCE TOTAL RETURN TRUST
24 Federal Street 9th Floor
Boston, MA 02110
1-800-225-6265
617-482-8260

Fund Classification:	GI
Total Assets:	$570 million
Fund Manager:	Edwin Bragdon
	M. Dozier Gardner
Year of Inception:	1981
Minimum Investment:	$1000
Sales Charge:	4.75%
12b-1 Charge:	Yes (.25%)
Expense Ratio:	1.54

Portfolio Mix:	%	*Issues*
Bonds	NA	NA
Corporate Bonds	NA	NA
Common Stock	NA	NA
Preferred Stock	NA	NA
U. S. Government Securities	NA	NA
Cash	NA	NA
Commercial Paper	NA	NA
Estimated Annual Portfolio Turnover	85%	

Estimates of Fund Performance:

Annual Return for Three Years:	28.9%
Annual Return for Five Years:	25.3%
Annual Return in Bull Markets:	
1985	40.2%
1986	31.9%
Annual Return in Bear Markets:	
6/30/83–6/30/84	3.38%
Representative Current Yield (12/31/86):	3.2%

Measures of Risk and Reward:

Alpha	12.0
Beta	0.70
R square	38
Standard deviation	4.76
Reward/risk ratio	6.1

Net Asset Value:	
9/25/87	10.36
10/28/87	8.17

PROFILE 11-3

EVERGREEN TOTAL RETURN FUND
550 Mamaroneck Avenue
Harrison, NY 10528
1-800-635-0003
914-698-5711

Fund Classification:	GI	
Total Assets:	$794 million	
Fund Manager:	Nola Maddox Falcone	
	Stephen A. Leiber	
Year of Inception:	1978	
Minimum Investment:	$2000	
Sales Charge:	No load	
12b-1 Charge:	No	
Expense Ratio:	1.11	
Portfolio Mix:	%	*Issues*
Bonds	34	55
Corporate Bonds	0	0
Common Stock	66	154
Preferred Stock	0	0
U. S. Government Securities	0	0
Cash	0	0
Commercial Paper	0	0
Estimated Annual		
Portfolio Turnover	65%	
Estimates of Fund Performance:		
Annual Return for Three Years:	21.8%	
Annual Return for Five Years:	24.2%	
Annual Return in Bull Markets:		
1985	31.5%	
1986	20.2%	
Annual Return in Bear Markets:		
6/30/83–6/30/84	4.76%	
Representative Current Yield (12/31/86):	5.4%	
Measures of Risk and Reward:		
Alpha	6.9	
Beta	0.60	
R square	76	
Standard deviation	2.80	
Reward/risk ratio	7.8	
Net Asset Value:		
9/25/87	18.83	
10/28/87	15.88	

PROFILE 11-4

MUTUAL QUALIFIED INCOME FUND
26 Broadway
New York, NY 10004
1-800-344-4515
219-908-4048

Fund Classification:	GI
Total Assets:	$517 million
Fund Manager:	Max L. Heine
	Michael F. Price
Year of Inception:	1980
Minimum Investment:	$1000
Sales Charge:	No load
12b-1 Charge:	No
Expense Ratio:	0.70

Portfolio Mix:	%	*Issues*
Bonds	20	NA
Corporate Bonds	0	0
Common Stock	60.38	173
Preferred Stock	0	0
U. S. Government Securities	0	0
Cash	0	0
Commercial Paper	0	0
Estimated Annual		
Portfolio Turnover	124%	

Estimates of Fund Performance:	
Annual Return for Three Years:	18.6%
Annual Return for Five Years:	21.0%
Annual Return in Bull Markets:	
1985	25.5%
1986	16.0%
Annual Return in Bear Markets:	
6/30/83–6/30/84	16.9%
Representative Current Yield (12/31/86):	5.2%

Measures of Risk and Reward:	
Alpha	6.0
Beta	0.41
R square	63
Standard deviation	2.14
Reward/risk ratio	8.7

Net Asset Value:	
9/25/87	24.92
10/28/87	19.18

PROFILE 11-5

MUTUAL SHARES FUND
26 Broadway
New York, NY 10004
1-800-344-4515
212-908-4048

Fund Classification:	GI	
Total Assets:	$1293 million	
Fund Manager:	Max L. Heine	
	Michael F. Price	
Year of Inception:	1949	
Minimum Investment:	$1000	
Sales Charge:	No load	
12b-1 Charge:	No	
Expense Ratio:	0.67	

Portfolio Mix:	%	*Issues*
Bonds	17	NA
Corporate Bonds	0	0
Common Stock	61.81	199
Preferred Stock	0	0
U. S. Government Securities	0	0
Cash	0	0
Commercial Paper	0	0
Estimated Annual		
Portfolio Turnover	122%	

Estimates of Fund Performance:	
Annual Return for Three Years:	19.0%
Annual Return for Five Years:	20.1%
Annual Return in Bull Markets:	
1985	26.5%
1986	16.5%
Annual Return in Bear Markets:	
6/30/83–6/30/84	15.0%

Representative Current Yield (12/31/86):	4.0%

Measures of Risk and Reward:	
Alpha	6.2
Beta	0.42
R square	68
Standard deviation	2.14
Reward/risk ratio	8.9

Net Asset Value:	
9/25/87	74.71
10/28/87	57.72

PROFILE 11-6

SELECTED AMERICAN SHARES
230 W. Monroe Street
Chicago, IL 60606
1-800-621-7321
In IL 1-800-572-4437
312-641-7862

Fund Classification:	GI
Total Assets:	$144 million
Fund Manager:	Donald A. Yacktman
Year of Inception:	1933
Minimum Investment:	$1000
Sales Charge:	No load
12b-1 Charge:	Yes (1%)
Expense Ratio:	0.87

Portfolio Mix:	*%*	*Issues*
Bonds	0	0
Corporate Bonds	0	0
Common Stock	94	45
Preferred Stock	6	2
U. S. Government Securities	0	0
Cash	0	0
Commercial Paper	0	0
Estimated Annual Portfolio Turnover	33%	

Estimates of Fund Performance:	
Annual Return for Three Years:	21.4%
Annual Return for Five Years:	22.0%
Annual Return in Bull Markets:	
1985	33.2%
1986	17.0%
Annual Return in Bear Markets:	
6/30/83–6/30/84	10.4%
Representative Current Yield (12/31/86):	3.5%

Measures of Risk and Reward:	
Alpha	5.7
Beta	0.69
R square	85
Standard deviation	3.11
Reward/risk ratio	6.9

Net Asset Value:	
9/25/87	14.97
10/28/87	11.53

PROFILE 11-7

STRONG TOTAL RETURN FUND
815 East Mason Street
Milwaukee, WI 53202
1-800-368-3863
414-765-0620

Fund Classification:	GI
Total Assets:	$452 million
Fund Manager:	Richard S. Strong
	William D. Corneliuson
Year of Inception:	1981
Minimum Investment:	$250
Sales Charge:	1.00%
12b-1 Charge:	No
Expense Ratio:	1.10

Portfolio Mix:	%	Issues
Bonds	0	0
Corporate Bonds	35	32
Common Stock	65	89
Preferred Stock	2	1
U. S. Government Securities	0	0
Convertible Securities	0.5	1
Commercial Paper	8	7
Estimated Annual Portfolio Turnover	154%	

Estimates of Fund Performance:	
Annual Return for Three Years:	18.4%
Annual Return for Five Years:	25.5%
Annual Return in Bull Markets:	
1985	25.4%
1986	20.0%
Annual Return in Bear Markets:	
6/30/83–6/30/84	3.62%

Representative Current Yield (12/31/86):	5.8%

Measures of Risk and Reward:	
Alpha	4.1
Beta	0.58
R square	70
Standard deviation	2.90
Reward/risk ratio	6.3

Net Asset Value:	
9/25/87	23.10
10/28/87	18.80

PROFILE 11-8

WINDSOR II FUND
Vanguard Financial Center
Valley Forge, PA 19482
1-800-662-7447 or (2739)
In PA 1-800-362-0530

Fund Classification:	GI	
Total Assets:	$730 million	
Fund Manager:	James Barrow	
Year of Inception:	1985	
Minimum Investment:	$1500	
Sales Charge:	No load	
12b-1 Charge:	No	
Expense Ratio:	0.76	

Portfolio Mix:	%	*Issues*
Bonds	0	0
Corporate Bonds	0	0
Common Stock	94.1	40
Preferred Stock	0	0
U. S. Government Securities	0	0
Convertible Securities	0	0
Commercial Paper	0	0
Estimated Annual Portfolio Turnover	NA	

Estimates of Fund Performance:	
Annual Return for Three Years:	NA
Annual Return for Five Years:	NA
Annual Return in Bull Markets:	
1985	NA
1986	21.4%
Annual Return in Bear Markets:	
6/30/83–6/30/84	-4.9%
Representative Current Yield (12/31/86):	3.3%

Measures of Risk and Reward:	
Alpha	3.0
Beta	0.75
R square	90
Standard deviation	3.4
Reward/risk ratio	6.2

Net Asset Value:	
9/25/87	15.01
10/28/87	11.80

Chapter 12
Growth Funds

BACKGROUND INFORMATION

Type of Security

A growth fund normally invests in companies whose long-term earnings are expected to grow significantly faster than the earnings of the stocks represented in the major unmanaged stock averages such as the S&P 500. Typically, a growth fund's holdings include blue-chip companies such as Exxon, IBM, AT&T, and General Motors. They seek relatively safe long-term growth and do not hold speculative stocks.

Risk/Stability

Like the aggressive growth funds, growth funds generally invest in stocks for growth of principal rather than for current income. The growth funds, however, generally invest for the longer term and are therefore considered more conservative in their approach. They are not as likely to invest in less stable, smaller companies that may provide substantial short-term gains at the risk of occasional or permanent substantial declines later on. Growth funds are more likely to invest in a company when it is well established and when it and the industry in which it operates are thought to have good long-term growth potential and less risk than speculative stocks.

Growth funds generally seek capital appreciation with an annual portfolio turnover rate of less than 100 percent while holding middle-of-the-road investments. They do not employ aggressive trading techniques, such as buying on margin or short-selling (that is, borrowing stock to sell in the hope of covering the sale by buying it at a cheaper price between the sale and the agreed delivery date).

The typical growth fund has a market return and risk. Thus, most growth funds have a beta between .90 and 1.0 (in contrast, aggressive growth funds will typically have betas greater than 1.0).

SPECIAL ADVANTAGES AND EXPOSURES

Like the aggressive growth funds, growth funds in general provide low current income. The investor's principal will be more stable than it would be in an aggressive growth fund. The potential for growth may be less over the short term, but over the long term many growth funds have superior performance records.

Although growth funds are more conservative than aggressive growth funds, they are still relatively aggressive and are suitable for growth-oriented investors, but not investors who are unable to assume risk or who are dependent on maximizing the level of current income they derive from their investments.

Market Effects

In general, growth funds tend to outperform the S&P 500 during ascending markets and nearly match the S&P 500 during declining markets. As a result, growth funds over the long term can be expected to return a relatively steady 14 percent annually. Of course, in making our selection we are looking for the above-average funds that can achieve 16 to 18 percent annually over the long term.

Basically, what a manager of a growth fund is seeking is common stocks whose growth of earnings and revenue are expected to be higher than average. Typically they should exhibit growth rates 1.5 to 2.0 times those of the market average as represented by the S&P 500.

PORTFOLIO FIT

Since growth funds seek companies whose long-term earnings are expected to grow faster than the earnings of the S&P 500, their risk and volatility tend to equal the market's. The investor who holds a growth fund should be willing to accommodate a market level of risk.

Through growth funds, the investor will participate in the growth of the U.S. economy, and, of course, in its ups and downs. It will not be unusual for a younger, well-paid individual to hold 50 percent of his or her portfolio in growth funds.

NINE REPRESENTATIVE GROWTH FUNDS

To illustrate, we have chosen nine growth funds that show the qualities that investors seek when purchasing shares of growth funds. Note that all of these examples are no-load funds. Table 12-1 contains a summary listing of the nine funds. It is followed by a more detailed description of each fund's objectives and investment philosophy and practice, as well as capsule Profiles of their recent performance.

Investors are reminded that past performance is no indicator of future performance.

Acorn Fund

The Acorn Fund's primary objective is capital growth, with income a secondary objective.

Table 12-1: Nine Representative Growth Funds

Fund	Annual Return % for 3 Years	Load
Acorn Fund	19.1	NL
Boston Capital Appreciation Fund	20.9	NL
Dodge & Cox Stock Fund	19.9	NL
Evergreen Fund	15.3	NL
Ivy Growth Fund	17.7	NL
Nicholas Fund	16.8	NL
Partners Fund	18.1	NL
T. Rowe Price Growth Stock Fund	17.6	NL
Quest for Value Fund	15.1	NL

The Fund seeks out areas of the economy that it believes will benefit from favorable trends for a number of years. The emphasized industries change from time to time. It particularly seeks smaller companies that have these characteristics: (1) superior, widely unrecognized growth potential; (2) strategic position in specialized markets because of technological, marketing, or managerial advantages; (3) the financial strength and stability of adequate capitalization. The Fund in 1987 had 20 percent of its assets in non-U.S. stocks.

The Fund has a risk that exceeds the market index (beta = 1.20), and yet it has done reasonably well in down markets. For example, Acorn declined 9.5 percent in 1981, while the S&P 500 declined 7.0 percent. Acorn returned 20.1 percent annually for the 10-year period ended December 31, 1986.

The Fund is managed by Ralph Wanger, who seeks stocks that grow in the longer term. Wanger first identifies industries with superior growth prospects. To do this, he considers technological or social trends that he expects to be important for five years or longer. Technology is only one of the themes running through Acorn. Sectors currently emphasized include information, real estate, banks, and foreign stocks. The largest holdings as of October 31, 1986, include Cray Research, Rouse Company, Macmillan, H.&R. Block, and the New York Times.

The Acorn Fund is an ideal investment for the longer-term investor who seeks a value-oriented growth fund with a proven manager.

Boston Company Capital Appreciation Fund

The Boston Company Capital Appreciation Fund, a popular equity fund, seeks long-term growth of capital. Current income is a secondary objective. For the twelve-month period ended December 1, 1986, the Fund provided a total return on investment of 22.5 percent.

The Fund invests preponderantly in common stocks of U.S. companies, with up to 10 percent of its assets in foreign stocks. The Fund returned 20.9 percent for the three years ended December 31, 1986. The performance of the Fund is shown in Figure 12-1.

Mr. Gerry Zukowski, who has managed the Fund since January 1983, favors a diversified portfolio. The five largest holdings are Warner Lambert, McDonalds, Sterling Drug, Browning Ferris, and Kimberley Clark.

Boston Company Capital Appreciation Fund has an excellent record and should be a valuable addition to any growth-oriented portfolio.

Figure 12-1: The Performance of Boston Capital Appreciation Fund Shown with Its 26-Week Moving Average. (Courtesy of Telescan.)

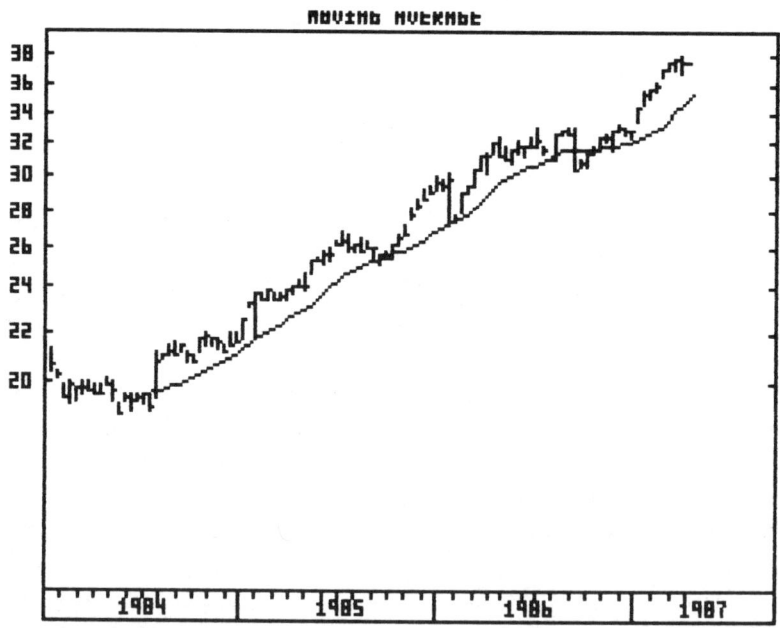

Dodge & Cox Stock Fund

The Dodge & Cox Stock Fund has as its primary objective providing shareholders with an opportunity for long-term growth of principal and income. A secondary objective is to achieve a reasonable current income.

The management of the Fund, in business since 1930, seeks out companies that have strong finances and good prospects for both earnings and dividend growth. As might be expected, the portfolio emphasizes blue-chip stocks. The Fund tries to stay fully invested in equities and currently has about 95 percent of its assets in stocks. As of September 30, 1986, the electronics and electrical equipment industry composed the largest segment (11.2 percent) of the Fund, followed by finance (10.8 percent), and office equipment (10.5 percent). As of December 31, 1986, the Fund's largest holdings were Digital Equipment, Teletronix, International Paper, Dow Chemical, and J. P. Morgan.

Purchases are considered for their long-term benefits, and turnover as a result is low. The Fund's performance is shown in Figure 12-2. The Fund has performed well during up and down markets, and its beta (.98) is near market level. It has performed steadily over both the short and the long term.

Figure 12-2: The Performance of Dodge and Cox Stock Fund Shown with Its 26-Week Moving Average. (Courtesy of Telescan.)

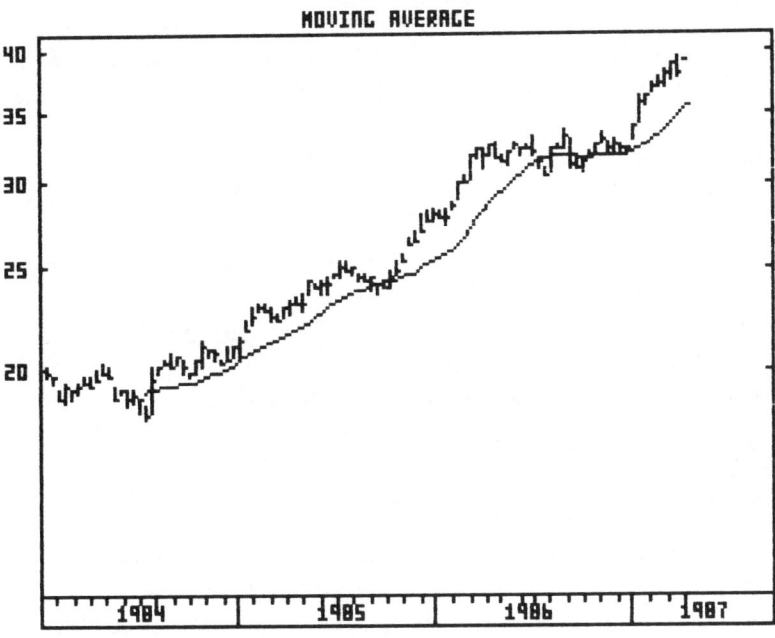

The Fund currently yields 3 percent in current earnings, making it attractive to investors who like to receive at least a modest dividend payout from their equity investments.

The Fund's attributes make the Fund a good choice for the conservative and moderately aggressive investor. The low turnover and low expense ratio help keep costs low, which makes the Fund an excellent value for the cost-conscious investor. The Fund is available only to residents of California, Oregon, Hawaii, Nevada, Utah, the District of Columbia, and New York.

The Evergreen Fund

The Evergreen Fund's objective is to achieve capital appreciation in the value of its shares. Income is not a factor in the selection of the Fund's portfolio.

The Fund seeks to achieve its objective through investments in common stocks and securities convertible into or exchangeable for common stock of little-known or relatively small companies. A little-known company is one whose market is regional or whose securities are closely held (i.e., only a small proportion are traded publicly). A relatively small company is one whose market share is small relative to its competitors or one that does business in a limited market, such as test equipment for electronics manufacturers.

Since its inception in 1971, president and portfolio manager Stephen Lieber hasn't changed his investment practice of buying takeover candidates without incurring undue risk. Evergreen has always benefited from takeovers. In seeking takeover candidates, Evergreen tries to capitalize on the price rises without becoming a participant in takeover "plays." The focus of the Fund has always been on stocks perceived by Lieber to be undervalued.

Lieber sees acquisitions, in a somewhat different form from what they have been, as prime beneficiaries of the new tax law of 1986. His mid-1986 report stated: "The future environment should be different. We see prospective acquirers as companies which have been paying taxes at top bracket rates, finding themselves with newly increased available earnings after taxes."

While the 1986 performance of Evergreen was a disappointing 13 percent, Evergreen is well managed for long-term growth. The volatility of the Fund is about that of the market, yet it can be expected to perform somewhat above the market.

Evergreen is particularly well-suited to the long-term growth investor.

Ivy Growth Fund

The Ivy Growth Fund seeks to achieve long-term growth of capital primarily through investment in equity securities. Income is a secondary consideration.

The top five holdings of the Fund are Contel, Eastman-Kodak, CBI, American Home products, and Weyerhaeuser. The Fund may invest up to 25 percent of its holdings in foreign securities.

The Fund has as excellent long-term record and is a very good buy on a risk-return basis. Its annual return over the ten-year period ended December 31, 1986, was 17.8 percent. The Fund's performance record is shown in Figure 12-3.

Chapter 12

Figure 12-3: The Performance of Ivy Growth Fund Shown with Its 26-Week Moving Average. (Courtesy of Telescan.)

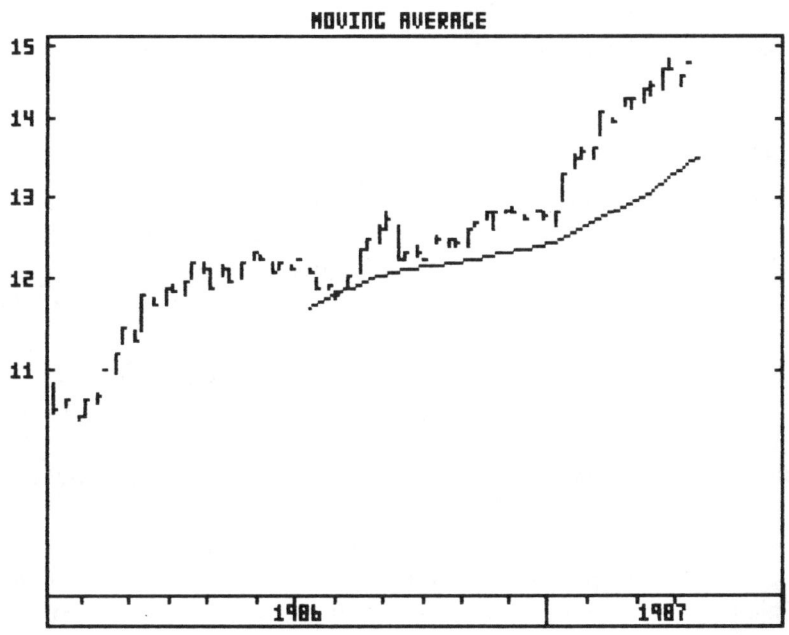

The Fund has changed the manager it uses several times during the Fund's 25-year history without affecting the quality of its performance. On December 1, 1986, Hingham Management assumed full control of the Fund and Fund officers Michael Peers and William Watson became the Fund's managers. Peers has been Fund Chairman since 1974 and Watson Fund President since 1975.

Nicholas Fund

The primary investment objective of the Nicholas Fund is capital appreciation, and current income is a secondary objective.

The Fund invests in securities believed to offer possibilities of growth in value—for the most part, common stocks of companies that the advisor considers to have favorable long-term prospects. The stocks sought are those with low price/earnings (P/E) ratios relative to their growth rates.

"We're stock pickers," said Albert O. Nicholas, president and portfolio manager for the 16-year-old fund. "We do not try to predict general market trends. We're bottom-up investors."

Nicholas, who founded the Fund after leaving a position as securities analyst for Marshall & Ilsley, has built up the Fund's assets to over $1 billion as of 1987, with a significant amount of cash. Despite its size, it still seeks values in its growth stock picks. Its long-term record has been good, but it returned a disappointing 12 percent in 1986. Nevertheless, the Fund has a 17-year record of achievement and remains a worthy investment for long-term growth.

Partners Fund

Partners Fund seeks capital growth as an objective.

The Fund invests principally in stocks and other equity securities; secondarily, it acquires bonds and debentures believed to have potential to appreciate in value.

The Fund disregards any distinctions between long- and short-term capital gains and ordinary income in its selections. The Fund holds each stock until a "target" price is reached, and then the stock is sold—regardless of whether the holding period was long enough to receive long-term capital gains treatment. Therefore, a substantial proportion of the Fund's portfolio may at times consist of securities selected for their short-term potential, and the Fund's turnover rate may at times be higher than that of parallel mutual funds.

On the other hand, since the tax distinction between short- and long-term capital gains has been eliminated in the 1986 tax law, the Fund's strategy is up to date.

"We are not market timers. We are individual stock timers. We are neither bulls nor bears. We pick individual securities that we think are undervalued," explained Philip H. Steckler, Jr., who manages the 16-year-old Fund with partner Dietrich Weismann. Allan Hunter, president of the Fund, observed on January 28, 1987, that the Fund "in the midst of this fast-moving market . . . has steered a relatively steady course. . . . We do not try to forecast the market trend, and we do not try to ride the trend."

The Fund has provided 20.1 percent annually for the ten years ended December 31, 1986. While its return was slightly below that of the market in 1986, it has a lower risk than the market with a beta of 0.79. The Fund is particularly suitable for the relatively conservative investor who wants to include a growth fund in his or her portfolio.

T. Rowe Price Growth Stock Fund

The T. Rowe Price Growth Stock Fund, begun in 1950, is one of the oldest current managed growth funds. The Fund's primary objective is capital appreciation, with increasing future dividends as a secondary goal.

The Fund invests primarily in medium-sized and larger, more established growth companies in the United States and abroad.

As of September 30, 1986, the Fund's five largest holdings were IBM, Upjohn, Digital Equipment, Union Pacific, and McDonald's. The Fund at that time held 120 stocks in most sectors of the U.S. economy, with 25 percent of the portfolio in foreign stocks.

Mr. T. Rowe Price pioneered the growth stock theory of investing more than 38 years ago, and his theory continues as the basis of the Fund's approach to investments today.

Management of the Fund defines a growth stock as a share in a business enterprise that is expected to reach a new peak in earnings per share during each consecutive business cycle.

From April 1950 to December 31, 1971, the Fund had returned 13 percent annually—superior to most funds at the time. The Fund languished through the late 1970s, as a result of the 1973–74 economic decline. The Fund averaged only 10.8 percent annually over the 10-year period ended December 31, 1986, which includes years from this period of difficulty for the Fund. For the 5-year period ended December 31, 1986, however, the Fund averaged 16.3 percent annually, demonstrating its recaptured vigor.

Since 1983 the Fund has been managed by M. David Testa and has performed exceedingly well, returning 17.6 percent annually for the three years ended December 31, 1986. Testa, who has been with the Price organization since graduating from Harvard Business School 15 years ago, keeps the Fund stocked with stalwarts such as General Electric, General Mills, Upjohn, Pfizer, Dayton-Hudson, and Boeing.

In later years, unfamiliar names (increasingly, foreign names) are entering the portfolio. Testa is using the overseas holdings to give the Fund new gains. Testa prefers to stay fully invested, replacing stocks when their price/earnings ratios get too high compared to those of other, equally solid growth firms. "There are not too many times when it pays very much to be in a cash position," says Testa.

The Fund today is solid, with improving prospects. It performs best during expansion years, such as 1985 and 1986, and poorly during recession or down periods, such as the year ended June 30, 1984. The Fund can serve nevertheless as a buy-and-hold fund for the growth investor.

Quest for Value Fund

The objective of the Quest for Value Fund is capital appreciation in the value of its shares.

As its name implies, the Fund seeks securities undervalued in relation to the companies' assets, earnings, cash flow, or growth potential.

The Fund's five largest holdings on April 30, 1986, were General Electric, Henley Group, Sears Roebuck, Morton Thiokol, and First Alabama Bank. Its portfolio turnover for the fiscal year ended April 30, 1986, was 68 percent.

The Fund had $165 million in assets on December 31, 1986, and it holds about 100 stocks, primarily in companies with low capitalization (capitalization = number of shares outstanding x share price). The Fund experienced relatively low volatility during the five years ended December 31, 1986, and the total return for those five years was 24.3 percent compounded annually. It is interesting to note that the Fund returned 5.3 percent annually during the bear market of 8/14/81 to 8/13/82, while the S&P 500 declined 16.6 percent. The Fund's beta is a relatively low .75.

The Fund's value-oriented approach is intended to minimize losses during market downturns while allowing for capital appreciation when values are rising. The Fund recently implemented another defensive measure with its *portfolio insurance,* or hedging. Hedging is done to protect the value of the portfolio's principal during declines.

The Fund has demonstrated its ability to weather downturns. It declined .8 percent from 6/30/83 to 6/30/84 while the S&P 500 declined 5 percent.

The investment manager is Paul Blaustein of Oppenheimer Capital Corporation, which also serves as a manager of pension funds and is a subsidiary of Oppenheimer and Company. Mr. Blaustein, who became portfolio manager in March 1986 after six years' association with the Fund, emphasizes capital preservation in tandem with the Fund's value criteria. He believes Quest for Value's difference is its ability to offer long-term appreciation potential with less risk and volatility than the market as a whole.

The Fund's expense ratio for the fiscal year ended April 30, 1986, was 2.2 percent. This includes the management fee of 2 percent for the first $50 million under management.

While Quest for Value did not match the gain of the S&P 500 in 1986, it is a well-positioned, long-term, lower-risk holding. Its value-oriented approach makes it a good long-term holding.

PROFILE 12-1

ACORN FUND
2 N. LaSalle Street
Chicago, IL 60602
312-621-0630

Fund Classification:	G	
Total Assets:	$395 million	
Fund Manager:	Ralph Wanger	
Year of Inception:	1970	
Minimum Investment:	$1000	
Sales Charge:	No load	
12b-1 Charge:	No	
Expense Ratio:	0.78	
Portfolio Mix:	*%*	*Issues*
Bonds	0	0
Corporate Bonds	0	0
Common Stock	85	128
Preferred Stock	0	0
U. S. Government Securities	0	0
Convertible Securities	0	0
Commercial Paper	0	0
Estimated Annual Portfolio Turnover	20%	
Estimates of Fund Performance:		
Annual Return for Three Years:	25.8%	
Annual Return for Five Years:	23.9%	
Annual Return in Bull Markets:		
1985	31.4%	
1986	23.2%	
Annual Return in Bear Markets:		
6/30/83–6/30/84	-9.53%	
Representative Current Yield (8/31/86):	1.2%	
Measures of Risk and Reward:		
Alpha	3.0	
Beta	0.76	
R square	73	
Standard deviation	3.72	
Reward/risk ratio	6.9	
Net Asset Value:		
9/25/87	47.73	
10/28/87	33.90	

PROFILE 12-2

BOSTON COMPANY CAPITAL APPRECIATION FUND
One Boston Place
Boston, MA 02108
1-800-343-6324
617-956-9740

Fund Classification:	G	
Total Assets:	$424 million	
Fund Manager:	Gerry Zukowski	
Year of Inception:	1979	
Minimum Investment:	$1000	
Sales Charge:	No load	
12b-1 Charge:	Yes	
Expense Ratio:	0.96	
Portfolio Mix:	%	*Issues*
Bonds	0	0
Corporate Bonds	0	0
Common Stock	83	111
Preferred Stock	0	0
U. S. Government Securities	0	0
Convertible Securities	0	0
Commercial Paper	0	0
Estimated Annual Portfolio Turnover	36.9%	
Estimates of Fund Performance:		
Annual Return for Three Years:	30.3%	
Annual Return for Five Years:	26.2%	
Annual Return in Bull Markets:		
1985	35.0%	
1986	22.5%	
Annual Return in Bear Markets:		
6/30/83–6/30/84	-5.62%	
Representative Current Yield (8/31/86):	1.1%	
Measures of Risk and Reward:		
Alpha	3.1	
Beta	0.90	
R square	93	
Standard deviation	3.88	
Reward/risk ratio	7.8	
Net Asset Value:		
9/25/87	38.39	
10/28/87	28.12	

PROFILE 12-3

DODGE AND COX STOCK FUND
One Post Street 35th Floor
San Francisco, CA 94104
415-981-1710

Fund Classification:	G	
Total Assets:	$46 million	
Fund Manager:	Joseph M. Fee	
	Peter Avenali	
Year of Inception:	1964	
Minimum Investment:	$250	
Sales Charge:	No load	
12b-1 Charge:	No	
Expense Ratio:	0.66	

Portfolio Mix:	%	*Issues*
Bonds	0	0
Corporate Bonds	0	0
Common Stock	94.22	47
Preferred Stock	0	0
U. S. Government Securities	0	0
Convertible Securities	0	0
Commercial Paper	0	0
Estimated Annual Portfolio Turnover	10%	

Estimates of Fund Performance:	
Annual Return for Three Years:	28.4%
Annual Return for Five Years:	27.1%
Annual Return in Bull Markets:	
1985	37.7%
1986	18.8%
Annual Return in Bear Markets:	
6/30/83–6/30/84	-1.98%
Representative Current Yield (8/31/86):	2.9%

Measures of Risk and Reward:	
Alpha	1.4
Beta	0.98
R square	93
Standard deviation	4.19
Reward/risk ratio	6.8

Net Asset Value:	
9/25/87	43.29
10/28/87	32.01

PROFILE 12-4

EVERGREEN FUND
550 Mamaroneck Avenue
Harrison, NY 10528
1-800-235-0064
914-698-5711

Fund Classification:	G	
Total Assets:	$639 million	
Fund Manager:	Steven A. Leiber	
	Nola Maddox Falcone	
Year of Inception:	1971	
Minimum Investment:	$2000	
Sales Charge:	No load	
12b-1 Charge:	No	
Expense Ratio:	1.08	
Portfolio Mix:	%	*Issues*
Bonds	0	0
Corporate Bonds	0	0
Common Stock	89.42	290
Preferred Stock	0	0
U. S. Government Securities	0	0
Convertible Securities	0	0
Commercial Paper	0	0
Estimated Annual		
Portfolio Turnover	82%	
Estimates of Fund Performance:		
Annual Return for Three Years:	24.9%	
Annual Return for Five Years:	25.4%	
Annual Return in Bull Markets:		
1985	34.6%	
1986	13.2%	
Annual Return in Bear Markets:		
6/30/83–6/30/84	-12.3%	
Representative Current Yield (8/31/86):	0.9%	
Measures of Risk and Reward:		
Alpha	1.4	
Beta	0.87	
R square	86	
Standard deviation	3.91	
Reward/risk ratio	6.4	
Net Asset Value:		
9/25/87	15.07	
10/28/87	10.79	

PROFILE 12-5

IVY GROWTH FUND
40 Industrial Park Road
Hingham, MA 02043
1-800-235-3322
617-749-1416

Fund Classification:	G	
Total Assets:	$165 million	
Fund Manager:	Michael Peers	
	William Watson	
Year of Inception:	1961	
Minimum Investment:	$1000	
Sales Charge:	No load	
12b-1 Charge:	No	
Expense Ratio:	1.25	

Portfolio Mix:	%	*Issues*
Bonds	NA	13
Corporate Bonds	0	0
Common Stock	NA	63
Preferred Stock	0	0
U. S. Government Securities	0	0
Convertible Securities	0	0
Commercial Paper	0	0
Estimated Annual Portfolio Turnover	132%	

Estimates of Fund Performance:	
Annual Return for Three Years:	23.6%
Annual Return for Five Years:	26.8%
Annual Return in Bull Markets:	
1985	29.4%
1986	16.8%
Annual Return in Bear Markets:	
6/30/83–6/30/84	1.12%

Representative Current Yield (8/31/86):	2.7%

Measures of Risk and Reward:	
Alpha	2.3
Beta	0.67
R square	87
Standard deviation	3.02
Reward/risk ratio	7.8

Net Asset Value:	
9/25/87	15.56
10/28/87	11.81

PROFILE 12-6

NICHOLAS FUND
700 N. Water Street
Milwaukee, WI 53202
414-272-6133

Fund Classification:	G	
Total Assets:	$1,053 million	
Fund Manager:	Albert O. Nicholas	
Year of Inception:	1968	
Minimum Investment:	$500	
Sales Charge:	No load	
12b-1 Charge:	No	
Expense Ratio:	0.86	
Portfolio Mix:	%	*Issues*
Corporate Bonds	0.9	1
Convertible Bonds	0.7	2
Common Stock	60.30	109
Preferred Stock	0.4	1
U. S. Government Securities	0	0
Municipal Bonds	0	0
Cash	38.3	10
Estimated Annual		
Portfolio Turnover	14%	
Estimates of Fund Performance:		
Annual Return for Three Years:	24.4%	
Annual Return for Five Years:	26.5%	
Annual Return in Bull Markets:		
1985	29.7%	
1986	11.7%	
Annual Return in Bear Markets:		
6/30/83–6/30/84	-6.87%	
Representative Current Yield (8/31/86):	2.5%	
Measures of Risk and Reward:		
Alpha	1.6	
Beta	0.69	
R square	82	
Standard deviation	3.21	
Reward/risk ratio	7.6	
Net Asset Value:		
9/25/87	37.58	
10/28/87	29.75	

PROFILE 12-7

PARTNERS FUND
342 Madison Avenue
New York, NY 10173
1-800-367-0770
212-850-8300

Fund Classification:	G
Total Assets:	$444 million
Fund Manager:	Phil Steckler
	Alan Hunter
	Dick Weissman
Year of Inception:	1967
Minimum Investment:	$500
Sales Charge:	No load
12b-1 Charge:	Yes
Expense Ratio:	0.89

Portfolio Mix:	%	*Issues*
Bonds	0	0
Corporate Bonds	0	0
Common Stock	71.7	63
Preferred Stock	0.5	1
U. S. Government Securities	1.6	4
U. S. Government Obligations	18.6	8
Cash	0	0
Estimated Annual Portfolio Turnover	181%	

Estimates of Fund Performance:	
Annual Return for Three Years:	25.3%
Annual Return for Five Years:	23.2%
Annual Return in Bull Markets:	
1985	29.8%
1986	17.3%
Annual Return in Bear Markets:	
6/30/83–6/30/84	-2.00%
Representative Current Yield (8/31/86):	2.2%

Measures of Risk and Reward:	
Alpha	1.7
Beta	0.79
R square	92
Standard deviation	3.42
Reward/risk ratio	7.4

Net Asset Value:	
9/25/87	19.32
10/28/87	14.95

PROFILE 12-8

T. ROWE PRICE GROWTH STOCK FUND
100 E. Pratt Street
Baltimore, MD 21202
1-800-638-5660
301-547-2000

Fund Classification:	G	
Total Assets:	$127 million	
Fund Manager:	M. David Testa	
Year of Inception:	1950	
Minimum Investment:	$1000	
Sales Charge:	No load	
12b-1 Charge:	No	
Expense Ratio:	0.59	

Portfolio Mix:	%	*Issues*
Bonds	0	0
Corporate Bonds	0	0
Common Stock	91	NA
Preferred Stock	0	0
U. S. Government Securities	0	0
U. S. Government Obligations	0	0
Cash	0	0
Estimated Annual Portfolio Turnover	64%	

Estimates of Fund Performance:	
Annual Return for Three Years:	28.8%
Annual Return for Five Years:	21.6%
Annual Return in Bull Markets:	
1985	35.1%
1986	21.7%
Annual Return in Bear Markets:	
6/30/83–6/30/84	-15.3%
Representative Current Yield (12/31/86):	1.9%

Measures of Risk and Reward:	
Alpha	0.1
Beta	0.92
R square	82
Standard deviation	4.24
Reward/risk ratio	6.8

Net Asset Value:	
9/25/87	21.41
10/28/87	15.05

PROFILE 12-9

QUEST FOR VALUE FUND
One New York Plaza
New York, NY 10004
1-800-525-7048
212-825-4497

Fund Classification:	G
Total Assets:	$75 million
Fund Manager:	Paul Blaustein
Year of Inception:	1979
Minimum Investment:	$2000
Sales Charge:	No load
12b-1 Charge:	No
Expense Ratio:	2.18

Portfolio Mix:	%	*Issues*
Bonds	0	0
Corporate Bonds	0	0
Common Stock	NA	129
Preferred Stock	72.6	NA
U. S. Government Securities	28.8	NA
U. S. Government Obligations	0	0
Cash	0	0
Estimated Annual Portfolio Turnover	68.4%	

Estimates of Fund Performance:	
Annual Return for Three Years:	21.6%
Annual Return for Five Years:	28.1%
Annual Return in Bull Markets:	
1985	27.4%
1986	14.3%
Annual Return in Bear Markets:	
6/30/83–6/30/84	-0.83%
Representative Current Yield (8/31/86):	0.7%

Measures of Risk and Reward:	
Alpha	0.5
Beta	0.66
R square	84
Standard deviation	2.98
Reward/risk ratio	7.2

Net Asset Value:	
9/25/87	30.03
10/28/87	21.98

Chapter 13
Aggressive Growth Funds

BACKGROUND INFORMATION

Type of Security

Aggressive growth funds seek to provide the investor with a maximum growth of capital with secondary emphasis on dividend or interest income. They invest in common stocks that have a high potential for rapid growth.

Some aggressive growth funds invest in companies in a broad range of industries; others concentrate on one or a few industry sectors. Because they invest in less stable securities, aggressive growth funds generally have higher portfolio turnover rates than average, and they may generate short-term capital gains or losses.

Risk/Stability

Because they invest in stocks that can experience wide swings up and down, they have relatively low stability of principal and very high potential for capital appreciation.

Aggressive growth funds generally incur higher risks than growth funds in their efforts to secure more rapid or more pronounced growth. Some of the most noted successes among mutual funds are aggressive growth funds whose managers have made wise choices in this high-risk, high-reward investing arena.

SPECIAL BENEFITS AND EXPOSURES

Speculative Strategies

These speculative funds are structured to obtain large gains. They often invest in newer, emerging companies, buy on margin, engage in borrowing, short-selling, options and warrants, and practice other speculative strategies to leverage their results.

Volatility

Aggressive growth funds are exciting to hold during bull markets, but they can be dreadful to own during market downturns. Since they are volatile, with betas of 1.30 or more, their rapid rises in up markets and quick declines in down markets are expected.

Specialty Funds

Some aggressive growth funds invest heavily in smaller, emerging, or high technology firms. Such specialties are covered more specifically in Chapter 15 (Technology Funds) and Chapter 17 (Small Company Growth Funds).

PORTFOLIO FIT

Aggressive growth funds seek to provide the investor with maximum growth of capital with little emphasis on income or dividends. They have a high potential for capital appreciation—and, of course, capital decline in down markets.

Such funds are suitable for investors who can afford to assume a risk—greater than the overall market's—of potential loss in the value of their investment in the hope of achieving substantial and rapid gains—again, greater than the overall market's. They are not suitable for investors who must conserve their principal or who must maximize the current income they derive from their investments.

If an aggressive growth fund begins to falter in its performance relative to the stock market, the investor must be ready to sell it and seek another aggressive growth fund.

Younger, aggressive investors might hold 10 to 20 percent of their portfolios in aggressive growth funds. Those who emphasize preservation of capital should have less than 10 percent of their portfolios in aggressive growth funds.

EIGHT REPRESENTATIVE AGGRESSIVE GROWTH FUNDS

To illustrate, we have chosen eight aggressive growth funds that show the qualities that investors seek when purchasing shares of aggressive growth funds. Note that all but one of these examples are no-load funds. Table 13-1 contains a summary listing of the eight funds. It is followed by a more detailed description of each fund's objectives and investment philosophy and practice, as well as capsule Profiles of their recent performance.

Investors are reminded that past performance is no indicator of future performance.

Bruce Fund

Bruce Fund is a fund aggressively seeking long-term appreciation.

The Fund has performed well due to a large holding of U.S. government zero-coupon bonds that constituted 48 percent of its portfolio on December 31, 1986. When interest rates declined, these bonds rose dramatically in value. Another interesting holding has been several Washington Public Power bonds in default, which accounted for 5 percent of the portfolio on December 31, 1986. The Fund's other holdings are 42 percent stocks and 6 percent in cash, due to a net cash inflow. Some common stock holdings are Kentucky Utilities, Inertia Dynamics, and RLI Corp.

Table 13-1: Eight Representative Aggressive Growth Funds

Fund	Annual Return (%) for 3 Years	Fund
Bruce Fund	28.9	NL
Fidelity Magellan Fund	39.0	LL
Lehman Capital Fund	26.8	NL
Loomis Sayles Capital Development Fund	40.8	NL
Manhattan Fund	35.1	NL
Pacific Horizon Aggressive fund	37.1	NL
Tudor Fund	30.2	NL
Twentieth Century Select Fund	343.0	NL

The assets of this small Fund have grown from $1.37 million on December 31, 1985, to $3.0 million on December 31, 1986. The Fund completed a strong 24-month performance with a 30 percent gain in calendar 1986.

Robert Bruce (a cofounder of the Mathers Fund), who has managed the Fund since October 1983, specializes in seeking unusual opportunities for capital appreciation.

Mr. Bruce stated recently that "there should be a settlement of the WPPS bonds since it makes good sense to Washington Public Power." One might look for a settlement yielding a doubling of value for the WPPS bonds. Bruce also still favors zero-coupon bonds for their capital appreciation.

The Fund's risk is average (beta = 1.0), but it could yield above-average returns if interest rates continue to decline and the WPPS settlement occurs before the end of 1988.

Fidelity Magellan Fund

Fidelity Magellan Fund is Fidelity Management's most aggressive fund. It actively seeks the most promising investment opportunities wherever they may be in the stock market. The Fund seeks to achieve capital appreciation by investing primarily in common stock and securities convertible into common stock. The Fund has often held 10 to 20 percent of its assets in international equities. Up to 20 percent of assets may also be invested in debt securities of all types and quality.

Peter Lynch, one of the most revered fund managers and stock pickers, has managed the Fund since June 1977. Since 1977, Fund assets have grown from $20 million to $7 billion, and it now holds 1300 stocks for 700,000 shareholder accounts.

A portfolio of $7 billion makes it difficult to beat the market, as Lynch himself admits. Nevertheless, the Fund was one of the few that beat the S&P 500 in 1986, and it returned 30 percent annually over the past five years.

Figure 13-1: The Performance of the Fidelity Magellan Fund Shown with Its 26-Week Moving Average. (Courtesy of Telescan.)

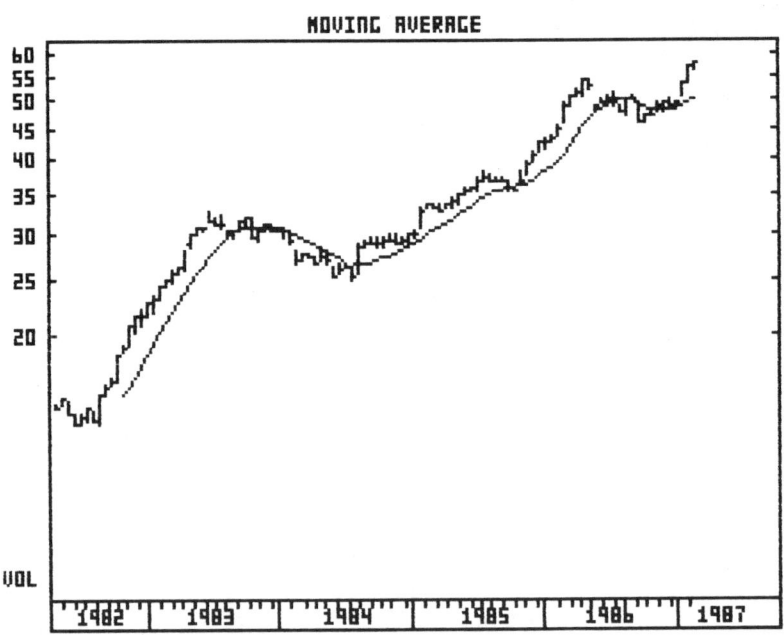

Lehman Capital Fund

Lehman Capital Fund seeks capital appreciation, with income a secondary consideration.

When Mr. Ronald Wiener became portfolio manager in 1986, he restructured the Fund's portfolio.

The Fund's 3-year record for the period ended December 31, 1986, was less than average. For the 5-year period ended December 31, 1986, its record was exemplary. It is too early to tell what effect the management change will have on the Fund's future.

Loomis Sayles Capital Development Fund

Loomis Sayles Capital Development Fund's objective is long-term capital appreciation.

The five largest holdings in 1986 were Texas Air, Marvin Labs, Standard Pacific, Home Shopping Network, and Marsh & McLennan.

Chapter 13   169

"We concentrate on companies with earnings evolution that will move their stock price up by at least 50 percent within a year from the point at which we invested," says portfolio manager Kenneth Heebner. The Fund in fact achieved a 29 percent annual return for the five years ended December 31, 1986; 28 percent annually in calendar 1986. The performance of the Fund is shown in Figure 13-2.

Figure 13-2: The Performance of the Loomis Sayles Capital Development Fund Shown with Its 26-Week Moving Average. (Courtesy of Telescan.)

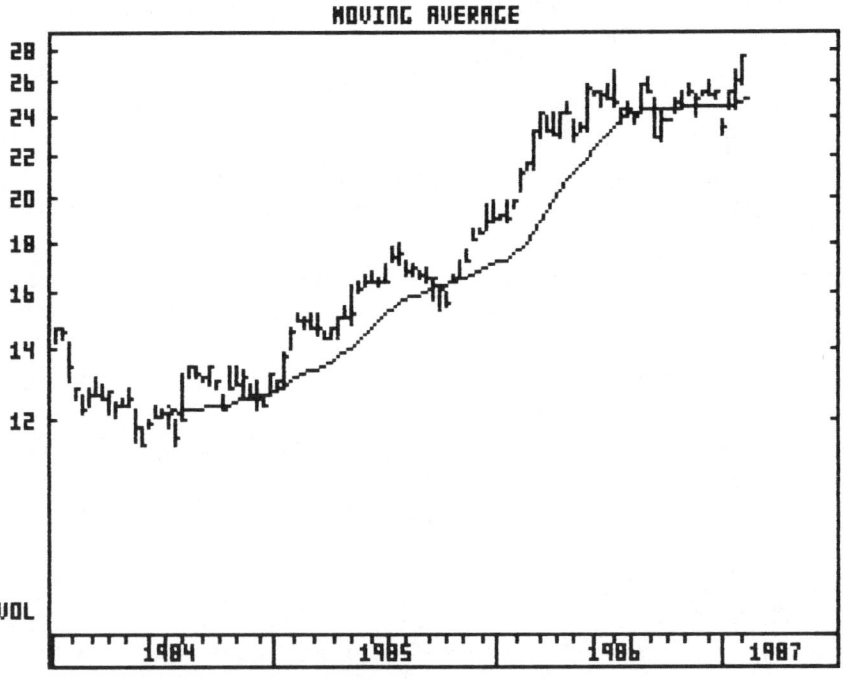

The Fund is closed to new shareholders within the SEC definitions, but those who own shares in Loomis Sayles Mutual Fund for six months may enter the Fund. The reason is that New England Life, who owns the Fund, also owns New England Life Growth Fund, a load fund with the same manager and strategy as Loomis Sayles Capital Development Fund. The SEC views it as unfair to market load and no-load versions of the same fund.

The Fund is best suited to the investor whose portfolio can accommodate the greater risk attendant on its aggressive investment approach in order to achieve better long-term returns.

Manhattan Fund

Manhattan is managed for capital appreciation.

The Fund, a member of the Neuberger and Berman family of funds, focuses on stocks with high-quality earnings and strong balance sheets. The five largest holdings as of September 30, 1986, were IBM, Digital Equipment, Ashland Oil, Monsanto, and General Re.

The Fund's total return has equalled the S&P 500 over the past five years. It has performed solidly in up markets and has had average dips in down markets.

Pacific Horizon Aggressive Growth Fund

Pacific Horizon Aggressive Growth Fund seeks to maximize capital appreciation by investing in common stocks and convertibles.

The strategies of the Fund will generally result in high portfolio turnover—about 200 percent annually. The Fund holds over-the-counter (OTC) emerging growth-company stocks that have appreciated well in the year prior to purchase. The criteria for selection are (1) rapid and accelerating growth, (2) rising relative strength, and (3) membership in an industry outperforming the market. Current emphasis is on retailers and the consumer sector.

On September 30, 1986, the Fund held 102 stocks and retained only 2 percent in cash. Its top ten holdings in 1986 were Home Shopping Network, Safecard Services, Reebok International, Days Inn, Arvin Industries, American Family Corp., Oshkosh Truck Corp., Prime Motor Inns, Crazy Eddy, Sizzler Restaurants, Manpower, Inc., and International Technology.

The Fund started on March 31, 1984, and had acquired assets of $96 million by late July 1986. At the end of 1986 its assets stood at $64 million.

The investment advisor is Security Pacific Bank. The Fund is distributed by the Dreyfus Corporation.

Mr. William Duncan, the portfolio manager, "expects the economy to surprise us on the downside," so he will "stay out of technology stocks." Financial stocks and other interest-sensitive securities are being considered. Duncan "plans on shifting strategies as market conditions change, while staying relatively fully invested."

The Fund's beta of 1.3 suggests it will do well in up markets. Its performance in bear markets has not been tested, but note that it dropped twice as far as the market in the third quarter of 1986. The Fund gained 37.5 percent in 1985 and 20 percent in 1986. Note its volatile behavior over the two years shown in Figure 13-3. This Fund is for the more aggressive investor.

Tudor Fund

Tudor Fund's objective is capital appreciation.

The Fund normally invests in common stocks or convertibles issued by companies operating in such industries as are believed to offer potential for capital appreciation. Equity securities constitute most of the Fund's portfolio, but the Fund may also

Figure 13-3: The Performance of the Pacific Horizon Aggressive Growth Portfolio for the 2 Years Ending 6/30/87. (Courtesy of Mutal Fund Chartist.)

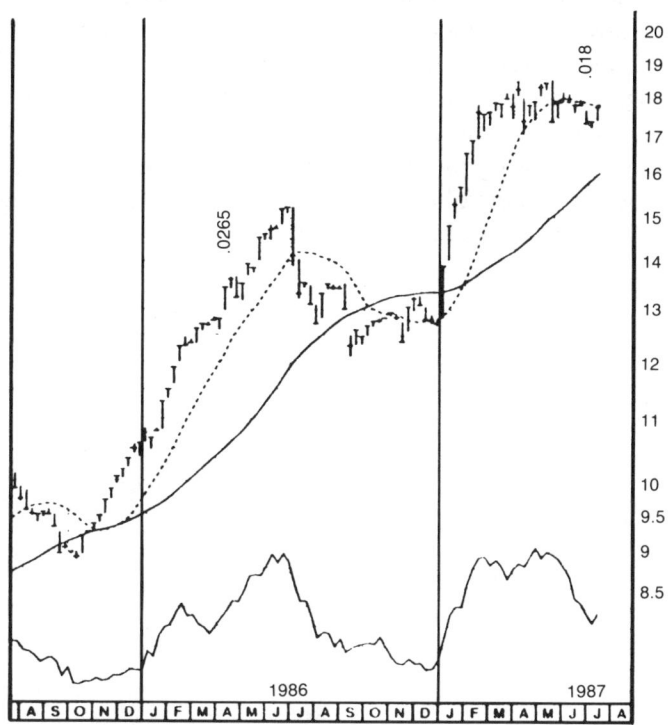

temporarily invest in high-grade preferred stock, debt securities, government securities, or cash. The top five holdings as of September 30, 1986, were Stone Container, FNMA, Federal Express, Trenwick, and Glaxo Holdings. The Fund's average annual turnover is 100 percent.

The Fund has been managed by Melville Strauss since 1973. It is an aggressive fund and moves fast when the market shifts. It increased 16 percent in January 1987 as the market jumped 15 percent. In the third quarter of 1986 the Fund dropped 7 percent, which equalled the market. Its return of 12.4 percent for calendar 1986 closed a ten-year period ended December 31, 1986, in which its annual return averaged 20 percent.

Twentieth Century Select Fund

Twentieth Century Select Fund seeks capital growth as the primary objective, but the Fund requires that the stocks it purchases pay current cash dividends, even if they are not significant.

The Fund invests in common stocks of well-established companies considered to have better-than-average prospects for appreciation. The Fund always remains fully invested.

The five largest holdings as of October 31, 1986, were Westinghouse, Aetna, Ford, Marsh & McLennan, and Polaroid.

The Fund was launched in 1958. Since 1970, James Stowers, the founder, has been the Fund's manager. Stowers's philosophy is to invest only in companies with accelerating earnings and revenues. To spot such prospects early, he and his management team rely on a computer program that isolates companies reporting sudden growth spurts.

Stowers won't touch a stock unless its trading volume is rising. "If you're the only one who knows about it, nothing's going to happen," argues Stowers. He reasons that as long as his stocks are sound, his portfolio will come out on top over the long run.

This Fund is for the more aggressive investor.

PROFILE 13-1

BRUCE FUND
20 N. Wacker Dr. Suite 1425
Chicago, IL 60606
312-236-9160

Fund Classification:	AG
Total Assets:	$5.4 million
Fund Manager:	Robert B. Bruce
Year of Inception:	1967
Minimum Investment:	$1000
Sales Charge:	No load
12b-1 Charge:	No
Expense Ratio:	2.57

Portfolio Mix:	%	*Issues*
Bonds	0	0
Corporate Bonds	0	0
Common Stock	37.42	11
Preferred Stock	0	0
U. S. Government Securities	50.51	3
Municipal Bonds	5.25	5
Cash	0	0
Estimated Annual Portfolio Turnover	0%	

Estimates of Fund Performance:	
Annual Return for Three Years:	23.5%
Annual Return for Five Years:	22.2%
Annual Return in Bull Markets:	
1985	37.0%
1986	29.6%
Annual Return in Bear Markets:	
6/30/83–6/30/84	-13.6%
Representative Current Yield (12/31/86):	1.2%

Measures of Risk and Reward:	
Alpha	5.3
Beta	0.90
R square	42
Standard deviation	5.85
Reward/risk ratio	4.0

Net Asset Value:	
9/25/87	102.87
10/28/87	82.25

PROFILE 13-2

FIDELITY MAGELLAN FUND
82 Devonshire
Boston, MA 02109
1-800-544-7777
617-523-1919

Fund Classification:		AG
Total Assets:		$6,555 million
Fund Manager:		Peter Lynch
Year of Inception:		1967
Minimum Investment:		$1000
Sales Charge:		3.00%
12b-1 Charge:		No
Expense Ratio:		1.08

Portfolio Mix:	%	Issues
Bonds	0	0
Corporate Bonds	0	0
Common Stock	93.96	1300
Preferred Stock	0	0
U. S. Government Securities	0	0
Municipal Bonds	0	0
Cash	0	0
Estimated Annual Portfolio Turnover	96%	

Estimates of Fund Performance:	
Annual Return for Three Years:	22.1%
Annual Return for Five Years:	30.2%
Annual Return in Bull Markets:	
1985	42.9%
1986	23.6%
Annual Return in Bear Markets:	
6/30/83–6/30/84	-13.6%
Representative Current Yield (12/31/86):	0.8%

Measures of Risk and Reward:	
Alpha	2.2
Beta	1.10
R square	92
Standard deviation	4.77
Reward/risk ratio	4.6
Net Asset Value:	
9/25/87	58.04
10/28/87	39.26

PROFILE 13-3

LEHMAN CAPITAL FUND
55 Water Street
New York, NY 10041
1-800-221-5350
212-668-8578

Fund Classification:	AG	
Total Assets:	$103 million	
Fund Manager:	Ronald Weiner	
Year of Inception:	1976	
Minimum Investment:	$1000	
Sales Charge:	5.0%	
12b-1 Charge:	No	
Expense Ratio:	1.13	

Portfolio Mix:	%	Issues
Bonds	0	0
Corporate Bonds	0	0
Common Stock	85.5	32
Preferred Stock	0	0
U. S. Government Securities	14.5	4
Municipal Bonds	0	0
Cash	0	0
Estimated Annual Portfolio Turnover	162%	

Estimates of Fund Performance:	
Annual Return for Three Years:	11.7%
Annual Return for Five Years:	22.0%
Annual Return in Bull Markets:	
1985	27.2%
1986	13.9%
Annual Return in Bear Markets:	
6/30/83–6/30/84	-8.09%
Representative Current Yield (12/31/86):	1.3%
Measures of Risk and Reward:	
Alpha	6.9
Beta	1.14
R square	86
Standard deviation	5.17
Reward/risk ratio	2.3
Net Asset Value:	
9/25/87	22.67
10/28/87	13.86

PROFILE 13-4

LOOMIS SAYLES CAPITAL DEVELOPMENT FUND
P.O. Box 449 Back Bay Annex
Boston, MA 02117
1-800-345-4048
617-578-6262

Fund Classification:	AG	
Total Assets:	$232 million	
Fund Manager:	G. Kenneth Heebner	
Year of Inception:	1961	
Minimum Investment:	$250	
Sales Charge:	No load	
12b-1 Charge:	No	
Expense Ratio:	0.79	
Portfolio Mix:	%	*Issues*
Bonds	0	0
Corporate Bonds	0	0
Common Stock	99	NA
Preferred Stock	0	0
U. S. Government Securities	0	0
Municipal Bonds	0	0
Cash	0	0
Estimated Annual Portfolio Turnover	208%	
Estimates of Fund Performance:		
Annual Return for Three Years:	20.0%	
Annual Return for Five Years:	28.8%	
Annual Return in Bull Markets:		
1985	46.2%	
1986	27.5%	
Annual Return in Bear Markets:		
6/30/83–6/30/84	-23.0%	
Representative Current Yield (8/31/86):	0.5%	
Measures of Risk and Reward:		
Alpha	1.1	
Beta	1.26	
R square	78	
Standard deviation	6.01	
Reward/risk ratio	3.3	
Net Asset Value:		
9/25/87	31.15	
10/28/87	17.93	

PROFILE 13-5

MANHATTAN FUND
342 Madison Avenue
New York, NY 10173
1-800-367-0770
212-850-8310

Fund Classification:	AG
Total Assets:	$241 million
Fund Manager:	Irwin Lainoff
Year of Inception:	1965
Minimum Investment:	$500
Sales Charge:	No load
12b-1 Charge:	Yes (1-2%)
Expense Ratio:	1.40

Portfolio Mix:	%	*Issues*
Bonds	0	0
Corporate Bonds	0	0
Common Stock	91.06	134
Preferred Stock	0	0
U. S. Government Securities	0	0
Municipal Bonds	0	0
Cash	0	0
Estimated Annual Portfolio Turnover	155%	

Estimates of Fund Performance:	
Annual Return for Three Years:	19.8%
Annual Return for Five Years:	22.9%
Annual Return in Bull Markets:	
1985	37.1%
1986	17.0%
Annual Return in Bear Markets:	
6/30/83–6/30/84	-4.84%
Representative Current Yield (12/31/86):	0.8%

Measures of Risk and Reward:	
Alpha	0.8
Beta	1.07
R square	95
Standard deviation	4.65
Reward/risk ratio	4.3

Net Asset Value:	
9/25/87	11.78
10/28/87	7.96

PROFILE 13-6

PACIFIC HORIZON AGGRESSIVE GROWTH FUND
767 Fifth Avenue
New York, NY 10153
1-800-645-3515

Fund Classification:	AG
Total Assets:	$64 million
Fund Manager:	William Duncan
Year of Inception:	1984
Minimum Investment:	$1000
Sales Charge:	4.5%
12b-1 Charge:	Yes (0.6%)
Expense Ratio:	1.50

Portfolio Mix:	%	*Issues*
Bonds	0	0
Corporate Bonds	0	0
Common Stock	97.2	75
Preferred Stock	0	0
U. S. Government Securities	0	0
Municipal Bonds	0	0
Cash	0	0
Estimated Annual Portfolio Turnover	234%	

Estimates of Fund Performance:	
Annual Return for Two Years:	28.5%
Annual Return for Five Years:	NA
Annual Return in Bull Markets:	
1985	37.5%
1986	20.1%
Annual Return in Bear Markets:	
6/30/83–6/30/84	-18.4%
Representative Current Yield (12/31/86):	0.2%
Measures of Risk and Reward:	
Alpha	NA
Beta	1.30
R square	NA
Standard deviation	6.0
Reward/risk ratio	4.75
Net Asset Value:	
9/25/87	17.84
10/28/87	13.04

PROFILE 13-7

TUDOR FUND
One New York Plaza
New York, NY 10004
1-800-223-3332
212-908-9582

Fund Classification:	AG
Total Assets:	$159 million
Fund Manager:	Melville Strauss
Year of Inception:	1986
Minimum Investment:	$1000
Sales Charge:	No load
12b-1 Charge:	No
Expense Ratio:	0.95

Portfolio Mix:	%	*Issues*
Bonds	0	0
Corporate Bonds	0	0
Common Stock	95.70	115
Preferred Stock	0	0
U. S. Government Securities	0	0
Municipal Bonds	0	0
Cash	0	0
Estimated Annual Portfolio Turnover	123%	

Estimates of Fund Performance:	
Annual Return for Three Years:	11.1%
Annual Return for Five Years:	20.6%
Annual Return in Bull Markets:	
1985	31.2%
1986	12.4%
Annual Return in Bear Markets:	
6/30/83–6/30/84	-23.9%
Representative Current Yield (12/31/86):	0.3%
Measures of Risk and Reward:	
Alpha	7.3
Beta	1.13
R square	84
Standard deviation	5.17
Reward/risk ratio	2.1
Net Asset Value:	
9/25/87	26.79
10/28/87	16.61

PROFILE 13-8

TWENTIETH CENTURY SELECT FUND
605 W. 47th Street
P.O. Box 200
Kansas City, MO 64141
816-531-5575

Fund Classification:	AG
Total Assets:	$1832 million
Fund Manager:	James Stowers
Year of Inception:	1958
Minimum Investment:	NA
Sales Charge:	No load
12b-1 Charge:	No
Expense Ratio:	1.01

Portfolio Mix:	%	Issues
Bonds	0	0
Corporate Bonds	0	0
Common Stock	99.81	76
Preferred Stock	0	0
U. S. Government Securities	0	0
Municipal Bonds	0	0
Cash	0	0
Estimated Annual Portfolio Turnover	85%	

Estimates of Fund Performance:	
Annual Return for Three Years:	14.3%
Annual Return for Five Years:	22.5%
Annual Return in Bull Markets:	
1985	33.8%
1986	20.7%
Annual Return in Bear Markets:	
6/30/83–6/30/84	−21.1%
Representative Current Yield (12/31/86):	1.5%

Measures of Risk and Reward:	
Alpha	5.3
Beta	1.20
R square	90
Standard deviation	5.31
Reward/risk ratio	2.7

Net Asset Value:	
9/25/87	42.59
10/28/87	29.61

Chapter 14
International Funds

BACKGROUND INFORMATION

Type of Security

International funds invest in the stocks of firms listed on the stock markets of countries and regions outside the United States.

Risk/Stability

It is wise to consider investing abroad since different economies experience intervals of prosperity and recession at different times. In the past, foreign markets have had periods in which they have outperformed the U.S. market. The Japanese economy, for example, grew twice as fast as the U.S. economy from 1953 to 1983.

"Record highs are consistently being achieved in [world] stock markets," says Michael O'Neill, president of G.T. Global Growth Funds. "But the continuously rising forecasts of corporate earnings mean prices can still go up without any hint of a speculative boom." The German market, for example, was up 87 percent in 1985; but because profits shot up too, the P/E ratio edged up only two points, from 11 to 13.

Another factor to consider is the value of the U.S. dollar relative to that of other countries' currencies. When the dollar's value declines, the returns from international funds improve, and vice-versa. When the U.S. dollar is strong, even when foreign stock markets do well in terms of their own currencies, good performances may not compensate for the weakness of the local currency relative to the dollar. For example, 1984 was a difficult year for international funds because the dollar strengthened against other currencies. The widely followed EAFE (Europe, Australia, Far East) market index was up 21.8 percent for 1984, but in U.S. dollar terms, the increase was only 8.1 percent. The decline of the dollar since 1985, however, has benefitted holders of international funds.

Risk and return performance for selected foreign stock markets for the five-year period ended September 30, 1983, is given in Table 14-1. It shows that the U.S. stock market was less volatile during this period than the other markets. As the economic recovery overseas continues and the dollar continues to decline over the next couple of years, we can expect international funds to increase in value significantly.

Table 14-1: Top Performing Major Stock Markets Worldwide Since 1980

Year	1st	2nd	3rd	4th	5th
1980	Italy 78	Hong Kong 71	Sing./Mal. 62	Australia 52	U.K. 39
1981	Sweden 36	Denmark 24	Sing./Mal. 18	Japan 15	Spain 11
1982	Sweden 23	U.S.A. 21	Holland 15	Germany 9	U.K. 8
1983	Norway 79	Denmark 68	Australia 53	Sweden 49	Holland 36
1984	Hong Kong 45	Spain 36	Japan 17	Belgium 12	Holland 11
1985	Austria 177	Germany 139	Italy 133	Switzerland 107	France 85
1986	Spain 107	Italy 105	Japan 86	France 79	Belgium 78

Source: G.T. Capital Management.

SPECIAL BENEFITS AND EXPOSURES

With over one-half of the world's companies outside the United States, international funds should be considered for a complete portfolio. A portfolio with international funds will, over time, produce better returns than a portfolio without them. Economic growth among industrial nations remains relatively independent: growth may be robust in one while another is experiencing a slump. As the economies of the world expand and interact, international participation is becoming more and more beneficial to the investor.

Volatility

A portfolio keyed to several nations will show less variability in its returns. Risk/return for U.S. versus global investments is shown in Figure 14-1. Moreover, from 1980 to 1986, for example, the investor would have found the top markets outside the United States, as Figure 14-2 shows. (Figure 14-2 is computed in U.S. dollars and reflect what the actual receipts would have been for a U.S. shareholder.)

Chapter 14

Figure 14-1: The Risk and Return for International Stock Markets

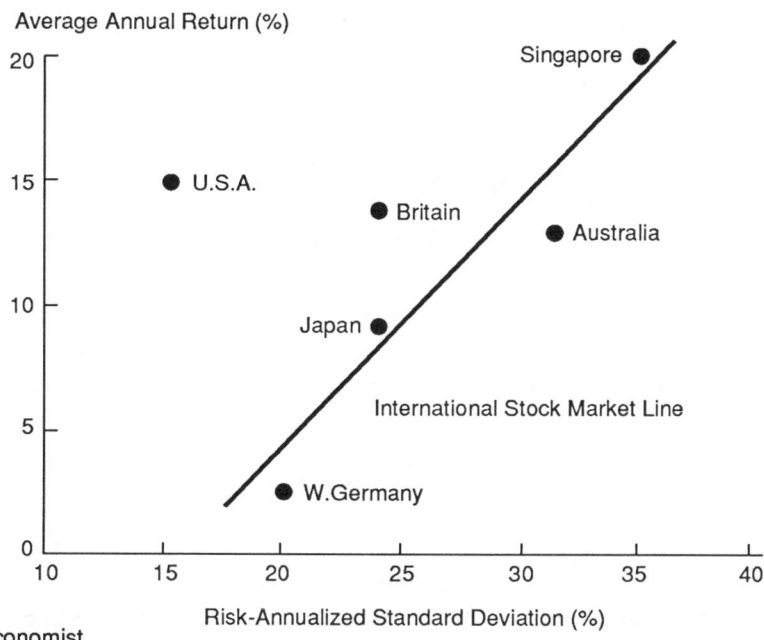

Source: The Economist.

Figure 14-2: Risk Reduction Benefits of International Diversification

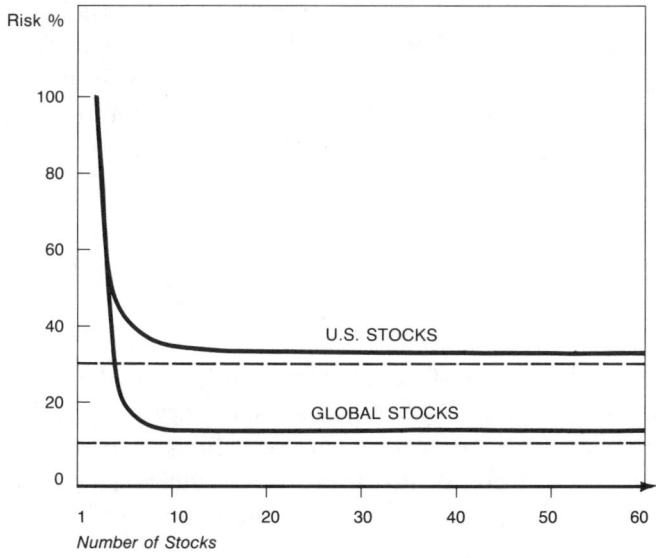

Regional Funds

Some funds, such as Price International or Scudder International, invest in many geographic areas, while others invest exclusively in one area. In general (as the attentive reader may infer from the presentation), I favor funds that represent worldwide non–U.S. markets. The smallest region to consider should be on the order of the Pacific Basin or Europe.

The Falling Dollar Factor in 1986

Investors looking for hot markets should know that returns on international investments may be somewhat above average for 1987 and 1988, perhaps, but the spectacular results of 1986 are unlikely to be repeated. Such successes resulted from several years of a rising foreign equity market coupled with a falling dollar—a confluence of events investors can rarely expect or anticipate. In the first quarter of 1987, in fact, international funds were laggards—up only 15 percent, while the U.S. market was up 21 percent.

PORTFOLIO FIT

International funds belong in most investors' portfolios since they provide worldwide diversification. Well-managed international funds offer participation in other markets.

The risk level of international funds varies, but they generally are only somewhat riskier than the U.S. market and somewhat less risky than aggressive growth funds.

Most advisers would suggest that investors keep a small portion of assets in international funds. "The whole object of international funds is to avoid the mine fields of investing in one market," says Henry B. W. de Vismes, president of Transatlantic Growth Fund.

Most investors should have 5 to 10 percent of their portfolios in international funds. The retired person might hold an international fund with a relatively lower risk than others. The size of the commitment in international funds for optimal diversification (greatest risk reduction, least reduction of return) is a matter open to debate.

The author's recommendation is between 10 and 20 percent.

TEN REPRESENTATIVE INTERNATIONAL FUNDS

To illustrate, we have chosen ten international funds that show the qualities that investors seek when purchasing shares of international funds. Note that only four of these examples are no-load funds. Table 14-2 contains a summary listing of the ten funds. It is followed by a more detailed description of each fund's objectives and investment philosophy and practice, as well as capsule Profiles of their recent performance.

Investors are reminded that past performance is no indicator of future performance.

Table 14-2: Ten Representative International Funds

Fund	Annual Return (%) for 3 Years	Load
Fidelity Overseas Fund	NA	LL
G. T. Pacific Growth Fund	21.7	L
Kemper International Fund	26.9	L
T. Rowe Price International Fund	30.0	NL
Putnam International Equities Fund	31.7	L
Scudder International Fund	30.6	NL
SoGen International Fund	19.6	L
Templeton World Fund	17.1	L
Transatlantic Fund	26.1	NL
Vanguard World-International Fund	34.4	NL

Fidelity Overseas Fund

The Fidelity Overseas Fund seeks long-term capital growth through investments in foreign securities.

The Fund has invested heavily in the domestic economies of Japan and Europe. It seeks stocks with excellent appreciation potential. Normally, at least 65 percent of the Fund's total assets will be invested in securities of companies from at least three countries outside North America. According to the prospectus, up to 35 percent may be in U.S. securities, but currently there are no U.S. securities among the 250 issues in the portfolio. The (foreign or U.S.) securities may include common stock and convertibles, as well as debt instruments of foreign businesses and foreign governments.

In 1984, George Noble became the manager of the Fund, after three years as stock selector for Lynch's Magellan Fund. The Fund returned 78.6 percent in 1985 and 68.9 percent in 1986. (Perhaps half of the 1986 gain was due to currency changes.) Noble's method is to study a stock's price/earnings (P/E) ratio, book value, and cash flow; yet he is not overly influenced by P/E ratios.

The Fund is popular; it grew in assets to over $2.6 billion by early 1987.

Noble favors railway stocks (Tokyu Corp. and Tobu Railway) and real estate (Mitsui Real Estate and Mitsubishi Estate, Ltd.) in Japan. The French market—and to a slightly lesser extent, the Spanish—represent the best current potential in Noble's view. While optimistic about the future of international markets, Noble says that "expectations need to be brought down. These are unusual times, and investors need to prepare themselves for the transition from unsustainable to normal rates of return."

The Fund's current concentration is Japan, 62 percent; France, 14 percent; Spain, 6 percent; United Kingdom, 6 percent; the remaining 12 percent is variously invested.

The Fund provides a means for investors to diversify their portfolios and participate in growth opportunities in companies and economies outside the United States. It is the most aggressive fund in this group.

G. T. Pacific Growth Fund

The G. T. Pacific Growth Fund seeks capital appreciation.

The Fund, founded in 1976, holds stocks from the Pacific Rim—Japan, Australia, Hong Kong, Singapore, and Malaysia. The G. T. Group has built up a reputation in international investing from its handling of accounts for major institutions, including five of the Fortune top ten and the BBC, over the years.

The Fund grew 114.8 percent for the five-year period ended December 31, 1986, for an annual gain of 18 percent. Recently, the amount of new cash flowing into the Fund has created the interesting problem for management of keeping pace in placing it.

The coordinator of the Fund since 1982 has been Paul Matthews, who is based in Hong Kong.

The Fund has benefitted from special circumstances that contributed to its performance: the decline of the dollar and the strength of overseas markets. G. T. intended to keep fully invested in 1987. It remained bullish about stock prices in countries where the currencies were weak in 1986—not so much because of currency gains in stock value as because of the beneficial effects of a weak currency on a domestic economy and the competitive export position created by a weak currency. Hong Kong, Singapore, and possibly Australia are areas G. T. considers potential gainers from weak currencies.

The G. T. Pacific Growth Fund is best suited to the more aggressive investor who wants to participate in the future of the Pacific Rim economies.

Kemper International Fund

The Kemper International Fund seeks total return, with capital appreciation and income as dual goals.

The Fund invests only in international (non-U.S.) markets and tends to favor stocks over bonds. At times the Fund has been in 17 countries, but in late 1986 its holdings were distributed in France, Japan, Switzerland, West Germany, the Netherlands, the United Kingdom, and Hong Kong. The Fund's total assets were $185 million in 1987.

Kemper is managed from Europe, by Kemper-Johnstone, Inc. (KMJI)—a joint firm composed of Kemper Financial Services of Chicago and Murray Johnstone, Ltd., an 80-year-old international securities firm of Glasgow, Scotland. KMJI's chief investment manager has been Michael Parlett of Murray Johnstone. The European connection and location often enable Kemper to identify trends in advance.

In 1987, Gavin Dobson, vice president and portfolio strategist of the Fund, expected certain markets to rise coupled with a continued decline in the dollar: perhaps a 10 percent appreciation from the latter and a 20 percent stock value appreciation in certain markets, particularly Europe. Dobson said the Fund made a big bet on the European market in 1986 by shifting some holdings from Japan to Europe. (The strategy was not completely successful for 1986, but the long-term results may yet prove the wisdom of the Fund managers.) When inflation in the United States begins to rise past 5 percent, Dobson favors Canadian and Australian mining issues.

The Fund takes a long-term view in managing its portfolio, and this patience has been a profitable virtue for the Fund, founded in mid-1981. Prepared for the inevitable drop in the dollar, the Fund was well rewarded in 1985. Its total return for the five years ended December 31, 1986, was 169 percent, a compound annual return of 21.9 percent. During the same period the S&P 500 grew by 147 percent for a compound annual return of 19.8 percent. For five or ten years the Fund should be expected to perform nearly the same as the market—18 percent annually under current predictions—with a risk about at the level of the market (beta = 1.04).

The Fund is best selected as a buy-and-hold for the long-term investor.

T. Rowe Price International Fund

The T. Rowe Price International Fund seeks both long-term growth of capital and income from a diversified portfolio of the marketable securities of non-U.S. issuers. The Fund places no limits (in percent or dollar figures) on the amount of assets managers may devote either to growth or to income.

The Fund remains well diversified, with 13 countries and 31 industries represented. The securities held were equally split (50 percent each) between Europe and the Far East.

The emphasis on total return allows the portfolio managers flexibility in choosing securities as warranted by changing conditions in world stock markets.

The adviser to the Fund—Rowe Price-Fleming International—has emphasized high-quality manufacturing and service companies. Overall, the Fund's managers believe the expected low inflation and slow, steady growth bode well for international equities. The Fund favors firms with strong earnings and specialized market niches. The largest concentration—35 percent—of assets is in Japan. Of late the Fund has been increasing its presence in Europe, especially France and Spain, which are believed to be able to derive the greatest benefit from the decline in energy costs.

Rowe Price-Fleming International is a joint venture between Price Associates (the well-known mutual fund management firm) and Robert Fleming Holdings (a respected international money manager). The venture is based in the United States but has offices in London and Tokyo to follow world events.

The Fund held $753 million in assets as of January 1, 1987, and returned 45.3 percent in 1985 and 60.5 percent in 1986. The annual average return was 24.6 percent for the five-year period ended December 31, 1986, and 30.0 percent for the three-year period ended December 31, 1986. The risk level is moderate (beta = 0.72).

Putnam International Equities Fund

The Putnam International Equities Fund's objective is capital appreciation.

The Fund seeks its objective by investing in the securities of U.S. and foreign companies.

The portfolio manager until the end of 1986 was Walter Oechsle, who has left Putnam with many of his staff. The current chief of international investments is Anthony Regan. The Fund received about $202 million in new investment during the first half of 1987, and the reports are that the Fund is still doing very well.

Under Oechsle the Fund achieved an average annual return of 26.3 percent for the five years ended December 31, 1986, earning 38.0 percent for 1986.

The Fund is best suited to the somewhat more conservative investor.

Scudder International Fund

The Scudder International Fund seeks long-term growth of capital through a diversified portfolio of marketable foreign equity investments.

The Fund invests in companies, wherever organized, that do business primarily outside the United States. The Fund intends to diversify among several countries and industries.

George S. Johnston, chairman of the Fund, stresses that the world is getting smaller. "The barriers are coming down everywhere. Consumers now shop, not by country of origin, but by quality of product," he says. Still, says Johnston, U.S. investors tend to be provincial about currency movements. "You want a strong company that can translate research into new products and will grow at above-average rates, whether the currency is weak or strong. We spend more time picking the right company than picking the right country."

The Fund does access country-by-country backgrounds: stock markets, currencies, and such industrial trends as labor costs and the availability of raw materials. But eventually the stock selection process comes down to searching out corporate fundamentals, company by company.

The five largest holdings are Olivetti, Siemens, Nestlé, Bekaert, and Cable and Wireless.

The performance of the Fund is shown in Figure 14-3.

"We seek opportunity in price," says Johnston. He thinks the price of stocks in Japan, fetching over 35 times earnings on average, is too high. "Some shares sell for 70 or 80 times earnings," he notes, adding that he also has concerns about the rising yen's impact on exporters. He is bullish on international investing, looking for oil prices and inflation rates to remain low and the dollar to stay weak. "The world economy is going to grow, and most of it is going to grow faster than the U.S."

The Fund is suitable for the less aggressive investor.

SoGen International Fund

The SoGen International Fund's primary objective is to provide long-term growth of capital.

Chapter 14

Figure 14-3: The Performance of Scudder International Fund Shown with Its 26-Week Moving Average. (Courtesy of Telescan.)

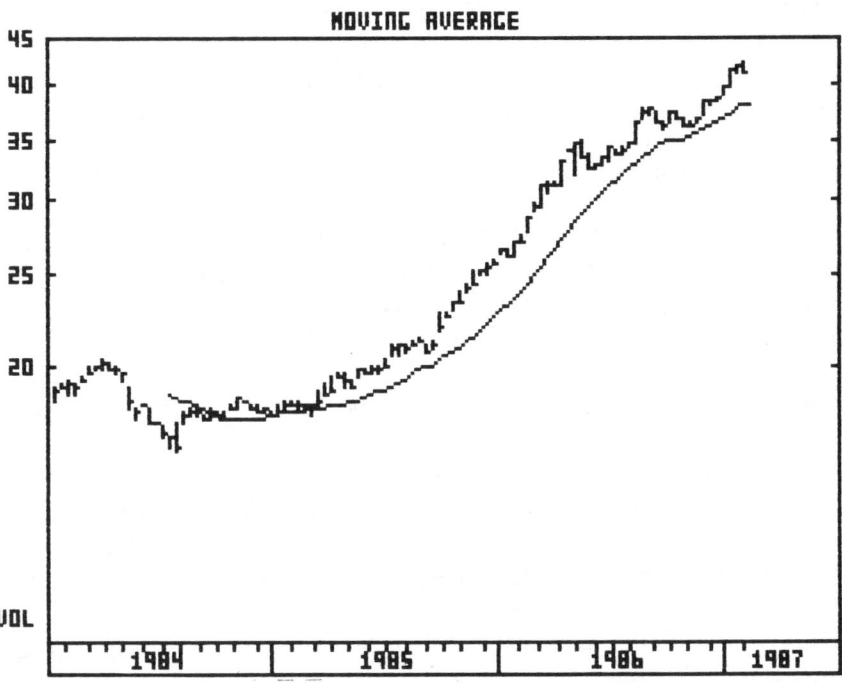

The Fund invests principally in the common stocks of companies organized and operating in the United States or elsewhere in the free world. The Fund will also invest in securities convertible into common stocks or in those accompanied by rights to purchase common stocks. There are no restrictions on what percentage of its assets the Fund may invest in the securities of issuers of any given country. At a given point of time, it is theoretically possible that all the Fund's assets could be invested in securities issued in a single country.

SoGen Securities Corporation (Sogensec) is the Fund's investment adviser. All outstanding voting securities of Sogensec are held by Société Générale of Paris, France. Société Générale is one of France's largest banks, and all its stock is owned by the French Republic. Sogensec conducts its regular business operations independently of Société Générale, and neither Société Générale nor the French government supervise the Fund's management or investment practices. The Fund is Sogensec's sole investment advisory client, although Sogensec provides research services to Société Générale.

The Fund is best described as a global fund, since it holds U.S. as well as non-U.S. securities. For example, in late 1986 it held 60 percent of its securities in U.S. stocks and bonds, with 40 percent in non-U.S. securities.

Since the Fund holds a large stake in U.S. securities, its return is affected by the U.S. stock market as well as foreign markets. As a result, the Fund returned 25.1 percent for 1986, while 32 international funds returned an average of 56.6 percent.

It should be noted that this Fund may not achieve the full diversification some investors may be seeking, since its U.S. holdings may partially duplicate the investor's portfolio allocation to that market. It is best suited to the investor seeking a global—rather than a non-U.S.—fund to round out a portfolio.

Templeton World Fund

Templeton World Fund has for its investment objective long-term capital growth.

The Fund has a flexible policy of investing in the stocks and debt obligations of the companies and governments of every nation. At present the Fund's assets are invested partly in the securities of U.S. issuers, but primarily in the securities of issuers outside the United States.

In late 1986, 90 percent of the Fund's investments were distributed over the Pacific Basin and European markets.

John M. Templeton, the investment manager, has built his reputation on an investment philosophy that emphasizes bargain-priced stocks. He has been perfecting this technique in a worldwide arena over more than 40 years, earning himself a reputation in the United States as a pioneer of global investing. He is still considered by industry insiders to be one of the field's shrewdest practitioners. Templeton is a leading light in the mutual fund industry and is probably the person most directly responsible for the existing interest in overseas investments.

His average holding period is almost five years per stock. "We are essentially long-range investors, and we don't think it pays to try to 'play the market' by trading it frequently. It's a mistake to think you can jump in and out of the market that frequently and still come out with a good record."

The Fund is a consistent performer, with an average annual return of 20.7 percent for the five years ended December 31, 1986. The Fund was up 18 percent for 1986 while the average global fund was up 31 percent (the Fund missed the Japanese market rise in 1986); nevertheless, its long-term record is very good. It is suitable for the relatively conservative investor.

Transatlantic Fund

The objectives of the Transatlantic Fund are long-term capital growth.

The Fund invests in companies domiciled outside the United States. More than half of the Fund's holdings are in the countries where the demand for equities is most pronounced: Germany (16 percent of assets) and Japan (35 percent of assets).

Final results in 1987 should show that corporate profits in Europe have outpaced those of the United States, and European stock markets as a result should keep growing. Holland, the United Kingdom, France, and Germany look like they offer the crème de la crème of European investments, says Henry de Vismes, portfolio manager for the Fund. The Fund's strategy helped it increase its share value by 51.7 percent in 1986.

Managers of the Fund emphasize equity investments in Europe (65 percent of assets) and the Far East (35 percent), with holdings diversified across many industries. Although the Fund has existed for about 25 years, it has been public only since 1982.

In 1987, the Fund focused on utilities, banks, and other companies that benefit from lower interest rates, because manager de Vismes believed interest rates would remain in check. "The domestic European investor is very yield-oriented," says de Vismes, who projects that dividend yields should rise to 4 or 6 percent. Such yields would make them competitive with European government bonds, which yield 5 to 6 percent. Another factor that should help keep European markets rolling ahead is the positive outlook of many finance ministers. "They're making some optimistic noises about the future," de Vismes said. One key development of 1985 and 1986 was the move to a "global industry trend," de Vismes said. The same groups are moving in all markets, he said, as institutions around the world become more and more sector-oriented.

Vanguard World-International Growth Fund

Vanguard World-International Growth Fund seeks long-term capital growth.

Fund investments have emphasized the international equity market and individual securities with above-average growth potential. The five largest holdings are Deutsche Bank, Unilever, Tokio Marine, Brown Bouveri, and Nishimatsu Construction.

Vanguard International Fund was founded in September 1981 as part of Ivest. The international portion of Ivest became the Vanguard World-International portfolio on August 31, 1985. The performance of the Fund is shown in Figure 14-4.

Schroder Capital Management International, a recognized international investment manager with access to the worldwide investment resources of the $12 billion Schroder Group, manages the Fund in its complex market.

For the five years of the portfolio's existence (4 as part of Ivest, 1 as an autonomous fund), the average annual return was 31.4 percent. Assets of the Fund are $444 million, and the Fund had a total return of 98.9 percent for the year ended August 31, 1986. For the year ended December 31, 1986, the Fund had low volatility (beta = 0.66) and a return of 56.6 percent.

Mr. Richard Foulkes of Schroder Management stated recently, "Our forecasts for economic growth outside the U.S. in 1987 are still encouraging." Mr. Foulkes believes that steering a fund through markets, some of which have gone "too far" and some of which haven't, is part of normal operating procedure for active management.

The Fund is broadly diversified and suitable for the investor interested in long-term growth and participation in international markets.

Figure 14-4: The Performance of Vanguard International Fund Shown with Its 26-Week Moving Average. (Courtesy of Telescan.)

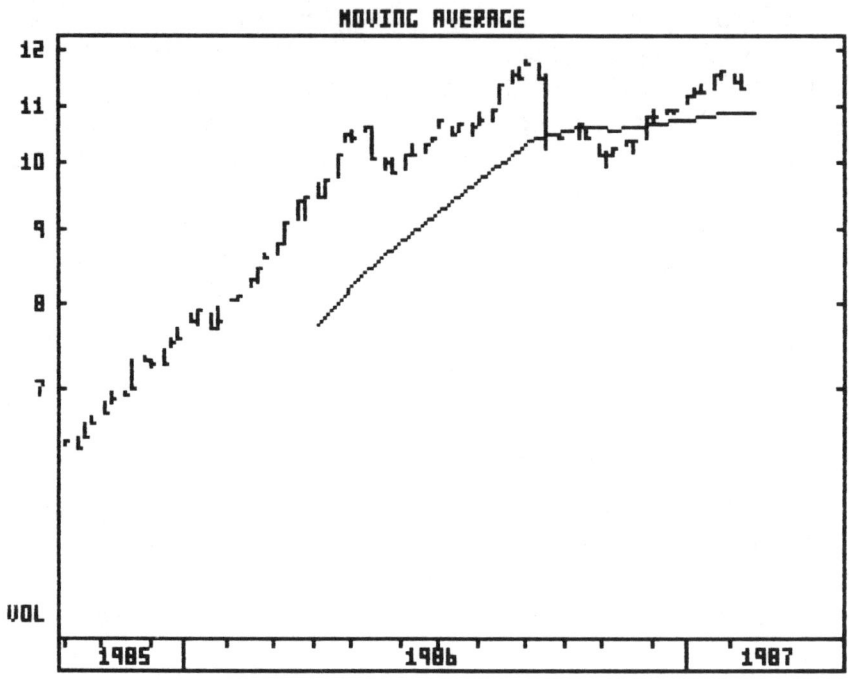

Chapter 14

PROFILE 14-1

FIDELITY OVERSEAS FUND
82 Devonshire
Boston, MA 02109
1-800-544-6666
1-617-523-1919

Fund Classification:	IN
Total Assets:	$2065 million
Fund Manager:	George Noble
Year of Inception:	1984
Minimum Investment:	2500
Sales Charge:	3.00%
12b-1 Charge:	No
Expense Ratio:	1.45

Portfolio Mix:	%	*Issues*
Bonds	0	0
Non Convertible Bonds	0.1	1
Common Stock	92.9	145
Preferred Stock	0	0
U. S. Government Securities	3.2	1
Municipal Bonds	0	0
Short-term Obligations	3.8	NA
Estimated Annual Portfolio Turnover	86%	

Estimates of Fund Performance:	
Annual Return for Two Years:	73.7%
Annual Return for Five Years:	NA
Annual Return in Bull Markets:	
1985	78.6%
1986	68.9%
Annual Return in Bear Markets:	
6/30/83–6/30/84	NA
Representative Current Yield (2/28/87):	3.3%

Measures of Risk and Reward:	
Alpha	NA
Beta	1.4
R square	NA
Standard deviation	6.0
Reward/risk ratio	12.3

Net Asset Value:	
9/25/87	39.45
10/28/87	30.62

PROFILE 14-2

G. T. PACIFIC GROWTH FUND
601 Montgomery St.
San Francisco, CA 94111
1-800-824-1580
415-392-6181

Fund Classification:	IN	
Total Assets:	$51 million	
Fund Manager:	G. Paul Matthews	
Year of Inception:	1976	
Minimum Investment:	500	
Sales Charge:	4.75%	
12b-1 Charge:	No	
Expense Ratio:	1.40	

Portfolio Mix:	%	*Issues*
Bonds	0	0
Non Convertible Bonds	0	0
Common Stock	95.2	46
Preferred Stock	0	0
U. S. Government Securities	0	0
Municipal Bonds	0	0
Short-term Obligations	0	0
Estimated Annual Portfolio Turnover	185.2%	

Estimates of Fund Performance:	
Annual Return for Three Years:	21.4%
Annual Return for Five Years:	20.8%
Annual Return in Bull Markets:	
1985	9.3%
1986	70.0%
Annual Return in Bear Markets:	
6/30/83–6/30/84	7.20%
Representative Current Yield (2/28/87):	0.0%

Measures of Risk and Reward:	
Alpha	6.7
Beta	0.59
R square	5
Standard deviation	5.81
Reward/risk ratio	3.7

Net Asset Value:	
9/25/87	27.82
10/28/87	21.16

PROFILE 14-3

KEMPER INTERNATIONAL FUND
120 S. LaSalle Street
Chicago, IL 60603
1-800-621-2414
312-781-1121

Fund Classification:	IN	
Total Assets:	$198 million	
Fund Manager:	Michael M. J. Parlett	
Year of Inception:	1980	
Minimum Investment:	1000	
Sales Charge:	8.50%	
12b-1 Charge:	No	
Expense Ratio:	1.08	
Portfolio Mix:	%	*Issues*
Bonds	0	0
Convertible Bonds	0	0
Common Stock	73.62	122
Preferred Stock	0	0
U. S. Government Securities	0	0
Municipal Bonds	0	0
Short-term Obligations	0	0
Estimated Annual Portfolio Turnover	111%	
Estimates of Fund Performance:		
Annual Return for Three Years:	28.0%	
Annual Return for Five Years:	25.4%	
Annual Return in Bull Markets:		
1985	55.3%	
1986	44.7%	
Annual Return in Bear Markets:		
6/30/83–6/30/84	0.48%	
Representative Current Yield (2/28/87):	1.1%	
Measures of Risk and Reward:		
Alpha	7.4	
Beta	0.64	
R square	23	
Standard deviation	4.85	
Reward/risk ratio	5.8	
Net Asset Value:		
9/25/87	23.93	
10/28/87	17.96	

PROFILE 14-4

T. ROWE PRICE INTERNATIONAL FUND
100 E. Pratt
Baltimore, MD 21202
1-800-638-5660
301-547-2308

Fund Classification:	IN	
Total Assets:	$790 million	
Fund Manager:	M. David Testa	
Year of Inception:	1980	
Minimum Investment:	1000	
Sales Charge:	No load	
12b-1 Charge:	No	
Expense Ratio:	1.10	

Portfolio Mix:	%	*Issues*
Bonds	0	0
Convertible Bonds	0	0
Common Stock	88.97	115
Preferred Stock	0	0
U. S. Government Securities	0	0
Municipal Bonds	0	0
Short-term Obligations	0	0
Estimated Annual Portfolio Turnover	54%	

Estimates of Fund Performance:	
Annual Return for Three Years:	33.1%
Annual Return for Five Years:	28.4%
Annual Return in Bull Markets:	
1985	45.2%
1986	60.5%
Annual Return in Bear Markets:	
6/30/83–6/30/84	5.27%
Representative Current Yield (2/28/87):	0.8%

Measures of Risk and Reward:	
Alpha	10.4
Beta	0.66
R square	24
Standard deviation	4.92
Reward/risk ratio	6.7

Net Asset Value:	
9/25/87	16.29
10/28/87	12.35

PROFILE 14-5

PUTNAM INTERNATIONAL EQUITIES FUND
One Post Office Square
Boston, MA 02109
1-800-225-1581
617-292-1000

Fund Classification:	IN	
Total Assets:	$426 million	
Fund Manager:	NA	
Year of Inception:	1966	
Minimum Investment:	500	
Sales Charge:	8.50%	
12b-1 Charge:	No	
Expense Ratio:	1.49	
Portfolio Mix:	%	*Issues*
Bonds	0	0
Convertible Bonds	0	0
Common Stock	92.04	78
Preferred Stock	0	0
U. S. Government Securities	0	0
Municipal Bonds	0	0
Short-term Obligations	0	0
Estimated Annual Portfolio Turnover	134%	
Estimates of Fund Performance:		
Annual Return for Three Years:	35.9%	
Annual Return for Five Years:	31.1%	
Annual Return in Bull Markets:		
1985	64.4%	
1986	38.0%	
Annual Return in Bear Markets:		
6/30/83–6/30/84	1.99%	
Representative Current Yield (2/28/87):	0.4%	
Measures of Risk and Reward:		
Alpha	13.2	
Beta	0.79	
R square	45	
Standard deviation	4.23	
Reward/risk ratio	8.5	
Net Asset Value:		
9/25/87	34.93	
10/28/87	26.09	

PROFILE 14-6

SCUDDER INTERNATIONAL FUND
175 Federal Street
Boston, MA 02110
1-800-453-3305
617-426-8300

Fund Classification:	IN	
Total Assets:	$711 million	
Fund Manager:	Nicholas Bratt	
Year of Inception:	1953	
Minimum Investment:	1000	
Sales Charge:	No load	
12b-1 Charge:	No	
Expense Ratio:	0.99	

Portfolio Mix:	%	*Issues*
Bonds	13	NA
Convertible Bonds	0	0
Common Stock	78.34	141
Preferred Stock	0	0
U. S. Government Securities	0	0
Municipal Bonds	0	0
Short-term Obligations	0	0
Estimated Annual Portfolio Turnover	36.0%	

Estimates of Fund Performance:	
Annual Return for Three Years:	31.6%
Annual Return for Five Years:	27.8%
Annual Return in Bull Markets:	
1985	48.9%
1986	50.5%
Annual Return in Bear Markets:	
6/30/83–6/30/84	5.27%
Representative Current Yield (2/28/87):	1.0%
Measures of Risk and Reward:	
Alpha	10.9
Beta	0.58
R square	25
Standard deviation	4.24
Reward/risk ratio	7.5
Net Asset Value:	
9/25/87	46.41
10/28/87	33.62

PROFILE 14-7

SO GEN INTERNATIONAL FUND
520 Madison Avenue
New York, NY 10022
212-832-0022

Fund Classification:	IN
Total Assets:	$74 million
Fund Manager:	Jean-Marie Eveillard
Year of Inception:	1969
Minimum Investment:	100
Sales Charge:	4.25%
12b-1 Charge:	Yes (0.25%)
Expense Ratio:	1.34

Portfolio Mix:	%	*Issues*
Bonds	30	NA
Convertible Bonds	0	0
Common Stock	72.25	107
Preferred Stock	0	0
U. S. Government Securities	0	0
Municipal Bonds	0	0
Short-term Obligations	0	0
Estimated Annual Portfolio Turnover	58.5%	

Estimates of Fund Performance:	
Annual Return for Three Years:	26.4%
Annual Return for Five Years:	26.9%
Annual Return in Bull Markets:	
1985	32.7%
1986	25.1%
Annual Return in Bear Markets:	
6/30/83–6/30/84	0.13%
Representative Current Yield (2/28/87):	3.1%

Measures of Risk and Reward:	
Alpha	3.7
Beta	0.65
R square	68
Standard deviation	2.83
Reward/risk ratio	9.3
Net Asset Value:	
9/25/87	23.53
10/28/87	18.39

PROFILE 14-8

TEMPLETON WORLD FUND
405 Central Ave. P. O. Box 3942
St. Petersburg, FL 33731
1-800-237-0738
813-823-8712

Fund Classification:	IN	
Total Assets:	$3374 million	
Fund Manager:	John M. Templeton	
Year of Inception:	1978	
Minimum Investment:	500	
Sales Charge:	8.50%	
12b-1 Charge:	No	
Expense Ratio:	0.71	
Portfolio Mix:	*%*	*Issues*
Bonds	5.6	NA
Convertible Bonds	0	0
Common Stock	72.5	NA
U. S. Government Securities	0	0
Municipal Bonds	0	0
Cash	21.9	NA
Estimated Annual Portfolio Turnover	15.7%	
Estimates of Fund Performance:		
Annual Return for Three Years:	23.3%	
Annual Return for Five Years:	25.9%	
Annual Return in Bull Markets:		
1985	30.3%	
1986	17.9%	
Annual Return in Bear Markets:		
6/30/83–6/30/84	1.33%	
Representative Current Yield (2/28/87):	2.4%	
Measures of Risk and Reward:		
Alpha	1.6	
Beta	0.84	
R square	87	
Standard deviation	3.48	
Reward/risk ratio	6.7	
Net Asset Value:		
9/25/87	18.86	
10/28/87	14.08	

PROFILE 14-9

TRANSATLANTIC FUND
100 Wall Street
New York, NY 10005
1-800-237-4218
212-747-0440

Fund Classification:	IN
Total Assets:	$92 million
Fund Manager:	Henry de Vismes
Year of Inception:	1963
Minimum Investment:	1000
Sales Charge:	4.50%
12b-1 Charge:	Yes (.05%)
Expense Ratio:	1.54

Portfolio Mix:	%	*Issues*
Bonds	0	0
Convertible Bonds	0	0
Common Stock	89.25	49
U. S. Government Securities	0	0
Municipal Bonds	0	0
Cash	0	0
Estimated Annual Portfolio Turnover	41%	

Estimates of Fund Performance:	
Annual Return for Three Years:	26.2%
Annual Return for Five Years:	21.9%
Annual Return in Bull Markets:	
1985	54.2%
1986	51.7%
Annual Return in Bear Markets:	
6/30/83–6/30/84	6.70%
Representative Current Yield (2/28/87):	0.0%

Measures of Risk and Reward:	
Alpha	6.8
Beta	0.73
R square	24
Standard deviation	5.46
Reward/risk ratio	4.8
Net Asset Value:	
9/25/87	29.33
10/28/87	22.01

PROFILE 14-10

VANGUARD WORLD INTERNATIONAL GROWTH FUND
Vanguard Financial Center
Valley Forge, PA 19482
1-800-662-7447
1-800-662-2739
In PA 1-800-362-0530

Fund Classification:	IN
Total Assets:	$444 million
Fund Manager:	Richard R. Foulkes
Year of Inception:	1981
Minimum Investment:	1500
Sales Charge:	No load
12b-1 Charge:	No
Expense Ratio:	0.90

Portfolio Mix:	%	*Issues*
Bonds	0	0
Convertible Bonds	0	0
Common Stock	95.06	77
U. S. Government Securities	0	0
Municipal Bonds	0	0
Cash	0	0
Estimated Annual Portfolio Turnover	38%	

Estimates of Fund Performance:	
Annual Return for Three Years:	34.2%
Annual Return for Five Years:	33.0%
Annual Return in Bull Markets:	
1985	56.9%
1986	56.6%
Annual Return in Bear Markets:	
6/30/83–6/30/84	6.9%
Representative Current Yield (2/28/87):	0.8%

Measures of Risk and Reward:	
Alpha	11.0
Beta	0.60
R square	25
Standard deviation	5.11
Reward/risk ratio	6.7

Net Asset Value:	
9/25/87	13.62
10/28/87	9.56

Chapter 15
Technology Funds

BACKGROUND INFORMATION

Type of Security

Mutual funds that hold primarily common stock of technology-based companies are called technology funds. Technology funds hold securities of companies that produce, for example, computers, electronics, ethical drugs, bioengineering, and communications services and equipment.

Risk/Stability

Technology funds enjoyed an excellent rise from August 1982 through July 1983 and then pulled back or leveled off through 1986. Science and technology mutual funds then rose as much in the first week of 1987 as they did in the whole of 1986. The average technology fund returned only 8.2 percent for 1986, but 16 percent for January 1987 alone. Many observers were taken aback by this blastoff. Yet managers of mutual funds that specialize in emerging companies have been saying that the opportunities in technology companies were dramatic.

There were two reasons for the sharp improvement: (1) the prices were previously artificially depressed, and (2) Wall Street shifted emphasis to issues that can participate in a faster-growing economy.

PORTFOLIO FIT

The volatility of technology securities makes selection of technology funds difficult.

Technology funds experience periods of excellent NAV growth punctuated with rapid downturns. Most, with the possible exceptions of Financial Strategic Technology Fund and Nova, are quite volatile and most suitable for the investor who believes in his or her own ability to catch the rises and avoid the big downturns.

Technology fund investors should be prepared to tolerate greater risk than average. The funds' up periods must be tracked and investments promptly liquidated when the market starts downward.

Technology funds are definitely not for the buy-and-hold investor. The aggressive investor who chooses a technology fund should place an upper limit of 10 percent of his or her portfolio in technology funds.

SIX REPRESENTATIVE TECHNOLOGY FUNDS

To illustrate, we have chosen six technology funds that show the qualities that investors seek when purchasing shares of technology funds. Note that only four of these examples are no-load funds. Table 15-1 contains a summary listing of the six funds. *Because of the volatile nature of these funds, it was considered more appropriate to provide 1986 and January (only) 1987 returns, since the three-year return is meaningful only for a buy-and-hold strategy.* The table is followed by a more detailed description of each fund's objectives and investment philosophy and practice, as well as capsule Profiles of their recent performance.

Investors are reminded that past performance is no indicator of future performance. This standard advice is particularly true of technology funds.

Table 15-1: Six Representative Technology Funds

Fund	*Jan. 1987*	*1986*	*Load*
Alliance Technology Fund	29.5	12.0	L
Fidelity Select Technology Fund	18.6	-7.4	LL
Financial Strategic Technology Fund	18.6	21.8	NL
Nova Fund	20.8	7.7	NL
Vanguard Technology Fund	15.4	5.7	NL
Medical Technology Fund	13.8	15.3	NL

Alliance Technology Fund

The objective of the Alliance Technology Fund is maximum capital appreciation.

The Fund invests in companies Alliance feels are poised to benefit from advances and improvements in science and technology.

The Fund's investments include the stocks of forty or fifty electronics and biotechnology companies, about two-thirds of which are based in the San Francisco Bay area.

The Fund was started in 1982 by Alliance Capital Management Company of New York. Richard Coons, portfolio manager for the Fund, said that the Fund has increased 177 percent since its inception, while most mutual funds have lagged. He also noted that during that period the Hambrecht and Quist index of technology stocks increased 59 percent and the NASDAQ index increased 93 percent.

Coons said a number of the smaller technology stocks have suffered from a perceived slump in the technology sector. In Coons words, "People have looked to IBM and the headlines, but a lot of the smaller companies have done great all along." Now that science and technology stocks are improving as a whole, investors are showing a lot of interest in technology issues that were undervalued all along, according to Coons.

Coons cited Seagate Technology, Maxtor Corporation, Autodesk, Inc., and Sun Microsystems as companies having contributed to the Fund's success. On the prospective longevity of the current trend, Coons observes, "When technology issues come into favor because of improved earnings, the group typically enjoys an extended run."

Coons does not believe science and technology stocks have peaked yet; he believes that present earnings and future orders show the stocks in the Fund are still undervalued: "Not only are orders picking up, but many companies have gone out of business. Often two or three solid companies have replaced twenty vulnerable ones. I expect the survivors to do very well." In a year, he adds, "we'll look back at these stocks and say 'how cheap they were.'"

The Fund's longer-term record is spotty. It can be expected to rise and fall faster than the market (beta = 1.45). It is nevertheless a good fund to hold when technology stocks are rising.

The Fund is designed for investors who seek to achieve maximum capital appreciation and who are willing to accept the greater risks in pursuing such an investment strategy.

Fidelity Select Technology Fund

Fidelity Select Technology Fund seeks capital appreciation.

The Fund invests in companies that develop products, processes, or services that contribute to or benefit from technological advances and improvements. The description of the technology sector is interpreted broadly by the Fund and includes such products or services as inexpensive computer power (personal computers, etc.), improved communication methods (satellite transmission and the like), and labor-saving machines or instruments (computer-aided design [CAD] equipment, etc.). The Fund looks particularly for companies that will benefit from advances in semiconductors, minicomputers and allied equipment, scientific instruments, computer software, communications technology, and office/factory automation.

The five largest holdings of the Fund as of October 31, 1986, were Western Digital, Mentor Graphics, Lex Service, Lockheed, and Daisy Systems.

The Fund had a roller-coaster ride from 1983 to 1986: +30 percent in 1983, -17 percent in 1984, +7.4 percent in 1985, and -7.4 percent in 1986; the Fund rose 18.6 percent for the month of January 1986.

The Fund is obviously very volatile! It is worth considering as a means of capitalizing on rising technology markets; it is clearly not a buy-and-hold fund.

Financial Strategic Technology Fund

Financial Strategic Technology Fund seeks capital appreciation.

The Fund's assets are invested primarily in the equity securities of companies principally engaged in technology. A company is deemed to be principally engaged in technology if it derives a substantial portion of its profits or sales from, or commits a substantial portion of its assets to, the development or application of products in one or more fields of technology. For the purposes of both the foregoing tests, "substantial" means no less than 25 percent, and generally at least 50 percent. Products and services currently deemed to constitute "engaged in technology" include mainly computers, communications, video, electronics, oceanography, office/factory automation, and robotics.

The three largest holdings on February 13, 1987, were Western Digital, Unisys, and Cipher Data Products.

The small and successful Fund has often been filled with biotech and medical technology stocks. Portfolio manager Dan Leonard plans to continue such investments—"the most exciting area of high tech—partly because of the new drugs these firms are producing and developments in genetic research." He mentions Genentech, Bio-Response, and Newport Pharmaceutical as his favorites. The Fund's commitments to Digital Equipment and IBM will continue.

Leonard projected continued market leadership for technology stocks through 1987, observing that companies are still using technology to cut costs. "I can't point to a specific area I don't want," he says.

The Fund grew in assets from $4 million on December 31, 1986, to $22 million on February 13, 1987, due to its excellent performance in 1985, 1986, and the first month of 1987.

The performance of the Fund is shown in Figure 15-1. Its record, management, and diversification make it an excellent choice.

The Fund is best suited to the slightly less aggressive investor.

Nova Fund

Nova Fund's primary investment objective is long-term growth of capital. Current income is not an objective, although the portfolio does include income-producing securities.

The Fund emphasizes investments in the common stocks of growing companies, whether established or emerging, that operate in scientific or technological fields or that have the potential because of changing circumstances to provide significant earnings growth. The Fund examines companies, industries, and microeconomic factors to inform its selections.

Figure 15-1: The Performance of Financial Technology Fund Shown with Its 26-Week Moving Average. (Courtesy of Telescan.)

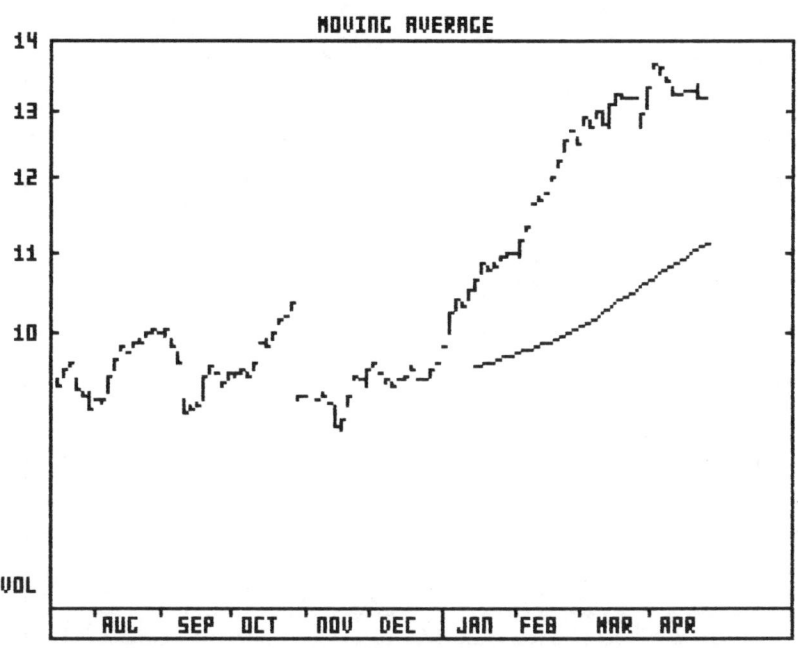

The Fund's five largest holdings on December 31, 1986, were Lotus Development, Seagate Technology, Millipore, Ashton-Tate, and Bristol-Myers.

Fund manager Bruce Everitt projected in the January 30, 1987, report that in 1987 "weighted earnings growth of Nova's portfolio [would be] 37 percent, or 3.7 times the 9 to 10% advance projected for the Standard & Poor's 500 Index."

Everitt noted in the same report that the Fund has virtually no current price/earnings premium (15.1 compared to 14.7 for the S&P 500), reflecting the fact that "the Market was just beginning to adjust to reflect the technology sector's superior earnings growth prospects."

Nova achieved excellent returns in 1982, 1983, and 1985; 1984 and 1986 were both disappointing. The Fund began strong in 1987. The Fund's performance is shown in Figure 15-2.

The Fund's erratic past performance suggests holding it for the short term only in up markets when the investor is convinced that technology will continue to gain. The Fund is suited to the slightly less aggressive investor.

Figure 15-2: The Performance of Nova Fund Shown with Its 26-Week Moving Average. (Courtesy of Telescan.)

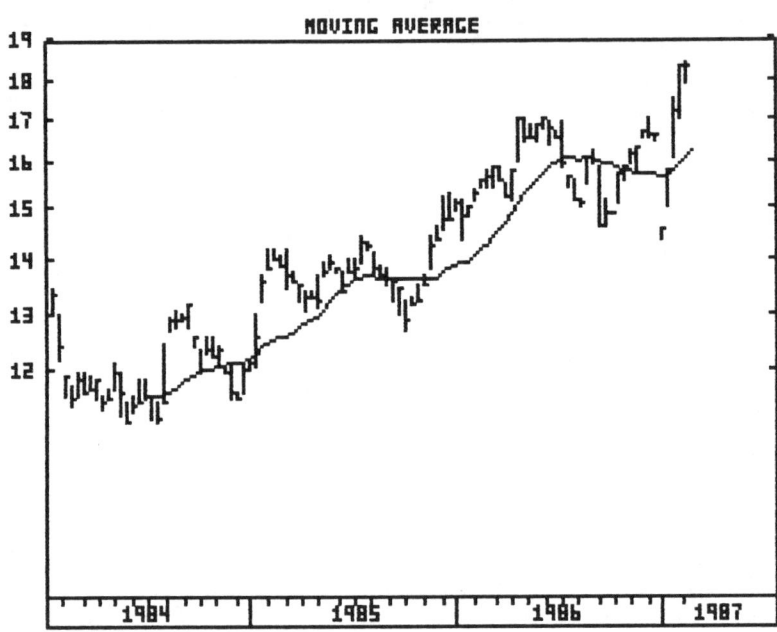

Vanguard Technology Fund

Vanguard Technology Fund seeks to capitalize on the opportunities created by rapid advances in technology.

Investments may be made in a variety of high-growth industries, such as computer hardware, telecommunications, semiconductors, aerospace and defense, medical technology, and consumer electronics.

The Fund's six largest holdings on July 31, 1986, were IBM, Digital Equipment, Hewlett-Packard, Burroughs, United Technologies, and Hexcel.

The Fund provided a weak return of 5.7 percent for 1986 and a fairly strong 15.4 percent return in January 1987. Its potential remains good during any rise in technology stock funds.

This conservatively managed Fund is particularly suitable for the investor who seeks a longer-term return from a technology fund. It remains nevertheless a fairly aggressive fund.

Medical Technology Fund

Medical Technology Fund was incorporated as a mutual fund in 1979. Its investment objective is capital growth through the concentration of investments in the common stocks of companies engaged in the design, manufacture, or sale of products or services derived from technology for use in medicine or health care.

The expected normal concentration in such investments is 80 percent; the minimum (when the Fund must take a temporary defensive position) is 25 percent. 1987 holdings in medical-care equities amounted to 93 percent of net assets. The remainder was held in cash or short-term investments.

The Fund currently concentrates on two major subsectors: therapeutic technology and supportive technology. The remainder of the medical-care portion of the portfolio is spread among the common stock of firms dealing in administrative, diagnostic, and preventive medicine. The Fund holds a significant number of nonrated equities from newer companies such as Genentech, Cetus, Centocor, California Biotechnology, and Chiron. Holdings do include stocks of highly rated pharmaceutical companies such as Merck and Syntex—most of which pay regular dividends.

The largest holding is Abbott Laboratories, one of the more established hospital supply companies.

The Fund is quite volatile—it benefited from the market upsurge in health-related stocks during 1986 and 1987; it provided an excellent return of 39 percent in 1985; it declined 35percent from June 30, 1983, to June 30, 1984 while the S & P 500 declined only 5 percent.

The Fund sums up as a speculative fund to be held during up technology markets and to be avoided when technology is out of favor on Wall Street. It is for the more aggressive investor who is in a position to assume some risk.

PROFILE 15-1

ALLIANCE TECHNOLOGY FUND
P.O. Box 997, Pine Street Station
New York, NY 10268
1-800-221-5672
In NY 1-800-522-2323

Fund Classification:	T
Total Assets:	$133 million
Fund Manager:	Richard Coons
Year of Inception:	1980
Minimum Investment:	250
Sales Charge:	8.50%
12b-1 Charge:	No
Expense Ratio:	1.14

Portfolio Mix:	%	*Issues*
Bonds	0	0
Convertible Bonds	0	0
Common Stock	96.17	56
U. S. Government Securities	0	0
Municipal Bonds	0	0
Cash	0	0
Estimated Annual Portfolio Turnover	259%	

Estimates of Fund Performance:	
Annual Return for Three Years:	28.8%
Annual Return for Five Years:	NA
Annual Return in Bull Markets:	
1985	26.2%
1986	12.0%
Annual Return in Bear Markets:	
6/30/83–6/30/84	-31.3%
Representative Current Yield (12/31/86):	0.0%
Measures of Risk and Reward:	
Alpha	14.5
Beta	1.45
R square	72
Standard deviation	7.26
Reward/risk ratio	4.0
Net Asset Value:	
9/25/87	33.88
10/28/87	19.67

PROFILE 15-2

FIDELITY SELECT TECHNOLOGY FUND
82 Devonshire
Boston, MA 02109
1-800-544-6666
In MA 1-800-225-6190
617-726-0200

Fund Classification:	T	
Total Assets:	$241 million	
Fund Manager:	Mark Boyer	
Year of Inception:	1980	
Minimum Investment:	1000	
Sales Charge:	3.00%	
12b-1 Charge:	No	
Expense Ratio:	1.26	
Portfolio Mix:	%	*Issues*
Bonds	0	0
Convertible Bonds	0.3	NA
Common Stock	87.7	95
U. S. Government Securities	0	0
Municipal Bonds	0	0
Short-term Obligations	12.0	NA
Estimated Annual Portfolio Turnover	85%	
Estimates of Fund Performance:		
Annual Return for Three Years:	9.7%	
Annual Return for Five Years:	14.5%	
Annual Return in Bull Markets:		
1985	7.4%	
1986	-7.4%	
Annual Return in Bear Markets:		
6/30/83–6/30/84	-24.7%	
Representative Current Yield (12/31/86):	0.0%	
Measures of Risk and Reward:		
Alpha	21.7	
Beta	1.13	
R square	29	
Standard deviation	8.94	
Reward/risk ratio	1.1	
Net Asset Value:		
9/25/87	27.38	
10/28/87	15.68	

PROFILE 15-3

FINANCIAL STRATEGIC TECHNOLOGY FUND
Box 2040
Denver, CO 80201
1-800-525-8085
303-779-1233

Fund Classification:	T	
Total Assets:	$22 million	
Fund Manager:	Daniel Leonard	
Year of Inception:	1984	
Minimum Investment:	250	
Sales Charge:	No load	
12b-1 Charge:	No	
Expense Ratio:	1.50	
Portfolio Mix:	%	*Issues*
Bonds	0	0
Convertible Bonds	0	0
Common Stock	91	NA
U. S. Government Securities	0	0
Municipal Bonds	0	0
Short-term Obligations	0	0
Estimated Annual Portfolio Turnover	368%	
Estimates of Fund Performance:		
Annual Return for Two Years Two Months:	38.4%	
Annual Return for Five Years:	NA	
Annual Return in Bull Markets:		
1985	27.7%	
1986	21.8%	
Annual Return in Bear Markets:		
6/30/83–6/30/84	-7.4%	
Representative Current Yield (12/31/86):	0.0%	
Measures of Risk and Reward:		
Alpha	NA	
Beta	1.10	
R square	NA	
Standard deviation	6.10	
Reward/risk ratio	6.3	
Net Asset Value:		
9/25/87	13.26	
10/28/87	7.19	

PROFILE 15-4

NOVA FUND
260 Franklin St.
Boston, MA 02110
1-800-572-0006
617-439-9683

Fund Classification:	T	
Total Assets:	$25 million	
Fund Manager:	Bruce W. Everitt	
Year of Inception:	1980	
Minimum Investment:	2000	
Sales Charge:	8.0%	
12b-1 Charge:	No	
Expense Ratio:	1.70	

Portfolio Mix:	%	*Issues*
Bonds	0	0
Convertible Bonds	0	0
Common Stock	90.79	39
U. S. Government Securities	0	0
Municipal Bonds	0	0
Short-term Obligations	0	0
Estimated Annual Portfolio Turnover	99%	

Estimates of Fund Performance:	
Annual Return for Three Years:	22.9%
Annual Return for Five Years:	13.2%
Annual Return in Bull Markets:	
1985	27.1%
1986	7.7%
Annual Return in Bear Markets:	
6/30/83–6/30/84	-16.6%
Representative Current Yield (12/31/86):	0.2%

Measures of Risk and Reward:	
Alpha	8.2
Beta	1.00
R square	67
Standard deviation	5.12
Reward/risk ratio	4.5
Net Asset Value:	
9/25/87	19.42
10/28/87	12.33

PROFILE 15-5

VANGUARD TECHNOLOGY FUND
Vanguard Financial Center
Valley Forge, PA 19482
1-800-662-7447
1-800-662-2739
In PA 1-800-362-0530

Fund Classification:	T	
Total Assets:	$33 million	
Fund Manager:	William Hicks	
Year of Inception:	1984	
Minimum Investment:	1500	
Sales Charge:	1.00%	
12b-1 Charge:	No	
Expense Ratio:	0.72	
Portfolio Mix:	*%*	*Issues*
Bonds	0	0
Convertible Bonds	0	0
Common Stock	98.22	46
U. S. Government Securities	0	0
Municipal Bonds	0	0
Short-term Obligations	0	0
Estimated Annual Portfolio Turnover	133%	
Estimates of Fund Performance:		
Annual Return for Two Years:	21.4%	
Annual Return for Five Years:	NA	
Annual Return in Bull Markets:		
1985	14.0%	
1986	5.7%	
Annual Return in Bear Markets:		
6/30/86–9/30/86	-9.6%	
Representative Current Yield (8/31/86):	0.7%	
Measures of Risk and Reward:		
Alpha	NA	
Beta	1.20	
R square	NA	
Standard deviation	6.10	
Reward/risk ratio	3.5	
Net Asset Value:		
9/25/87	15.05	
10/28/87	8.93	

PROFILE 15-6

MEDICAL TECHNOLOGY FUND
Fire Sentry Parkway West Suite 120
P.O. Box 1111
Blue Bell, PA 19422
1-800-523-0864
215-825-0400

Fund Classification:	T
Total Assets:	$66 million
Fund Manager:	Jennifer L. Byrne
Year of Inception:	1979
Minimum Investment:	1000
Sales Charge:	No load
12b-1 Charge:	Yes (0.50%)
Expense Ratio:	1.41

Portfolio Mix:	%	*Issues*
Bonds	0	0
Convertible Bonds	0	0
Preferred Stock	0	0
Common Stock	94.29	64
U. S. Government Securities	0	0
Cash	0	0
Estimated Annual Portfolio Turnover	15%	

Estimates of Fund Performance:	
Annual Return for Three Years:	25.6%
Annual Return for Five Years:	14.0%
Annual Return in Bull Markets:	
1985	39.0%
1986	15.3%
Annual Return in Bear Markets:	
6/30/83–6/30/84	-34.6%
Representative Current Yield (12/31/86):	0.0%

Measures of Risk and Reward:	
Alpha	8.9
Beta	1.39
R square	86
Standard deviation	6.35
Reward/risk ratio	4.0

Net Asset Value:	
9/25/87	13.46
10/28/87	9.04

Chapter 16
Energy and Utility Funds

ENERGY AND NATURAL RESOURCE FUNDS

Background Information

Type of Security. Energy and natural resource funds typically invest more than half their net assets in companies that produce or distribute natural resources or energy and related products and equipment.

Typical investments would be in companies that produce oil, gas, coal, and forest products; in real estate sales or development companies; and developers and producers of mineral and precious-metal mines.

Risk/Stability. The value and yield of energy stocks are subject to swift changes because of external factors that affect the price and supply of the energy product itself. The drop in the price of crude oil during 1986 is shown in Figure 16-1.

Special Benefits and Exposures

Energy and natural resource funds form a class because they both benefit from the assumption that ownership of commodities ultimately preserves capital during times of inflation.

Price and Supply. Energy securities, however, are greatly affected by changes in the prices and the supplies of oil and other energy fuels; prices and supplies, in turn, experience significant short-term fluctuations because of changes in numerous external factors: international politics, policies of the Organization of Petroleum Exporting Countries (OPEC), relations between OPEC members, energy conservation practices and laws, the regulatory environment in general, governmental tax policies, and the economic climate in energy-consuming countries.

Inflation. The large number of external factors affecting the returns of energy stocks makes natural resource stocks more attractive investments when inflation is present but mild. When inflation is strong, as it was before 1980, the uncertainties of price and supply are weaker deterrents in the face of potential gains.

Figure 16-1: The Price of Crude Oil in Dollars per Barrel for 1984-86.

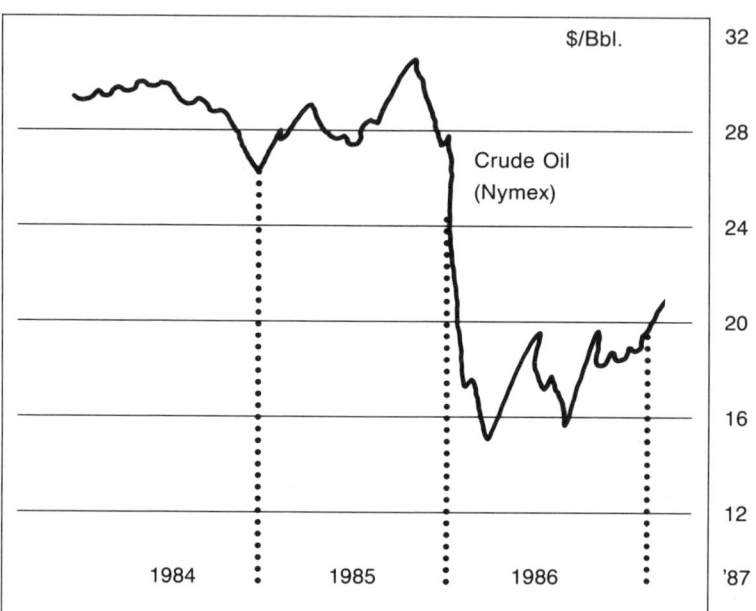

The Future. Overall, natural resource funds showed weak performance for 1986. For the long term, these funds are positioned for future gains—a number of commodity experts are convinced that prices for 1986 are near bottom. In addition, the 1987 inflation rate of 5 percent revived interest in some natural resource stocks.

UTILITY FUNDS

Background Information

Type of Security. Public utility investments include securities of companies engaged in the manufacture, production, generation, transmission, and sale of gas and electric energy; and companies engaged in the communications field in various ways, including telephone, telegraph, and satellite communications.

Risk/Stability. Public utility stocks have traditionally produced above-average dividend income, but investments in such funds are usually made on the basis of their potential for capital appreciation.

Because electric utility stocks usually pay high dividends, analysts consider them sensitive to interest rates: their prices usually rise when interest rates decline and fall when interest rates rise. In the longer term, price movements depend on inflation as well. When inflation grows at modest rates and interest rates are stable or declining, electric utility stocks should do well.

Special Benefits and Exposures

The Nature of the Business. A public utility company offers a public service such as gas, water, or electricity in a designated region and receives a monopoly in return for the service. Since it has a monopoly, a utility is regulated by state and federal agencies.

Gas and electric public utility industries are subject to such uncertainties as difficulties of obtaining adequate return on investments, exposure to environmental issues, the prices of fuel, adequacy of supply for market demand, and (in the case of electric utilities) the risks of constructing and operating nuclear power facilities.

Nuclear Power Issues. It is worthwhile to briefly consider nuclear power costs. In the past 20 years, electric utilities moved toward nuclear power, and construction costs increased fivefold. Nuclear power plants are expensive to build and maintain—too expensive in general to finance out of current revenues.

The Future. The fundamentals of electric utilities are still strong: they've slowed down their construction costs, generated a lot of cash, and improved their balance sheets. They should as a result be able to generate earnings on current and past investments without having to depend on the granting of rate increases or bond referendums.

Still, the public debate generated by the industry's need for financing altered the political environment in which electric utilities operated. The electric utility industry has been transformed from one with a predictable, regulated income into one operating in a volatile free market in many senses. The political and economic forces that revolutionized long-distance communications and air travel are also sweeping power companies toward deregulation. By 1990, deregulation may replace construction costs as the primary concern in the industry. The one is, nevertheless, a legacy of the other.

PORTFOLIO FIT

Energy and Natural Resource Funds

Energy and natural resource funds are typically used as a hedge against inflation and to participate in the growth of energy and resource industries. Risk in such funds is about equal to that of the stock market.

Investors who believe inflation is about to rise might put 5 to 10 percent of their portfolios in energy and natural resource funds. Such funds should be avoided when deflation is expected.

Utility Funds

Utility funds are quite attractive for investors needing defensive holdings and lower risk. They are, however, sensitive to interest rate changes, since they pay higher dividends than the general stock market. Retired investors find them attractive because of their relatively secure and steady income.

Over a period of years utilities have demonstrated an ability to raise the dividends they pay.

Utility funds are sound investments for those seeking lower risk and solid income. A retired person, for example, might have up to 25 percent of his or her portfolio in utility funds.

SEVEN REPRESENTATIVE ENERGY AND UTILITY FUNDS

To illustrate, we have chosen seven energy and utility funds that show the qualities that investors seek when purchasing shares of energy and utility funds. Four are energy funds: Fidelity Select Energy, Neuberger, T. Rowe Price, and Vanguard. Three are utility funds: Fidelity Select Utilities, Prudential-Bache, and Stratton Monthly Dividends. Note that only four of these examples are no-load funds. Table 16-1 contains a summary listing of the seven funds. It is followed by a more detailed description of each fund's objectives and investment philosophy and practice, as well as capsule Profiles of their recent performance.

Investors are reminded that past performance is no indicator of future performance.

Table 16-1: Seven Representative Energy and Utility Funds

Fund	Annual Return (%) for 3 Years	Load
Fidelity Select Energy Fund	8.4	LL
Fidelity Select Utilities Fund	25.4	LL
Neuberger & Berman Energy Fund	12.3	NL
T. Rowe Price New Era Fund	13.9	NL
Prudential-Bache Utility Fund	24.9	12b-1
Stratton Monthly Dividend Shares	23.6	NL
Vanguard Energy Fund	NA	NL

Fidelity Select Energy Fund

Fidelity Select Energy Fund invests in companies in the energy field, including those involved in the conventional energy sources of oil, gas, electricity, and coal, and those involved in newer sources such as nuclear, geothermal, oil shale, and solar. The business activities of companies in the Fund's portfolio may include production, generation, transmission, marketing, control, or measurement of energy or energy fuels; providing component parts or services to companies engaged in such activities; and environmental activities related to the solution of energy problems, such as energy conservation or pollution control. Companies participating in new activities resulting from technological advances or research discoveries in the energy field are also considered for the Fund's portfolio.

The Fund held 65 securities as of April 30, 1986. The Fund's five largest holdings on April 33, 1986, were Southland Corporation, Total Petroleum, British Petroleum, Coastal Corporation, and Occidental Petroleum.

While the Fund was a laggard performer from 1984 to 1986, it may be well positioned for investors who want an energy fund in their portfolios. If the industry comes back, Fidelity should be one of the better performers.

Fidelity Select Utilities Fund

Fidelity Select Utilities Fund is one of many Fidelity Select Portfolio funds. Its objective is capital appreciation, and does not emphasize yield.

Normally 80 percent of the portfolio consists of utility equity securities. The Fund incorporates securities both of companies in the public utilities industry and of companies deriving a substantial majority of their revenues from supplying public utilities.

On August 30, 1986, the Fund held 75 common stocks, 3 preferred stocks, and 4 bonds, all in the utility classification. In percentages of assets, by classification, 80 percent of the securities held were in electric and gas utilities, 10 percent in communications utilities, 6 percent in gas companies, and 4 percent in bonds and preferred stocks. The assets of the Fund on December 31, 1986, were $195 million.

The Fund's R squared coefficient of 38 percent indicates that the Fund is significantly less diversified than the general market—this is to be expected in a sector fund. Portfolio turnover reported for the year ended April 30, 1986, was 96 percent.

During 1986 a declining interest-rate environment greatly benefited the performance of utility stocks. At the time, the Fund focused on electric, telephone, and combination utilities. As yields fell on utility issues, the Fund increased its position in high-quality bonds. The Fund avoided utilities involved in regulatory or construction difficulties with nuclear facilities. Fund positions in companies negatively affected by the fall in oil and gas prices were also reduced at that time. This strategy has proved successful for the Fund.

The Fund, with its de-emphasis on yield, is somewhat more risky than, say, Stratton Monthly Dividend Shares. Nevertheless, from 1984 through mid-1987, the beta was a relatively low 0.56 and the alpha an impressive 13.4 percent. The Fund's income for the period ended April 30, 1986, was 6.3 percent; actual dividends paid to shareholders were 2 percent for that period.

Managed more as a sector fund than a utility fund (with its low yield and high portfolio turnover), this Fund should not be considered an income-oriented investment, but a capital-appreciation investment. The Fund should experience market-like rises and falls; from

1984 to 1987 the Fund has outperformed the S&P 500. The expense ratio for the year ended April 30, 1986, was 1.3 percent. The performance of the Fund is shown in Figure 16-2.

Figure 16-2: The Performance of Fidelity Utilities Fund Shown with Its 26-Week Moving Average. (Courtesy of Telescan.)

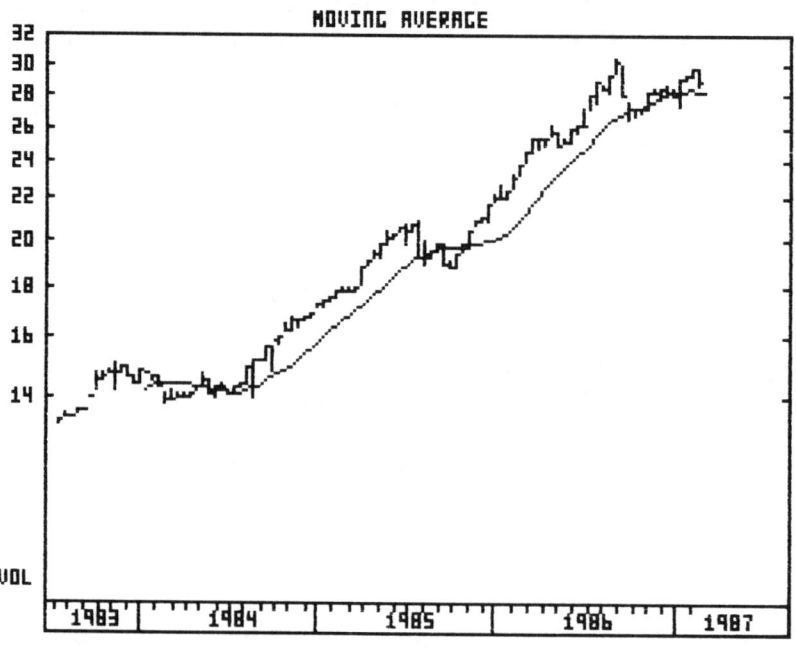

The Fund is one of 31 portfolios of the Fidelity Select Fund, which are treated as one fund for tax purposes. Thus, gains for the Fund are merged with losses of other portfolios and not distributed if such offsetting is possible. This creates a favorable tax position for shareholders of the Fund as long as the Fund generates capital gains.

The Fund is well poised for capital appreciation and best suits investors with that as their primary goal.

Neuberger & Berman Energy Fund

The investment objective of Neuberger & Berman Energy Fund is long-term capital appreciation. The Fund was first publicly offered in 1955.

The Fund pursues its investment objective primarily through investment in companies whose activities are directly or indirectly related to energy. At least 80 percent of the value of the Fund's investments are normally in companies whose activities are related to energy. Energy source and product companies account for 46 percent of the Fund's portfolio.

The Fund's seven largest holdings on December 31, 1986, were Royal Dutch, A. G. Bayer, Waste Management, Baltimore Gas & Electric, Morton Thiokol, Chevron, and Mapco.

Investments include both newer sources such as thermal and solar power and familiar sources such as oil, gas, and coal, as well as various transformed varieties of energy such as electricity and gasoline. The Fund management intends to participate in all advances and new developments in energy's broad and rapidly changing technology and not confine its investments only to old or new methodology.

Fund management believes that the development of new energy resources and applications will be a necessary and integral part of the U.S. economy's growth and expansion. President Bernard Stein expects an accord between oil-producing nations, which would cause prices to rebound and stocks to recover; this development would strengthen the Fund's large holdings in energy source and product companies.

T. Rowe Price New Era Fund

T. Rowe Price New Era Fund seeks long-term growth of capital.

The Fund invests in a diversified group of companies whose tangible asset value and/or earnings are expected to grow faster than the rate of inflation over the long term. Primary investments are in natural-resource-related companies.

Six significant holdings in the Fund on December 31, 1986, were IBM, Dow Chemical, Cyprus Minerals, Union Camp, Echo Bay Mines, and Newmont Mining.

Management believes that the most attractive opportunities that satisfy the Fund's objective are in companies that own or develop natural resources and in companies in which management has the flexibility to adjust prices and control operating costs.

George Roche, manager of the Fund since 1979, says, "I favor, more than my colleagues, very strong economic growth, and if I can get inflation along with it, so much the better. That's ideal for me." Many of the stocks Mr. Roche typically invests in benefit from inflation.

The Fund was created in 1969 to provide a hedge against inflation by investing mostly in natural resource companies with valuable tangible assets—such as precious metals, operating metal mines, timber, and energy-related industries.

Roche assumed the presidency of the Fund while inflation was in double digits, and in his first two years the Fund posted gains of almost 60 and 52 percent. Since that time inflation has been in sharp remission; high real interest rates, a strong dollar (until 1985 at least), and moderate economic growth have taken a toll on commodity-related producers.

To cope with the changes, Roche increased investment emphasis on less cyclical resource businesses and more traditional growth companies in consumer products, science, and technology. (Such stocks have always been a part of the Fund's assets; the amount has varied with economic conditions.)

The flexible tactics occasioned a 23.4 percent advance in 1985, while other natural resource mutual funds averaged a 14.4 percent return. The Fund returned 13.9 percent for 1986. The Fund nevertheless lagged behind the general market because of the effects of a weak economy on commodity prices. Chemical stocks and consumer- and service-related holdings performed well, but the diversified resource, diversified metals, and precious metals holdings were a drag on performance. Fund managers said an anticipated pickup in economic growth in 1987 would significantly enhance the operating environment for industrial and resource firms.

The Fund has returned 15.4 percent annually over the ten-year period ended December 31, 1986. Its performance is shown in Figure 16-3

The Fund is well designed for protection against inflation; investors requiring such protection in their portfolios should look into T. Rowe Price New Era Fund.

Prudential-Bache Utility Fund

The Prudential-Bache Utility Fund's investment objective is to seek high current income and moderate capital appreciation.

Investments are in equity and debt securities of utility companies, principally electric, gas, and telephone companies. In normal circumstances, the Fund expects to invest at least 80 percent of its assets in such securities. Utility common stocks are anticipated to be the primary type of security in the portfolio; the Fund has the option, however, of investing in utility preferred stocks and debt securities when they appear better able to meet the Fund's objective or when the Fund is in a temporary defensive position.

There is no initial sales charge for shares of the Fund; a contingent deferred sales charge (5 to 0 percent) may be imposed on redemptions of shares held less than five years.

Prudential-Bache acts as distributor of the Fund's shares pursuant to a Plan of Distribution adopted by the Fund under Rule 12b-1 with an annual charge of 1 percent. The covers commissions and other Prudential-Bache expenses as distributor. (Such commission credits approximate 5 percent of the offering price of shares sold.)

The Fund achieved a 24.9 percent annual average return over a three-year period ended December 31, 1986, with relatively low risk (beta = 0.46). The Fund's performance is shown in Figure 16-4 (page 226).

An investor can favorably hold shares in the Fund for several years and thus avoid the contingent deferred sales charge. The Fund is appropriate for the utilities investor who has relatively more need for current income than for capital appreciation, such as an investor in early retirement years.

Stratton Monthly Dividend Shares

Stratton Monthly Dividend Shares seeks as its objective a high rate of return from interest and dividend income. The Fund pays a monthly dividend to its shareholders.

Chapter 16   225

Figure 16-3: Performance of T. Rowe Price New Era Fund Shown with Its 33-Week Moving Average. (Courtesy of Telescan.)

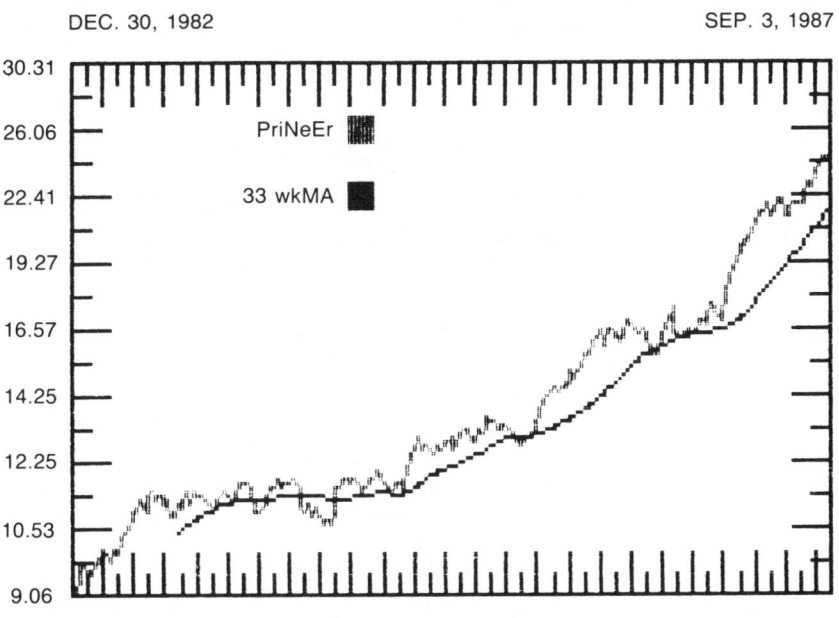

The Fund invests in common stock and securities convertible into common stock. The Fund must hold at least 25 percent of its assets in public utility companies engaged in electric, energy, gas, water, or telephone service.

As of December 31, 1986, the Fund held 72 percent of its portfolio in electric and gas utilities and 12 percent in regional banks. Total assets were $43 million. The portfolio turnover for the fiscal year ended January 31, 1986, was only 13.6 percent. The remaining 16 percent was widely distributed in other sectors of the economy.

On January 31, 1985, the Fund's assets were $10.4 million, so the size of the Fund almost quadrupled in 24 months.

Stratton Management became manager of the Fund began on May 31, 1980. The Fund became a mutual fund in November 1981. Formerly known as Energy and Utility Shares, the Fund changed its name in May 1985 so that it would no longer be required to hold 80 percent of its portfolio in utility shares. The Fund's investment advisor is Stratton Management Company of Blue Bell, Pennsylvania, and the Fund managers are James Stratton, Gerard Heffernan, and John Affleck. Mr. Heffernan described the basic strategy as "a dedication to yield" with "provisions for diversification with low impact on yield."

The year ended December 31, 1986, produced a total return of 20.4 percent and an average yield of 7.0 percent. Over 11 years (1976–86) the annual dividend increased at an annual average of 6.1 percent. For the year ended December 31, 1986, the yield was 6.9 percent. The Fund has a surprisingly high return for a low-risk fund (beta = 0.50): 180.6 percent over the five years ended February 28, 1986, for an average annual return of 22.9 percent.

Figure 16-4: The Performance of Prudential Bache Utility Fund Shown with Its 26-Week Moving Average. (Courtesy of Telescan.)

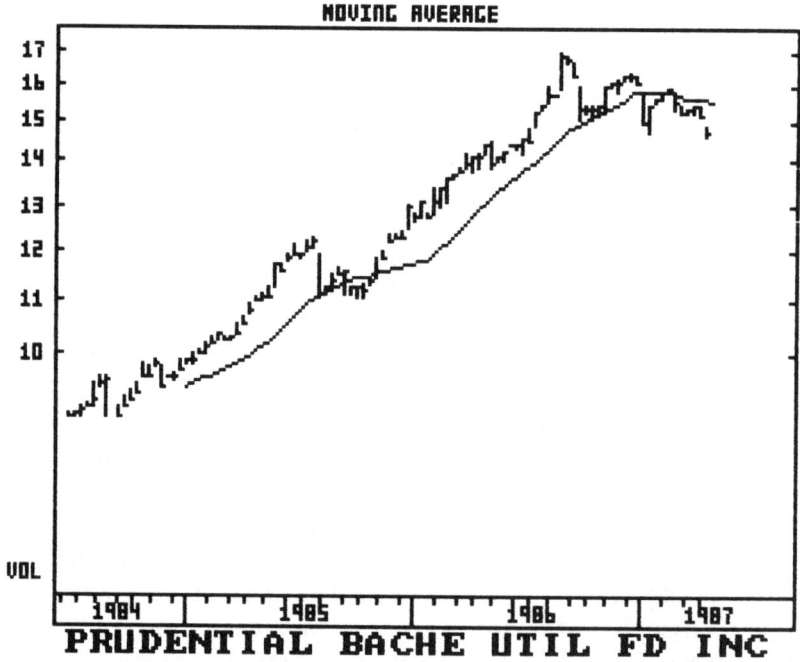

The Fund's expense ratio for the fiscal year ended January 31, 1986, was 1.49 percent. Mr. Heffernan described the Fund as a low-risk buy-and-hold fund, adding that the Fund managers are "long-term investors." The Fund is a good choice for an investor seeking total return with significant interim income.

Vanguard Energy Fund

The Vanguard Energy Fund seeks capital appreciation.

The Fund invests in the securities of companies whose activities are directly related to energy. The activities may be production, transmission, marketing, control or measurement of energy or energy fuels, manufacture of component products for energy activities, energy research or experimentation, or energy conservation and pollution control, and related activities. The company may be involved with newer sources of energy such as geothermal, nuclear, and solar power or more traditional sources of energy such as oil, natural gas, or coal. As new sources or methods are developed, the companies involved in them will also be considered. Natural gas distributors and natural gas pipeline firms are permitted candidates; the Fund will not, however, purchase the securities of electric utility companies.

The portfolio manager, Ernst von Metzsch, has focused the Fund on the oil and gas business, both here and abroad. The Fund retains major holdings in quality companies such as Amerada Hess, Royal Dutch, Kerr McGee, Mobil, Britoil, Shell Transport, and Questar.

The Fund underperformed the market during 1986 as the market reflected fears about weakened oil prices. World oil demand remained lackluster during 1986 while oil production outside OPEC increased. It was no surprise that oil prices weakened and energy stocks declined that year, after a good performance in 1985. Capital budgets were still being revised sharply downward in mid-1987, and a significant portion of cash flow was earmarked for reducing equity base or reducing long-term debt in the industry.

As oil and gas prices stabilize, energy investments will become more profitable, and the better restructured companies should perform better. The Fund plans to take advantage of this foreseen restructuring in the industry by looking for opportunities to acquire revitalized companies early on.

The outlook for oil pricing remains clouded, and a volatile, crisislike atmosphere may remain well into 1988. It is in the best interests of most governments to promote stability within the industry; the Fund is watching for the opportunities resulting from restructuring as well as share repurchases and the elimination of major pricing uncertainties. If the industry comes back, Vanguard should be one of the better performers.

PROFILE 16-1

FIDELITY SELECT ENERGY FUND
82 Devonshire
Boston, MA 02109
1-800-544-6666
617-523-1919

Fund Classification:	EU
Total Assets:	$71 million
Fund Manager:	Richard C. Habermann
Year of Inception:	1980
Minimum Investment:	1000
Sales Charge:	3.00%
12b-1 Charge:	No
Expense Ratio:	1.54

Portfolio Mix:	%	Issues
Bonds	0	0
Convertible Bonds	10.3	NA
Common Stock	81.6	52
U. S. Government Securities	0	0
Municipal Bonds	0	0
Short-term Obligations	0	0
Estimated Annual Portfolio Turnover	141%	

Estimates of Fund Performance:	
Annual Return for Three Years:	11.6%
Annual Return for Five Years:	13.0%
Annual Return in Bull Markets:	
1985	17.9%
1986	5.5%
Annual Return in Bear Markets:	
6/30/83–6/30/84	2.10%
Representative Current Yield (8/31/86):	0.0%

Measures of Risk and Reward:	
Alpha	5.0
Beta	NA
R square	29
Standard deviation	4.84
Reward/risk ratio	2.4
Net Asset Value:	
9/25/87	14.96
10/28/87	10.54

PROFILE 16-2

FIDELITY SELECT UTILITIES FUND
82 Devonshire
Boston, MA 02109
1-800-544-6666
617-523-1919

Fund Classification:	EU	
Total Assets:	$195 million	
Fund Manager:	Warren A. Casey	
Year of Inception:	1980	
Minimum Investment:	1000	
Sales Charge:	3.00%	
12b-1 Charge:	No	
Expense Ratio:	1.34	

Portfolio Mix:	%	*Issues*
Bonds	0	0
Convertible Bonds	0	0
Common Stock	97.13	74
U. S. Government Securities	0	0
Municipal Bonds	0	0
Short-term Obligations	0	0
Estimated Annual Portfolio Turnover	96%	

Estimates of Fund Performance:	
Annual Return for Three Years:	28.8%
Annual Return for Five Years:	24.7%
Annual Return in Bull Markets:	
1985	31.7%
1986	24.0%
Annual Return in Bear Markets:	
6/30/83–6/30/84	9.84%
Representative Current Yield (8/31/86):	0.7%

Measures of Risk and Reward:	
Alpha	9.3
Beta	0.67
R square	49
Standard deviation	4.03
Reward/risk ratio	7.1
Net Asset Value:	
9/25/87	26.84
10/28/87	24.82

PROFILE 16-3

NEUBERGER & BERMAN ENERGY FUND
342 Madison Avenue
New York, NY 10173
1-800-367-0770
212-850-8300

Fund Classification:	EU
Total Assets:	$376 million
Fund Manager:	Bernard Stein
Year of Inception:	1955
Minimum Investment:	500
Sales Charge:	No load
12b-1 Charge:	No
Expense Ratio:	0.89

Portfolio Mix:	%	*Issues*
Bonds	0	0
Convertible Bonds	0	0
Common Stock	80.67	82
U. S. Government Securities	0	0
Municipal Bonds	0	0
Short-term Obligations	0	0
Estimated Annual Portfolio Turnover	18%	

Estimates of Fund Performance:	
Annual Return for Three Years:	17.8%
Annual Return for Five Years:	17.5%
Annual Return in Bull Markets:	
1985	22.5%
1986	10.1%
Annual Return in Bear Markets:	
6/30/83–6/30/84	13.0%
Representative Current Yield (11/30/86):	4.3%

Measures of Risk and Reward:	
Alpha	2.5
Beta	0.72
R square	73
Standard deviation	3.43
Reward/risk ratio	4.0
Net Asset Value:	
9/25/87	23.69
10/28/87	14.48

PROFILE 16-4

T. ROWE PRICE NEW ERA FUND
100 E. Pratt Street
Baltimore, MD 21202
1-800-638-5660
301-547-2308

Fund Classification:	EU	
Total Assets:	$494 million	
Fund Manager:	G. A. Roche	
Year of Inception:	1968	
Minimum Investment:	1000	
Sales Charge:	No load	
12b-1 Charge:	No	
Expense Ratio:	0.73	

Portfolio Mix:	%	*Issues*
Bonds	0	0
Convertible Bonds	0	0
Common Stock	87.09	49
U. S. Government Securities	0	0
Municipal Bonds	0	0
Short-term Obligations	0	0
Estimated Annual Portfolio Turnover	32%	

Estimates of Fund Performance:	
Annual Return for Three Years:	21.6%
Annual Return for Five Years:	21.5%
Annual Return in Bull Markets:	
1985	22.9%
1986	16.2%
Annual Return in Bear Markets:	
6/30/83–6/30/84	3.00%
Representative Current Yield (8/31/86):	2.4%

Measures of Risk and Reward:	
Alpha	2.5
Beta	0.93
R square	82
Standard deviation	4.03
Reward/risk ratio	5.4
Net Asset Value:	
9/25/87	24.72
10/28/87	17.37

PROFILE 16-5

PRUDENTIAL-BACHE UTILITY FUND
One Seaport Plaza
New York, NY 10292
1-800-872-7787
212-214-1234

Fund Classification:	EU
Total Assets:	$1,212 million
Fund Manager:	Steve Ballentine
	Theresa Hamacher
Year of Inception:	1981
Minimum Investment:	1000
Sales Charge:	5.00%
12b-1 Charge:	Yes (1.0%)
Expense Ratio:	1.13

Portfolio Mix:	%	*Issues*
Bonds	0	0
Convertible Bonds	0	0
Common Stock	91.55	58
U. S. Government Securities	0	0
Municipal Bonds	0	0
Short-term Obligations	0	0
Estimated Annual Portfolio Turnover	36%	

Estimates of Fund Performance:	
Annual Return for Three Years:	27.0%
Annual Return for Five Years:	22.0%
Annual Return in Bull Markets:	
1985	33.4%
1986	27.6%
Annual Return in Bear Markets:	
6/30/83–6/30/84	NA
Representative Current Yield (8/31/86):	4.7%

Measures of Risk and Reward:	
Alpha	10.6
Beta	0.46
R square	28
Standard deviation	3.63
Reward/risk ratio	7.4
Net Asset Value:	
9/25/87	14.30
10/28/87	12.79

PROFILE 16-6

STRATTON MONTHLY DIVIDEND SHARES
610 W. Germantown Pike
Plymouth Meeting, PA 19462
1-800-634-5726
215-941-0255

Fund Classification:	EU
Total Assets:	$43 million
Fund Manager:	James W. Stratton
	Gerald E. Hefferman
Year of Inception:	1971
Minimum Investment:	1000
Sales Charge:	No load
12b-1 Charge:	No
Expense Ratio:	1.49

Portfolio Mix:	%	Issues
Bonds	0	0
Convertible Bonds	0	0
Common Stock	63.3	31
U. S. Government Securities	3.4	2
Municipal Bonds	0	0
Convertible Debentures	30.6	16
Estimated Annual Portfolio Turnover	18%	

Estimates of Fund Performance:	
Annual Return for Three Years:	27.4%
Annual Return for Five Years:	22.5%
Annual Return in Bull Markets:	
1985	29.7%
1986	20.4%
Annual Return in Bear Markets:	
6/30/83–6/30/84	-4.3
Representative Current Yield (8/31/86):	6.9%

Measures of Risk and Reward:	
Alpha	9.2
Beta	0.50
R square	39
Standard deviation	3.34
Reward/risk ratio	8.2
Net Asset Value:	
9/25/87	26.40
10/28/87	23.39

PROFILE 16-7

VANGUARD ENERGY FUND
Valley Forge, PA 19482
1-800-662-7447
215-648-6000

Fund Classification:	EU
Total Assets:	$14 million
Fund Manager:	Gene Tremblay
Year of Inception:	1984
Minimum Investment:	1500
Sales Charge:	No load
12b-1 Charge:	No
Expense Ratio:	.65

Portfolio Mix:	%	*Issues*
Bonds	NA	NA
Convertible Bonds	NA	NA
Common Stock	NA	NA
U. S. Government Securities	NA	NA
Municipal Bonds	NA	NA
Convertible Debentures	NA	NA
Estimated Annual Portfolio Turnover	31%	

Estimates of Fund Performance:	
Annual Return for Two Years:	18.1%
Annual Return for Five Years:	NA
Annual Return in Bull Markets:	
1985	14.4%
1986	12.5%
Annual Return in Bear Markets:	
6/30/83–6/30/84	NA
Representative Current Yield (12/31/86):	3.9%

Measures of Risk and Reward:	
Alpha	NA
Beta	0.75
R square	NA
Standard deviation	4.0
Reward/risk ratio	4.5

Net Asset Value:	
9/25/87	15.09
10/28/87	10.84

Chapter 17
Small-Company Growth Funds

BACKGROUND INFORMATION

Type of Security

A small-company growth fund maintains prospectus language and portfolio practice that limits its investment to companies that have low market capitalizations. (Size here is measured by the total market value of the company's outstanding shares.) Typically, the stock of the companies held in their portfolios are traded on the over-the-counter (OTC) market.

The OTC market provides the means through which securities of hundreds of leading U.S. corporations; many billions of dollars are traded in the aggregate. Securities traded "over the counter" are not traded on any exchange because they do not meet the requirements of the New York Stock Exchange or the American Stock Exchange, and are sold through other distribution media. At the end of 1984, more than 30,000 issues were trading yearly in the OTC market and the stocks of over 15,000 corporations were trading daily.

Risk/Stability

Small-company stocks had declined in relative favor as of this writing and may go in and out of favor periodically.

While small- and medium-sized companies often have a limited market for their securities and limited financial resources—and are usually more affected by changes in the economy in general—they may also have the potential for more rapid, and greater, long-term growth because of newer and more innovative products.

The years 1982 through 1986 were particularly good to blue chips and less so to small-company stocks. In the five years through January 31, 1987, when the S&P 500 was up 128 percent (excluding dividends), the NASDAQ index of over-the-counter issues managed only a 108 percent rise. The Hambrecht & Quist Technology Index weighed in with just an 86 percent rise during the same five years. In 1986 alone, while the Dow shot ahead 22.6 percent, the over-the-counter market and the American Stock Exchange rose only 7.3 percent and 7 percent, respectively.

Secondary issues finally began to show some muscle in 1987, encouraging the hope that they would lead the market to new highs. While the Dow Jones Industrial Average soared a spectacular 17 percent in the first two months of 1987, the NASDAQ composite index posted an even stronger 20 percent return for the OTCs.

Experiences like these have taught us to be extremely skeptical about market generalizations and about expectations that market patterns will repeat themselves.

The return of small-company stocks compared to other investments is shown in Table 17-1.

Table 17-1: Investment Return by Investment Class: 1964-83

Investment Category	Total Annual Return (%)
Small-Company Stocks	17.6
Common Stocks	8.3
Long-Term Corporate Bonds	4.7
Long-Term Government Bonds	4.0
Treasury Bills	6.8

Source: "Stocks, Bonds, Bills and Inflation: 1984 Yearbook." Chicago, IL: R. G. Ibbotson Associates, Inc. 1984.

SPECIAL BENEFITS AND EXPOSURES

Volatility

Theoretically, if the market pricing for small-company stocks is as efficient as that of larger stocks, the two should perform similarly when prices decline; but before the 1986-87 bull market, smaller issues fell faster in corrections and rose faster in bull markets. In this light, it is not surprising to find that mutual funds have moved into the arena of small firms in an effort to capitalize on the attractive returns.

Price/Earnings Ratios

Smaller companies frequently offer the possibility of more rapid sales and profit expansion than most larger and more mature businesses. Because they grow more rapidly than larger companies, small stocks usually command a higher price.

Small stocks typically sold at about a 50 percent premium to the overall market in 1987. In early 1987, the price/earnings (P/E) multiple (or price/earnings ratio—price per share compared with earnings per share) for small companies was on average close to that of the big companies that make up the S&P 500 index. This has happened only a few times since the early 1960s—and then only fleetingly. Normally the average P/E multiple has

Chapter 17 237

been anywhere from 20 to 60 percent above the S&P 500. (In 1983, small stocks had been selling at twice the P/E of the overall market.)

Continuing Effects of the 1986–87 Bull Market

A big thrust by institutional investors into small stocks altered the way those shares performed in the 1986–87 bull market, and the change could be irreversible. The sudden interest in small firms can most likely be attributed to the discovery that small-firm common stocks tend to outperform the stocks of large firms, even after adjusting for risk. (In fact, portfolios of small-firm stocks have historically earned, on average, 5 percentage points per year *more than they should for their level of risk*.)

PORTFOLIO FIT

Small-company growth funds are for those seeking above-average returns while accommodating above-average risk. Generally, these funds need to be held through market ups and downs to provide above-average return. You must avoid selling them when they drop in price and buying them again at the top.

These are high-risk–high-return funds and should be less than 10 percent of your total portfolio. Nevertheless, the person who is willing to hold them over a business cycle can reap good returns. Be prepared, however, for sharp volatility in returns. Note that Fidelity OTC went up 69 percent in 1985 but only returned 11 percent in 1986.

SEVEN REPRESENTATIVE SMALL-COMPANY GROWTH FUNDS

To illustrate, we have chosen seven small-company growth funds that show the qualities that investors seek when purchasing shares of small-company growth funds. Note that five of these examples are no-load funds. Table 17-2 contains a summary listing of the seven funds. It is followed by a more detailed description of each fund's objectives and investment philosophy and practice, as well as capsule Profiles of their recent performance.

Investors are reminded that past performance is no indicator of future performance.

Babson Enterprise Fund

Babson Enterprise Fund's objective is to seek smaller, fast-growing companies that have good potential for long-term growth. The companies selected generally have market capital of $15 million to $300 million and are listed on a national exchange or are sold over the counter.

As of November 30, 1986, the Fund held 64 common stocks. The portfolio was well-diversified with building and construction stocks (11.5 percent), consumer products (10.8

percent), and leisure companies (13.7 percent) accounting for the largest sectors in the Fund. Its performance is shown in Figure 17-1 (page 240).

Table 17-2: Seven Representative Small-Company Growth Funds

Fund	Annual Return (%) for 3 Years	Load
Babson Enterprise Fund	16.8	NL
Fidelity OTC Fund	43.1*	LL
Janus Venture Fund	35.0**	NL
Mathers Fund	18.6	NL
Nicholas II Fund	24.9	NL
Over-the-Counter Securities Fund	15.0	L
Twentieth Century Vista Fund	20.9	NL

Note: In this same 3-year period, the S&P 500 annual return was 23.7 percent.

*Annualized from the 25 months through 1/31/87.

**Annualized from the period 4/26/85 through 1/31/87.

The Portfolio Manager, Peter Schliemann, stated in late 1986: "It appears that this period of adjustment for small companies is very close to being over and today's values are the best seen in many years. For the long-term investor looking for both growth and value, small stocks are compelling."

Small-company growth funds live with volatility. All of them concede the possibility of unforeseen setbacks. But Babson's Schliemann puts a view that could stand for all of them: "At this stage in the stock market, all the signs are that the potential for best relative performance is in the smaller companies."

In November 1986, the price/earnings ratio of the Fund was 15.7 while it was 17.7 for the S&P 400.

Fidelity OTC Fund

Fidelity OTC Fund seeks to achieve capital appreciation by investing primarily in securities traded on the OTC securities market.

The Fund has 322 securities and has held stocks in the insurance, finance, and retail drug sectors, among others.

Fidelity OTC was managed in 1985 by Paul Stuka. After Stuka left in July 1986, Morris Smith took over as Manager. Fidelity achieved a remarkable return of 69 percent in its first year, 1985. It returned a disappointing 12 percent, however, in 1986.

Fidelity OTC Fund is for the person who wants to have a portion of his funds in a high-risk–high-return fund.

Janus Venture Fund

The Janus Venture Fund seeks capital appreciation by emphasizing investments in the common stocks of small companies that may experience strong growth in revenues, earnings, and assets.

James Craig, the Fund's Portfolio Manager, says he "rejects the high-visibility darlings covered by big funds." The 30 stocks in his portfolio, which include shares of a Colorado slaughterhouse and a jewelry store, have as little as $15 million in market capitalization. As Mr. Craig sees it, Janus's size is an important advantage. "If it got too big, we would probably close it," he says.

Mr. Craig has been with Janus Capital since 1983 and is President of Janus Venture Fund. He was formerly an investment analyst with Trust Company of the West.

Janus Venture Fund is a high-risk–high-return fund for the investor whose portfolio has room for some proportion of high-risk investments in small companies.

Mathers Fund

The primary investment objective of Mathers Fund is long-term capital appreciation, and securities are selected for its portfolio primarily on this basis. Current income is only a secondary factor in the selection of investments.

The policy of the Fund is to invest in securities that offer the possibility of increase in value: for the most part, common stocks of companies that appear to the adviser to have favorable long-term prospects.

This Fund has provided good returns over the 3-year and 5-year periods ending January 31, 1987. Also, it only declined 5 percent during the third quarter of 1986 while the S&P 500 declined 7 percent and all the other smaller company funds declined even more. The Fund was up 16 percent for the month of January 1987. The performance of the Fund is shown in Figure 17-2.

Nicholas II Fund

Nicholas II has the primary objective of long-term growth, and securities are selected for its portfolio on that basis. Current income will be only a secondary factor in considering the selection of investments.

Figure 17-1: The Performance of the Babson Enterprise Fund Shown with Its 33-Week Moving Average. (Courtesy of Mutual Fund Chartist.)

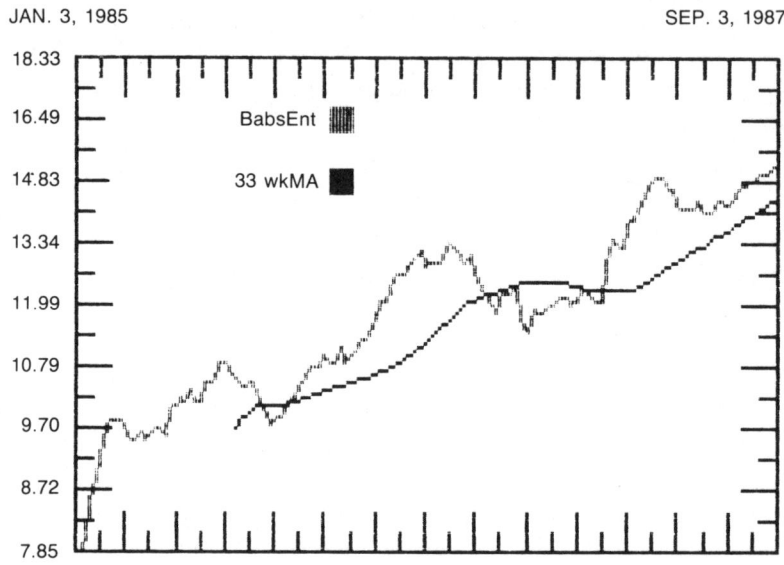

Figure 17-2: The Performance of the Mathers Fund Shown with Its 26-Week Moving Average (Courtesy of Telescan.)

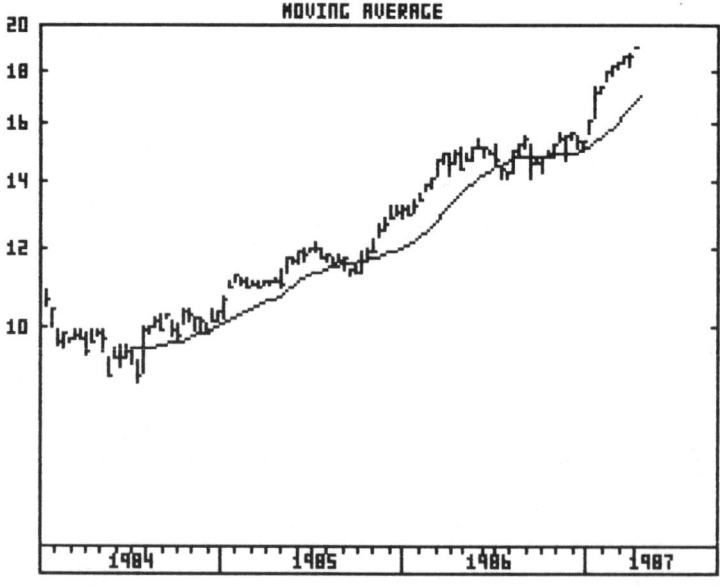

The Fund's investment philosophy is basically a long-term growth philosophy, inherent in which is the assumption that if a company achieves superior growth in sales and earnings, eventually the company's stock will achieve superior performance.

The top five holdings as of December 31, 1986, were Godfrey Company, Standard Commercial Tobacco, Community Psychiatric Centers, Block Drug, and Pansophic Systems. Albert Nicholas, the Fund's Manager, seeks out-of-favor stocks of small companies with good growth patterns.

The Fund has a very good record over the 3 years ending January 31, 1987, with an average annual return of 25 percent. The performance of the Fund is shown in Figure 17-3.

Figure 17-3: The Performance of Nicholas II Fund Shown with Its 26-Week Moving Average. (Courtesy of Telescan.)

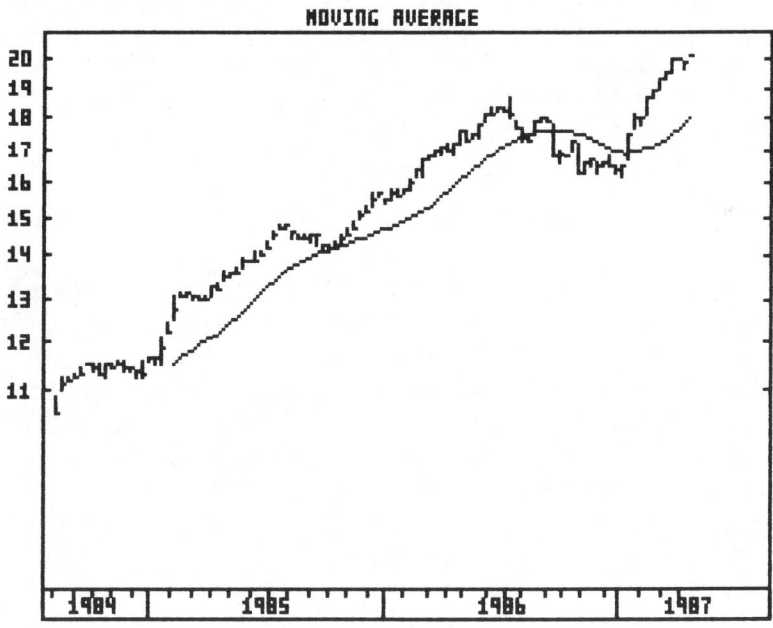

The Fund has relatively less risk than many other small-company funds, which makes it appropriate for investors whose portfolios have only a moderate tolerance for risk.

Over-the-Counter Securities Fund

Over-the-Counter Securities Fund is organized to invest in companies whose securities are traded in the over-the-counter securities market. The Fund is designed to meet the needs of individual investors for investing in a diversified group of over-the-counter securities with continuous professional supervision.

Since 1955, OTC Securities has been investing in the stocks of small, emerging growth companies traded, as the Fund's name implies, over the counter. As soon as a stock moves to one of the major exchanges, it is sold. The portfolio continues to be one of the most diversified of any mutual fund in terms of number of holdings and diversity of businesses.

Manager Binkley Shorts remains as fully invested as possible while seeking new opportunities among the more than 40,000 OTC equities currently available.

Shorts has managed the Fund, the oldest mutual fund dealing solely in OTC stocks, since 1980. "We try to discover and invest in obscure, thinly traded companies," he said, noting he doesn't like stocks with market capitalizations of more than $100 million and prefers to stay with firms under $50 million.

In screening undiscovered stocks, Shorts prefers to see historical earnings growth of about 15 percent. But it doesn't have to be steady, he said, calling consistency a "false god that institutions pay way too much money for."

The Fund has a good long-term record, but it underperformed in 1986. Since the Fund takes a long-term view, investors who choose this above-average fund should also take a longer-term view. The Fund is more appropriate for the buy-and-hold investor, and less so for the investor looking to small-company stocks for short-term gains.

Twentieth Century Vista Fund

Twentieth Century Vista is considered one of Twentieth Century's most aggressive funds, seeking growth as the paramount objective.

The Fund invests in small, growing companies that demonstrate accelerating earnings and revenues. This investment strategy, along with Vista's smaller size, tends to increase both its share price volatility and its long-term growth potential.

Despite the Fund's high volatility of share price and monthly return, its performance was very attractive for the 3 years ended January 31, 1987, and it gained 20.8 percent for the month of January, 1987. Note, however, that it had the largest decline of the five representative funds for the third quarter of 1986.

Mr. James Stowers, the Fund's Manager, stated in the October 31, 1986, report: "While we cannot predict the future, we anticipate the market volatility of 1986 to continue. As is always our policy, we will remain fully invested in the common stock funds and will not attempt to 'time' the market. We will continue to carefully execute the investment policies that have guided our activities for the past 15 years."

Vista is a high-risk–high-return fund for the investor who foresees a rising market for emerging growth companies for the next several years. It is definitely for the more aggressive investor.

PROFILE 17-1

BABSON ENTERPRISE FUND
2440 Pershing Road
Kansas City, MO 64108
1-800-821-5591
1-816-471-5200

Fund Classification:	SCG
Total Assets:	$47 million
Fund Manager:	Peter C. Schliemann
Year of Inception:	1983
Minimum Investment:	$1000
Sales Charge:	No load
12b-1 Charge:	No
Expense Ratio:	1.37

Portfolio Mix:	%	*Issues*
Bonds	0	0
Convertible Bonds	0	0
Common Stock	95	64
U. S. Government Securities	0	0
Municipal Bonds	0	0
Convertible Debentures	0	0
Estimated Annual Portfolio Turnover	32%	

Estimates of Fund Performance:	
Annual Return for Three Years:	16.8%
Annual Return for Five Years:	NA
Annual Return in Bull Markets:	
1985	38.6%
1986	7.5%
Annual Return in Bear Markets:	
6/30/86–9/30/86	-9.2%
Representative Current Yield (1/31/87):	0.9%
Measures of Risk and Reward:	
Alpha	NA
Beta	1.02
R square	71
Standard deviation	5.09
Reward/risk ratio	3.30
Net Asset Value:	
9/25/87	14.95
10/28/87	9.92

PROFILE 17-2

FIDELITY OTC FUND
82 Devonshire
Boston, MA 02109
1-800-544-6666
617-523-1919

Fund Classification:	SCG
Total Assets:	$631 million
Fund Manager:	Morris Smith
Year of Inception:	1984
Minimum Investment:	2500
Sales Charge:	3.00%
12b-1 Charge:	No
Expense Ratio:	1.31

Portfolio Mix:	%	*Issues*
Bonds	0	0
Convertible Bonds	0	0
Common Stock	99	322
U. S. Government Securities	0	0
Municipal Bonds	0	0
Convertible Debentures	0	0
Estimated Annual Portfolio Turnover	32%	

Estimates of Fund Performance:	
Annual Return for Two Years:	43.1%
Annual Return for Five Years:	NA
Annual Return in Bull Markets:	
1985	69.0%
1986	11.2%
Annual Return in Bear Markets:	
6/30/86–9/30/86	-13.9%
Representative Current Yield (1/31/87):	0.1%

Measures of Risk and Reward:	
Alpha	NA
Beta	1.20
R square	NA
Standard deviation	7.0
Reward/risk ratio	6.10
Net Asset Value:	
9/25/87	22.61
10/28/87	14.08

PROFILE 17-3

JANUS VENTURE FUND
Box 44339
Denver, CO 80201

Fund Classification:	SCG	
Total Assets:	$43 million	
Fund Manager:	James Craig	
Year of Inception:	1985	
Minimum Investment:	1000	
Sales Charge:	No load	
12b-1 Charge:	No	
Expense Ratio:	1.80	

Portfolio Mix:	%	*Issues*
Bonds	0	0
Convertible Bonds	0	0
Common Stock	65	45
U. S. Government Securities	35	NA
Municipal Bonds	0	0
Convertible Debentures	0	0
Estimated Annual Portfolio Turnover	248%	

Estimates of Fund Performance:

Annual Return for One Year:	35.0%
Annual Return for Five Years:	NA
Annual Return in Bull Markets:	
1985	31.4%
1986	20.2%
Annual Return in Bear Markets:	
6/30/86–9/30/86	-8.0%
Representative Current Yield (1/31/87):	4.9%

Measures of Risk and Reward:

Alpha	NA
Beta	1.20
R square	NA
Standard deviation	6.0
Reward/risk ratio	5.83

Net Asset Value:
9/25/87	34.23
10/28/87	27.53

PROFILE 17-4

MATHERS FUND
125 S. Wacker Drive
Chicago, IL 60606
312-236-8215

Fund Classification:	SCG	
Total Assets:	$135 million	
Fund Manager:	Henry G. VanderEb, Jr.	
	Richard Glenn	
Year of Inception:	1965	
Minimum Investment:	1000	
Sales Charge:	No load	
12b-1 Charge:	No	
Expense Ratio:	0.74	
Portfolio Mix:	%	*Issues*
Bonds	0	0
Convertible Bonds	0	0
Common Stock	89.12	59
U. S. Government Securities	0	0
Municipal Bonds	0	0
Convertible Debentures	0	0
Estimated Annual		
Portfolio Turnover	64%	
Estimates of Fund Performance:		
Annual Return for Three Years:	18.6%	
Annual Return for Five Years:	17.9%	
Annual Return in Bull Markets:		
1985	27.5%	
1986	12.9%	
Annual Return in Bear Markets:		
6/30/86–9/30/86	-5.0%	
Representative Current Yield (1/31/87):	3.7%	
Measures of Risk and Reward:		
Alpha	6.1	
Beta	1.08	
R square	89	
Standard deviation	4.82	
Reward/risk ratio	3.86	
Net Asset Value:		
9/25/87	19.73	
10/28/87	16.40	

PROFILE 17-5

NICHOLAS II FUND
700 Water Street
Milwaukee, WI 53202
414-272-6133

Fund Classification:	SCG
Total Assets:	$293 million
Fund Manager:	Albert Nicholas
Year of Inception:	1983
Minimum Investment:	1000
Sales Charge:	No load
12b-1 Charge:	No
Expense Ratio:	0.86

Portfolio Mix:	%	Issues
Bonds	0	0
Convertible Bonds	0	0
Common Stock	90	108
U. S. Government Securities	0	0
Municipal Bonds	0	0
Convertible Debentures	0	0
Estimated Annual Portfolio Turnover	15%	

Estimates of Fund Performance:	
Annual Return for Three Years:	24.9%
Annual Return for Five Years:	NA
Annual Return in Bull Markets:	
1985	33.8%
1986	10.3%
Annual Return in Bear Markets:	
6/30/86–9/30/86	-8.5%
Representative Current Yield (1/31/87):	2.3%
Measures of Risk and Reward:	
Alpha	NA
Beta	0.67
R square	77
Standard deviation	3.23
Reward/risk ratio	7.71
Net Asset Value:	
9/25/87	19.39
10/28/87	14.19

PROFILE 17-6

OVER-THE-COUNTER SECURITIES FUND
511 Pennsylvania Ave., Suite 325
Fort Washington, PA 19034
1-800-523-2578
215-643-2510

Fund Classification:	SCG	
Total Assets:	$247 million	
Fund Manager:	Binkley Shorts	
Year of Inception:	1955	
Minimum Investment:	500	
Sales Charge:	8.00%	
12b-1 Charge:	No	
Expense Ratio:	1.25	
Portfolio Mix:	%	*Issues*
Bonds	0	0
Convertible Bonds	0	0
Common Stock	86.22	384
U. S. Government Securities	0	0
Municipal Bonds	0	0
Convertible Debentures	0	0
Estimated Annual Portfolio Turnover	31%	
Estimates of Fund Performance:		
Annual Return for Three Years:	15.0%	
Annual Return for Five Years:	19.4%	
Annual Return in Bull Markets:		
1985	34.9%	
1986	5.4%	
Annual Return in Bear Markets:		
6/30/86–9/30/86	-12.6%	
Representative Current Yield (1/31/87):	0.3%	
Measures of Risk and Reward:		
Alpha	3.3	
Beta	0.72	
R square	68	
Standard deviation	3.66	
Reward/risk ratio	4.10	
Net Asset Value:		
9/25/87	19.95	
10/28/87	14.21	

PROFILE 17-7

TWENTIETH CENTURY VISTA FUND
Box 200
Kansas City, MO 64141
1-800-531-5575
1-816-531-5575

Fund Classification:	SCG	
Total Assets:	$153 million	
Fund Manager:	James Stowers	
Year of Inception:	1983	
Minimum Investment:	NA	
Sales Charge:	0.5%	
12b-1 Charge:	No	
Expense Ratio:	1.01	
Portfolio Mix:	%	*Issues*
Bonds	NA	NA
Convertible Bonds	NA	NA
Common Stock	NA	NA
U. S. Government Securities	NA	NA
Municipal Bonds	NA	NA
Convertible Debentures	NA	NA
Estimated Annual Portfolio Turnover	121%	
Estimates of Fund Performance:		
Annual Return for Three Years:	20.9%	
Annual Return for Five Years:	NA	
Annual Return in Bull Markets:		
1985	22.5%	
1986	26.5%	
Annual Return in Bear Markets:		
6/30/86–9/30/86	-18.3%	
Representative Current Yield (1/31/87):	0.0%	
Measures of Risk and Reward:		
Alpha	-13.3	
Beta	1.60	
R square	78	
Standard deviation	7.72	
Reward/risk ratio	2.71	
Net Asset Value:		
9/25/87	8.49	
10/28/87	4.57	

Chapter 18
Gold and Precious Metals Funds

BACKGROUND INFORMATION

Type of Security

Gold funds invest primarily in shares of gold or other mineral producing firms and sometimes directly in gold bullion. Purchased with care, they can provide excellent growth when other funds are faltering, since their growth and decline cycles are often opposite to those of the stock market.

Risk/Volatility

Gold funds generally increase when inflation heats up, and they serve as an excellent hedge against inflation. This effect is illustrated by Figure 18-1, which shows how gold prices grew rapidly from 1975 to 1980, with both inflation and gold peaking in early 1981 and again in 1983.

On August 21, 1985, the London spot (cash) price for gold had been $335.90/ounce; one year later, the spot price was $381.15/ounce—an increase of 13.5 percent. In contrast, the consumer price index, the most widely watched measure of inflation, rose 1.6 percent during 1986. "The fact that gold has been rising in the face of low inflation could signal the start of an upward trend in the price of gold," commented William Stack, Portfolio Manager of the Lexington Goldfund.

Gold-oriented funds soared, on average, 28.6 percent in 1986—enough to make them the second-best performers for the year. Rallies always prompt a question: Is this move for real? The investor should keep in mind that gold fund managers typically view gold through tinted, or maybe gilded, glasses—the metal is always going to rise in price.

Gold probably performed so well in 1986 because of the fact that investors had lost confidence in the dollar during the third quarter of that year and began moving their assets into gold. Commodity-market prices for gold as a result jumped nearly 25 percent in the last three months of the year—from about $330 an ounce in January 1986, to $452—before falling back to $400 at year-end. That, in a nugget, is the story behind mutual fund performances reported for that quarter.

Figure 18-1: The Price of Gold on the London Market (dollars/ounce).

Many advisers foresaw in 1987 and 1988 the fundamental conditions for a precious metals rebound: a creeping inflation rate, expanded industrial needs, and the ever-present specters of Third World debt, South African unrest, and the federal deficit. A new factor also entered the picture at about that time—the retail investor in gold funds. Today's retail investor is acting not on expectations of inflation but on the strategy of holding a diversified portfolio.

Gold funds do not move along with the stock market, so the R squared measured is normally zero and the beta and the alpha are not meaningful measures of risk. For gold funds we use standard deviation as the risk measure. The standard deviation of a gold fund is about twice that of (that is, twice as risky as) an average growth fund.

SPECIAL BENEFITS AND EXPOSURES

Short Response Time

"Those who are interested in gold need to be invested already," says Milton Berg, portfolio manager of Oppenheimer Gold and Special Minerals. "The market reacts so rapidly to developments nowadays that those who wait for conditions to change have already missed the boat."

Gold as Anxiety Hedge

Because gold is seen as a "store of value," or an asset that can be used as currency when paper money decreases in value, gold normally increases in value when inflation rises and decreases in value when inflation is declining.

It should be noted that gold is not only an inflation hedge, but also an anxiety hedge. During 1986, for example, gold prices went upward despite relatively low inflation (probably because a rise in inflation was *anticipated*). A market watcher will notice that the slightest rumor of discord among nations, which could result in an outbreak of war, will cause precious metal prices to rise rapidly. In uncertain times, no one wants to be holding anything but "the real stuff."

South Africa and the Supply Question

South Africa is now worrying everybody. On the one hand, the dumping of stocks by investors who have had enough or have decided to divest for political reasons could force down prices of gold-mining companies, and a collapse of the currency is not out of the question.

On the other hand, any interruption of supplies should in all normal circumstances force up gold prices. For most people, owning the metal itself is too cumbersome and costly to store and insure. For others, the choice of individual gold-mining companies is too risky.

Fears of an interruption in gold supplies from South Africa, some rekindling of fear s that inflation may pick up again in the months ahead, and lower expectations for other financial assets have sent gold up around the highest levels in several years.

Marginal Producers

What has helped all the gold funds is that the highest price of gold has made any previously marginal North American and Australian gold mines profitable again. More productive techniques, bigger output, and, above all, gold at around $400 an ounce have given North American producers—and shareholders—opportunities that have not existed in years.

PORTFOLIO FIT

Gold funds are for those who seek an inflation hedge. Investment advisers were recommending in 1987 that as much as 15 percent of a portfolio be put into bullion, both as an inflation hedge and as a counterweight to equities (whose fall often parallels an upturn in metals).

My own opinion is that most investors should generally keep only 2 percent of their portfolios in gold funds and increase that percentage when they see inflation heating up. For example, I might increase gold funds to 5 percent when the inflation rates exceed 6 percent. If inflation then went on to the 10 percent level, I would increase holdings in gold funds to 10 percent.

An investor who fears recurring inflationary surges should hold a small portion of her portfolio in a gold fund. Then as inflation really heats up, you can switch an increasing percentage of your assets to the gold fund.

Gold funds, as a useful part of an investor's portfolio, may be overemphasized by many investment commentators. In general, gold fund prices are very volatile and very difficult to anticipate. The risk level of a gold fund (as measured by standard deviation) is about twice that of the average growth fund.

FIVE REPRESENTATIVE GOLD AND PRECIOUS METALS FUNDS

To illustrate, we have chosen five gold and precious metals funds that show the qualities that investors seek when purchasing shares of gold and precious metals funds. Note that four of these examples are no-load funds. Table 18-1 contains a summary listing of the five funds. It is followed by a more detailed description of each fund's objectives and investment philosophy and practice, as well as capsule Profiles of their recent performance.

Investors are reminded that past performance is no indicator of future performance.

Table 18-1: Five Representative Gold and Precious Metals Funds

Fund	Annual Return (%) for 3 Years	S.D.*	Load
Fidelity Precious Metals	18.1	10.3	LL
Golconda Investors Fund	26.0	7.2	NL
Lexington Goldfund	28.4	7.7	NL
United Services Gold Shares	7.4	15.1	NL
Vanguard Specialized Gold & Precious Metals Fund	25.2	8.0	

*Standard deviation: special measure of risk for precious-metal funds. The higher the standard deviation, the greater the risk.

Fidelity Precious Metals Fund

Fidelity Precious Metals Fund seeks capital appreciation.

The Fund holds companies engaged in exploration, mining, processing, or dealing in gold, silver, platinum, diamonds, or other precious metals or minerals. The Fund may also invest in securities of companies that themselves invest in companies engaged in these activities. The Fund is authorized to invest up to 25 percent of its assets in gold bullion and coins.

The five largest holdings as of February 28, 1987, were Free State Consolidated Gold, Vaal Reefs Exploration and Mining, Western Deep Levels Ltd., Hartebeefsfontein Gold Mining, and Southvaal Holdings Ltd.

Investments in gold bullion may help to hedge against inflation and fluctuations in the Fund's securities because at certain times the price of gold has fluctuated less widely than the value of permitted investments in securities. When the Fund purchases bullion, it will only be in a form that is readily marketable and that will be delivered to and stored with a qualified U.S. bank.

As of October 31, 1986, the Fund had 50 percent of its investments in South African gold mine stocks, with 20 percent of its holdings in Canadian mining stocks.

The Fund was the best performing Select (sector) portfolio for Fidelity in 1986. Nevertheless, its annual return for the 3-year period ending January 31, 1987, was only 1.0 percent.

The Fund is over twice as volatile as the typical common stock fund and its performance changes rapidly. It should only be held as a small portion of a portfolio, unless the investor is convinced that runaway inflation is about to occur.

Golconda Investors Fund

Golconda Investors Fund has as its objective capital appreciation, with income secondary.

The Fund concentrates its investments in gold bullion and an internationally diversified portfolio of gold mining shares; it may also invest in other foreign securities. It thereby offers investors seeking to hedge against the loss of purchasing power of the dollar a convenient way to participate in the possible growth and current income from the Fund's securities investments, together with the advantages and appreciation potential of gold itself. The Fund may hold a portion or all of its cash in the form of foreign currencies, part or all or which may be in the form of gold coins.

The Fund will typically hold a significant portion of its assets in gold bullion. The Fund has a relatively high expense ratio since it has a 1 percent 12b-1 annual charge.

The Fund returned 2.6 percent for 1985 and 35 percent for 1986. It is worth considering for a small portion of a portfolio as an inflation hedge. However, remember you are giving up a 1 percent annual charge for the 12b-1 distribution fee.

Lexington Goldfund

Lexington Goldfund's investment objective is to attain capital appreciation and such hedge against loss of buying power as may be obtained through investment in gold and equity securities of companies throughout the world engaged in mining or processing gold.

The Fund will normally hold at least 65 percent of its assets in gold and gold-related securities. In mid-1986, the Fund held over 40 percent of its portfolio in gold bullion.

The Fund had a good return in 1985 and 1986 and returned 28 percent for the three-year period ended August 31, 1987, with a risk level at or below that of other gold funds. The Fund is a solid candidate for those who seek a gold fund as a hedge against inflation.

United Services Gold Shares

The primary investment objective of the United Services Gold Shares Fund is to seek long-term growth of capital as well as protection against inflation and monetary instability. Current income is a secondary objective.

The Fund concentrates its investments in the common stock of companies involved in the exploration for, mining of, processing of, or dealing in gold, with emphasis on stocks of foreign companies. Normally, at least 80 percent of the Fund's total assets are invested in the securities of companies involved in gold operations. The Fund may also invest in the securities of issuers engaged in operations related to silver and other precious metals.

The Fund was started in 1974 and had a long and solid track record during the 1970s. The Fund is quite volatile; it returned -27 percent in 1985 and +38 percent in 1986. Most investors would find that kind of swing unsettling. The annual return for the five years ended January 31, 1987, was only 7 percent.

The Fund is worth considering when you are sure that inflation is up and gold will rise also.

Vanguard Specialized Gold and Precious Metals Fund

Vanguard Specialized Gold and Precious Metals Fund seeks capital appreciation.

The Fund invests in the securities of foreign and domestic companies engaged in the exploration, mining, fabrication, processing, or distribution of gold, silver, platinum, diamonds, or other precious and rare metals and minerals.

The five largest holdings of the Fund as of July 31, 1986, were American Barrick, De Beers, Consolidated Gold, Pan Continental, and Eastmagne Gold Mines. The Fund at that time held 80 percent of its portfolio in common stocks, 8.5 percent in gold bullion, and 6.1 percent in short-term investments. The assets of the Fund as of February 20, 1987 were $54 million.

The Fund declined 5 percent in 1985 and then returned 49.5 percent in 1986. The Fund continued its rise in 1987, reporting a 73.6 percent return in the first eight months of 1987. The performance of the Fund is shown in Figure 18-2.

Chapter 18

Figure 18-2: The Performance of Vanguard Gold Fund Shown with Its 26-Week Moving Average. Note the Cyclical Volatility of the Fund. (Courtesy of Telescan.)

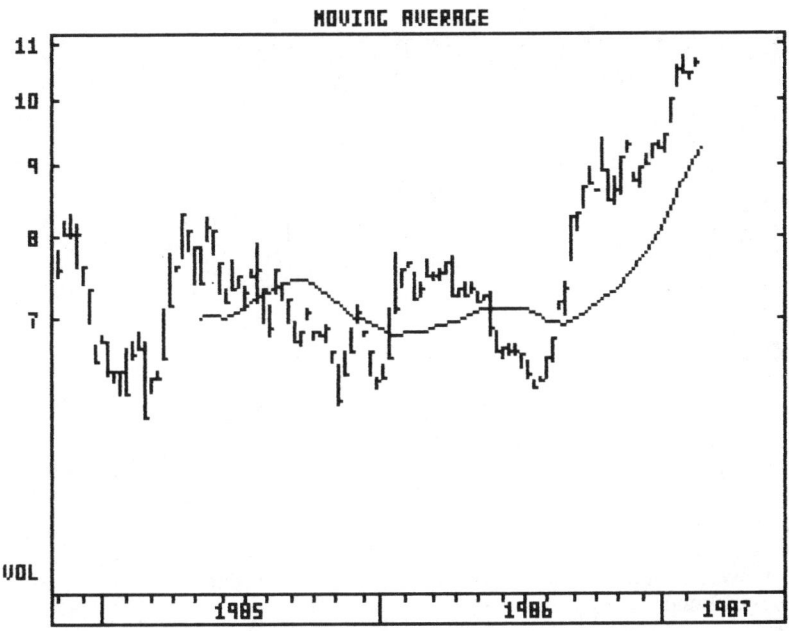

The Fund's net asset value is about twice as volatile as that of the market, as shown in Figure 18-2. Beginning in mid-1986, the Fund's price jumped significantly.

This well-managed Fund is for those who see inflation rising in the near future. Alternatively, secure a prospectus for the Fund and keep it ready for the time that inflation returns. When the Consumer Price Index breaks above 5 or 6 percent, it is time to hold this or a similar fund in your portfolio.

PROFILE 18-1

FIDELITY PRECIOUS METALS FUND
82 Devonshire
Boston, MA 02109
1-800-544-6666
617-523-1919

Fund Classification:	ME
Total Assets:	$188 million
Fund Manager:	Malcolm McNaught
Year of Inception:	1980
Minimum Investment:	1000
Sales Charge:	3.00%
12b-1 Charge:	No
Expense Ratio:	1.48

Portfolio Mix:	%	*Issues*
Bonds	0	0
Convertible Bonds	0	0
Common Stock	90	71
U. S. Government Securities	0	0
Municipal Bonds	0	0
Cash	0	0

Estimated Annual Portfolio Turnover	65%

Estimates of Fund Performance:

Annual Return for Three Years:	0.9%
Annual Return for Five Years:	10.6%
Annual Return in Bull Markets:	
1985	-10.5%
1986	32.8%
Annual Return in Bear Markets:	
6/30/83–6/30/84	-9.89%
Representative Current Yield (1/31/87):	0.7%

Measures of Risk and Reward:

Alpha	NA
Beta	NA
R square	0
Standard deviation	10.27
Reward/risk ratio	0.09

Net Asset Value:	
9/25/87	20.60
10/28/87	14.37

PROFILE 18-2

GOLCONDA INVESTORS FUND
11 Manover Square
New York, NY 10005
1-800-431-6060
212-785-0900

Fund Classification:	ME	
Total Assets:	$33 million	
Fund Manager:	Robert W. Radsch	
Year of Inception:	1957	
Minimum Investment:	1000	
Sales Charge:	No load	
12b-1 Charge:	Yes (1%)	
Expense Ratio:	2.39	

Portfolio Mix:	%	Issues
Bonds	0	0
Convertible Bonds	4.55	3
Common Stock	55.17	34
Preferred Stock	1.42	1
U. S. Government Securities	0	0
Gold Bullion	38.47	NA
Cash	0	0
Estimated Annual Portfolio Turnover	30%	

Estimates of Fund Performance:	
Annual Return for Three Years:	5.9%
Annual Return for Five Years:	5.4%
Annual Return in Bull Markets:	
1985	2.6%
1986	35.0%
Annual Return in Bear Markets:	
6/30/83–6/30/84	-13.3%
Representative Current Yield (1/31/87):	0.2%

Measures of Risk and Reward:	
Alpha	NA
Beta	NA
R square	0
Standard deviation	7.15
Reward/risk ratio	0.83
Net Asset Value:	
9/25/87	22.85
10/28/87	16.28

PROFILE 18-3

LEXINGTON GOLDFUND
P.O. Box 1515 Park 80 West Plaza Two
Saddle Brook, NJ 07662
1-800-526-0057
1-800-526-7443
201-845-7300

Fund Classification:	ME
Total Assets:	$25 million
Fund Manager:	Robert DeMichele
	Bill Stack
Year of Inception:	1975
Minimum Investment:	1000
Sales Charge:	No load
12b-1 Charge:	Yes (0.250%)
Expense Ratio:	1.50

Portfolio Mix:	%	*Issues*
Bonds	0	0
Convertible Bonds	0	0
Common Stock	57.3	27
U. S. Government Securities	0	0
Gold Bullion	40.6	NA
Cash	2.1	1
Estimated Annual Portfolio Turnover	22%	

Estimates of Fund Performance:	
Annual Return for Three Years:	9.6%
Annual Return for Five Years:	NA
Annual Return in Bull Markets:	
1985	13.0%
1986	32.7%
Annual Return in Bear Markets:	
6/30/83–6/30/84	-6.31%

Representative Current Yield (1/31/87):	0.3%

Measures of Risk and Reward:	
Alpha	NA
Beta	NA
R square	0
Standard deviation	7.70
Reward/risk ratio	1.25

Net Asset Value:	
9/25/87	8.14
10/28/87	6.00

PROFILE 18-4

UNITED SERVICES GOLD SHARES
Box 29467
San Antonio, TX 78229
1-800-824-4653
512-696-1234

Fund Classification:	ME
Total Assets:	$292 million
Fund Manager:	Brad Heaston
Year of Inception:	1974
Minimum Investment:	500
Sales Charge:	No load
12b-1 Charge:	No
Expense Ratio:	1.27

Portfolio Mix:	%	*Issues*
Bonds	0	0
Convertible Bonds	0	0
Common Stock	98	31
U. S. Government Securities	0	0
Gold Bullion	0	0
Cash	0	0
Estimated Annual Portfolio Turnover	14%	

Estimates of Fund Performance:	
Annual Return for Three Years:	-7.1%
Annual Return for Five Years:	6.7%
Annual Return in Bull Markets:	
1985	-27.0%
1986	37.5%
Annual Return in Bear Markets:	
6/30/83–6/30/84	-7.0%
Representative Current Yield (1/31/87):	1.04%

Measures of Risk and Reward:	
Alpha	NA
Beta	NA
R square	0
Standard deviation	15.1
Reward/risk ratio	0.64

Net Asset Value:	
9/25/87	7.23
10/28/87	5.40

PROFILE 18-5

VANGUARD SPECIALIZED GOLD AND PRECIOUS METALS FUND
Vanguard Financial Ctr.
Valley Forge, PA 19482
1-800-662-7447
1-800-662-2739
In PA 1-800-362-0530

Fund Classification:	ME
Total Assets:	$53 million
Fund Manager:	L. E. Linaker
Year of Inception:	1974
Minimum Investment:	1500
Sales Charge:	1.00%
12b-1 Charge:	No
Expense Ratio:	0.73

Portfolio Mix:	%	*Issues*
Bonds	4.2	1
Convertible Bonds	0	0
Common Stock	80.2	56
U. S. Government Securities	0	0
Gold Bullion	8.5	NA
Cash	0	0
Estimated Annual Portfolio Turnover	41%	

Estimates of Fund Performance:	
Annual Return for Three Years:	NA
Annual Return for Five Years:	NA
Annual Return in Bull Markets:	
1985	-5.1%
1986	49.5%
Annual Return in Bear Markets:	
6/30/83–6/30/84	NA
Representative Current Yield (1/31/87):	2.0%

Measures of Risk and Reward:	
Alpha	NA
Beta	NA
R square	5
Standard deviation	8.0
Reward/risk ratio	3.23
Net Asset Value:	
9/25/87	16.34
10/28/87	11.73

Chapter 19
Specialized and Sector Funds

BACKGROUND INFORMATION

Type of Security

A specialized common stock fund seeks to achieve its objective by concentrating its holdings in a single industry or group of related industries, in a single geographical region, or in companies that have some common characteristics. These funds usually invest in the common stocks of high-quality companies that offer unique investment opportunities. Long-term capital growth is a common objective, although current dividend income is also sought. Specialty industries such as electronics, gold, chemicals, and the health field are popular candidates for specialty funds.

Sector funds, a form of specialty mutual funds, offer investors the opportunity to own portfolios concentrated on various segments of the stock market. Unlike well-diversified funds that embrace many different industries, these funds focus on areas of the stock market that tend to be very active. If you think energy, technology or health stocks are ready for gains, this is a convenient way to buy that sector of the market and obtain a diversified, working portfolio of stocks that will benefit if the sector moves. If your hunch proves correct, the potential rewards are great.

In the past half-dozen years, sector mutual funds have multiplied more than five times in numbers to 112 and nearly sevenfold in assets to $11.6 billion.

An investor can obtain sector funds that specialize in technology issues, utilities, banks, insurance companies, defense and aerospace firms, leisure and entertainment stocks, medical technology, government securities, regions of the United States and financial services.

Gold funds are discussed in Chapter 18, energy and utility funds in Chapter 16, and technology funds are covered in Chapter 15.

Another way in which funds can specialize is by selecting stocks whose common characteristics are defined by the makeup of an index. These index funds have an objective of duplicating the composite performance of an index such as the S&P 500 index. The returns of funds match the performance of the index.

Risk/Stability

During periods of stagnant overall stock market activity, specific sectors within the market will perform well. If you can choose the right sector funds, you can gain while the rest of the market is stalled. And by using a family of specialized funds, you can try to anticipate when market leadership begins to rotate from one sector to another and then switch to the more promising sector fund.

Specialty funds offer the opportunity of sharp capital gains in cases where the fund's industry is "in favor," but they also entail the risk of capital losses when the industry is out of favor. Consequently, they are suitable for investors who can monitor industry performance regularly and alter investment strategies accordingly.

One must recognize that investing in single industry involves unsystematic risk that can be avoided with broader diversification. (Unsystematic, or diversifiable, risk is that which is unique to an industry. Labor strikes and shifts in consumer preferences are examples of unique risks that can cause industry returns to vary.) However, there are times when you may want to target your investments to a particular industry—perhaps one that you perceive as currently undervalued.

To their critics, sector funds defeat the main purpose of mutual-fund investing—risk reduction through diversification. Sector funds offer more risk and no better performance long-term for most investors. Many critics contend that most investors aren't smart enough to pick which sector will do well and which will nose-dive.

Excluding gold funds, which are really a separate breed, just 27 percent of sector funds beat the S&P 500 index for all of 1986 (which gained 18.7 percent with dividends reinvested).

SPECIAL BENEFITS AND EXPOSURES

Control

The excitement of sector investing lies in the control it gives you over your investment decisions. When you buy a broad-based mutual fund, you're choosing an investment objective—the portfolio manager is free to allocate the fund's assets in whatever way he or she feels will best meet that objective.

With a sector fund, *you* decide what part of the economy seems most promising to you and choose a sector. Once that important decision is made, you should monitor the events taking place in that sector. But you don't have to spend your time researching companies and making buy and sell decisions. The portfolio's expert manager works full time to provide you with the best possible performances—taying on top of developments in the industry and in individual companies, and actively trading stocks within the portfolio.

Downside Risk

Because such funds invest primarily in one sector, they do not offer the element of downside risk protection found in mutual funds that invest in a broad range of industries. However, such funds do enable investors to diversify holdings among many companies within an industry, a more conservative approach than investing directly in the shares of one particular company.

A calculation by Massachusetts Financial Services underlines the opportunities—and hazards—of switching between different sectors of the stock market. It shows that an investor who started out with $10,000 in 1980 and made the right switch every year would have had $97,043 at the end of 1986. But one who made all the wrong switches would have had only $3,314.

Timing Expertise

"Unfortunately, there is plenty of evidence to suggest that ordinary investors are more likely to make their moves at the wrong, rather than the right, time," says Paul McMahon, Portfolio Manager of MFS Managed Sectors Trust.

McMahon says most people move into a sector of the market only when a strong rise has attracted attention to it. "By then it is often too late. Winning sectors generally do not remain on top for long—and when they fall, they can fall fast."

PORTFOLIO FIT

A specialized fund or a sector fund are concentrated in one part of the market. Thus, they are not as diversified as the stock market and growth funds. Consequently, they will fluctuate widely as the special sector changes in performance or favor with investors.

Specialized funds are typically more risky than the general market and fluctuate more. On the other hand, they enable you to select one industry that you believe will do very well. For example, you can purchase a health-care fund and participate in the general growth of the health-care industry. Similarly, you can select the financial services or the leisure industries. Sector funds are about as volatile as an aggressive growth fund and belong in the portfolio of an aggressive investor.

Vanguard Index Trust is a specialized fund that mirrors the stock market in return and risk. Many investors will want to hold a portion of their portfolio in such a fund since it is a simple, low-cost way to participate in the overall market return.

Families of specialty funds are offered by Fidelity, Vanguard, and Financial Programs. Sector investing can be an attractive strategy. But because they carry somewhat higher risk and require more involvement on your part, it may be best to allocate only a portion of your investments to specialized or sector funds. My suggestion is no more than 10 percent.

EIGHT REPRESENTATIVE SPECIALIZED AND SECTOR FUNDS

To illustrate, we have chosen eight specialized and sector funds that show the qualities that investors seek when purchasing shares of specialized and sector funds. Note that five of these examples are no-load funds. Table 19-1 contains a summary listing of the eight funds. It is followed by a more detailed description of each fund's objectives and investment philosophy and practice, as well as capsule Profiles of their recent performance.

Investors are reminded that past performance is no indicator of future performance.

Table 19-1: Eight Representative Specialized and Sector Funds

Fund	Annual Return (%) for 3 Years	Return to Risk Ratio	Load
Century Shares Trust Fund	28.5	5.6	NL
Fidelity Select Financial Services Portfolio Fund	30.9	6.6	LL
Fidelity Select Health Care Portfolio Fund	40.2	6.3	LL
Fidelity Select Leisure Fund	34.6	7.1	LL
IAI North Star Regional Fund	26.7	6.5	NL
Vanguard Index Trust Fund	26.3	6.3	NL
Vanguard Specialized Health Care Portfolio	33.0	6.6	NL
Vanguard Specialized Service Economy Portfolio	27.3	5.6	NL

Century Shares Trust Fund

Century Shares Trust Fund seeks capital appreciation.

The Fund is concentrated in the securities of insurance companies and banks. In other words, it holds a sector of the U.S. service economy and reaps its benefits from specialized, long-term research analysis and portfolio management in the insurance and bank sector.

The insurance business has grown more rapidly than the economy and not all stocks move together so the value of analysis can be high. Century has a low turnover rate of about 5 percent annually and holds stocks long-term. Most companies held in the portfolio are medium capitalization firms with revenues of $500–$800 million. The price/earnings ratio of the holdings are less than the market ratio.

While Century has an at-market risk (beta = 1.01), it has returned an excellent performance over up and down periods. Century Shares has grown to $141 million by 2/28/87 with a yield of 2.4 percent. It has a sterling 3-year and 5-year record and has returned 16 percent for the first two months of 1986.

The Fund had an annual return of 22.9 percent over the 5-year period ended 2/28/87 and only dropped 5.7 percent in contrast to -16.5 percent for the S&P 500 during the recessionary period 11/30/80–7/31/82.

Century was founded in 1928 and is managed by Mr. Allan Fulkerson, who joined Century in 1966 and became Chairman in 1976. Mr. Fulkerson and Mr. William Dyer manage the daily operations and specialize in following 150 insurance and bank stocks.

Mr. Allan Fulkerson, Chairman and Managing Trustee, said on February 6, 1987: "Currently, we look for a sustained period of further progress for earnings and dividends which should, over time, be reflected in continued worthwhile investments. ...We believe that Trust is positioned to benefit from the growth and profitability of exciting industries. While markets are transitory and short-term results will fluctuate, we look forward to producing competitive returns in the years immediately ahead."

The life insurance business has doubled every eight to ten years since the turn of the century. Insurance needs grow and the companies keep coming up with new products. The Fund has a modest expense ratio of 0.77 and an R-squared coefficient of 71. The R coefficient means 71 percent of the Fund's risk is market-related and the other 29 percent is attributable to the Fund's unique characteristics.

The Fund is an excellent sector fund for the long-term investor.

Note on the Fidelity Sector Family

Hourly Pricing. The Fidelity Select funds are specialized or sector funds with several portfolios concentrated in specific industries. Fidelity Select portfolios are priced every hour during the New York Stock Exchange's normal business hours, whereas most other mutual funds are priced only once a day. Hourly pricing allows you to more closely match your transactions to what is taking place on the trading floor. It gives you more control over the timing of your investment transactions.

Short Selling. Fidelity also permits "shorting" eight of their sector funds. Selling a fund or a stock short means that you're betting that the price will fall. To do so, you sell borrowed stock in the hope of buying it back later at a lower price.

In a sense Fidelity Select funds are a cross between a mutual fund and individual stocks with hourly trading and the possibility of shorting them. To participate in short selling, one must have an account with Fidelity Brokerage.

Zero Net Income. Another unique characteristic of Fidelity Select funds is the statement in the prospectus: "Although we have multiple Portfolios, we are treated as a single entity for federal income tax purposes. Consequently, gains from one Portfolio will not be distributed if they can be offset by losses in another Portfolio." This means that none of the Fidelity sector funds can be expected to produce income, even if securities in its sector are traditionally income-producing, as in the case of Select Utilities and Select Energy.

Fidelity Select Financial Services Portfolio Fund

Fidelity Select Financial Services Portfolio is one portfolio sponsored by Fidelity Investments of Boston. The objective of the Fund is to "provide focused growth in the financial services industry," as described by Michael Hines of Fidelity.

Fidelity Financial holds common stocks and bonds, convertible stocks, and a minority of corporate bonds of financial institutions such as banks, insurance companies, real estate investment trusts, securities brokers, and savings and loans. The Fund searches for companies that can capitalize on lower interest rates, new efficiencies, and the demands for mortgages and insurance.

The seven largest holdings are Meridian Bankcorp, Student Loan Marketing, NBD Bankcorp, Marine Midland, Security Pacific, Shawmut Bank, and Loews Corp. The Fund holds approximately 100 stocks focused in the financial services sector, which accounts for 6.5 percent of the total stock market. The Fund had a portfolio turnover of 136 percent for the year ended April 30, 1986. The expense ratio for the year ended October 31, 1986, was 1.26 percent and the Fund has a 3 percent load (2 percent at purchase and 1 percent at redemption). On October 31, 1986, the Fund held its assets in: banks, 51 percent; insurance, 19.3 percent.

Fidelity Financial had $93 million in assets on February 28, 1986, and had a return of 15.1 percent for 1986. The Fund performed well over the five-year period ended 2/28/87, resulting in a compound average annual return of 30 percent. This was achieved with a beta of only 0.97. The performance of the Fund is shown in Figure 19-1.

"Financial services fits the disinflation, low-interest rate theme," Michael Hines stated. Beginning in mid-1982, Fidelity Financial has performed amazingly well due to the disinflationary movements. As long as the nation is protected from inflationary pressures, the Fund should do well. It has a risk factor about equal to the S&P 500 (beta = 0.96) and yet has outperformed the market over the past four years.

As the Manager, Mr. Warren Casey, stated recently: "In my viewpoint, one characteristic is that, generally, this Portfolio will perform well in a low interest rate environment. The Portfolio is composed of companies in the areas of commercial and retail banking and lending—like money center banks, regional banks, savings and loan associations and finance companies. There are also insurance companies of all kinds—including life or property and casualty—securities investment, leasing and real estate. And all of these stocks are sensitive to interest rate changes."

Fidelity Financial Services should do well as long as interest rates and inflation remains low.

Figure 19-1: The Performance of the Fidelity Financial Services Fund Shown with Its 26-Week Moving Average. (Courtesy of Telescan.)

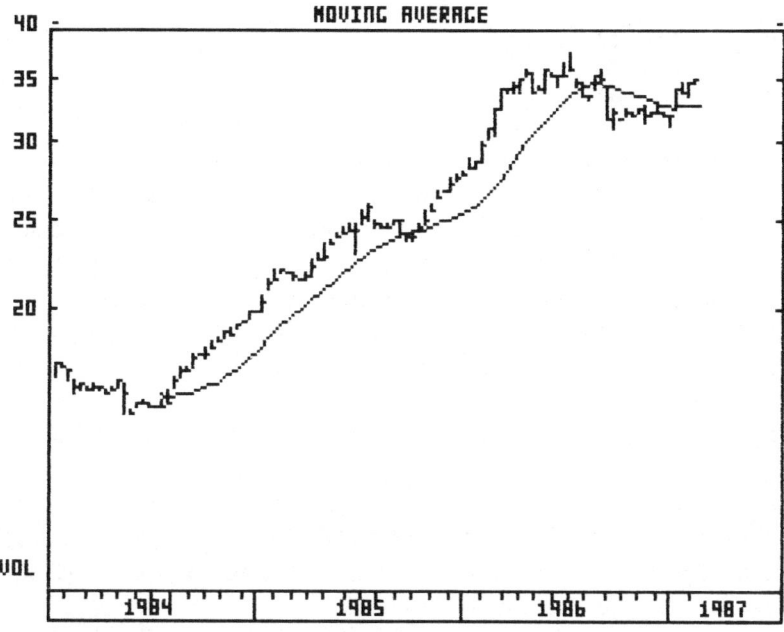

Fidelity Select Health Care Portfolio Fund

Fidelity Select Health Care Portfolio seeks capital appreciation.

The Fund invests in companies engaged in the design, manufacture, or sale of products or companies used for or in connection with health care or medicine. Companies in the health-care field include pharmaceutical companies; firms that design, manufacture, sell or supply medical, dental, and optical products, hardware, or services; companies involved in biotechnology, medical diagnostic, and biochemical research and development, as well as companies involved in the operation of health-care facilities. Many of these companies are subject to governmental regulation of their products and services, a factor that could have a significant and possibly unfavorable impact on the price and availability of such products or services. Furthermore, the types of products or services produced or provided by these companies may become obsolete quickly.

Fidelity Health Care provided excellent returns for 1985 and 1986 as well as a very good return over the 5 years ended 2/28/87. However, this is a volatile fund with a standard deviation of 6.38 percent (50 percent above that of the market). If it is a long-term holding, it should do well, but it is a very difficult sector to switch in and out of. Note that the Fund dropped 26 percent during the down market of 6/30/83–6/30/84—compared to the drop of the S&P of 5 percent. On the other hand, the Fund was up 32 percent for the first two months of 1987.

In spite of the risk, it may be attractive to invest in the Fund, since it represents a growing and vibrant sector of the economy.

Fidelity Select Leisure Fund

Fidelity Select Leisure Fund seeks capital appreciation.

The Fund has 150 securities in the portfolio and is very well diversified across several industries. The Fund invests in companies engaged in the design, production, or distribution of goods or services in the leisure industries, such as television and radio broadcast (including cable television), motion pictures and photography, recordings and musical instruments, publishing (including newspapers and magazines), sporting goods and camping and recreational equipment, and sports arenas. Some other activities of companies in the Fund's portfolio are those related to toys and games (including video and electronic), amusement and theme parks, travel-related services, hotels and motels, fast-food and other restaurants, and gaming casinos.

The five largest holdings are Harcourt, Brace, Jovanovich; Washington Post Co.; Rogers Cable Systems; Macmillan Inc.; and Hasbro Bradley Co.

The Fidelity Select Leisure Fund is a sector fund that was initiated on May 8, 1984. The assets have grown to $94 million over the 3-year period of its existence. The Fund had provided a total return of 81 percent over the 2-year period ended 12/31/86. The beta of the Fund is estimated to be a relatively low 1.05.

When oil prices decline, as they did in 1986–87, the tendency is for people to vacation in the U.S., and we can expect the leisure sector to benefit. In addition, when the stock market increases and the GNP rises, people feel more wealthy and tend to spend more on leisure products, restaurants, travel, lodging, sporting goods, and the like.

The Portfolio Manager is Carol Ramsey, who says: "If an investor wants to be in cash, he'll do it in his account. I do the best I can to be fully invested."

As Michael Hines, Manager of the sector funds, stated: "The best strategy for the Leisure Fund would have been to have bought it on day one and held on to it." This low-load Fund is well managed to obtain the benefits of a growing leisure services sector. The profits of companies in this sector grew during 1986.

The leisure sector represents about 5 percent or more of the total stock market. This sector fund is well-diversified and suitable for a buy and hold strategy. Fidelity Leisure is a good selection for the growth-oriented investor. The performance of the Fund is shown in Figure 19-2.

Figure 19-2: The Performance of Fidelity Select Leisure for the Period 6/1/84 to 9/4/87. (Courtesy of Equity Fund Research.)

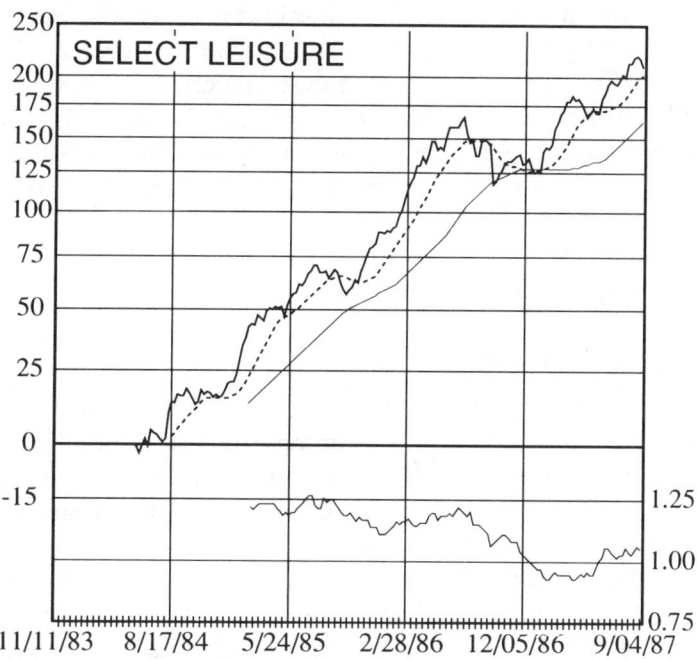

IAI North Star Regional Fund

The objective of IAI North Star Regional Fund is capital appreciation.

The Fund pursues its objective by investing at least 80 percent of its equity investments in companies that have their headquarters in Minnesota, Wisconsin, Iowa, Nebraska, Montana, North Dakota, or South Dakota. Along with investments in nationally recognized companies, Regional Fund's portfolio generally includes some companies not as well known because they are newer or have a small capitalization, but that offer the potential for capital appreciation.

The northern Midwest region may not seem the most likely area for a young fund to look for growth. But the Fund believes it is in the best possible place to find and monitor a variety of growth-oriented companies.

While IAI North Star Regional Fund focuses on small companies, it looks for all investment opportunities that have not yet gone public. The heavy concentration of business in the area "spawns the entrepreneurial" and there are spinoffs of good ideas, he said. The $90 million-in-assets Fund is allowed to invest up to 10 percent of its assets in restricted securities.

The five largest holdings of the Fund are Medtronic Inc., Pillsbury Co., Minnesota Mining & Manufacturing Co., Snap-On Tools Corp., and NWA Inc.

The Fund Manager, Julian Carlin, is based in Minneapolis and relies on close contact with the regional companies he invests in. He said it is especially important to be near small companies, since larger ones, such as Dayton-Hudson Corp. and Minnesota Mining & Manufacturing Co., are followed by analysts nationally. Carlin joined Investment Advisors, Inc. (IAI) in 1974 and has managed other portfolios for the firm. He has been in charge of IAI North Star Regional Fund since its inception in 1980.

The risk of IAI North Star Regional is about that of the S&P 500. However, its performance has exceeded that of the Index.

The Fund is for the investor who seeks capital appreciation through the growth of the northern Midwest region of the United States.

Vanguard Index Trust Fund

It is an investor's goal to find mutual funds that consistently provide returns that exceed the market return on a risk-adjusted basis. For the five-year period December 31, 1981, to December 31, 1986, the average equity mutual fund rose 137 percent while the market as measured by the S&P 500 rose 147 percent. Over the past 15 years almost two-thirds of all mutual funds underperformed the S&P 500.

According to the efficient market theory, attempting to beat the market is futile. So while an investor is searching for funds that provide above-average risk-adjusted returns, why not consider purchasing a fund that provides the full market return as measured by the S&P 500 index? This type of fund is appropriately called an *index fund*.

One of the few such funds available is the Vanguard Index Trust. The trust managers simply maintain a portfolio that matches the S&P 500 as closely as practical. For example, in 1985, it outperformed 77 percent of all equity and bond funds with a total return of 31.2 percent, while the S&P 500 actually returned 31.6 percent. The Index Trust had a very low expense ratio of 0.28 percent.

Vanguard Index returned 26.3 annually over the 3-year period ended February 28, 1987. It is an excellent choice during strong up markets and can be exchanged for a money market or bond fund during obvious down markets.

As John Bogle of Vanguard recently said: "Having set forth the advantages of indexing, allow us to debunk an indexing myth: 'Indexing guarantees mediocrity.' What is so mediocre about achieving a 'top quartile' performance over time, while virtually eliminating your risk of being 'at the bottom of the heap'?"

Vanguard Index is bought by those who seek the market return at the regular market risk (beta = 1.0). It will capture the good years and you can switch out in the bad years. If you believe that the market will climb upward for the next two or three years, you can buy the Index Trust and simply put it in a safe place for semi-annual review. The person who likes

Chapter 19 273

the efficient market theory or simply desires the market return during the good years should consider Vanguard Index Trust.

Vanguard Specialized Health Care Portfolio

Vanguard Special Health Care Portfolio is one of five specialized or sector portfolios in the Vanguard family of funds. The Portfolio seeks capital appreciation.

The Portfolio invests in the securities of companies engaged in the development, production, or distribution of products and services related to the treatment or prevention of diseases and other medical infirmities. Companies in this field include pharmaceutical firms; companies that design, manufacture, or sell medical supplies, equipment and support services; and companies that operate hospitals and other health-care facilities. The Portfolio also considers for investment companies engaged in medical, diagnostic, biochemical, and biotechnological research and development.

Vanguard Health currently has $43 million in assets. Its portfolio turnover was 32 percent and its expense ratio 0.83 percent for the year ended December 31, 1986. The five largest holdings are Sterling Drug, Schering-Plough, Hospital Corp. of America, National Medical Enterprises, and Novo Industries. The performance of the Portfolio is shown in Figure 19-3.

Figure 19-3: The Performance of the Vanguard Health Care Fund Shown with Its 26-Week Moving Average. (Courtesy of Telescan.)

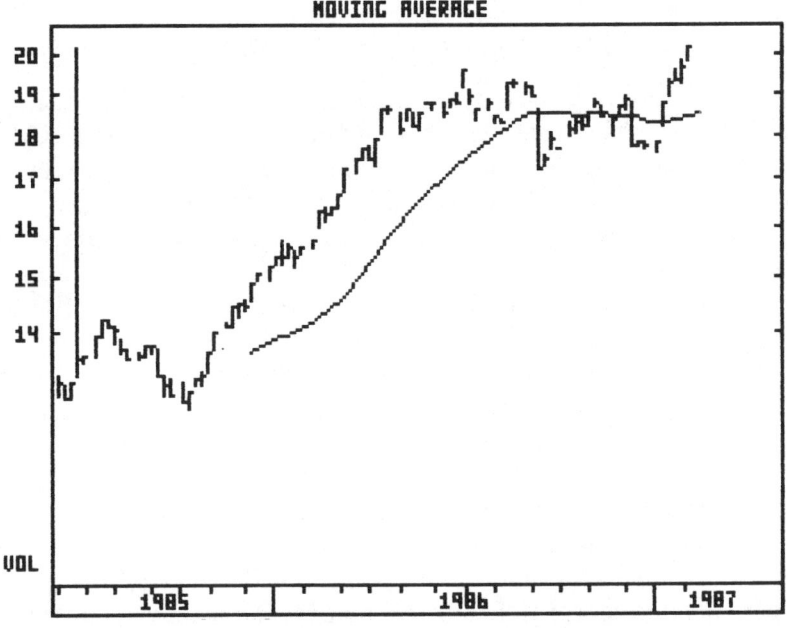

One of the risks in the health-care sector is the highly regulated environment for drugs and instruments.

The continuing management of this Portfolio by the team of Ed Owens and Joseph Schwartz of Wellington Management Co. is important to its success.

Ed Owens joined Wellington after receiving his Harvard MBA in 1974, while Joe Schwartz joined Wellington in 1983 after 11 years in the financial analysis business. Schwartz follows the medical services (25 percent of assets) and the medical technology industries (15 percent) while Owens tracks pharmaceuticals (45 percent) and international health stocks (15 percent). They follow a longer-term, value-oriented approach in their stock selections and currently hold a portfolio of about 60 common stocks.

Owens and Schwartz seek companies that provide consistent innovation. They describe the health sector as a "dynamic sector." They explained, "It is 10 percent of the economy and of growing significance due to the aging of the population." They expect health-care companies to be beneficiaries of tax reform due to lower tax rates. The health-care sector, it should be noted, is fairly well insulated from the effects of both inflation and recession.

Vanguard Health has performed well since its inception in May 1984. It also held up well during the 1986 third quarter drop due to its diversification into international stocks. Vanguard Health Care is an excellent fund for a portfolio. Many should consider it for 5 percent of their total portfolio of funds.

The Portfolio is suitable for the longer-term investor who seeks good returns by participating in the consistently increasing health-care sector and can accommodate occasional swings.

Vanguard Specialized Service Economy Portfolio

Vanguard Service Economy is one of five specialized or sector portfolios offered by Vanguard Group. As the name indicates, it focuses on the service sector of the U.S. economy. Its objective is long-term capital appreciation through investment in the service sector.

The Portfolio has a low expense ratio of 0.57 percent for the year ended December 31, 1986. The portfolio turnover for the same period was 54 percent. The Portfolio holds about 80 stocks and the top five holdings are Commerce Clearing House, Gap Stores, Capital Cities Communication, May Department Stores, and City Federal Financial.

There has been a shift in the U.S. economy from companies that produce capital goods (including manufacturing, mining, and agricultural firms) to firms that produce consumer goods and that provide services and products to both consumers and corporations. The Portfolio uses the term "service economy" to designate this expanding group of industries. Specifically, the Portfolio focuses on the securities of companies that provide financial services, information and media services, business services, and consumer services.

Financial service companies include banks, savings and loans, insurance carriers, leasing companies, and providers of financial technology. Companies involved in providing media and information services and products include newspaper publishers, book publishers, radio and television broadcasters, motion picture companies, transportation companies, computer service companies, waste-service firms, package express companies, and distributors of industrial and pharmaceutical products. Companies providing consumer services and/or distributing consumer-related products include hotels and providers of amusement and recreation services. Finally, retail and distribution includes food service, retailers, and department stores.

The Portfolio has performed quite well since its inception on May 23, 1984. As a result, the Portfolio has grown to $48 million in assets. Wellington Management Company is the portfolio manager.

According to Mr. Silvester Marquardt of Wellington Management, one of a team responsible for the Portfolio, the service sector offers "excellent pricing flexibility, excess cash flow for expansion, and low risk of international competition." He stated that "earnings growth is good for this sector and it is advisable to consider this fund as a buy and hold."

As long as the nation's economy is relatively strong and consumers maintain strong buying patterns, one can profit from the Portfolio's strong performance. One could buy and hold this Portfolio, perhaps selling during a large economic downturn. One can switch at no charge to a money-market fund or one of the other sector funds, which include a gold fund as well as an energy sector fund. The perofrmance of the Fund is shown in Figure 19-4.

Figure 19-4: The Performance of Vanguard Specialized Service Economy for the Period 6/1/84 to 9/4/87.

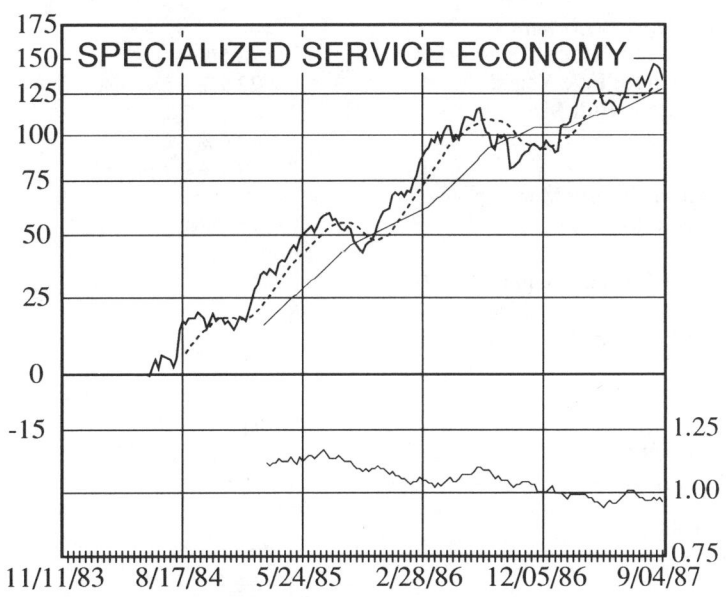

PROFILE 19-1

CENTURY SHARES TRUST FUND
One Liberty Square
Boston, MA 02109
1-800-321-1928
617-482-3060

Fund Classification:	S	
Total Assets:	$141 million	
Fund Manager:	Allan Fulkerson	
Year of Inception:	1928	
Minimum Investment:	$500	
Sales Charge:	No load	
12b-1 Charge:	No	
Expense Ratio:	0.77	

Portfolio Mix:	%	*Issues*
Bonds	4	4
Convertible Bonds	0	0
Preferred Stock	0	0
Common Stock	96	33
U. S. Government Securities	0	0
Cash	0	0
Estimated Annual Portfolio Turnover	6%	

Estimates of Fund Performance:	
Annual Return for Three Years:	28.5%
Annual Return for Five Years:	22.9%
Annual Return in Bull Markets:	
1985	42.6%
1986	9.4%
Annual Return in Bear Markets:	
6/30/83–6/30/84	-1.85%
Representative Current Yield (2/28/87):	2.4%

Measures of Risk and Reward:	
Alpha	2.7
Beta	1.01
R square	71
Standard deviation	5.07
Reward/risk ratio	5.6

Net Asset Value:	
9/25/87	20.14
10/28/87	16.33

PROFILE 19-2

FIDELITY SELECT FINANCIAL SERVICES PORTFOLIO FUND
82 Devonshire
Boston, MA 02109
1-800-544-6666
617-523-1919

Fund Classification:	S	
Total Assets:	$93 million	
Fund Manager:	Warren Casey	
Year of Inception:	1980	
Minimum Investment:	$1000	
Sales Charge:	3.0%	
12b-1 Charge:	No	
Expense Ratio:	1.26	
Portfolio Mix:	%	*Issues*
Bonds	0	0
Convertible Bonds	0	0
Preferred Stock	0	0
Common Stock	89.9	116
U. S. Government Securities	0	0
Short-Term Obligations	9.2	NA
Estimated Annual Portfolio Turnover	136%	
Estimates of Fund Performance:		
Annual Return for Three Years:	30.9%	
Annual Return for Five Years:	29.6%	
Annual Return in Bull Markets:		
1985	41.2%	
1986	15.1%	
Annual Return in Bear Markets:		
6/30/83–6/30/84	-0.40%	
Representative Current Yield (2/28/87):	0.6%	
Measures of Risk and Reward:		
Alpha	5.3	
Beta	.97	
R square	77	
Standard deviation	4.67	
Reward/risk ratio	6.6	
Net Asset Value:		
9/25/87	34.12	
10/28/87	25.15	

PROFILE 19-3

FIDELITY SELECT HEALTH CARE PORTFOLIO FUND
82 Devonshire
Boston, MA 02109
1-800-544-6666
617-523-1919

Fund Classification:	S	
Total Assets:	$229 million	
Fund Manager:	William Hayes	
Year of Inception:	1980	
Minimum Investment:	$1000	
Sales Charge:	3.00%	
12b-1 Charge:	No	
Expense Ratio:	1.28	
Portfolio Mix:	%	*Issues*
Bonds	0	0
Convertible Bonds	0	0
Preferred Stock	0	0
Common Stock	92.3	110
U. S. Government Securities	0	0
Short-Term Obligations	7.7	NA
Estimated Annual Portfolio Turnover	217%	
Estimates of Fund Performance:		
Annual Return for Three Years:	40.2%	
Annual Return for Five Years:	32.8%	
Annual Return in Bull Markets:		
1985	59.4%	
1986	22.0%	
Annual Return in Bear Markets:		
6/30/83–6/30/84	-25.6%	
Representative Current Yield (2/28/87):	0.0%	
Measures of Risk and Reward:		
Alpha	1.6	
Beta	1.35	
R square	81	
Standard deviation	6.38	
Reward/risk ratio	6.3	
Net Asset Value:		
9/25/87	45.16	
10/28/87	29.96	

PROFILE 19-4

FIDELITY SELECT LEISURE FUND
82 Devonshire
Boston, MA 02109
1-800-544-6666
617-523-1919

Fund Classification:	S
Total Assets:	$94 million
Fund Manager:	Carol Ramsey
Year of Inception:	1984
Minimum Investment:	$1000
Sales Charge:	3.0%
12b-1 Charge:	No
Expense Ratio:	1.41

Portfolio Mix:	%	*Issues*
Bonds	0	0
Corporate Bonds	2.0	NA
Preferred Stock	0	0
Common Stock	83.7	141
U. S. Government Securities	0	0
Short-Term Obligations	14.2	NA
Estimated Annual Portfolio Turnover	148%	

Estimates of Fund Performance:	
Annual Return for Three Years:	NA
Annual Return for Five Years:	NA
Annual Return in Bull Markets:	
1985	56.6%
1986	15.7%
Annual Return in Bear Markets:	
6/30/86–9/30/86	-1.57%
Representative Current Yield (2/28/87):	0.0%

Measures of Risk and Reward:	
Alpha	NA
Beta	1.05
R square	NA
Standard deviation	4.9
Reward/risk ratio	7.1
Net Asset Value:	
9/25/87	28.67
10/28/87	19.18

PROFILE 19-5

IAI NORTH STAR REGIONAL FUND
1100 Dain Tower
P.O. Box 1160
Minneapolis, MN 55440
612-371-2884
612-371-7780

Fund Classification:	S	
Total Assets:	$89 million	
Fund Manager:	Julian P. Carlin	
Year of Inception:	1980	
Minimum Investment:	$2500	
Sales Charge:	No load	
12b-1 Charge:	No	
Expense Ratio:	0.80	

Portfolio Mix:	%	*Issues*
Bonds	0	0
Corporate Bonds	0	0
Preferred Stock	0	0
Common Stock	81.47	37
Restricted Securities	5.1	11
U. S. Government Securities	0	0
Cash	12.6	7
Estimated Annual Portfolio Turnover	112%	

Estimates of Fund Performance:	
Annual Return for Three Years:	26.7%
Annual Return for Five Years:	26.3%
Annual Return in Bull Markets:	
1985	38.4%
1986	22.8%
Annual Return in Bear Markets:	
6/30/83–6/30/84	-12.7%

Representative Current Yield (2/28/87): 1.8%

Measures of Risk and Reward:	
Alpha	1.0
Beta	1.90
R square	83
Standard deviation	4.13
Reward/risk ratio	6.5

Net Asset Value:	
9/25/87	21.20
10/28/87	15.81

PROFILE 19-6

VANGUARD INDEX TRUST FUND
Valley Forge, PA 19482
1-800-662-7447
In PA 1-800-362-0530

Fund Classification:	S
Total Assets:	$485 million
Fund Manager:	Kevin Johnson
Year of Inception:	1975
Minimum Investment:	$1500
Sales Charge:	No load
12b-1 Charge:	No
Expense Ratio:	0.28

Portfolio Mix:	%	*Issues*
Bonds	0	0
Convertible Bonds	0	0
Preferred Stock	0	0
Common Stock	NA	505
U. S. Government Securities	0	0
Municipal Bonds	0	0
Cash	0	0
Estimated Annual Portfolio Turnover	36%	

Estimates of Fund Performance:	
Annual Return for Three Years:	26.3%
Annual Return for Five Years:	24.9%
Annual Return in Bull Markets:	
1985	31.2%
1986	18.2%
Annual Return in Bear Markets:	
6/30/83–6/30/84	-4.87%
Representative Current Yield (2/28/87):	2.9%

Measures of Risk and Reward:	
Alpha	0.2
Beta	1.00
R square	100
Standard deviation	4.19
Reward/risk ratio	6.3
Net Asset Value:	
9/25/87	32.32
10/28/87	23.43

PROFILE 19-7

VANGUARD SPECIALIZED HEALTH CARE
Vanguard Financial Ctr.
Valley Forge, PA 19482
1-800-662-7447
1-800-662-2739
In PA 1-800-362-0530

Fund Classification:	S	
Total Assets:	$43 million	
Fund Manager:	Ed Owens	
	Joseph Schwartz	
Year of Inception:	1984	
Minimum Investment:	$1500	
Sales Charge:	1.00%	
12b-1 Charge:	No	
Expense Ratio:	0.61	

Portfolio Mix:	%	*Issues*
Bonds	0	0
Convertible Bonds	1.7	3
Preferred Stock	0	0
Common Stock	89.6	59
U. S. Government Securities	0	0
Cash	0	0
Estimated Annual		
Portfolio Turnover	32%	

Estimates of Fund Performance:	
Annual Return for Three Years:	NA
Annual Return for Five Years:	NA
Annual Return in Bull Markets:	
1985	45.7%
1986	21.5%
Annual Return in Bear Markets:	
6/30/86–9/30/86	-6.5%
Representative Current Yield (2/28/87):	1.1%

Measures of Risk and Reward:	
Alpha	NA
Beta	1.0
R square	NA
Standard deviation	5.0
Reward/risk ratio	6.6

Net Asset Value:	
9/25/87	22.46
10/28/87	15.33

Chapter 19   283

PROFILE 19-8

VANGUARD SPECIALIZED SERVICE ECONOMY
P.O. Box 2600
Valley Forge, PA 19482
1-800-662-7447
1-800-662-2739
215-648-6000

Fund Classification:	S
Total Assets:	$48 million
Fund Manager:	Gene Tremblay
	Silvester Marquardt
Year of Inception:	1984
Minimum Investment:	$1500
Sales Charge:	1.00%
12b-1 Charge:	No
Expense Ratio:	0.48

Portfolio Mix:	%	Issues
Bonds	2.1	5
Convertible Bonds	0	0
Preferred Stock	0	0
Common Stock	93.0	79
U. S. Government Securities	0	0
Cash	0	0
Estimated Annual Portfolio Turnover	91%	

Estimates of Fund Performance:	
Annual Return for Three Years:	NA
Annual Return for Five Years:	NA
Annual Return in Bull Markets:	
1985	43.6%
1986	12.8%
Annual Return in Bear Markets:	
6/30/86–9/30/86	-13.9%
Representative Current Yield (2/28/87):	1.8%

Measures of Risk and Reward:	
Alpha	NA
Beta	.95
R square	NA
Standard deviation	4.90
Reward/risk ratio	5.6

Net Asset Value:	
9/25/87	18.92
10/28/87	12.67

Chapter 20
Money-Market Funds

BACKGROUND INFORMATION

Type of Security

For the cautious investor, money-market funds provide very high stability of principal while seeking moderate to high current income. They invest in highly liquid, virtually risk-free, short-term debt securities of agencies of the U.S. and foreign governments and also securities of foreign banks and corporations. They have no potential for capital appreciation.

This chapter describes money-market funds that invest in taxable securities. The next chapter describes funds that invest in tax-exempt securities.

Risk/Stability

Because they invest in short-term investments, money-market mutual funds are able to keep a constant share price; only the yield fluctuates. Because of the price stability, many investors see in money-market funds an attractive alternative to bank accounts.

Money-market fund yields are generally competitive with—and usually somewhat higher than—yields on bank certificates of deposit (CDs). The average of the 7-day yield for 284 money-market funds is given in Table 20-1. The yield of money-market funds dropped steadily in 1984, 1985, and 1986 and then rose again in 1987. However, a number of funds have provided above-average returns, as shown in the representative funds chosen for Table 20-2.

Unlike banks, money-market funds are not insured by the FDIC or FSLIC. But money-market funds invest only in highly liquid, short-term, top-rated money-market instruments. Such instruments are usually inaccessible to the average investor because of the high minimum purchase requirements. By pooling the funds of many investors, money-market funds afford the individual investor the dual ad-vantage of high yields and maximum safety.

Table 20-1: Average of 7-Day Yields for 284 Money-Market Funds

	12/83	12/84	12/85	12/86	3/87	7/87
Yield (%)	8.73	8.38	7.23	5.39	5.35	6.10

SPECIAL BENEFITS AND EXPOSURES

Money-market funds have several advantages over CDs.

Liquidity

With money-market mutual funds, you may withdraw your money without penalty any time you wish. With CDs, you must leave your funds on deposit for a fixed period of time. Should you need your money earlier than the maturity date of a CD, the bank will usually charge you a stiff penalty for early withdrawal.

Check-Writing Access

Money-market funds offer you check-writing privileges. You may draw checks against your fund balance and use them as you would any check, such as to pay bills or to make deposits to your checking account.

Cash Management

Some investors use money-market funds as a convenient and lucrative place to "park" the proceeds of recently sold investments awaiting reinvestment in some other form, such as stocks, bonds, or growth funds. Others use money-market funds as a place to hold recently received income from earnings or investments until it is spent issuing a check for some personal expenditure. The funds earn income until the check clears the fund.

PORTFOLIO FIT

Every investor will want to invest in a money-market fund. It can serve as a parking place for short-term money and a place to put the proceeds of the sales of other funds. Any investment fund not committed to other types of investments can be held in a money-market fund. The investor may wish to accumulate reserves in such a fund for future investments in other funds. The risk of loss of principal is negligible and interest rates will fluctuate over time. This is a low-risk–low-return investment.

EIGHT REPRESENTATIVE MONEY-MARKET FUNDS

To illustrate, we have chosen eight money-market funds that show the qualities that investors seek when purchasing shares of money-market funds. Note that all of these examples are no-load funds. Table 20-2 contains a summary listing of the eight funds. No detailed description of the funds' objectives and investment philosophy and practice will be offered in this chapter, since they are similar for all money-market funds. Similarly, any differences in performance are within the realm of chance. Selection is usually made on the basis on features and convenience.

Investors are reminded that past performance is no indicator of future performance.

Table 20-2: Eight Representative Money-Market Funds

Fund	Return (%) for 1 Year to 2/28/87	Minimum Investment	Load
Dreyfus Liquid Assets	5.98	2500	NL
Fidelity Cash Reserves	6.08	1000	NL
Kemper Money Market	6.16	1000	NL
T. Rowe Price Prime Reserve	5.85	1000	NL
Scudder Cash Investment Trust	5.82	1000	NL
Stein Roe Cash Reserves	5.78	2500	NL
Value Line Cash Fund	6.09	1000	NL
Vanguard Money Market Reserves	6.39	1000	NL

For demonstration purposes, the yield of the Kemper Money-Market Fund and the average 7-day yield for 238 money-market funds for the 77-week period ended March 27, 1987, is shown in Figure 20-1.

288 Chapter 20

Figure 20-1: The Yield for Kemper Money Market Fund and the Average 7-Day Yield for 238 Money Market Funds for the 77-Week Period Ending March 27, 1987.

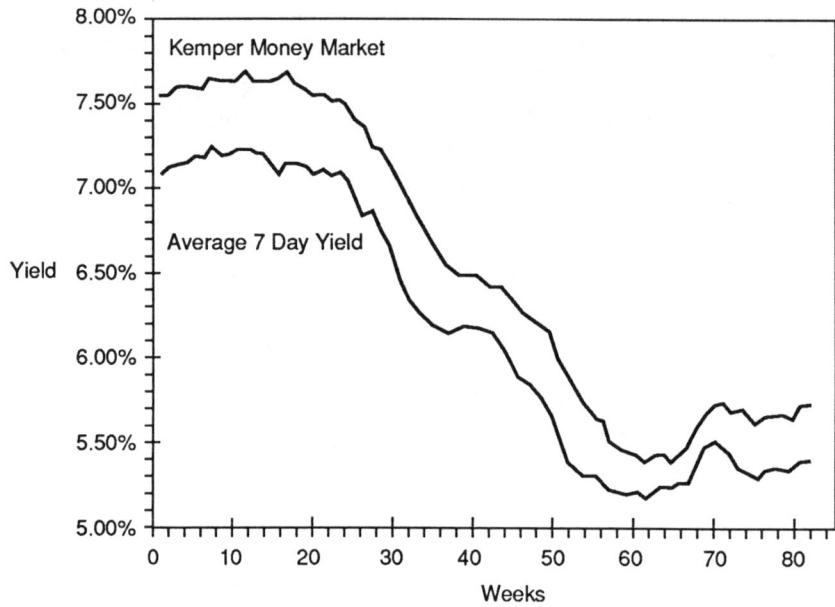

PROFILE 20-1

DREYFUS LIQUID ASSETS
666 Old Country Road
Garden City, NY 11530
1-800-645-6565 or 221-4062
718-895-1206

Fund Classification:	MM
Total Assets:	$7089 million
Fund Manager:	Joseph DiMartino
Year of Inception:	1974
Minimum Investment:	$2500
Sales Charge:	No load
12b-1 Charge:	No
Expense Ratio:	0.66
One-Year Return to (2/28/87):	5.98%
Representative Current Yield (3/10/87):	5.5%
Average Maturity:	57 days
Minimum Check Withdrawal:	$500
Net Asset Value:	
9/25/87	1.0
10/28/87	1.0

PROFILE 20-2

FIDELITY CASH RESERVES
82 Devonshire
Boston, MA 02109
1-800-544-6666
617-726-0200

Fund Classification:	MM
Total Assets:	$5122 million
Fund Manager:	Bernie Scehman
Year of Inception:	1979
Minimum Investment:	$1000
Sales Charge:	No load
12b-1 Charge:	No
Expense Ratio:	0.82
One-Year Return to (2/28/87):	6.08%
Representative Current Yield (3/10/87):	5%
Average Maturity:	46 days
Minimum Check Withdrawal:	$500
Net Asset Value:	
9/25/87	1.0
10/28/87	1.0

PROFILE 20-3

KEMPER MONEY MARKET
120 S. LaSalle Street
Chicago, IL 60607
1-800-621-1048
312-781-1121

Fund Classification:	MM
Total Assets:	$4175 million
Fund Manager:	Frank Rachwalski
Year of Inception:	1974
Minimum Investment:	$1000
Sales Charge:	No load
12b-1 Charge:	No
Expense Ratio:	0.77
One-Year Return to (2/28/87):	6.16%
Representative Current Yield (3/10/87):	5.7%
Average Maturity:	42 days
Minimum Check Withdrawal:	$500
Net Asset Value:	
9/25/87	1.0
10/28/87	1.0

PROFILE 20-4

T. ROWE PRICE PRIME RESERVE
100 E. Pratt Street
Baltimore, MD 21202
1-800-638-5660
301-547-2308

Fund Classification:	MM
Total Assets:	$2616 million
Fund Manager:	Edward Taber
Year of Inception:	1976
Minimum Investment:	$1000
Sales Charge:	No load
12b-1 Charge:	No
Expense Ratio:	0.65
One-Year Return to (2/28/87):	5.85%
Representative Current Yield (3/10/87):	5.5%
Average Maturity:	43 days
Minimum Check Withdrawal:	$500
Net Asset Value:	
9/25/87	1.0
10/28/87	1.0

PROFILE 20-5

SCUDDER CASH INVESTMENT TRUST
175 Federal Street
Boston, MA 02110
1-800-225-2470 or 453-9500
617-426-8300

Fund Classification:	MM
Total Assets:	$1165 million
Fund Manager:	Robert Pruyne
Year of Inception:	1976
Minimum Investment:	$1000
Sales Charge:	No load
12b-1 Charge:	No
Expense Ratio:	0.68
One-Year Return to (2/28/87):	5.82%
Representative Current Yield (3/10/87):	5.3%
Average Maturity:	40 days
Minimum Check Withdrawal:	$500
Net Asset Value:	
9/25/87	1.0
10/28/87	1.0

PROFILE 20-6

STEIN ROE CASH RESERVES
Box 1143
Chicago, IL 60690
1-800-621-0320
312-368-7826

Fund Classification:	MM
Total Assets:	$821 million
Fund Manager:	Anthony Zulfer
	Jane Naeseth
Year of Inception:	1976
Minimum Investment:	$2500
Sales Charge:	No load
12b-1 Charge:	No
Expense Ratio:	0.72
One-Year Return to (2/28/87):	5.78%
Representative Current Yield (3/10/87):	5.4%
Average Maturity:	44 days
Minimum Check Withdrawal:	$50
Net Asset Value:	
9/25/87	1.0
10/28/87	1.0

PROFILE 20-7

VALUE LINE CASH FUND
711 Third Avenue
New York, NY 10017
1-800-223-0818
212-687-3965

Fund Classification:	MM
Total Assets:	$421 million
Fund Manager:	Marie Conway
Year of Inception:	1979
Minimum Investment:	$1000
Sales Charge:	No load
12b-1 Charge:	No
Expense Ratio:	0.79
One-Year Return to (2/28/87):	6.09%
Representative Current Yield (3/10/87):	5.4%
Average Maturity:	55 days
Minimum Check Withdrawal:	$500
Net Asset Value:	
9/25/87	1.0
10/28/87	1.0

PROFILE 20-8

VANGUARD MONEY MARKET RESERVES
Valley Forge, PA 19482
1-800-662-7447
In PA 1-800-362-0530

Fund Classification:	MM
Total Assets:	$2130 million
Fund Manager:	Ian Mackinnon
Year of Inception:	1975
Minimum Investment:	$1000
Sales Charge:	No load
12b-1 Charge:	No
Expense Ratio:	0.51
One-Year Return to (2/28/87):	6.39%
Representative Current Yield (3/10/87):	5.7%
Average Maturity:	42 days
Minimum Check Withdrawal:	$250
Net Asset Value:	
9/25/87	1.0
10/28/87	1.0

Chapter 21
Tax-Exempt Money-Market Funds

BACKGROUND INFORMATION

Type of Security

During recent years, an entirely new type of money-market fund has emerged: *tax-exempt money-market funds*. Tax-exempt money-market funds combine the features of municipal bond funds with those of money-market funds. Tax-exempt money-market funds invest exclusively in municipal bonds that are close to maturity, typically having only two to four months of remaining life, and in various types of short-term municipal notes and bonds.

Tax-exempt money-market funds purchase short-term debt securities, called municipal notes, and hold them until they mature 60 to 120 days later.

Risk/Stability

They resemble regular money-market funds in that the net asset value of the fund remains stable. Also, they provide check-writing privileges. They differ in that the income earned by shareholders is exempt from federal income taxes.

Tax-exempt money-market funds are suitable for persons who ordinarily would invest in regular money-market funds for all the reasons investors use such funds (see description of money-market funds in Chapter 20) but whose marginal income tax bracket is such that their after-tax yield is higher with the tax-exempt money-market fund. Because the difference (or "spread") in yields between the taxable and tax-exempt funds fluctuates, investors should compare their after-tax return on both before deciding which type of fund to purchase.

SPECIAL BENEFITS AND EXPOSURES

By using short-term securities, tax-exempt money-market funds attempt to hold the net-asset value at $1.00 so that you may write a check on any day without concern for fluctuations in the net asset value.

Since the fund is tax-exempt, it can be compared readily to a regular, taxable money-market fund. For a person in a 30-percent tax bracket, 4 percent tax-free is equivalent to a 5.7 percent taxable yield. When the current yield of a taxable money-market fund is 5.4 percent, we find a significant advantage for tax-exempt money-market funds.

The comparable tax-exempt return is calculated as:

$$\text{TFR} = \frac{\text{TFY}}{1 - \text{TR}}$$

where
TFR = comparable tax-exempt return
TFY = tax-exempt yield
TR = tax rate

The features you should look for will include good performance over the past year, reasonable current yield, and acceptable minimum required investment.

PORTFOLIO FIT

Tax-exempt money-market funds are similar to regular money-market funds in that they are a low-risk–low-return investment. They provide a lower return than regular money-market funds, but they may provide higher after-tax returns. For example, a taxable money-market fund may return 6.0 percent when a tax-exempt fund would provide 4.0 percent. However, if you are in the 40-percent tax bracket, the return on the taxable fund is only 3.6 percent after taxes. Many people in higher tax brackets use tax-exempt money-market funds as a place to accumulate cash.

SEVEN REPRESENTATIVE TAX-EXEMPT MONEY-MARKET FUNDS

To illustrate, we have chosen seven tax-exempt money-market funds that show the qualities that investors seek when purchasing shares of tax-exempt money-market funds. Note that all of these examples are no-load funds. Table 21-1 contains a summary listing of the seven funds. No detailed description of each fund's objectives and investment philosophy and practice is provided because of the strong resemblance between such funds. Differences in performance are within the realm of chance.

Investors are reminded that past performance is no indicator of future performance.

Table 21-1: Seven Representative Tax-Exempt Money-Market Funds

Fund	Return (%) for 1 Year to 2/28/87	Yield 3/9/87	Minimum Investment
Calvert Tax-Free Reserves	4.55	4.0	2000
Dreyfus Tax-Exempt Money Market Fund	4.08	3.4	5000
Fidelity Tax-Exempt Money Market Fund	4.13	3.5	5000
Neuberger & Berman Tax-Free Money Fund	3.95	3.3	2000
T. Rowe Price Tax-Exempt Money Fund	4.22	3.6	1000
USAA Tax-Exempt Money Market Fund	4.48	3.9	10,000
Vanguard Municipal Bond Money Market	4.33	3.4	3000

PROFILE 21-1

CALVERT TAX-FREE RESERVES
1700 Pennsylvania Ave.
Washington, D. C. 20006
1-800-368-2748
301-951-4820

Fund Classification:	MMTF
Total Assets:	$682 million
Fund Manager:	Reno Martini
Year of Inception:	1981
Minimum Investment:	$2000
Sales Charge:	No load
12b-1 Charge:	No
Expense Ratio:	0.50
One-Year Return to (2/28/87):	4.55%
Representative Current Yield (3/9/87):	4.0%
Average Maturity:	71 days
Minimum Check Withdrawal:	$250
Net Asset Value:	
9/25/87	1.0
10/28/87	1.0

PROFILE 21-2

DREYFUS TAX-EXEMPT MONEY MARKET FUND
666 Old Country Road
Garden City, NY 11530
1-800-645-6561
718-895-1206

Fund Classification:	MMTF
Total Assets:	$3001 million
Fund Manager:	Richard Moynihan
Year of Inception:	1980
Minimum Investment:	$5000
Sales Charge:	No load
12b-1 Charge:	No
Expense Ratio:	0.56
One-Year Return to (2/28/87):	4.08%
Representative Current Yield (3/9/87):	3.4%
Average Maturity:	59 days
Minimum Check Withdrawal:	$500
Net Asset Value:	
9/25/87	1.0
10/28/87	1.0

PROFILE 21-3

FIDELITY TAX-EXEMPT MONEY MARKET FUND
82 Devonshire
Boston, MA 02109
1-800-544-6666
617-523-1919

Fund Classification:	MMTF
Total Assets:	$3748 million
Fund Manager:	Raymond Hender
Year of Inception:	1980
Minimum Investment:	$5000
Sales Charge:	No load
12b-1 Charge:	No
Expense Ratio:	0.35
One-Year Return to (2/28/87):	4.13%
Representative Current Yield (3/9/87):	3.5%
Average Maturity:	58 days
Minimum Check Withdrawal:	$500
Net Asset Value:	
9/25/87	1.0
10/28/87	1.0

PROFILE 21-4

NEUBERGER AND BERMAN TAX-FREE MONEY FUND
342 Madison Avenue
New York, NY 10173
1-800-367-0776
212-850-8300

Fund Classification:	MMTF
Total Assets:	$187 million
Fund Manager:	Theresa Havell
Year of Inception:	1984
Minimum Investment:	$2000
Sales Charge:	No load
12b-1 Charge:	No
Expense Ratio:	0.59
One-Year Return to (2/28/87):	3.95%
Representative Current Yield (3/9/87):	3.3%
Average Maturity:	49 days
Minimum Check Withdrawal:	$200
Net Asset Value:	
9/25/87	1.0
10/28/87	1.0

PROFILE 21-5

T. ROWE PRICE TAX-EXEMPT MONEY FUND
100 E. Pratt Street
Baltimore, MD 21202
1-800-638-5660
301-547-2308

Fund Classification:	MMTF
Total Assets:	$1142 million
Fund Manager:	Peter J. D. Gordon
Year of Inception:	1981
Minimum Investment:	$1000
Sales Charge:	No load
12b-1 Charge:	No
Expense Ratio:	0.61
One-Year Return to (2/28/87):	4.22%
Representative Current Yield (3/9/87):	3.6%
Average Maturity:	69 days
Minimum Check Withdrawal:	$500
Net Asset Value:	
9/25/87	1.0
10/28/87	1.0

PROFILE 21-6

USAA TAX-EXEMPT MONEY MARKET FUND
9800 Fredricksburg Road
San Antonio, TX 78288
1-800-531-8000
512-690-6062

Fund Classification:	MMTF
Total Assets:	$308 million
Fund Manager	Kenneth Willmann
Year of Inception:	1984
Minimum Investment:	$10,000
Sales Charge:	No load
12b-1 Charge:	No
Expense Ratio:	0.59
One-Year Return to (2/28/87):	4.48%
Representative Current Yield (3/9/87):	3.9%
Average Maturity:	72 days
Minimum Check Withdrawal:	$250
Net Asset Value:	
9/25/87	1.0
10/28/87	1.0

PROFILE 21-7

VANGUARD MUNICIPAL BOND MONEY MARKET
Vanguard Group
Valley Forge, PA 19482
1-800-662-7447
In PA 1-800-362-0530

Fund Classification:	MMTF
Total Assets:	$1358 million
Fund Manager:	Ian Mackinnon
Year of Inception:	1980
Minimum Investment:	$3000
Sales Charge:	No load
12b-1 Charge:	No
Expense Ratio:	0.39
One-Year Return to (2/28/87):	4.33%
Representative Current Yield (3/9/87):	3.8%
Average Maturity:	93 days
Minimum Check Withdrawal:	$500
Net Asset Value:	
9/25/87	1.0
10/28/87	1.0

PART II: FUND SELECTION AND TIMING

Chapter 22
Mutual Funds: More Choices Than Ever Before
by Reg Green, Green Communications

The mutual fund industry is the fastest-growing industry in the United States. In the past year alone it has shot up by almost 50 percent. Total assets invested in mutual funds were $730 billion at the beginning of 1987; 10 years earlier the comparable figure was $50 billion. For a large and mature industry—over 60 years old—that rate of advance is almost unheard of.

It amounts to a revolution in the way ordinary shareholders are saving and investing their money. Until the mid-70s mutual funds were simply a way of getting into the main currents of the stock market—and consequently were of interest to a fairly well-defined group of buyers. Characteristically, these buyers were quite affluent, college-educated and mature, with quite long investment horizons, willing to take moderate risks and used to the idea that stock prices fluctuate.

Since then the picture has changed dramatically. First, of course, it has expanded. Twenty five million Americans now own mutual fund shares, compared with one-third as many only a few years ago. Second, millions of these newer investors have less risk tolerance than the traditional mutual fund owners: roughly one-third of all fund assets are in money market funds, the near-ultimate in investment safety, and more than one-third are in bonds. Third, many more shareholders are not just new to mutual funds, they are new to any form of investing.

As a result, many more older people, including retirees, both buy and own funds. So do more younger people, more people in lower income brackets, more two-income families, and many, many more women.

To meet these changes, mutual funds themselves have undergone an equally decisive change. Ten years ago the bulk of the few hundred funds available invested in conventional stocks. Now, 1700 funds are searching for investment opportunities everywhere from overnight Treasury securities to bankrupt companies. Where there were once a handful of different investment objectives, common usage now identifies 18 main categories; within each category there are sub-categories; and within sub-categories, literally every fund has a different portfolio and management style from every other.

The broad distinctions are still fairly clear: common stock funds range from those intent on maximizing capital appreciation to those which invest in solid middle-of-the-road companies, much of whose attraction lies in their record of consistently paying high dividends. Bond funds include corporate, municipal and US Government issues, and even the money market funds offer a choice of taxable and tax-free securities.

Then the complications start. Take just one category, municipal bonds. Some funds will buy such bonds anywhere in the United States, looking for the highest yield relative to safety; others confine themselves to the bonds of a single state, thereby offering returns free of both federal and state taxes; some buy lower-rate bonds for investors willing to face more risk for higher yields; and still others are insured. Or, to look at it another way, maturities in these funds run from a few weeks to 30 years, and consequently their share values can range from constant to skittish.

The upshot is that whatever degree of risk you are prepared to run to get tax-free income, there are funds appropriate to your decision. Leaders in this sector of the industry offer many choices even within one organization so that you can adjust your preferences at any time: at a recent count, a leader in this field, J.&W. Seligman & Co., was offering no fewer than seventeen alternatives among tax-free funds alone. But even this is not all. Outside the broad reaches of the industry, a number of funds have carved out a special niche for themselves. They are, in fact, investments tailor-made for particular investors. To give just a few examples: Benham Target Maturities Trust invests in US Treasury zero-coupon bonds, the only type of fund permitted by the SEC to quote an anticipated growth rate and so heavily favored by those planning for retirement; Colonial has an international index fund which tracks the performance of companies in major stock markets around the world, an investment in the world economy requiring no expertise by the investor; Massachusetts Financial Services Managed Sectors Trust offers a bridge for those who like the exciting potential of moving between different sectors of the market but who prefer to have those decisions made by the fund managers; Delaware has invented a fund, its Treasury Investor Series, that puts its money in short-to-intermediate Government bonds, thus paying significantly more than money market funds but with much more modest fluctuations than conventional bond funds; National Real Estate Stock Fund pioneered the concept of investing in property-related companies through a mutual fund, abolishing at a stroke the main drawback of investing in property, its illiquidity.

Similarly, the investment techniques used by funds vary widely. The Value Line funds lean heavily on the objectivity of their statistically sophisticated ranking system, which has outperformed the stock market for 19 of the last 22 years. The successful Strong funds supplement their objective analysis with a continuous round of visits to companies that interest them: in a recent twelve-month period one member of the team alone, Richard Strong, the chairman, visited 250 companies. Venture Income Plus and Venture Muni-Plus have that "Plus" in their title because they aim for the highest yields available and are not afraid to go into threatening territory to get them. As their manager, Talton Embry puts it, "I don't care how sick the securities I look at are. I only want to know: can they recover?" He too travels extensively on the lookout for the sort of opportunity that daunts other investors. The G.T. group has offices around the world gathering information that is fed into its international mutual funds: shareholders have the reassurance of knowing that G.T. handles the international investments of some of the largest institutions in the world, including three of the Fortune Top Ten.

Most funds have a portfolio manager who, although relying to varying degrees on the research and analysis of colleagues, makes the final decisions. Some are national figures, like Peter Lynch, long-time manager of the Fidelity Magellan Fund. Others, like Harry Hutzler, who manages both the outstandingly successful Weingarten Equity and Constellation Growth funds, are known by name only to admiring fellow professionals. By contrast the American Funds Group relies on a team approach, with perhaps four managers all investing a portion of a fund's assets. Unusual though it is, this approach has worked so well that over meaningful periods—that is, 10 years or more—all 6 common stock funds in the group have beaten the stock market throughout their entire lifetime.

These wide-ranging choices have stimulated another major change in the way Americans handle their investments. At one time, shareholders typically put money into an investment, checked it from time to time, and only pulled out when completely disillusioned with the results or when the original objective—money for retirement, children's school fees, buying a new home—had been reached. Now anyone in a family of funds can switch between those funds just about as often as economic conditions or their own circumstances change.

This can be just a minor change of emphasis—a little more or a little less in equities. On the other hand, it can be a wholesale switch. If, for instance, interest rates look like shooting up again, a telephone call can take you from long-term bonds into money market funds all in one day. If, on the other hand, interest rates are low and getting lower, another telephone call can put you 100 percent into stocks—or 80, or 60. Ten years ago exchanges like this totalled about $1 billion a year; now they are running at around $50 billion a year. In short, ordinary Americans now have a degree of control over their assets that not long ago a millionaire would have envied.

What that degree of control gives them is access to broadly-diversified portfolios selected to meet defined investment objectives and watched over by teams of full-time money managers. The diversification spreads the risks so that the failure of any one holding is not serious, as it could be in an individual holding. It also gives the managers the confidence to reach out for special opportunities, knowing that the rest of the portfolio will cushion any miscalculations.

Professional managers are not infallible. But over time professionals will tend to beat amateurs in investing as anywhere else. They have so many advantages, including training, instant access to information and broadly-based research. Moreover, for them it is a full-time job not subject to the distractions of those who try to follow the market in their spare time. Investors can buy into these portfolios for small sums—generally a few hundred dollars, sometimes no minimum at all. They can redeem on any business day at their share of the value of the fund's assets—and by law the fund is bound to honor that obligation. And they can switch between funds in a group for a few dollars at a time and sometimes at no charge. Reassuringly, close regulation at federal and state level has kept them the most open of all investment alternatives.

Put like that, the concept has so many material advantages that its popularity is self-explanatory. It does, however, have its own dangers.

Among others: professional money managers may not perform up to expectations and you have no redress if they do not; if they aren't performing over a reasonable period their methods may simply be ill-conceived and shareholders should cash in. Some funds may become too specialized—restricting their investments to some narrow sector of the market or one small foreign country. At times that portfolio may do well, but for most people the dangers are too great unless they are prepared to keep vigilant all the time.

Some funds get their results by taking much bigger risks than others. That need not be a problem of shareholders recognize it and have long enough ahead of them to recover from setbacks. But it can seriously hurt elderly or less affluent investors.

Both the stock and bond markets have been unusually profitable in the last two or three years: shareholders should not be lulled into thinking they will always be so. The sheer variety of investment alternatives has caused considerable confusion about what is available, let alone what is appropriate. Investors really must undertake more study of their own—either to narrow down the sort of funds they want or to find a financial advisor with whom they can work comfortably.

That said, mutual funds are an extraordinarily flexible way for people of all types to invest with reasonable prospects of success. Best of all, the existence of a multitude of competing products not only spurs innovation but gives any dissatisfied shareholder a host of other places to go.

Chapter 23
Choosing an Aggressive Growth Fund
by Sheldon Jacobs, No-Load Fund Investor, Inc.

The analysis of past and present performance is the primary method for selecting funds. However, performance is really the end product. It is the net result of several factors, all of which contribute to a fund's performance—or lack of it. Since the goal is to obtain top future performance, you should understand the factors that explain why some funds outperform others. While they won't guarantee success, these criteria can turn the odds of choosing a superior fund in your favor. One of the most important is cash inflow.

CASH INFLOW

Unlike closed-end funds or stocks, open-end mutual funds attract new money by selling additional shares. If a fund is selling more shares than it is redeeming, it is said to have a positive cash flow. Conversely, if more shares of a fund are being redeemed than sold, the fund is experiencing a negative cash flow, or an outflow. Reinvested distributions and dividends are not counted as capital inflow. Neither are increases in the fund's assets as a result of mergers with other funds. These don't provide new money.

For many years it was thought that cash inflow or outflow was a function of performance. If a fund did well, it attracted new money; if it did poorly, investors would redeem their shares, causing a negative outflow. However, another school of thought emerged, contending just the reverse: positive cash flow produces superior performance and negative cash flow causes inferior market performance. The person who popularized this latter theory is Alan Pope of Albuquerque, New Mexico, a mutual fund buff who charts fund performance. He is the author of a book, *Successful Investing in No-Load Funds* (John Wiley & Sons), that discusses cash flow in greater detail.

Pope's conclusions came after he noticed that no fund, however well managed, ever maintained front-rank performance for more than a few years. Size, while one factor, did not sufficiently explain why funds inevitably stumbled. After all, many small funds achieved superior performance for a short time, then declined, even though they had not grown to unmanageable size. So why did they slow down? Pope concluded that cash inflow was a key variable. His reasoning:

- With new money coming into a fund, management can buy securities on market dips.
- A positive cash flow means a fund need not sell good or promising equities in order to meet redemptions, or to raise cash for defensive purposes.
- With fresh money coming in, a fund need not sell existing holdings to take advantage of new or special market situations. Thus decision-making is simpler; a manager need decide only what to buy, rather than what to buy and what to sell.
- A positive cash flow minimizes a fund's investment mistakes. Bad investments compose an increasingly smaller proportion of the fund's asset base. In effect, incoming cash flow dilutes losses.
- With more money to spend, a fund can attract the advice of the best analysts.
- With ample cash, fund managers try harder to find promising new investment opportunities.
- A fund can "bootstrap," directing new money into additional shares of stocks already in its portfolio. If the stock's "float" is not too large, such investments can raise its price—and the value of the fund's shares.

To what extent does cash flow aid performance? Pope's research indicates that 100 percent cash flow increases performance by 10-14 percent over the market average. Less than 10 percent cash flow doesn't help much.

Another analyst who has investigated cash flow is Melvin Roebuck, a now-retired expert who spent considerable time investigating fund performance. Mr. Roebuck believes: "If a fund has net new-money gains equal to 200 percent or more of its assets within a year, then it is almost certain to excel. In 95 percent of the cases it will wind up in the top 25 percent of its group. If the net new-money flow is between 30 percent and 200 percent of assets, the fund will probably outperform the average of its group. With a flow of -5 percent to +30 percent it can go either way. If the flow is below -5 percent (that is, it's experiencing net redemptions) the fund will probably never again turn up among the top 25 percent."

Using the method described below, we estimated 1985 cash inflow for all aggressive growth funds and found a strong correlation between cash flow and their performance. Those funds which had a cash flow exceeding 100 percent last year achieved an average gain of 38.6 percent. The average gains declined steadily as inflow decreased and turned into outflow. However, because 1985 was such a good year, even the aggressive growth funds with cash outflow turned in a 24.5 percent gain in 1985 (see Table 23-1).

Cash inflow also explains why big funds inevitably slow down. They cannot maintain the same rate of cash inflow over long periods of time. If a $2 million fund maintained a 100 percent rate of new money inflow it would have $4 million in assets at the end of the first year (excluding the effects of per share price changes), $8 million at the end of the

Table 23-1: Aggressive Growth Funds Cash Flow in 1985

Cash Inflow	1985 % Gain
100% +	38.6
50-100%	30.4
0-50%	26.9
minus	24.5

second year—and over $2 billion by the end of the tenth year. It is not possible for large funds to grow at the same rate as they did when they were small.

Cash flow typically starts after investors note that a small fund is turning in an outstanding performance. Cash inflow then enables the fund to maintain superior performance until the additions of new money are no longer meaningful in relation to the size of the fund.

Cash inflow analysis fell into disuse during the bear markets of the Seventies because few stock funds had significant amounts of new money coming in. The situation changed in 1980, and by 1983 incredible amounts of cash were flowing into the best-performing funds. Fidelity Select Technology began 1983 with $46.9 million in assets. It ended the year with assets of $718 million. Its 56 percent increase in per share value accounted for only a small portion of this gain. Similarly, Twentieth Century Select's assets rose from $130 million to $743 million over the course of 1983.

How to Determine Cash Inflow

Usually, the Statement of Changes in Net Assets in a fund's annual or quarterly report has date titled "Capital Share Transactions." Entries in this section show the number and dollar value of shares sold or redeemed. If you don't have the reports, you can estimate a fund's cash flow by noting its per share performance and total net asset figures. Then measure the growth of assets due to the fund's per share gain for the year. The net inflow of capital is the fund's assets above this gain. Here are the specific calculations: Assume a fund started the year with $1 million in net assets. During the year its per share value increased 40 percent. The fund ended the year with $2 million in total assets. By itself, the 40 percent per share gain would account for $400,000. Thus $600,000 is the amount of new money that flowed into the fund. This new-money inflow percentage is 60 percent of the fund's initial assets. The figures you need to make these calculations are readily available in our Statistical section.

As Alan Pope points out, the operative word is "flow." Ideally cash should come into the fund at a steady rate. If a fund is inundated with new money, it will have trouble investing it wisely.

NET REDEMPTIONS HURT PERFORMANCE

While excessive cash inflow occasionally presents problems, net cash outflow clearly hurts performance. A fund in net redemptions must either keep abnormally large cash positions, thus diluting its performance in up markets, or it's forced to sell stocks to meet redemptions. The fund tries first to sell the stocks with the least hope of gain. But eventually it may be forced to sell assets it wouldn't have otherwise. A fund in net redemptions can't be aggressive, unless it is authorized and prepared to use margin to maintain its stock positions.

SELL AGGRESSIVE GROWTH FUNDS IN BEAR MARKETS

Aggressive growth funds lack defensive capabilities. The speculative stocks they hold can take terrible drubbings. In 1969–70 and in 1973–74, the average performance fund declined by about half. In 1984, a mixed year that saw conservative funds gaining, the aggressive growth funds had sizeable declines. They were off 10.6 percent on average, and the worst declined 59.6 percent. Certainly, the below-average performers should have been sold.

Here's a case history of a great fund that went sour, and how its shareholders reacted. The 44 Wall Street Fund was by far the outstanding success in the stock market cycle that began in 1975 and ended with the 1981–82 decline. Since then it has been one of the worst funds. To see how no-load fund investors reacted, we tracked 44 Wall shareholders through the fund's gyrations since 1975.

44 Wall emerged from the 1973–74 bear market with only 1,500 shareholders (see Table 23-2). It took investors a while to recognize the fund's outstanding performance. As late as 1978, 44 Wall had only 3,000 shareholders. The next year the number of shareholders doubled, and the following year, 1980, with its achievements widely publicized, its shareholder role zoomed to 15,000. In 1980, the fund's minimum investment was raised to $250,000 and some of the 9,000 new 1980 shareholders bought just before the new minimum went into effect. Between 1975 and 1980 the fund gained 1,423 percent, but no more than 1,500 shareholders fully participated in this huge increase. Most bought along the way; a good percentage bought in near the top.

The next year, 1981, was a down year for the market, and the high flyers, as usual, fared the worst. 44 Wall declined 23.6 percent and then declined another 21.5 percent in the first half of 1982. Relatively few of 44 Wall shareholders reacted to the fund's poor performance by selling. In 18 months, only 2,200 of 44 Wall's shareholders redeemed. (This is the net loss, taking into account new shareholders.) 44 Wall still had 13,000 shareholders in June 1982 when it was the worst performing of all aggressive growth no-loads. Many more should have sold out, particularly considering 44 Wall's convenient telephone switch privilege. Just a phone call would send a shareholder's money scuttling to the Reserve Fund, a money fund.

Table 23-2: 44 Wall Street Fund

	Annual Performance	Number of Shareholders (At year-end)	Total Net Assets In Millions (At year-end)
1974	-52.2	1,500	$ .6
1975	184.1	2,000	6.7
1976	46.5	2,000	18.3
1977	16.5	2,000	16.4
1978	32.9	3,000	30.6
1979	71.4	6,300	107.7
1980	36.1	15,322	193.5
1981	-23.6	13,516	122.2
June 1982	*(-21.6)	(13,105)	(98.1)
1982	6.9	13,365	200.9
1983	6.9	12,915	182.7
1984	-59.6	11,497	67.8
1985	-20.1	9,795	42.3

*Jan-June 1982.

When the market took off in August 1982, 44 Wall was still a logical choice for the aggressive investor. While the number of new investors added by year-end was small, the fund's assets grew rapidly, far more than could be accounted for by the fund's 36.4 percent gain in the last six months of the year. Obviously, the big, smart money had come in to reap the bull market profits.

The money stayed in until the end of January, 1984. At that time, stocks turned sharply downward and the smart money moved out of 44 Wall. In one month, the fund's assets plunged from $208 million to $93.5 million, far more than the 16 percent decline in the NAV per share in the same period. But that was the smart money—the large holdings of a relatively few investors. Most investors hung on and absorbed 1984's punishing 59.6 percent decline. More parted in 1985, but at year-end 44 Wall still had close to 10,000 shareholders.

Chapter 24
Selecting Mutual Funds and Market Timers
by Paul A. Merriman, Paul A. Merriman & Assoc., Inc.

What if people really told each other the truth about the success of their investing in the stock market? The result might be something like this:

The Scene: An intimate cocktail party attended by ten adults, all of whom are long-term, amateur investors. They stand around the room, sipping their iced drinks and sharing news of their fortunes.

"I lost my shirt on that last trade, and it was supposed to be a hot buy-out candidate. ..."

"Sure, I made good-sized gains a few times, but my losses have outnumbered them two to one!"

"Frankly, I would have done better keeping my money in the credit union. ..."

The fact is, current statistics say that only one of the ten guests would be able to honestly say, "Yes, I've continued to make good money on my investments."
The reason for this one-in-ten estimate is simple: Making money in the stock market is as tough as making money in any other business.
Only about one out of the next 16 businesses started today will be around in five years—and it is not a coincidence that the percentage of losers is approximately the same in the stock market.
Usually it is the lack of certain factors that lead to failure in both business and investing. Lack of experience, discipline, the inability to deal with adversity when things don't develop as planned, and lack of a detailed, well-researched business plan lead the list. Following those are the faults of too-little money to weather difficult periods and an inability to measure and manage risk.

Last and far from least is the one characteristic most likely to be present in abundance—dreams of easy profits.

Experience and discipline can't be taught, but the development of a detailed business plan can be learned by the business person or investor.

A detailed business plan should address most of the topics that will later lead to the success or failure of a business. It should consider short- and long-term sales goals, marketing, competition, compensation, new product development, personnel, use of outside professionals, physical space, inventory controls, and accounting systems, to name a few.

Numerous professionals are consulted, such as accountants, bankers, engineers, investment advisors, real estate specialists, and transportation experts.

I offer the following advice on the decisions you must make to begin investing in the stock market. These points can be applied to stock investments of any size and can bring most of the nine cocktail party guests described above over to the side of the lone market winner.

1. Unless you are investing for fun, forget about trying to buy individual stocks on your own or with the help of a stockbroker. In this business, professionals win and amateurs lose. Stockbrokers are professional salespeople motivated by commissions, not professional portfolio managers or analysts.

2. Buy mutual funds. Treat yourself like a millionaire and invest in a professionally diversified portfolio of stocks. Be sure you buy into funds that are part of a family of funds where you can move from one to another without a commission.

3. Buy no-load mutual funds. No-load funds are bought and sold commission-free. But be careful, the load fund industry has gotten clever and found ways to hide the costs of sales. A no-load fund must now be defined as a fund you can buy on Monday and sell on Tuesday without any early liquidation penalties. Plus, the true no-load fund does not have ongoing 12b-1 annual sales and promotional fees.

4. Buy at least five different no-load mutual funds. Each fund portfolio is managed by one stock picker supported by a group of research analysts. Buying five funds eliminates the bias of one person's view of the market. Further, it is unlikely that any portfolio manager will be number one under all market conditions.

5. Buy mutual funds that allow liberal switching. You must be able to move out of your equity fund when the market is falling. Although mutual funds would like you to buy their funds and go away, that is not in your best interest. Mutual funds protect you from stock risk through diversification, but they do little to protect you from the risks of the market. (Even the famed Fidelity Magellan went down 42 percent in 1973 and 28 percent in 1974. The losses were not due to stock selection, but rather a broad market decline.)

6. Use market timing to increase your profits and reduce your risk. The purpose of a market timing program is to capture most of a market's advances, participate in only a small portion of the declines and, over a complete cycle, retain more of the gains. The primary benefit of a timing program is its ability to participate in bull markets without taking the extraordinary risks of bear markets.

Chapter 24

7. Hire a trend-following market timer or buy a trend-following market timing system to protect your investment from major market declines. There are two basic approaches to market timing—trend following and forecasting.

Forecasting market timers generally evaluate a number of technical and fundamental variables that they say can help them foresee the future. *The Mutual Fund Forecaster*, a very popular newsletter, uses market forecasting. This service forecasts where mutual funds will be a year from now—something that simply cannot be predicted accurately. There are too many unknowns to know where the market is going to be 12 months from now.

Trend-following market timing is usually based on monitoring the direction of broad market indices. This is the most conservative market timing an investor can use, because the system can never take a bullish posture in the face of a major market decline.

8. Make use of at least two market timers or market timing systems. This advice is based on the same logic as diversifying among funds. Even the best long-term timing systems have years of disappointing results. By spreading the risk among timers, you will give yourself an extra chance to be successful in most market environments.

Since most timers have funds they recommend, the timer and/or system becomes the first prime decision you must make. The system and fund selection must match *your* risk comfort level. If your choice of timing system and mutual funds is too aggressive, it's likely you will not have the patience or discipline to see it through as a long-term investment.

The following eight important questions should be answered when you are considering a timing system.

1. How long has the system been in use or back-tested? Be wary of timing disciplines that only go back to 1975. The market has been in a major uptrend since then and only systems tested back from 1970 to 1968 will show how they held up during the long-term downtrends such as those experienced between 1968 and 1974.

2. What is the average number of trades in a year? Most long-term systems trade one to two times; intermediate term systems trade three to six times each year on the average. The advantage of a more actively traded system is that the buy and sell signals are normally generated closer to the top or bottom of the market. The disadvantage of the same system is the greater occurrence of "whipsaws" or false starts. Whipsaws are buy signals that turn into relatively short-term sell signals, often at a small loss. While both kinds of systems may give similar results after very long periods of time, I find most investors would rather get out closer to the top, get in closer to the bottom, and suffer some small losses due to whipsaws, as opposed to the substantial losses that occur with the longer-term systems.

3. How often does the system trade at a profit or loss? Most strict trend-following systems, based on the direction of the price of major market indices, are correct 60 to 75 percent of the time. Typically, long-term systems generate more profitable trades on a percentage basis than the more actively traded systems, but the *overall* returns of the more active systems tend to be better.

4. What are the average losses and gains per trade? This may be one of the most important questions for many investors. The gains and losses of a system will largely be dependent on the volatility of the mutual funds. For example, one of the systems generates average profits per trade of 16 to 20 percent with aggressive funds, but average losses of 4 to 6 percent. The same system applied to conservative funds has produced average gains of 9 to 11 percent, and average losses of only 2 percent. Therefore, the nature of investors who use conservative funds is more "risk averse" than those who use the aggressive funds.

5. What is the worst loss per unprofitable trade? Market timing does not protect against loss, it works to manage and minimize losses. Make sure you can accept the worst-case scenario on a trade or you will find yourself abandoning the fund and the system and going back to a bank. You must assume that the worst-case situation could happen on your first trade.

6. How often does the system buy back into the market at a price higher than the last sale? This question represents one of the most emotionally unacceptable transactions for investors. The idea of buying an investment at a price higher than last sold is very difficult to accept, because we all want to buy low and sell high. Be prepared—a characteristic of trend-following systems is to buy into strength and sell into weakness.

7. How much of the time is the system putting you at risk and how much of the time are you without risk? While you are in the money market fund you are theoretically at no risk. If two systems have approximately the same rates of return over many years, choose the system that keeps you out of the market the greater percentage of the time.

8. How do all the years (profitable and unprofitable) of a fund compare with and without market timing? Table 24-1 shows the impact of one equity switch model on Fidelity Magellan, the number one growth fund for the past 17 years. This model is based on a price-oriented trend-following timing technique. The results assume an original investment of $10,000, the reinvestment of dividends, interest and capital gains, with no fees or taxes and average annual T-bill rates while out of the market. The past success of this or any other fund, with or without market timing, is no guarantee of future profitability.

If you compare buy-and-hold to market timing one year at a time, it might be difficult to note the effectiveness of the system. Take special note of the column headed "Advantage or Disadvantage with Market Timing." In 11 out of 17 years, a buy-and-hold approach outpaced market timing. Yet at the end of the period, market timing produced a 100 percent higher overall gain.

The results of Fidelity Magellan with or without market timing are phenomenal. But what happens when you apply the same timing to a fund with a below average return? Table 24-2 shows the impact of the same equity switch model on Value Line Special Situations.

Chapter 24   315

Table 24-1: Fidelity Magellan

Year	Buy/Hold		Market Timing		Advantage Or Disadvantage With Market Timing
1970	-15.7%	$ 8,430	24.5%	$ 12,450	40.2%
1971	35.1	11,389	31.7	16,397	-3.4
1972	30.1	14,817	28.9	21,135	-1.2
1973	-42.1	8,579	-7.5	19,550	34.6
1974	-28.3	6,151	7.9	21,094	36.2
1975	44.4	8,882	23.5	26,051	-20.9
1976	35.5	12,035	32.4	34,492	-3.1
1977	16.3	13,997	4.4	36,010	-11.9
1978	31.7	18,434	26.4	45,517	-5.3
1979	51.7	27,964	26.9	57,761	-24.8
1980	69.9	47,511	74.3	100,677	4.4
1981	16.4	55,303	20.4	121,215	4.0
1982	48.1	81,904	43.1	173,459	-5.0
1983	38.6	113,519	35.8	235,557	-2.8
1984	2.0	115,789	10.3	259,819	8.3
1985	43.1	165,694	40.5	365,046	-2.6
1986	23.7	204,963	16.5	425,279	-7.2

Table 24-2: Value Line Special Situations

Year	Buy/Hold		Market Timing		Advantge Or Disadvantage With Market Timing
1970	-34.4%	$ 6,560	10.5%	$ 11,050	44.0%
1971	17.6	7,715	35.9	15,017	18.3
1972	-11.0	6,866	-4.5	14,341	-6.5
1973	-45.5	3,742	-1.6	14,112	43.9
1974	-29.5	2,638	7.9	15,227	37.4
1975	47.0	3,878	34.0	20,404	-13.0
1976	52.7	5,922	57.8	32,197	5.1
1977	12.3	6,650	3.5	33,324	-8.8
1978	21.2	8,060	17.0	38,990	-4.2
1979	43.6	11,575	26.0	49,127	-17.6
1980	54.4	17,871	78.4	87,642	24.0
1981	-2.2	17,478	8.5	95,092	10.7
1982	23.1	21,515	30.7	124,285	7.6
1983	19.4	25,689	21.4	150,882	2.0
1984	-25.5	19,138	-5.7	142,282	19.8
1985	21.1	23,176	19.3	169,742	-1.8
1986	5.1	24,358	-7.5	157,011	-12.6

The volatility of aggressive equity funds leads to the greatest returns on a long-term basis, but at a relatively high risk. What are the results of the same system when applied to a conservative fund? Table 24-3 displays the buy-and-hold versus market timed results of a representative low risk fund, Value Line Income fund.

Gold funds have a history of high volatility. Table 24-4 represents a comparison of a buy-and-hold versus using a price-based trend-following timing technique on United Services Gold Shares.

Table 24-3: Value Line Income Fund

Year	Buy/Hold		Market Timing		Advantage Or Disadvantage With Market Timing
1970	6.7%	$10,670	19.3%	$11,930	12.6%
1971	13.5	12,110	19.4	14,244	5.9
1972	9.1	13,213	2.0	14,529	-7.1
1973	-15.9	11,112	8.8	15,807	24.7
1974	-16.1	9,323	7.9	17,055	24.0
1975	41.7	13,210	22.3	20,859	-19.4
1976	34.5	17,768	29.2	26,950	-5.3
1977	1.8	18,088	4.2	28,082	2.4
1978	11.1	20,095	16.5	32,716	5.4
1979	27.6	25,642	15.5	37,786	-12.1
1980	26.8	32,514	35.0	51,012	8.2
1981	16.4	37,846	6.2	54,174	10.2
1982	29.7	49,086	20.6	65,334	-9.1
1983	6.5	52,277	8.4	70,822	1.9
1984	2.7	53,688	14.1	80,808	11.4
1985	23.9	66,520	20.6	97,455	-3.3
1986	16.8	77,695	7.8	105,056	-9.0

In addition to understanding the risk and returns of a market timing system, an investor has the responsibility to find out everything he or she can about a timer and their system. Here are some questions you should ask a market timer

What kinds of funds do you manage with market timing? (Ask about aggressive and conservative growth funds, tax-exempt bond funds, GNMA, international, growth-income, corporate and gold funds, as well as funds on margin.)

When did you start using your timing model?

Are the results of your timing model simulated prior to your actual start date? For how long?

Table 24-4: United Services Gold Shares

Year	Buy/Hold		Market Timing		Advantage Or Disadvantage With Market Timing
1975	-38.9%	$ 6,110	-5.%	$ 9,470	33.6%
1976	-41.1	3,599	5.0	9,944	46.1
1977	39.9	5,035	11.8	11,117	-28.1
1978	9.0	5,488	-8.4	10,183	-17.4
1979	187.2	15,762	142.6	24,704	-44.6
1980	78.9	28,198	78.4	44,072	-0.5
1981	-28.0	20,303	1.1	44,557	29.1
1982	72.4	35,002	107.6	92,500	35.2
1983	1.0	35,352	6.3	98,328	5.3
1984	-29.6	24,888	1.0	99,311	30.6
1985	-26.8	18,218	-21.7	77,760	5.1
1986	37.9	25,123	28.7	100,077	-9.2

Do you provide your timing management with both load and no-load funds? (Beware of timers bearing only load funds.)

Do you depend on fundamental or technical analysis in determining your timing dates? (Fundamental analysis examines factors such as earnings, net worth, inflation, and the state of the economy. Technical analysis just monitors the supply and demand for stocks.)

Is your timing model proprietary or fully disclosed? (Very few of the best systems are totally revealed to investors. The timer's model is his or her stock in trade.)

Are your switches always documented? (Documentation is preferable.)

Is your timing model based on a strict formula or do you use subjective analysis? (Use of a formula takes the emotion and ego out of these crucial decisions. Gut decisions may be dangerous to your financial health.)

Do you provide long-term results of your timing strategies versus a buy-and-hold strategy on the funds you time? (One year's performance does not a timer make.)

What is your management fee structure? (Fees range from one to three percent. Do not pay more than two percent.)

What is your minimum account size?

How much is your set-up fee?

How often do you bill clients? (Some actually bill a year in advance!)

How much notice must a client give before termination of an account? (Many have a 30-day lead time. Consider that should you wish to terminate, it will most likely be because you want to get out *immediately*.)

Do you have a termination fee?

Do you send a regular newsletter to your managed accounts? (Ask for samples from firms you are considering. It will help you see the attitude toward clients. Is it friendly? Informative? Impersonal?)

What is the total value of mutual funds currently under management? Twenty million and up is the answer to look for to avoid beginners who will be learning with your money.

What is your previous business experience in the securities market? Outside the securities market? (A good market timer needs experience in both areas. And a person with a record of success tends to continue to be successful.)

Keeping these questions in mind, along with the basic points noted earlier, will give you an edge in the confusing world of investments and market timing.

Remember, any successful business needs advance research and planning. Do your homework and then look forward to being the one in ten people at the cocktail party who can honestly say "Yes, I've continued to make good money on *my* investments."

Chapter 25
Market Timing and Selecting Growth Funds

*by William E. Donoghue and Mary C. Driscoll
The Donoghue Organization, Inc.*

Buy low, sell high. This old stock market adage has intrigued investors since day one. After all, the highest returns go to the clever few who can select securities at bargain prices and sell out when those securities have peaked in value. Notice that we said "the clever few." Many investors, acting alone, simply do not have the time, energy, or skill it takes to run a "buy low, sell high" strategy. And, unfortunately, no stock carries a label saying that the current price is either low or high. Unsure which way to turn, too many individual investors become overly dependent on brokers' recommendations. Others blindly plunk their money down in the most heavily advertised equity mutual funds. Then the praying starts.

There's got to be a better way. For over a decade, we've been teaching investors to avoid the dangerous buy-hold-pray syndrome. We explain that the buy-hold approach can lead to mediocre returns or, worse, painful losses. We point out that there is a safer and potentially more profitable way to invest: following the principles of sound market timing and strategic selection of growth mutual funds. Moving in and out of the stock market at opportune moments is the goal of market timing. Investors who do this successfully will earn higher rates of return than investors who simply buy and hold. But market timing is only half the battle. Buying funds with the potential for top performance, and selling funds that are beginning to decline, is the other half. The idea here is to buy funds as they are making their way up the performance charts—not after they've won yesterday's race.

THE RISKS OF THE BUY-HOLD APPROACH

It doesn't take too much preaching on our part to convince investors that a buy-hold posture is like a car with faulty brakes and a poorly tuned engine. For one thing, if a buy-hold investor faces an unexpected need for cash and has to liquidate an equity position when the stock market or a particular fund is declining steadily, that investor may lose prior gains. That investor may even lose principal. For another, the buy-hold approach sacrifices the profit potential of strategy-minded portfolio management.

The numbers tell the story. A reasonable assumption: On January 1, 1986, a reader of *Donoghue's MONEYLETTER* invested in the Scudder Stevens & Clark fund family. He followed our percentage allocation advice (explained later in this chapter), committed to reinvesting all capital gains and dividends, and bought shares in Scudder's Capital Growth Fund, its International Fund, and its money fund, the Cash Investment Trust. (Both equity funds were on our top-five performance list for the twelve months ended December 1985. Thus, it's reasonable to assume that on January 1, 1986, the investor could have chosen these funds.)

If he invested $10,000 on January 1, 1986 and followed our advice throughout the year, he would have owned shares worth $11,959 on December 31. That's a total return of 19.6 percent. Now, compare that to a buy-hold approach based on the S & P 500 for the same period: 18.7 percent. Or, compare our reader's return to the average performance delivered by the largest aggressive growth funds: 17.56 percent. The average performance of all equity funds was 13.56 percent during 1986. The most popular aggressive growth fund, Fidelity Magellan, earned 23.8 percent. (20 percent if you adjust for the sales charge), but investors who "bought and held" Magellan spent many hairy moments during the year. Magellan certainly has a superior long-term track record (a 30-percent average annual total return from 1982 to 1986), but it produced negative returns at times during 1986. Many people are not comfortable with high levels of investment risk, and they don't think the extra long-term return justifies losing sleep when Magellan falters.

THE DONOGHUE ALTERNATIVE

We offer an investment alternative that has two basic ingredients: market timing and the ability to spot the strongest growth mutual funds before the race for the top-ten list is over. Once you get your personal portfolio set up, the idea is to own funds demonstrating relative strength at the right time, not to invest in a fund simply because its average, long-term performance looks good. After all, if the market is rising while yesterday's number one fund is suffering a temporary slide—as all funds eventually do—investors in that fund are losing prior gains and missing today's opportunities. Buying and holding yesterday's winner means you risk buying in at the peak of that fund's performance and perhaps having to sell at the bottom.

Our strategy recommends specific stock market mutual funds, which may be either no-load or low-load, when the stock market is rising and calls for switches into money-market mutual funds or short-term bond funds when the market is clearly on a downward trend. We also urge people to invest in overseas stock and bond markets—through mutual funds, of course—when attractive opportunities exist and portfolio diversification is desired.

How do we time the market? First, by analyzing interest rates, we spot strong economic trends in their infancy, and thus move in or out of the market long before the market's direction is obvious to one and all. Second, we analyze the market's own dynamics to gain a sense of how it might behave in the short run. For example, we try to anticipate how stock prices will respond to world politics, global trade imbalances, the value of the U.S. dollar, and assorted indicators of domestic economic strength. Overall, our aim is to predict the major stock market moves. We want to "get while the gettin's good" but switch gears and pursue safe money-market yields just before the party breaks up.

Why the heavy emphasis on interest rate analysis? It's no secret that over the long run the movement of interest rates determines stock market direction. Students majoring in finance can recite a number of reasons why stock prices decline when rates are rising. They can also explain why the reverse is also true: stock prices rise when rates are falling. Figure 25-1 below illustrates this point.

Figure 25-1: S & P 500 versus MF Yields

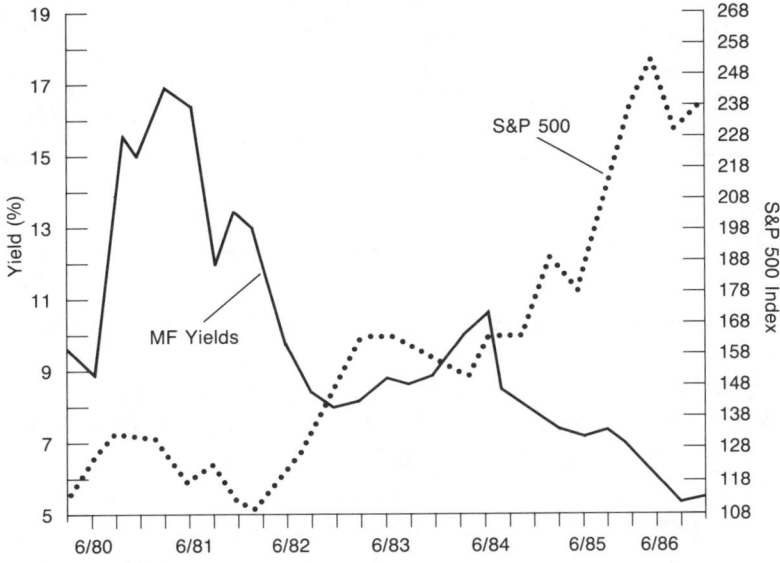

Money fund yields are a good measure of interest rates.

Because the stock market adjusts its overall direction in response to changing interest rate trends, a timing strategy based on interest rate movements will outperform the buy-hold posture over the long haul. Specifically, when the market is declining, we'll be earning safe money-market yields while the buy-hold investors are fretting over negative returns. When it's time to buy back into the stock market, we will be fortified by preserved capital as well as yields earned in the money market. Meanwhile, buy-hold investors will be playing "catch-up." (See Figure 25-2.)

Figure 25-2

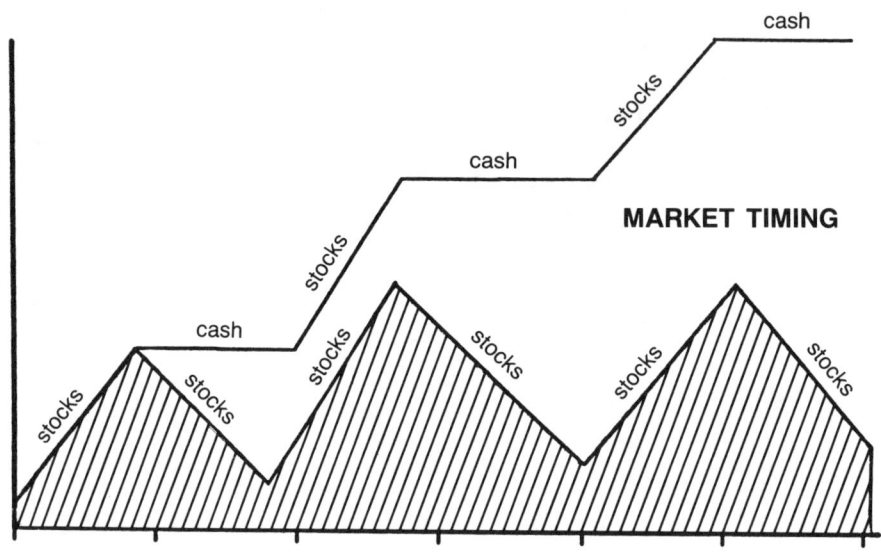

A quick look at recent interest rate movements, and the stock market's response, proves our point. In August 1982, the stock market blasted off on what proved to be a record-breaking surge. By the end of January 1987, stock prices, as measured by the Dow Jones Industrial Average, had jumped over 180 percent. It's no coincidence that in 1982 interest rates peaked and beat a hasty retreat from super-high levels. As the bull market emerged, growth stock mutual funds were the smart place to be. The top performers earned over 200 percent between the summer of 1982 and the end of 1986. During this period, as interest rates continued their steady decline, bond funds also produced healthy capital gains.

Now, if you had owned a crystal ball in 1982, you would have known to load up on growth funds. Without the benefit of clairvoyance, however, you could have tried "timing the market" as the sustained downward interest rate trend clearly emerged. And that's where our strategy would have come in handy. It would have advised you to put increasing percentages of your investment dollars in growth mutual funds as the bull market gathered steam. Obviously, at the beginning of a bull market, share prices are relatively low and substantial profits are possible. Our strategy would also have identified which growth funds promised the best relative performance.

If you were following our advice during 1986, you would have also protected your bull market earnings from violent market drops during July and September and captured the mouth-watering returns produced by international growth mutual funds. For example, in the fall of 1985, we signalled a partial move into no-load international funds. We recommended T. Rowe Price International Stock Fund and Scudder International. During 1986, these funds delivered total returns of 62 percent and 52 percent, respectively.

This signal was based on our own analysis of currency trends and market strength overseas. We sensed as well that in 1986 the domestic stock market, while still quite bullish, was set for volatile swings and several spells of sideways trading after a long upward climb. Note, however, that all along our timing system flashed eventual new highs for the domestic market. In January 1987, it rose dramatically with the Dow surging over 200 points in the first three weeks of January alone.

It's important to note that our approach is geared toward major stock market moves, changes in the Dow of at least 10–15 percent. We do not attempt to call short-term market swings. It has never been proven that anyone can consistently call market tops or bottoms over the short term. The lack of evidence notwithstanding, many aggressive traders try to do just that.

The market timing component of our strategy is based on long-term indicators tested for their ability to identify significant changes in market direction. Why focus only on major market moves? Our system is conservative by nature—the primary aims are to earn above-average returns through early participation in a strong bull market and to safeguard assets by avoiding losses when the bull has retired. Our system was built for investors who do not want to alter their mutual fund portfolios more frequently than several times a year.

Timing Indicators

Every indicator has its own strengths and weaknesses. Some are good at calling market tops (sell signals), others market bottoms (buy signals). In general, it is easier to find indicators that are good at calling bottoms. We base our timing on a mix of indicators that enable us to call both tops and bottoms. There is of course no one glorious indicator that unlocks the door to stock market riches. Our timing system also strives for simplicity—one can endlessly multiply the number of indicators without significantly improving timing calls.

We settled on three indicators. One proved to be very good at calling market bottoms; another does well with market tops. The third serves to confirm what we learn analyzing the first two. The three indicators are: (1) mutual fund cash positions, (2) the relationship—yield curve—between long- and short-term interest rates, and (3) the average maturity index of institutions-only money market funds. We adjust the first indicator for the influence of interest rates. We also calculate various rates of change in the second indicator to elicit a signal. We then use well-known statistical techniques to get a handle on the "extreme" values of the indicators.

With three indicators, and thus three calls on the market, we need a way to combine them to arrive at one unambiguous signal. (The indicators don't always agree on the direction the market will take next.) The solution comes from assigning weights to the indicators, based on what we know about the market's current direction. For example, if we are looking for a market top, we give the most weight to the indicator whose strength is calling market tops.

Looking at our system's calls since 1975, we find that it leans toward conservatism. It kept us out of the market when there were two large moves up—they took place during a period of high and fluctuating interest rates. The system turned bullish in August 1982 and has been bullish ever since.

Moreover, when the indicators are in complete agreement, the system will call for either maximum, 100 percent investment in equity funds or 0 percent, that is, no stock market participation. When the indicators disagree, our timing system will call for only partial investment in stock funds. How much depends on the weights assigned to the positive indicators.

Note that interest rates play a key role in our system. Two of the indicators are interest rates or market responses to them. This system is an evolution of the original tenet that interest rates drive the stock market.

What we now have is a mechanical tool for allocating assets, including new money coming available for investment, between money funds or short-term bond fund and growth funds. We apply this advice to three categories of mutual fund investors: (1) the true conservatives, (2) the more risk-oriented, or active, people, and (3) the clearly venturesome.

Fund Selection

The strategy also spots the most promising no-load and low-load growth funds within a universe of funds we track. How do we determine that universe? To be included, a growth fund must offer telephone exchange privileges, so that investors can easily move back and forth between money funds and growth funds. The fund must also have at least $50 million in assets, be managed by a well-respected money management firm, sport a strong track record and be a relatively consistent performer. Extreme volatility is a "no-no." We favor no-load funds, but we also include the top-performing low-load funds.

We search for growth funds that promise to beat the pack by analyzing fund performance over key time periods. Analyzing past performance over various time periods helps us spot the up-and-comers and simultaneously weed out "flash-in-the-pan" funds that land by fluke on the short-term, top-ten performance lists. Our fund selection system yields strong performance results in both up and down markets. Realize, however, that our market timing signals will have us either totally or partially out of equities during market declines.

Each fund is assigned a numerical rank, reflecting a blend of short- and long-term performance. A built-in trend confirmation factor attempts to spot funds that will most likely deliver the best results in the future. Just as important, it spots funds that are losing ground—and those that will most likely remain behind the competition.

Our system recognizes that there is no such thing as a consistent winner. Even the fund with the best average long-term performance suffers occasional declines. What's more, the fact that the market in general is rising doesn't guarantee that all funds will move up in sync. Our goal is to recommend the funds which are gaining relative strength at any point in a bull market.

By its nature, our fund selection system offers a fail-safe mechanism: it will move you quickly out of a growth fund that is nosediving and into one that is moving up into the winner's circle. That said, it's important to note that our fund selection system is not built on a hair trigger.

If a fund is performing well, our tracking system will pick it up, and we will continue to recommend it as long as it delivers a relatively attractive investment result. On the other hand, if one of our "buy" recommendations ceases to perform and stumbles badly, we'll issue a "sell" recommendation on that fund.

The primary goal is to move you in and out of funds based on how they are performing compared to all the funds in our universe. In addition, by flagging the currently best performing funds, our advice helps you allocate new money that's just become available for growth fund investing.

Our system is designed to help you avoid painful losses and those sleepless nights that come from investing in a fund before it slumps, and waiting for it to rebound just so you can break even.

For a sample copy of our newsletter, write to *Donoghue's MONEYLETTER*, Dept. P-1, Box 540, Holliston, Mass., 01746 or call 800-343-5413.

Chapter 26
The Upgrading Strategy
by Burton Berry, DAL Investment Company

"Buy low, sell high," the lullaby of old Wall Street. But can the market be beaten with any degree of consistency? Many investors spend a lifetime poring through the growing library of books, magazines, financial newspapers, newsletters, and the latest rage, TV and radio talk-shows, exploring the world of finance and investing. Much of this enormous flow of intelligence has to do with market timing coming from the gurus who claim the secrets of how to sell near the top, park your cash until the market bottoms out, and then reinvest for the big killing! The appeal of such a fountain of wealth is so great as to almost irresistible, whether it works or not.

The tremendous growth of mutual funds and the advent of computerized shareholder recordkeeping and toll-free telephoning have enabled funds to participate in this trend by providing and promoting switching. The primary use of telephone exchanging is to put your money in the right place at the right time. Paralleling the bull market that started mid-1982, the use of funds for market timing became epidemic, generally to the delight of the fund industry.

Sector funds are the latest products developed, offering investors the opportunity to telephone-switch their money into the various stock market sectors or international areas for the purpose of swinging into the right sector at the right time. This sector trading strategy also includes the use of money funds so that if all sectors go to hell at the same time, money can be switched to the sector money fund. To date, studies on the records of investors playing the sector game seem to conclude that the chances of being in the right sector at the right time hold about the same promise of success as market timing between growth funds and money funds. Note that professional money managers who use market timing or sector-switch investing are few and far between. Most professionals accept the futility of trying to beat the market by timing or sectoring.

The fact is that there are so many forces influencing the direction of the stock market, as well as interest rates (which in themselves influence movements in the stock market) that they make accurate forecasting, particularly in the short term, principally a matter of luck. And the financial markets get more complex with computerization and the speed of communication. Consequently the forces influencing the markets, many of them new, continue growing.

So what are the alternatives? We believe staying with the winning funds—upgrading—may offer the best opportunity for investment success.

"Upgrading" is an investment strategy that is practical only with no-load funds. We started using it in 1969, when DAL Investment Co.® became registered as an investment adviser. The purpose was to use the little-known or understood no-load mutual funds as the principal investment vehicle for client portfolios. Taking advantage of commission-free trading, our objective was to keep client assets in the best-performing funds. And when their funds were no longer doing well, we "upgraded" to the winners.

As our advisory business grew, the statistical data developed for rating no-load funds worked so well that it was put together in the form of a monthly newsletter, **NoLOAD FUND*X®

The universe of no-load funds had grown from around 60 in 1969 to 120 when we published the first issue of the newsletter in April 1976. Today, **NoLOAD FUND*X® includes over 500 no-load and low-load funds (and subscribers around the world). By the end of 1986 the mutual fund industry, including full-load funds, grew to some 1900 funds, a greater number than all stocks on the New York Stock Exchange!

All funds in the newsletter are divided into ten classes and subclasses so that only similar funds are compared with one another. Every month the top funds in each category are identified with two stars (**) so that subscribers can quickly identify the winning funds in the various categories. There are three classes of common stock growth funds, *Very Aggressive*, *Aggressive*, and *Conservative*; and three classes of income funds, *Total Return Funds*, *Bond Funds* (divided into corporate, U.S. government, and tax-exempt), and *Money-Market Funds* (divided into diversified, U.S. government, and tax-exempt).

The upgrading strategy is not market timing and certainly not buy-and-hold. Most investment experts today consider buy-and-hold an outdated and usually unsuccessful investment strategy (without lots of luck). Upgrading is really a basic, fundamental concept—keeping money in the top-performing funds in the investment categories, or classes, selected by the investor. Obviously in the world of mutual funds the greatest difference in performance between best and worst is in the stock funds. And in this area by far the best record has been in **NoLOAD FUND*X® Class 3, the higher-quality growth funds.

Because of the momentum in the fund industry, particularly among the more conservative funds, leadership endures for many months, sometimes years, so the upgrading strategy does not involve constant buying and selling.

We have monitored investment results of upgrading since August of 1976, using one top fund in each of the three common stock classes. (That's when the Vanguard Index Trust was first offered, a fund that invests in the Standard & Poor's 500 Stock Index. This provided excellent comparison of any investment strategy against the "market.") Starting in August 1976 with the number one fund in each of the three stock fund classes, the fund was held until it no longer was among the top five in its class in the monthly ratings. A fallen fund was sold on the first Friday following the approximate receipt date of our newsletter. The proceeds of the sale were reinvested on the next Friday in what was then the new number one fund in each class. This theoretically allowed time for receipt of the newsletter and making the trades. In all classes, the strategy outperformed the "market" dramatically. But Class 3, the conservative growth fund category, was by far the best. For the ten-year-and-seven-month period 8/31/76 to 3/31/87, the Class 3 upgrading model would have gained 1539 percent, which is an annual compound growth rate of 30.1 percent. This assumes reinvestment of dividends and capital gains when paid. Taxes were not considered.

There are about 1000 financial newsletters, over 50 specializing in mutual funds. The *Hulbert Financial Digest*, a monthly newsletter, monitors the performance of about 100 leading newsletters, using its own statistical calculations, analyzing all recommendations and the investment results as their subscribers would have experienced them in the real world. (Needless to say, individual "guru" claims were frequently far greater than those discovered by Mr. Hulbert.) In measuring results of ***NoLOAD FUND*X* ®, Hulbert uses all five top-rated funds in Classes 1, 2, and 3, sells them all each month upon the receipt of the newsletter, and reinvests proceeds equally in the current issue's top five funds in each class. Naturally this dilutes the performance since the same funds are often sold and immediately repurchased. But despite this, ***NoLOAD FUND*X*® rates not only among the very best of mutual fund newsletters, but among the best of *all* financial newsletters followed in the *Hulbert Financial Digest*.

The success of the upgrading strategy surprises many experts, perhaps because it is so simple. But consider the logic—it is obvious that so long as you stay with the best-performing funds on a continuing basis, your investment results should be superior. Particularly when trading is commission-free.

Before 1987, taxable investors needed to watch capital gains holding periods. The Tax Reform Act of 1986 ended favorable treatment for long-term capital gains. Now federal taxes imposed on short-term gains are the same as long-term gains and investors need not be discouraged from upgrading their holdings just because they haven't owned funds for six months. This caution was never necessary in tax-deferred plans such as IRAs, Keoghs, and pension plans. (State taxes may still distinguish between long- and short-term tax rates.)

While the strategy is quite simple, it does require attention. What should be done in the event of a repeat of the 73-74 bear market when the S&P 500, for example, declined 37 percent including dividends over the two-year market collapse? Obviously all investments involve risk and so do all investment strategies. With upgrading, market declines can be dealt with in two ways. First of all, it is possible to use a "stop-loss" based on declines in a given fund's price, or using the "market" overall as an indicator to sell after a certain percentage drop. The risk here is getting whipsawed by selling just as the market bottoms out, rebuying near the top, and then reselling again near the bottom. This can be controlled to some extent by setting a larger decline as the target, for example, 15 percent on the S&P 500. Or similar declines in individual funds. You must also have a plan for re-entering the market.

For investors with greater risk tolerance there's a strategy of hanging in or moving into more conservative funds during a sharp market decline. Funds that hold portfolios of higher-yielding stocks, convertible preferreds, and convertible debentures and often larger cash positions are more defensive. What happens in this "hanging in" strategy is that in a prolonged market decline the "top-performing" funds themselves may have gone heavily into cash, sometimes well over 50 percent. So in effect, investors have market-timed, but indirectly through the funds to which they have upgraded in declining markets.

The upgrading strategy is no magic beat-the-market, get-rich-quick "system." But there have been countless techniques promoted over the years for dealing with the irrational behavior of securities markets. Unfortunately they don't have a good record. There is no science to the markets' moods because the major force driving stock and bond prices is the psychology of the marketplace, often led by unpredictable and conflicting human emotions of greed and fear. With the introduction of computers in the operation of both the markets and the funds, and the explosion of media attention to the financial markets, aggressive trading has soared. Investors of all types are going for it, from the $2000-a-year IRA investor to the billion-dollar institutions. But the bottom line in any investment strategy is how it works. While upgrading does not carry the excitement of active trading through stock brokers, or telephone switching among sector funds or between stock and money-market funds, the results speak for themselves. The strategy of staying with winners makes sense. There *is* an alternative to buy-and-hold and market timing.

Chapter 27
Using Moving Averages
by John Waggoner, Personal Investing

The idea behind market timing is to buy at the bottom and sell at the top. This is an idea that sounds good, of course—but so does turning lead into gold. The fact of the matter is that no one has discovered a way to time the stock market perfectly, and no one is likely to do so in the near future. Even if someone did figure out how to buy at the bottom and sell at the top, it's doubtful that he or she would want to share it with anyone else.

But that doesn't necessarily mean that you should simply buy a stock or a mutual fund and hold it forever, either. Although a buy-and-hold strategy will generally make money, the payback period could be a long time coming if you buy close to the top. And you could put your money to much more productive use than waiting for the stock market to retrace its gains—like stuffing it in your mattress, for example.

Instead of attempting to predict the market's tops and bottoms, however, many investors simply try to follow the market, buying when the market appears oversold and selling when the market appears overbought. Again, given the stock market's penchant for wild gyrations, this is easier said than done. On April 7, 1987, for instance, the Dow Jones average shot up nearly 60 points in one day—which, for many investors, was a sure sign that the market was on its way up. They were sadly mistaken—the market resumed the decline that began in March and finished the month 100 points lower than its April 7 peak.

One way of smoothing out the market's up-and-down movements is charting moving averages, which are running tallies of the average price action of a stock, mutual fund, or market index. As with many similar trend-following techniques, moving averages have their drawbacks. At worst, moving averages can whip you in and out of the market in search of elusive gains. And even at their best, moving averages won't get you in at the bottom or out at the top. But many times, moving averages can give you 60 percent to 80 percent of a gain—and help you avoid losses of similar magnitude.

HOW THEY WORK

A moving average is simply the average price of a security or index over a given period of time. The difference between a moving average and an ordinary average, however, is that a moving average is updated at regular intervals by deleting the oldest price from the average and inserting the most recent price. A 30-week moving average of the Dow Jones Industrial Average, for example, is simply the average price of the index over a 30-week period. Each subsequent week, the oldest index price is dropped and the most recent one is added.

For example, suppose you wanted to calculate the 10-week moving average of the Raging Bull fund, an aggressive growth fund. Each week, you'd look up the fund's Friday closing price and write it down. Your list might look like this:

Weekly Fund Price	Ten-Week Total	Ten-Week Moving Average
Week 1: $10.00		
Week 2: $10.13		
Week 3: $10.44		
Week 4: $10.37		
Week 5: $10.15		
Week 6: $10.53		
Week 7: $11.07		
Week 8: $10.87		
Week 9: $11.02		
Week 10: $11.23	$105.81	$10.58

The next week, you would repeat the procedure, dropping the oldest figure (Week 1) and adding the newest (Week 11):

Weekly Fund Price	Ten-Week Total	Ten-Week Moving Average
Week 1: $10.00		
Week 2: $10.13		
Week 3: $10.44		
Week 4: $10.37		
Week 5: $10.15		
Week 6: $10.53		
Week 7: $11.07		
Week 8: $10.87		
Week 9: $11.02		
Week 10: $11.23	$105.81	$10.58
Week 11: $11.15	$106.96	$10.69

Plotted over time, the moving average will give you a smoothed line, rather than the typical "fever line" typical of most securities price charts. Essentially, the average is a long-term view of price action, discounting week-to-week fluctuations and showing overall price trends.

TIME SPAN

The best time span for a moving average is a matter of hot debate. As you can see from the previous examples, however, the shorter the time period you use, the closer the moving average will resemble the actual price trend. Longer-term moving averages will result in smoother lines and show less resemblance to actual price movements.

The most popular time spans for short-term movements are 10-week and 13-week moving averages. Technicians with longer-term outlooks tend to choose either 30-week or 39-week moving averages.

When deciding on the time span, however, your most important decision should already have been made: That is, what kind of investor are you? If you're an aggressive market-timer seeking maximum capital gains, then a 10- or 13-week moving average would probably best suit your needs. If you're an extremely active trader (and if you are, I know several brokers who'd love to meet you), you could use a moving average as short as 2 or 3 weeks.

If your major concern is avoiding a large loss on your long-term holdings, then a 30- or 39-week average is probably all you'd need. Averages longer than 39 weeks, however, are so insensitive to price fluctuations as to be next to useless. If you used a 100-week moving average in 1929, for example, you probably wouldn't have gotten out of the market until after the Korean War.

MARKET TIMING WITH MOVING AVERAGES

Market timing with moving averages is a trend-following approach. Rather than attempting to anticipate price movements, investors attempt to spot follow uptrends and downtrends and make their moves accordingly. When the Dow moves upwards, trend followers buy stock. When the Dow moves downwards, trend followers sell stock and move to cash positions.

There are three different ways to follow trends with moving averages. For the sake of example, suppose you're charting the moving average of the Dow Jones Industrial Average against the actual price movements of the index. (The technique works not only for deciding whether or not to buy stock, but also whether to buy or sell a mutual fund or an individual stock.)

The first method, and the one most frequently used, is:

1. When the Dow rises above its moving average and the moving average is trending upward, buy stock.
2. When the Dow falls below its moving average and the moving average is trending downward, sell stock.

With this method, the time span of your moving average is crucial; if your moving average's time span is too short, you run the risk of making too many trades. Frequent trading can be hazardous to your wealth: You'll run up large commission costs and capital gains, and you'll run the risk of getting whipped in and out of the market too quickly. And a moving average that's too long won't time the market at all. Most investors who use this technique use a 30- or 39-week moving average.

Figure 27-1 shows the basic moving average market timing technique in action. Here the Dow is plotted against a 30-week moving average. Using this method, you would buy into the stock market sometime after the second month in August and sell just after the second week in September—just after a near record-breaking Dow plunge, incidentally. Your next buy signal would happen in December, 1986, shortly before the Dow started soaring to record heights.

Figure 27-1

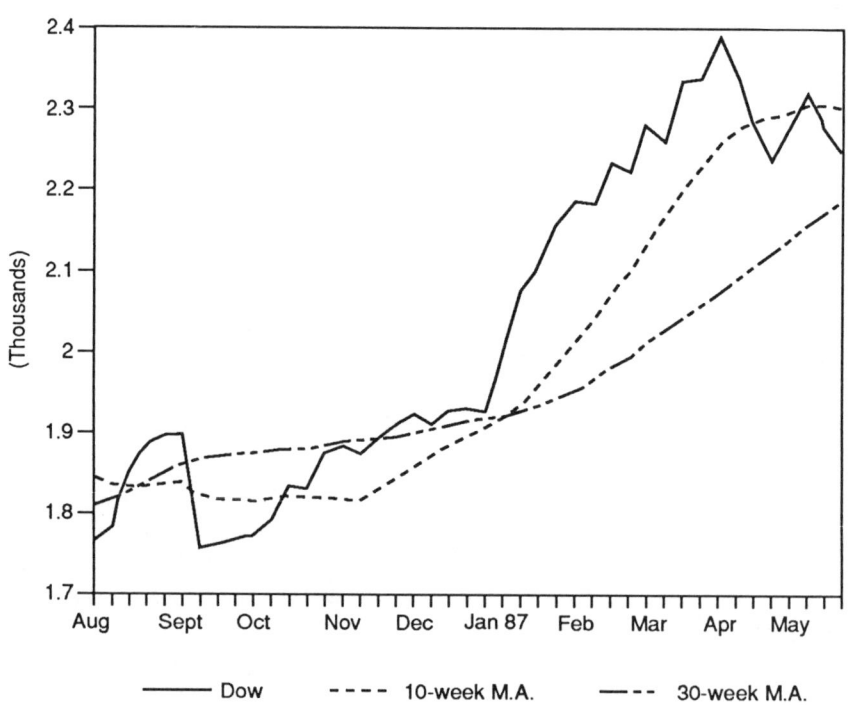

Note that the 30-week moving average touched the Dow line in October. Until the index price moves above the moving average *and* the index is moving upwards, however, you wouldn't buy into the market. Note also that, despite a nearly 10-percent drop in the Dow through April and May 1987, no sell signal had been generated by the end of May. So if you use the basic moving average timing technique, be aware that you will take losses from time to time: no method is foolproof. In general, however, this method would have had you in the market during significant rises most of the time.

A more serious drawback is the dreaded "whipsaw"—moving in and out of the market when the overall trend is flat. There was some small whipsawing action in Figure 27-1, when an investor would have been in the market for a little over a month between August and September 1986.

Figure 27-2 shows some of the dangers of using a shorter-term moving average; here the Dow is plotted against a 10-week moving average. An investor would have been in and out of the market four times during a one-and-a-half-year period. And a heart-stopping journey it would have been: Two of the round trips (in August and November) would have been virtually profitless. The foray in late August to late September would have made some money, and, of course, the entry in December would have been a doozy. Still, the costs and annoyance of trading in and out so rapidly may not have made the short-term average worth the effort.

Figure 27-2

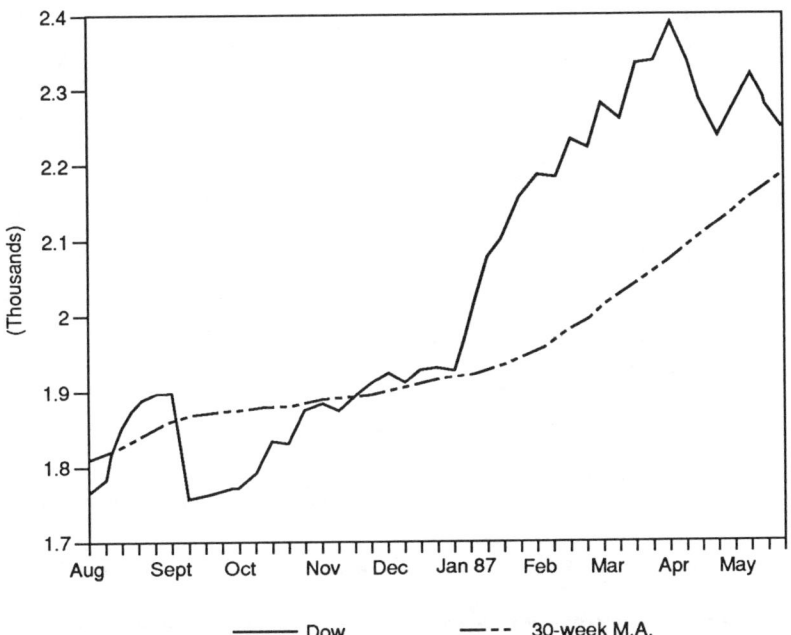

Variations on a Theme

Another method uses two sets of moving averages. Using an equity fund as an example, the rules for this method are:

1. Plot the fund's 30-week moving average, its 13-week moving average, and its weekly closing price.
2. When the 10-week moving average crosses below the 30-week moving average, sell your fund shares and park your money in a money fund.
3. When the equity fund's 10-week moving average crosses above the 39-week moving average, use your money market investment to buy shares of the equity fund.

Fans of this system say that it cuts down on the possibility of getting whipsawed. Because the method uses two averages, it takes some time for another switch signal to be generated after one has just occurred.

Figure 27-3 shows the two-average method at work.

Figure 27-3

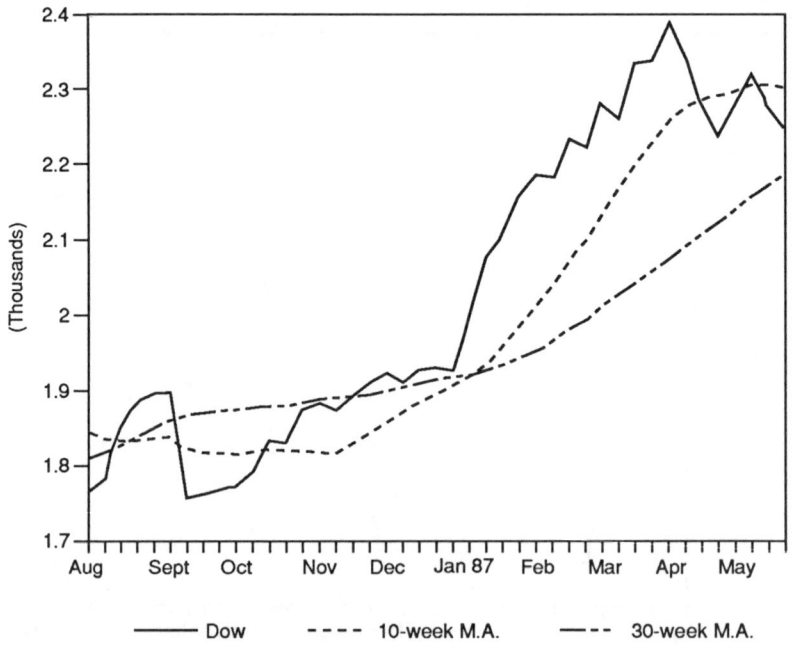

Here the investor would get a sell signal in late August, and a buy signal in mid-January. This method would have avoided some of the whipsawing caused by the first technique, but at a cost: The investor's entry in the red-hot January 1987 market would have been somewhat delayed. On the other hand, the investor would also have avoided the precipitous September 1986 slide, when the Dow fell over 120 points in two days.

Keep in mind, however, that an especially volatile market would still result in whipsawing. If you invested in the average gold fund between 1985 and 1986, for example, you would have moved in and out of the fund several times in search of elusive gains.

One final technique often employed by true moving average fans is the weighted moving average. This technique makes the moving average more sensitive by giving a higher value to recent prices and a lower value to older ones. Here's how it works:

1. Select the time span you would like to use. (In this example, I'm using a 10-week moving average to save space.)
2. Multiply the oldest price by one, the second-oldest price by two and so on until you reach the most recent price.
3. Total up the multiplied prices.
4. Total up the multipliers.
5. Divide the multiplied prices by the multipliers.

Here's a sample calculation of the weighted moving average of the Raging Bull fund:

Weekly Fund Price	*Multiplier*	*Column1 X Column 2*
Week 1: $10.00	* 1	10.00
Week 2: $10.13	* 2	20.26
Week 3: $10.44	* 3	31.32
Week 4: $10.37	* 4	41.48
Week 5: $10.15	* 5	50.75
Week 6: $10.53	* 6	63.18
Week 7: $11.07	* 7	77.49
Week 8: $10.87	* 8	86.96
Week 9: $11.02	* 9	99.18
Week 10: $11.23	*10	112.30

Sum of column 2: 55
Sum of column 3: 592.92
Sum of column 3 divided by sum of column 2 (592.92/55): 10.78.

In general, this technique gives greater emphasis to more recent data and downplays older information. And it makes your moving average more sensitive. Again, however, overly sensitive moving averages are not always an investor's best friend.

The Joys of the Average

Moving averages aren't the most sophisticated investment technique. But that's probably their greatest appeal. If you invest by using moving averages, you need only to spend about five minutes a week calculating and plotting your averages. If you have a computer at your mercy and a reasonably decent spreadsheet program, such as Lotus 1-2-3, the time you'll need to make your investment decisions will be relatively brief. And, if you don't want to be bothered with plotting your own moving averages, there are several excellent newsletters which will do so for you. I've included the addresses of three of them for your convenience.

The major drawback with moving averages, of course, is also their simplicity. As with any mechanical, widely followed system, they won't work all the time with every fund and with every market. And they're murder in a sideways or flat market.

To be truly successful in investing, you need to keep your eyes open at all times. This is especially true with moving averages. If, for example, you see hundreds of investment advisors hurling themselves off Wall Street buildings, it would probably be a good idea to sell, no matter what your charts tell you. But in general, moving averages can keep you invested during the best part of a bull market and safely in cash when the bears come out to play.

MOVING AVERAGE NEWSLETTERS

Telephone Switch Newsletter, Box 2538, Huntington Beach, CA 92647
The Mutual Fund Chartist, Box 6600, Rapid City, SD 57709
The Mutual Fund Specialist, Box 1025, Eau Claire, WI 54701

Chapter 28
Switch Strategies
by James McKeever, The Mutual Fund Advantage

The key to successful investing in mutual funds is correct timing of your moves from fund to fund. One of the reasons we recommend families of funds such as Fidelity, Lexington, and Financial Strategic funds is the ease with which you can switch from one fund to another. But equally important is picking the proper time to make the switch, which is one of the benefits of a subscription to *Mutual Fund Advantage*.

Here at MFA headquarters, we maintain data on several hundred funds—funds that generally fulfill the basic requirements for our recommendations. We diligently track these funds, using both computers and manual data-gathering, and we maintain charts of the performance of these funds for use both in our own research and for presentation here at MFA. In addition, however, we keep track of many other factors that can affect switching decisions, some of which we will be discussing below.

There are a large number of indicators available in the economy on which one can base his financial decisions. The government releases quite a few "economic indicators" each month, including such things as the Consumer Price Index (CPI), the various money supply figures, durable goods orders, and so forth. All of these indicators have some meaning to the investor, especially those invested in stocks and bonds. Since most mutual funds use stocks and bonds as their investment vehicles, these indicators also affect our decisions.

In this article, we will examine in some detail four of the indicators we watch closely, to see their effect on the various classes of mutual funds. We will relate each of these indicators to four groups of funds—growth funds, income funds, international funds, and precious metals funds. We will see whether, and how, these various indicators are reliable in helping us make our switch decisions and develop a strategy based on these indicators to maximize our profits.

The four indicators we will be examining are:

1. Discount rate
2. Swiss franc exchange rate
3. London gold price
4. Dow Jones Industrial Average

We will evaluate each of these indicators as to its relationship, if any, to the four mutual fund groups mentioned above. We will find that an investment strategy can be based on any one of these indicators, but that a combination may provide the best all-around strategy.

Since mutual fund investments tend to be fairly long-term, with switching taking place only a few times a year at most, we do not want to make switch decisions based on minimal changes in the indicators we watch. Instead, we are looking for changes in direction, such as the start of a new bull or bear market or a reversal of a trend in interest rates.

It is these changes in direction that will give us clues as to the need for changes in our fund portfolio. But we will see that detecting a change in direction is not always simple, nor will it always be as prompt as we would like. Let's take a look at some of these areas to see what we mean.

THE DISCOUNT RATE

The discount rate is the rate of interest charged by the Federal Reserve to its member banks when they borrow from the Fed. As you will see in Figure 28-1, the discount rate tends to drive the prime rate, which is the rate of interest charged by banks to their best customers. If the discount rate rises, the prime rate will have to follow, and if the discount rate falls, so will the prime rate.

Figure 28-1: Monthly Prime Rate/Discount Rate Graph

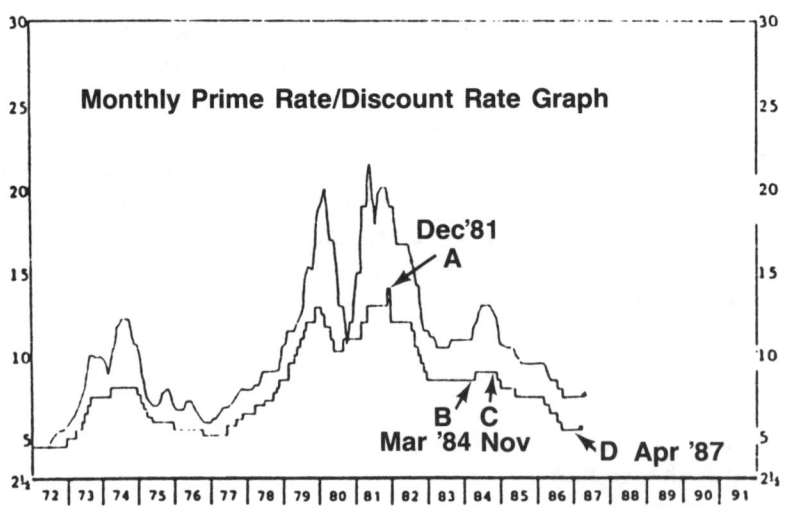

The prime rate will, of course, influence all other interest rates, including the cost of consumer financing, but these other rates may lag behind the changes in prime and discount rates by some period of time, perhaps measured in months. One indication of this is the extremely slow decline in the rates for credit card interest. Although the prime rate fell from 14 percent to 5-1/2 percent over the last 5 years, we have seen very little in the way of relief for the credit card consumer. While the banks were quick to raise their rates during the preceding rise in discount and prime rates, they have been extremely slow to reduce them again.

As you can see, detecting a change in direction in the discount rate is very simple. Once a direction is established, it rarely changes for at least two years—the exception being the brief up-turn in rates between March and November of 1984. We have marked the changes in direction as points A, B, C and D on the graph for comparison with the same points in time in the various fund graphs we will present.

First, let us look at the relationship between the reversals in discount rate and the growth funds. Generally speaking, it would seem reasonable that falling interest rates would be beneficial to business and would result in rising stock prices across the board. Thus, we would expect to see the growth funds react upward during times of falling interest rates, and react downward during times of rising interest rates.

The Manhattan Fund bears out this belief (see Figure 28-2). Had an investor bought this fund whenever the interest rate trend turned down and sold when it turned up, the result would have been a profit of 110 percent over the five year period involved.

Figure 28-2: Manhattan Fund

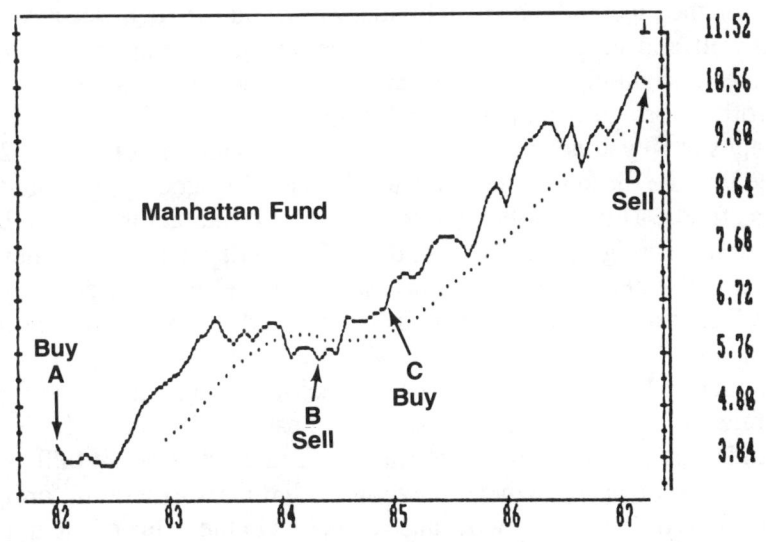

The same trend can be seen on the graph of Fidelity Puritan fund (Figure 28-3), although the growth is not as great. The buy and sell signals in the growth funds, based on the discount rate alone, provide an impressive result.

Figure 28-3: Puritan Fund

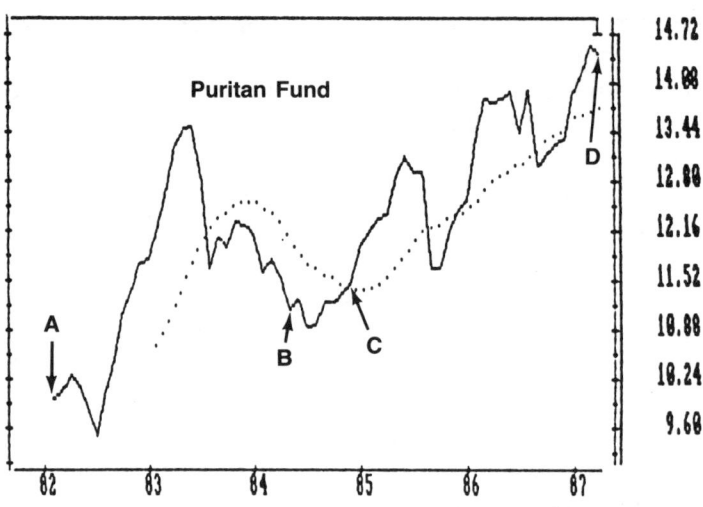

A similar, though less impressive, pattern can be seen in the income funds (Figures 28-4 and 28-5). As interest rates rise, bonds decline in value, and vice versa. Since much of the investment in the income funds is in bonds, we would expect to see a contra-trend in these funds as well, and such is the case. As can be seen in the graphs, however, the bond market would seem to anticipate the interest rate turns, and the actual indicator loses quite a lot of the profit before giving a firm signal to sell.

From the graphs of Keystone and Rowe Price International funds (Figures 28-6 and 28-7), we can see that the discount rate indicator does a fairly good job of predicting turns in the overseas funds. This is probably due primarily to the fact that when U.S. interest rates rise, it attracts foreign investment in the U.S. and depresses investment in foreign markets. When U.S. interest rates drop, investors move elsewhere, pushing the foreign stocks higher. This same phenomenon will be observed when we analyze the currency markets and the overseas funds.

We will find that, in looking at the graphs of precious metals funds (see Figures 28-8), the discount rate indicator provides as good an indication of trends as it did with the international funds, and for much the same reasons. If interest rates are falling in the U.S., and investors seek to invest elsewhere, they must sell dollars to acquire foreign currency for investment. This dollar selling will cause a decline in the value of the dollar, and will result in higher prices for the precious metals, in terms of dollars.

Chapter 28

Figure 28-4: Fidelity High Yield Fund

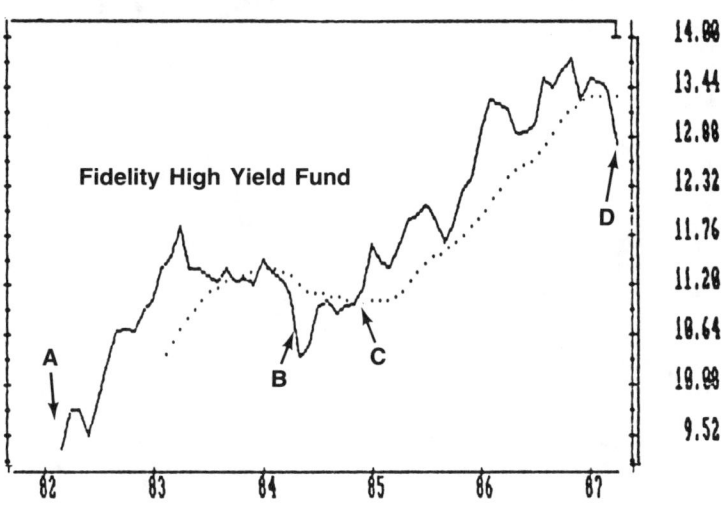

Figure 28-5: Fidelity High Income Fund

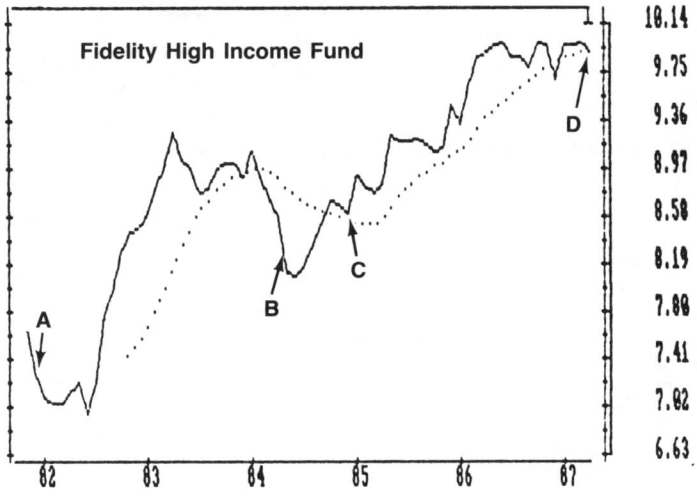

Figure 28-6: Keystone International

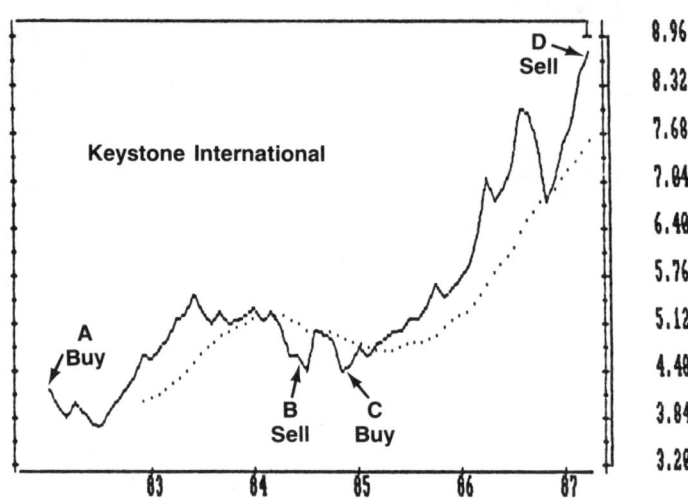

Figure 28-7: Rowe Price International Fund

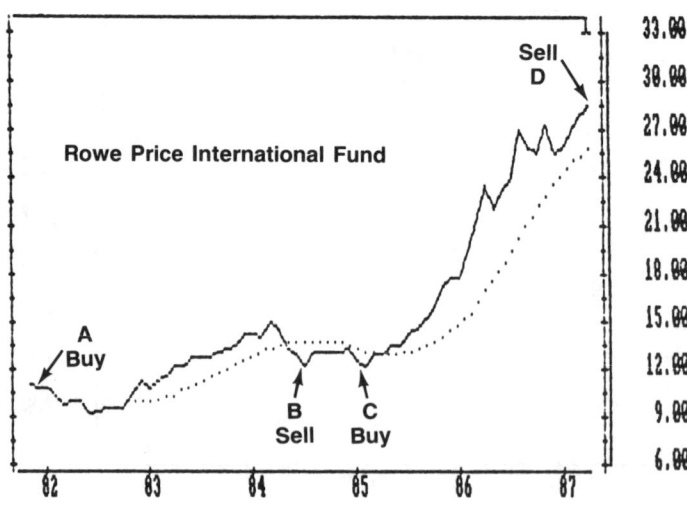

Figure 28-8: Lexington Gold Fund

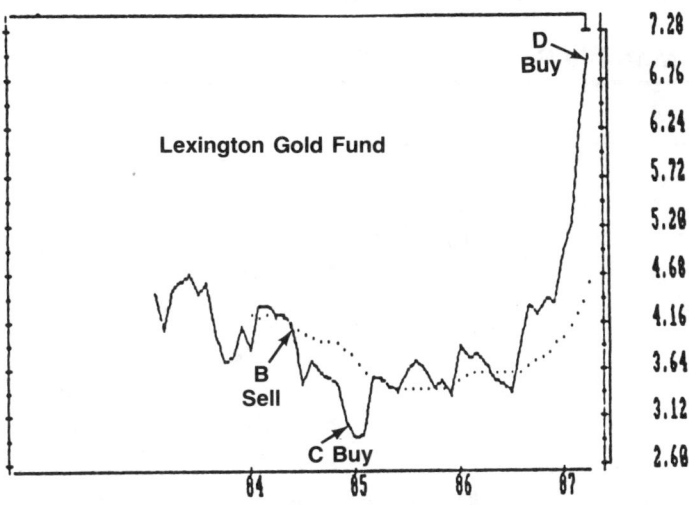

The Swiss Franc

Because of the similarities between the use of the discount rate as an indicator and the use of currencies, we will discuss the Swiss franc while the relationships mentioned earlier are fresh in your mind.

We chose the Swiss franc for this study simply because it is representative of the major foreign currencies. We could just as easily use the Deutschemark or the Japanese yen, as all of these currencies trend together for the most part. We would not use the British pound or the Canadian dollar, however, as they are totally different in their patterns.

Due to the relationship between interest rates in the U.S. and the value of the dollar, as mentioned above, we will see a distinctly similar pattern in the use of the Swiss franc and the discount rate for making switch decisions. However, we will see that the Swiss franc is not as reliable an indicator, since it will let more of our profits dwindle away before giving a signal.

This is because, while we know of interest rate changes in direction immediately, we must wait for a trend line to be broken in the currencies before being confident enough of a turn to call for a switch. A brief look at the graph of the Swiss franc will make this clear (Figure 28-9). We can see that the trend in fact changed direction only once during the lifetime of many of the funds we follow, and that occurred in February 1985 (marked as point A).

But we had seen brief upturns in the value of the franc before, several of them quite significant, yet the downtrend remained intact. Therefore, we were not sure enough of a change in direction until the downtrend line was broken to the upside, and that didn't occur until July, 1985, as indicated at point B. Thus, we missed out on some of the value of the indicator, as we will see in detail below.

Figure 28-9: Monthly Swiss Franc Graph

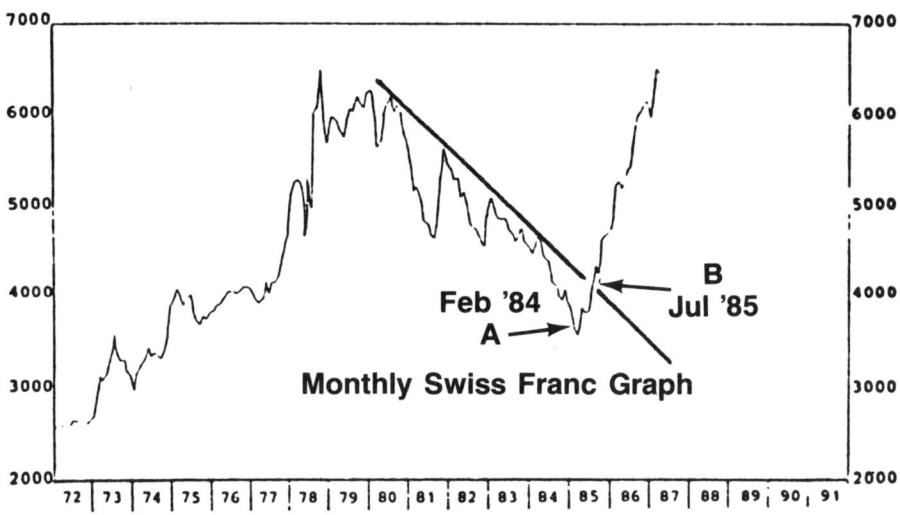

A cursory glance at graphs for growth and income funds will suffice to demonstrate that the currency trend is nearly useless in these funds (Figures 28-10 and 28-11).

However, as we could have anticipated from all of the discussion above, the indicator works very well indeed in signaling changes in the precious metals and international funds. Although the discount rate indicator did a better job of finding the best buy points in these funds as well, the currency play would have produced a handsome profit.

London P.M. Gold Fixing

Each morning and each afternoon, a group of gold dealers gets together in a room in London. They bid on gold as a group, and the resulting price at which the trades take place determines what is called "the London fixing." There is a morning fixing and an afternoon fixing, and nearly everyone interested in gold keeps an eye on the afternoon fixing as a harbinger of the direction of gold. In the trade, it is called the "PM fix." (See Figures 28-12 and 28-13.)

We have presented a graph of the PM fix, on which we have again drawn the trend lines and points at which the trends have been broken, thus indicating a change in direction (Figure 28-14).

As with the Swiss franc, we will find that the PM fix is a very poor indicator for use in determining changes in trend in the growth and income funds. While it would have ap-

Chapter 28

peared to work somewhat over the short term shown in these graphs, it would also have caused you to miss out on a significant part of the uptrend in these funds. (See Figures 28-15 and 28-16.)

Figure 28-10: Puritan Fund

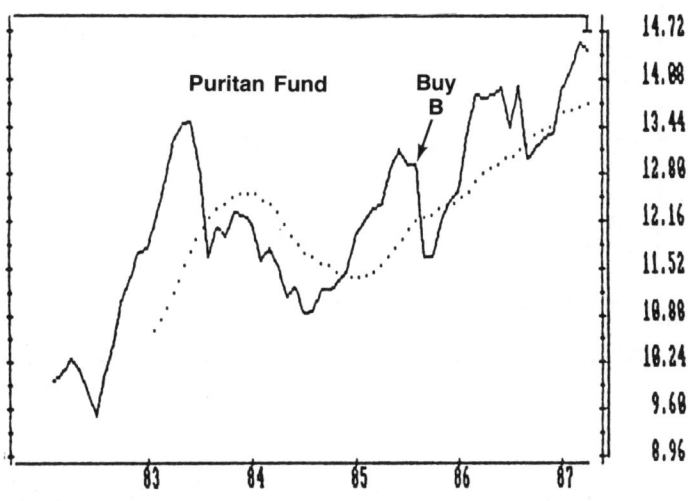

Figure 28-11: Fidelity High Income Fund

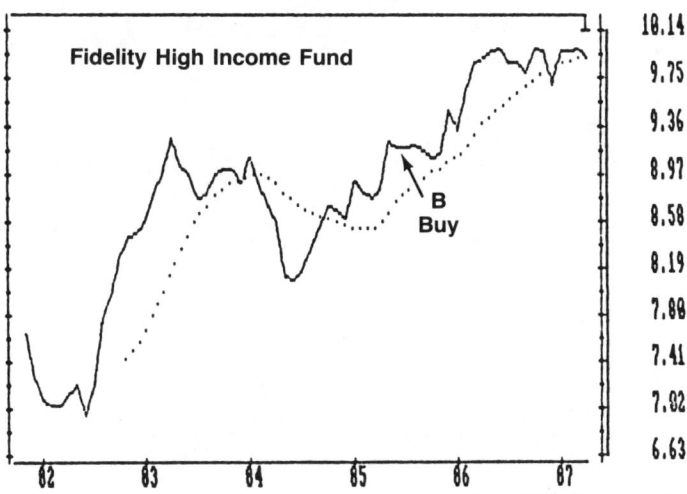

348 Chapter 28

Figure 28-12: Keystone International

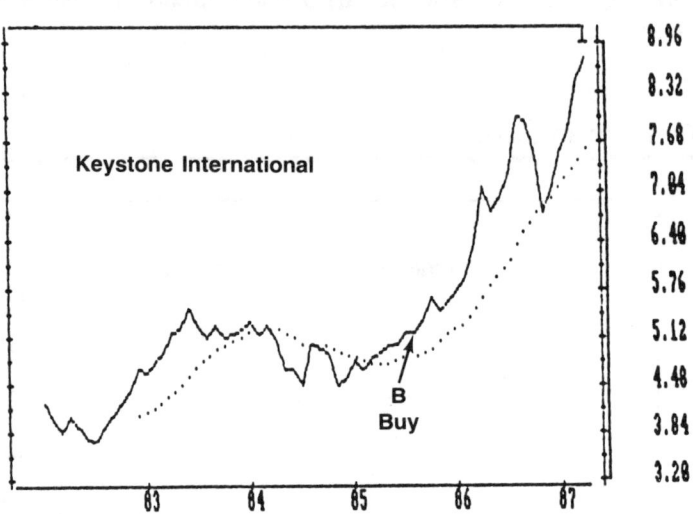

Figure 28-13: Lexington Gold Fund

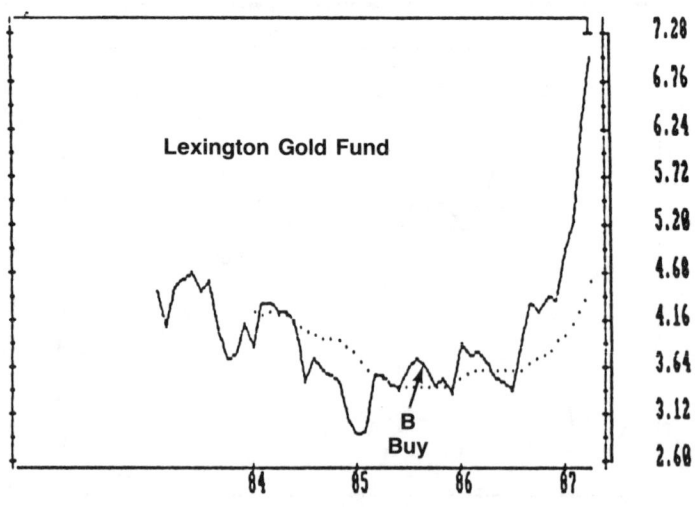

Chapter 28   349

Figure 28-14: Monthly Gold Graph

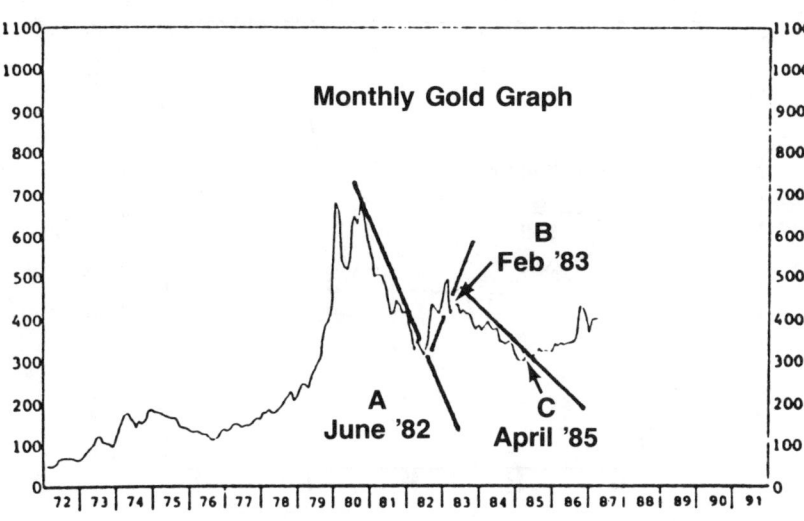

Figure 28-15: Manhattan Fund

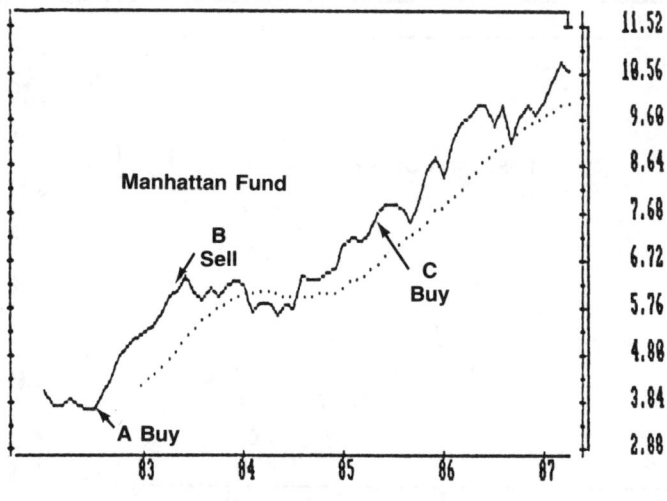

Figure 28-16: Fidelity High Yield Fund

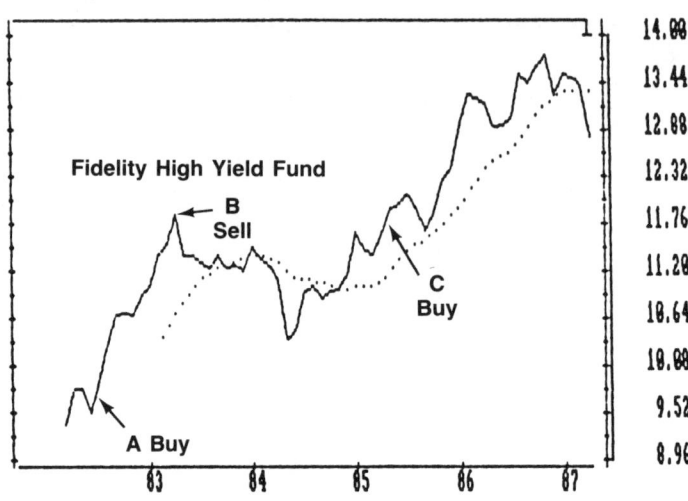

When it comes to the precious metals and international funds, however, it is a different matter. The PM fix indicator caught the uptrend beginning in January 1985, giving a trend change in April and yielding a healthy percentage of the potential profit of the trend. (See Figure 28-17.)

Figure 28-17: Lexington Gold Fund

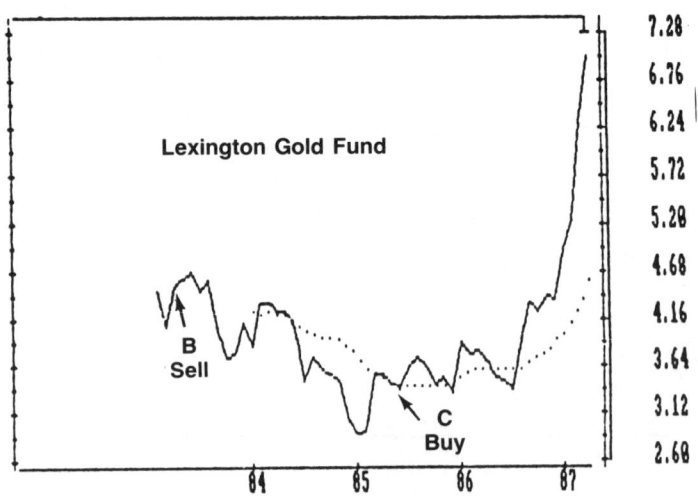

Interestingly, the PM fix also provides an excellent indicator for the international funds. Following this indicator alone would have resulted in a gain of nearly 140 percent in the Rowe Price International fund and nearly 110 percent in the Keystone International fund over the five-year period. (See Figure 28-18.)

Figure 28-18: Keystone International

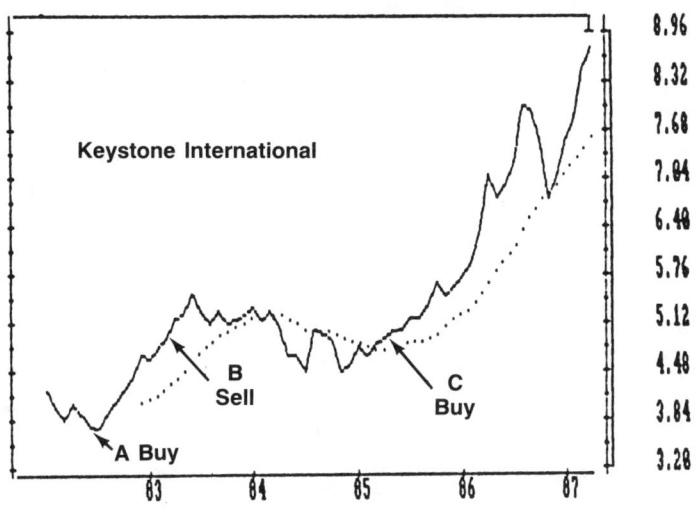

Dow Jones Industrial Average

Lastly, we will take a look at the DJIA as an indicator for switching mutual funds. The DJIA is a composite of the prices of thirty selected industrial stocks traded on the New York Stock Exchange. Although the mix of stocks is occasionally changed to reflect changes in the investment world, the indicator has remained a fairly good one over the years. (See Figure 28-19.)

We would expect that the DJIA would be a good indicator for growth funds, as indeed it is. The graphs of just a couple of the growth funds will suffice to make the point. (See Figures 28-20 through 28-24.)

The surprising thing is that the DJIA seems to afford a reliable indicator for the income funds and the international funds as well.

The DJIA appears almost useless as an indicator for the precious metals funds, even though these funds are largely made up of domestic stocks. This is probably because gold is an anxiety hedge, and when investors are nervous about the stock market in general they will tend to move into something solid like gold. This results in the gold mining shares running contrary to the general market.

Figure 28-19: Monthly DJIA Graph

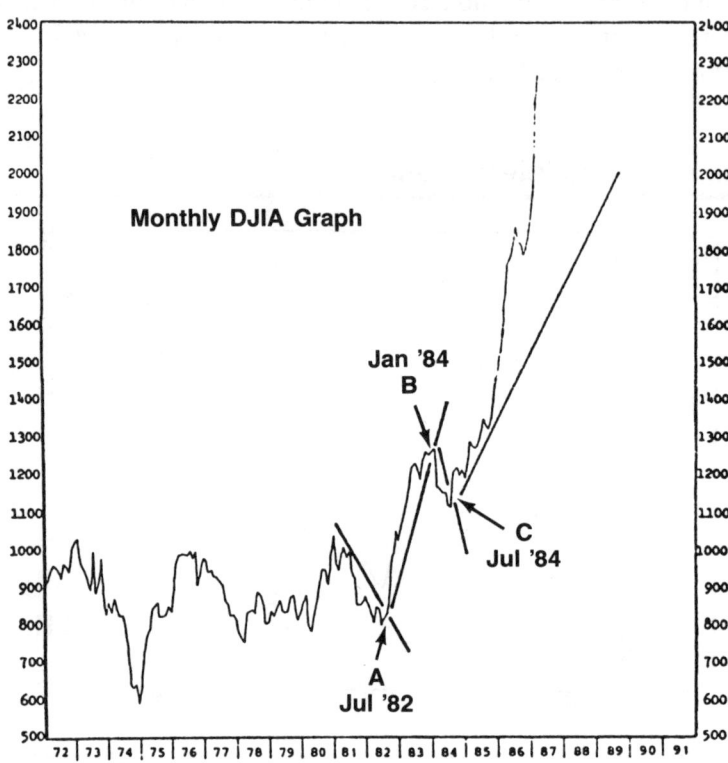

Figure 28-20: Puritan Fund

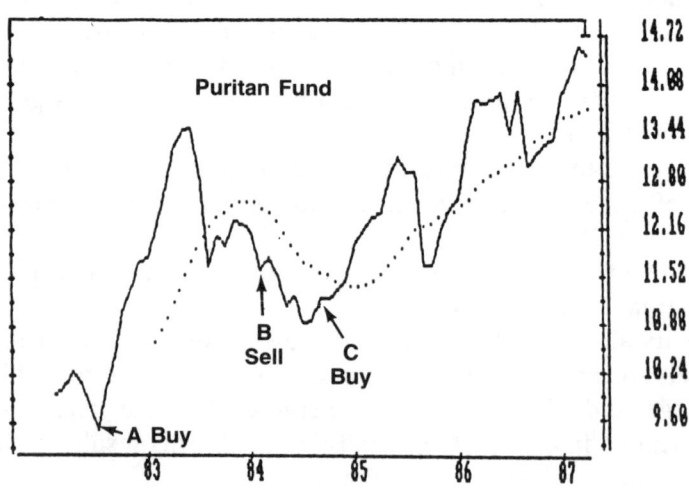

Chapter 28

Figure 28-21: Manhattan Fund

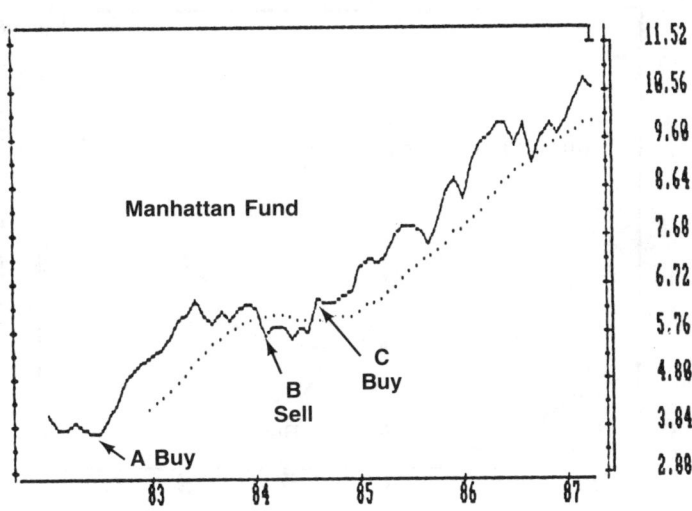

Figure 28-22: Fidelity High Yield Fund

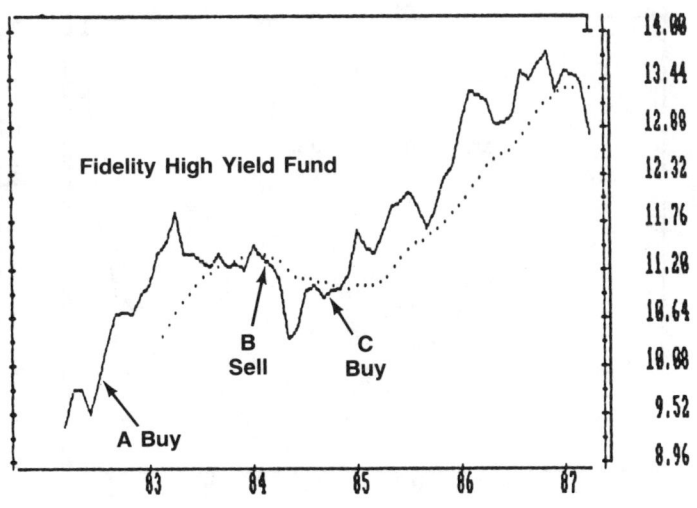

Figure 28-23: Rowe Price International Fund

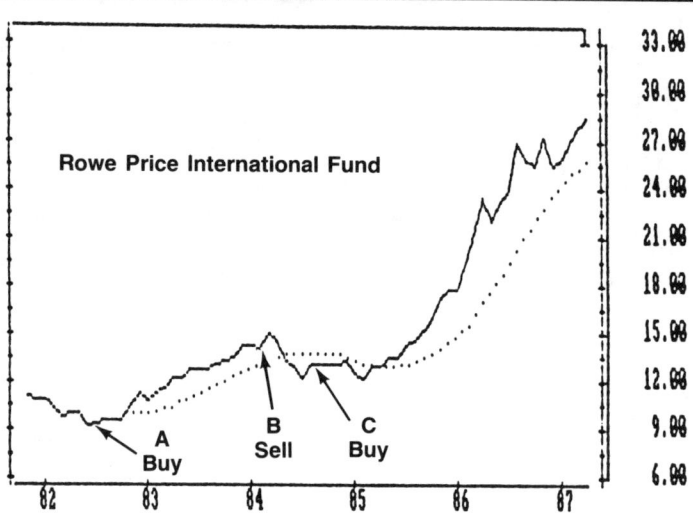

Figure 28-24: Lexington Gold Fund

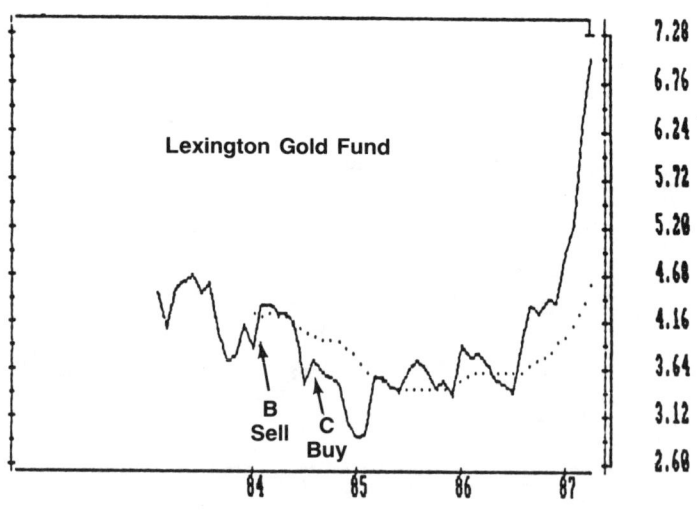

SELECTING A SYSTEM

Any one of the indicators examined above could be used exclusively as your only means of entering or leaving the various markets. If an investor chose to take that approach, of course, he would be faced with the choice of which funds to invest in, since his indicator would simply tell him to buy or sell—not which funds to buy or sell. Even so, if an investor were to simply split his investment funds evenly across four mutual funds (one of each of the types we've been discussing) and buy and sell according to his chosen indicator, he wouldn't do all that badly. Using this technique, our calculations show that the relative effectiveness of the four techniques discussed above would be:

Indicator used	Percentage of Available profit actually earned
Discount rate	87%
Swiss franc exchange rate	62%
London PM fixing	86%
DJIA	85%

This example assumes that the investor places an equivalent amount of money in all four areas—precious metals, growth, income and international funds. It can easily be demonstrated that following a combination of indicators, and stressing one sector over another depending on those indicators, will improve overall profit greatly. It will also result in your investment always being at work, rather than having periods of inactivity as would result from the use of an individual indicator only.

Chapter 29

Sector Funds Investing on Margin through a Broker

by Cato Ohrn, Sector Funds Newsletter

An investor is now in a position to benefit from three new developments in mutual fund investing. You may now trade no- and low-load sector funds through a discount broker in a margin or cash account. This particular combination was just not possible prior to 1984. To realize how recent this investment approach is, consider the following:

1. Only since 1980 has it been possible to "order out" your mutual fund certificates and borrow up to 50 percent against them through your broker, that is, "go on margin."
2. Prior to 1981, sector funds were not specifically marketed as such, although there were a few gold funds, bond funds, etc. It was only after Fidelity started its first four Select portfolios that the sector fund concept really caught the public's fancy.
3. Only since 1984 have you been able to buy no-load funds through any broker. This task was assumed by some discount brokers as soon as it became lawful. Full-service brokers have long marketed load funds, and are not interested in selling no-loads, for obvious reasons.

The *Sector Funds Newsletter* was started in 1985 to advocate this powerful new investment approach. The strategy is still relatively unknown.

Some analysts say that sector funds are too speculative, to which my answer is, "Compared to what?" Compared to balanced mutual funds, the answer is definitely yes. However, I maintain that sector funds are not nearly as speculative as common stocks.

THE ADVANTAGES OF SECTOR FUNDS

Sector funds provide extensive diversification within an industry. The legendary trader Jesse Livermore may have been the first to proclaim his preference for sector trading when he said, "First I identify the strongest industries, then I pick my stocks from those industries."

Academic studies have shown that when a stock advances, 20 percent of the gain is accounted for by the general market, 60 percent is due to industry strength, and only 20 percent is caused by the stock itself I happen to believe that a great many investors are spending 95 percent of their time trying to capture the 20 percent to be gotten from the stock.

There are thousands of stocks to choose from, but there are only a few dozen industries. If you identify the sectors that have the highest relative strength, I believe you can safely leave the job of picking the strongest stocks to the sector fund managers. Most of them are awfully good at it, and they spend all their time doing what you cannot possibly do yourself.

The sector concept can be based on geography, interest rate direction, currency trends, industry groups, inflation-deflation, megatrends (e.g., service vs. manufacturing), and so on. Space does not allow for an extensive discussion here, but it becomes evident that some sectors will advance when others go down, even in a declining market. This is because some of the sectors' trends will be in direct conflict with others. For example, during inflationary periods, gold funds will go up, bond funds down; if the price of oil goes up, energy funds will advance, but air transports will decline, and so on.

THE ADVANTAGES OF TRADING THROUGH A DISCOUNT BROKER

The numerous advantages of trading through a discount broker may be listed under a few broad categories:

Saving Legwork

You don't have to run to a bank for a signature guarantee or stand in line at the post office to mail "receipt requested."

Saving Time When Switching

Instead of waiting 3 to 4 weeks for a check from one fund to clear so you can buy another fund, using a broker enables you to switch the same day.

No "Fund Family" Restrictions

Don't break into jail. You want to be able to go with the strongest funds, wherever they are. Doing all your trading within one fund family made a lot of sense prior to the S.E.C. ruling that allows discount brokers to sell no-load funds. But not anymore. Fidelity may have the best overseas fund, but Financial may have the strongest technology sector fund, and Vanguard is still the only one to offer a "service" sector.

Simplified Bookkeeping

This is self-explanatory, but more important than most investors realize at first.

The Ability to Hedge Your Portfolio

Occasions may arise when you may want to hedge. Most funds have a rule in the prospectus enabling them to suspend cash redemptions. If there is a free-fall market, trading in individual stocks may be halted, and the funds can't get out, which means that they don't have the cash for redemptions. They may then be forced to pay you "in kind," meaning send you your equity in stocks from their portfolio. If this should happen, you may want to hedge instead, by shorting a closed-end fund, by puts, or some similar procedure. For this, you need a broker.

Leverage

Using a discount broker makes it possible to buy funds "on margin," which means that you can borrow up to 50 percent of the value of your funds from the broker. But leverage is a two-edged sword and should be used only in strong up markets. I prefer to use the NYSE Advance-Decline line to determine when to be on margin.

TIME SECTORS

It has helped me in the past to expand the sector concept to include time sectors. What I am referring to is not so much the rotating strength amongst the various industries during a business cycle, because that type of growth will show up in the individual industry sectors. What I have in mind is the fact that a bull market can be divided into three stages.

The first stage is characterized by high relative strength in the blue chips, the very large, well-known companies that are found in the Dow averages and the Standard & Poor 500 index.

Investor interest gradually shifts from these blue chips to so-called junior growth stocks, which are medium-sized, well-managed firms with good earnings and sales growth.

The third and final stage of a bull market is when the public finally joins in, and speculation is rampant. During this stage, everything goes up, but lower-priced "cats and dogs" advance faster than the rest of the market and so do new issues.

There are funds that fit the different stages of the market, from index funds, those that clone a market average, all the way to aggressive growth and new issues funds; there are even "venture capital" funds.

THE NEED FOR A STRATEGY

Money management is without doubt the most important ingredient in investment success. It isn't that most investors don't have a plan—they do, but when push comes to shove, they don't follow it.

In my newsletter, I use two entirely different indicators for buying and selling. For buying, I use relative strength comparisons. For selling, I use two simple moving average lines crossovers. There are specific reasons for this approach. When I buy a fund, I want to buy the one with the highest relative strength, because history shows that a trend, once established, has a tendency to continue much further than anyone expects. I do *not* want to buy laggards, in hopes that they will catch up.

Relative strength comparisons are no good for sell signals, however. This is simply because you can outperform the S&P 500 and still lose your shirt, if the market is bad enough. This is why I use the moving average lines crossovers for selling.

This technique works much like a stop-loss system. Moving averages are done easily on a computer, and when it comes to picking the *periods for* the two moving averages, you should let your pain threshold guide you. You can tailor-make the system so as to get out when your fund is 5, 8, 10, or whatever percentage from the most recent high. I have found the 20/65-day combination helpful in most sector funds. Many analysts use longer periods—up to 40 weeks. I am not that brave, since I believe any decline can turn into another 1929.

SOME CHART ILLUSTRATIONS

The following charts illustrate the steps to be taken in order to implement a plan of using relative strength and moving-average crossovers. There are other methods equally good, or better; this just happens to be the one I prefer, for the following reasons:

1. Safety, or preservation of capital, is the most important part of money management. Regardless of what the general market is doing, there has to be a method for cutting the losses in *each one of your funds*. The moving-average crossovers will do that—they work like a stop-loss order, based on the fact that taking a small loss, say 8 percent, prevents this loss from turning into a big one. This is important, because taking a loss is contrary to human nature.

2. As long as there is a plan for getting out whenever a position goes against you, such as that described in item 1, an investor can be more aggressive in the selection of funds. So I prefer to buy the funds with the highest relative strength, regardless of their historical performance in down markets. A high beta does not have to scare you when you have preselected a moving average combination for selling that fits your personal threshold for pain.

3. For anyone to stick to a plan for any length of time, it must be simple. The method described here is actually quite simple, being based on technical factors. In other words,

my belief is that everything that is known about an investment such as a mutual fund is reflected in the price, and "the trend is your friend."

Here, then, is the sequence of steps I take before buying or selling a fund.

1. Before an *initial* purchase, the general market must be in an uptrend. This means that the Dow Jones Industrials show the simple moving average (SMA) lines to be in a "buy mode," with the shorter-term SMA positioned above the longer-term SMA. The SMA crossover combination used here is the 20 day/65 day (see Figure 29-1), but the optimum (most profitable) combination is continuously tested to fit the market.

Figure 29-1: Dow Jones Industrials

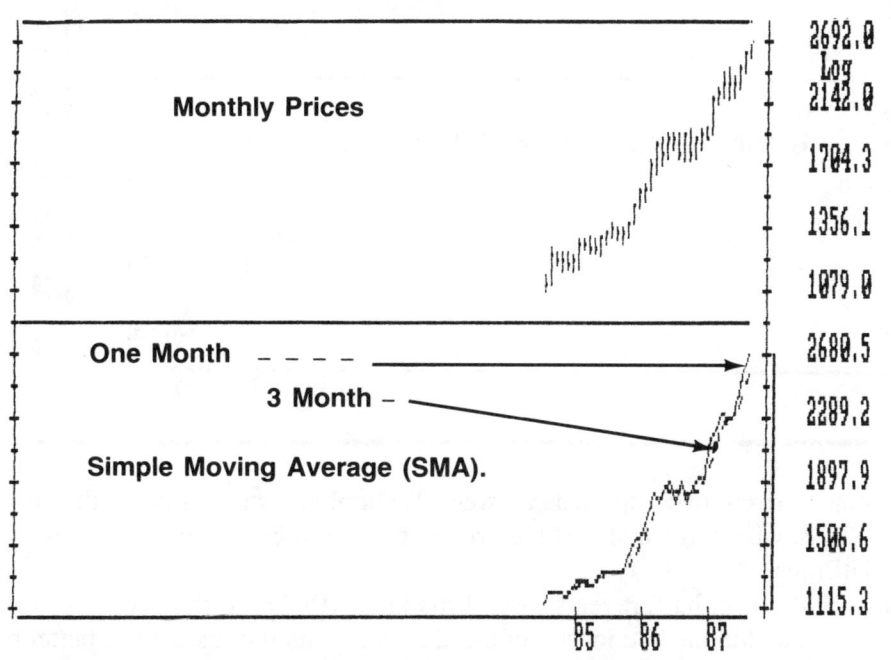

2. Once the general market is in a "buy mode," we are interested in finding the funds with the highest relative strength. Simple scanning of the charts will identify the top 20–30, each of which is then compared with the S&P 500 on a relative strength basis. Only the funds that are outperforming the S&P 500 are considered any further. Figure 29-2 shows Fidelity Select Technology: monthly prices (upper half) and a relative strength comparison with the S&P 500 (lower half). The latter has a declining tops line (dotted line A–B), which was broken to the upside at the arrow. This is the point at which this

fund started outperforming the general market. Does that mean a buy signal? Not yet. First, we want to compare Technology with other funds that are also outperforming the S&P 500. Two comparisons are shown: Fidelity Select Utilities and 20th Century Vista.

Figure 29-2: Fidelity Select Technology

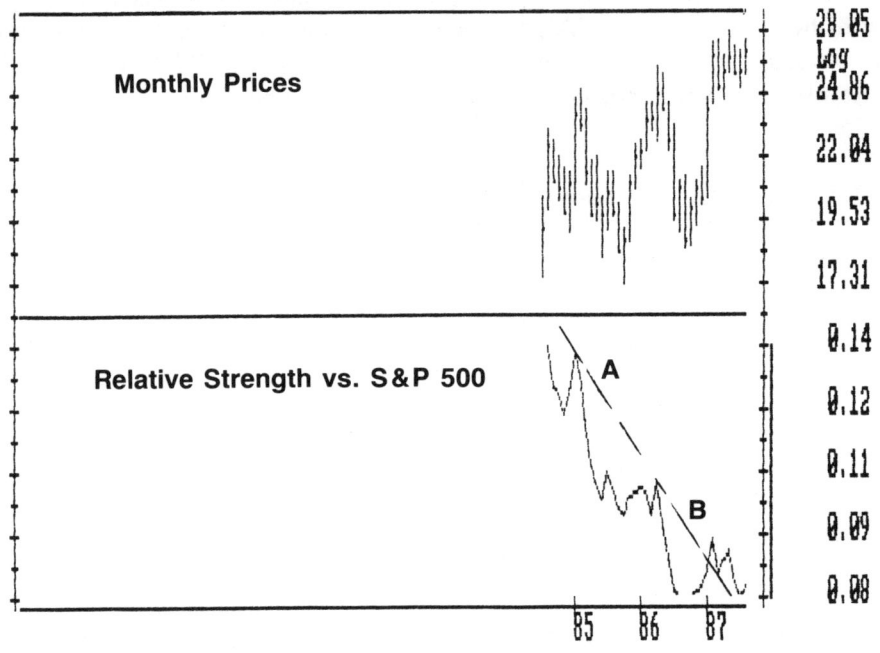

3. The relative strength comparison between Technology and Utilities is the bottom half of Figure 29-3, which again shows the arrow at which point Technology started to outperform Utilities.

4. Figure 29-4, lower half, reveals a trend channel, ABCD (dotted lines). As long as the solid line stays within the boundaries of the channel, Vista is considered a better buy than Technology.

This process of comparing relative strengths of all our buy candidates, two at a time, is continued until we end up with the strongest 6 or 8 funds (out of 1800).

5. The final decision to make in a buy program is whether or not to be on margin. I feel the extra risk of margin is warranted only when the Advance-Decline line on the New York Stock Exchange is in an uptrend. This can be found in *Investor's Daily* every day on page 8. The only way I know to interpret the trend of this indicator is old-fashioned chart reading, using trendlines as defined by ascending tops and bottoms, double and triple tops and bottoms, head-and-shoulders, flags, and all the other patterns.

Chapter 29   363

Figure 29-3: Fidelity Select Technology

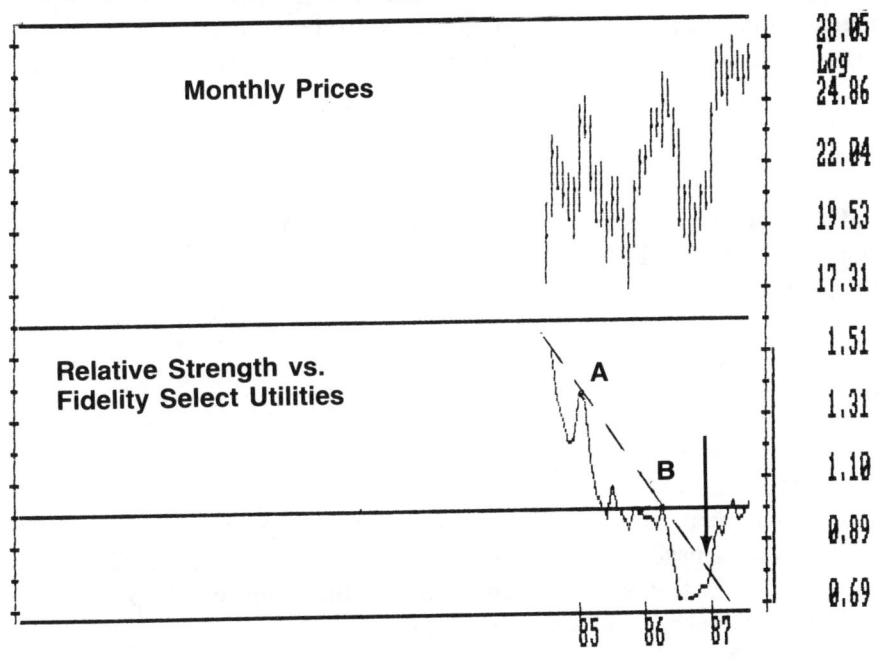

Figure 29-4: 20th Century Vista

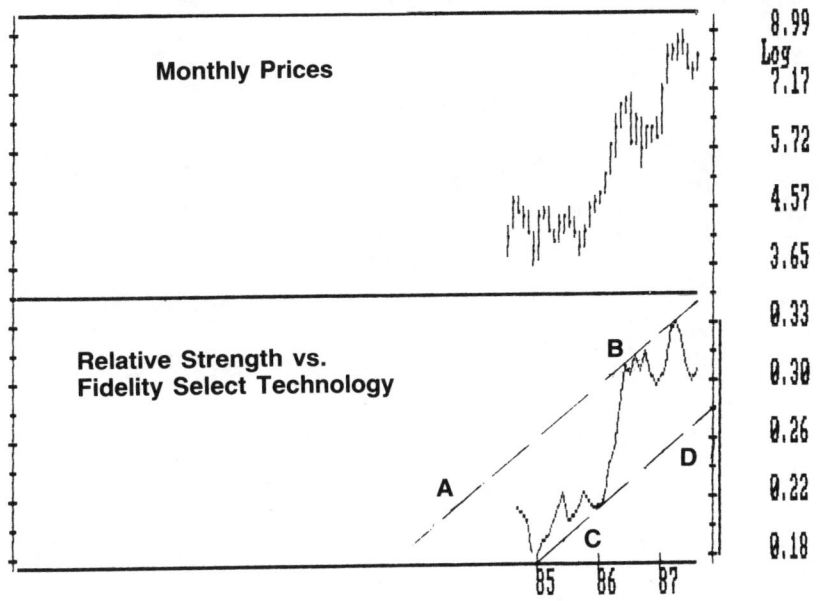

Whenever the Advance-Decline line turns down, the margin debt is paid off by selling a proportionate share of each fund in the portfolio. From then on, I am 100-percent invested, because some sector funds can go up in a general market decline. Each fund is on its own, so to speak, and is sold only if and when the SMA lines cross to the downside.

SELL SIGNALS

After a fund is in the portfolio, profitability studies by computer determine the optimum SMA combination (may be different for different funds). A downside SMA crossover is used for a sell signal.

CONCLUSION

Like most directions, this plan may seem complicated at first glance. Considering the number of trades the average investor does per month, however, very little time is required. Access to a computer is mandatory, and there are many software packages that offer the indicators discussed above. I believe it has been documented that most people spend more time in selecting a car than they do selecting a retirement program or an investment strategy. It does not have to be that way.

CHAPTER 30
Building an All-Weather Portfolio
by Gerald Perritt, Mutual Fund Letter

It's no secret that varying economic scenarios affect alternative investments differently. Gold, precious metals and real estate perform best in an inflationary environment, while bonds perform poorly. During periods of deflation, gold and real estate investors suffer while bondholders reap abnormally high real returns. Falling interest rates and an economic rebound generally mean sharply higher stock prices. A falling dollar, coupled with a large trade deficit, favors international investments over domestic investments. While investors should position their overall portfolios to take advantage of the best-performing assets, optimal asset allocation requires that investors anticipate changes in economic trends and take appropriate action before such trends are well underway. This, of course, is much easier said than done.

As an alternative to forecasting varying economic trends, some investors prefer to layer their portfolios with investments in each asset class. Thus, over varying economic cycles, the losses suffered by those assets declining in value are offset by gains in those assets increasing in value. Furthermore, since investment returns from varying classes of assets tend to move in opposite directions at times, individuals who invest "across the board" obtain additional risk reduction due to the low correlation of investment returns among the classes of assets.

Table 30-1 illustrates the total annual investment returns for five classes of assets (U.S. stocks, foreign stocks, U.S. government bonds, real estate, and gold bullion) over the period 1968–84. In addition, the figure contains the investment returns for a portfolio consisting of equal investments made in each of the five classes. Investors in gold bullion reaped the greatest rewards over this period (a compound total return of 776 percent). However, they also experienced the greatest variability of investment return (annual returns ranged from 91.7 percent to -32.2 percent, or a spread of 123.9 percent). Bonds were the poorest-performing asset (157 percent total compound return). However, bond returns were one of the least variable. Although real estate appears to provide the least variable returns (the difference between the best and worst years is only 13.5 percent), these returns assume all equity investment. Generally, real estate investments are leveraged (e.g., put up $20 and borrow $80 to make a $100 investment). Thus, investing in real estate using borrowed funds makes investment returns much more variable (risky).

For example, if investors financed projects with 80 percent debt at an interest rate of 12 percent, the worst year's return (1981) falls from 5.4 percent to -21 percent while the best year's return (1979) climbs from 18.9 percent to 46.5 percent. (i.e., the difference in returns between the best and worst years increases from 13.5 percent for unleveraged projects to 67.5 percent for leveraged projects).

Note that the portfolio consisting of all five assets provides the greatest return per unit of variability (after assuming that the investment in real estate used borrowed funds). The portfolio's value climbed 450 percent during this 17-year period, yet its maximum annual loss amounted to only 6.4 percent. Thus, this all-weather portfolio appears to give investors the best of two worlds: a high rate of return and modest investment risk.

Of course, the return data contained in Table 30-1 are hypothetical. These are not actual portfolio returns but rather arithmetic returns calculated by taking the beginning and ending values of various indices. To put the theory to the test of practicality, we arbitrarily selected one asset (a mutual fund when possible) which invests in each specific asset class. We then tracked the returns for a portfolio consisting of equal dollar investments maintained in each of the specific assets (i.e., 20 percent of the portfolio allocated to each asset). The specific funds from each class were randomly selected and, thus, do not necessarily represent the best-performing fund in that class. Our goal here was to examine the behavior of the actual returns which could have been earned by an investor and not to illustrate the best possible outcome. Also, we made an equal allocation of investment dollars to each asset since we did not want to bias the results by benefiting from hindsight.

United Services Gold Shares Fund produced the greatest investment return over this 10-1/2 year period (see Table 30-2). However, it also contained the greatest amount of investment risk (the range of returns equaled 212 percent). On the other hand, the portfolio of all five assets again performed quite well. It returned a total of 594 percent, yet had only one losing year (a -5.8 percent return during 1981).

While an all-weather portfolio may not produce the greatest investment returns, it usually provides the greatest returns per unit of investment risk. Thus, for those investors who cannot or do not wish to bounce from one investment to another or for those who wish to reduce total investment risk, the all-weather portfolio approach offers a suitable alternative. Furthermore, due to their wide degree of diversification, mutual funds appear to be the ideal vehicle for investment in each asset class. Once an investor establishes an all-weather portfolio, he then needs only to monitor the funds in each asset class and select those which promise the best future investment return regardless of economic scenario.

Table 30-1: Total Investment Returns from Various Investment Alternatives

Year	S&P 500	Foreign Stocks	U.S. Gov't Bonds	Real Estate	Gold Bullion	Equally Weighted Portfolio
1968	11.1%	32.8%	−0.3%	8.6%	12.3%	3.2%
1969	−8.5	6.4	−5.1	9.7	5.6	1.6
1970	4.0	−7.4	12.1	11.1	−12.3	1.5
1971	14.3	27.4	13.2	9.7	13.2	15.5
1972	19.0	40.9	5.7	9.2	42.2	23.4
1973	−14.7	−14.1	−1.1	11.9	66.9	9.8
1974	−26.5	−24.0	4.4	14.0	63.3	6.2
1975	37.2	37.5	9.2	13.3	1.1	19.7
1976	23.8	6.0	16.8	9.9	−22.4	6.8
1977	−7.2	15.7	−0.7	11.1	18.4	7.5
1978	6.6	34.3	−1.2	15.0	30.6	17.1
1979	18.4	12.9	−1.2	18.9	58.8	21.6
1980	32.4	25.1	−4.0	14.1	91.7	31.9
1981	−4.9	−2.1	1.8	5.4	−32.2	−6.4
1982	21.4	−0.6	40.3	8.9	13.9	16.8
1983	22.5	25.1	0.7	7.1	−16.5	8.0
1984	6.3	5.3	15.4	8.5	−19.2	2.4
Total	225%	526%	157%	481%	776%	450%
Best	37.2%	40.9%	40.3%	18.9%	91.7%	31.9%
Worst	−26.5	−24.0	−5.1	5.4	−32.2	−6.4
Range	63.7	64.9	45.4	13.5	123.9	38.3

Table 30-2: The All-Weather Portfolio: Putting the Theory to the Test

Year	Fund for U.S. Gov't Sec.	Vanguard Index Trust	United Services Gold Shares	Scudder Int'l	Property Cap(REIT)	Portfolio
1977	1.8%	−7.8%	51.8%	−0.5%	10.0%	10.9%
1978	1.6	5.9	2.2	21.3	1.7	6.5
1979	0.1	18.1	182.4	19.2	57.6	55.5
1980	−2.3	31.9	80.1	26.9	85.0	44.3
1981	−0.5	−5.3	27.7	−2.7	7.2	−5.8
1982	40.2	21.0	70.5	0.8	34.1	33.2
1983	11.1	21.4	1.0	29.8	9.1	14.5
1984	12.8	5.7	−29.8	−0.7	19.0	1.4
1985	16.7	31.1	−27.0	48.9	12.4	17.8
1986	8.6	18.6	37.5	50.5	27.9	28.6
1987	2.4	25.3	42.3	18.4	5.5	18.8
Total	129%	342%	884%	511%	821%	594%
Best	40.2%	31.9%	182.4%	50.5%	85.0%	55.5%
Worst	−2.3	−7.8	−29.8	−2.7	1.7	−5.8
Range	42.5	39.7	212.2	53.2	83.3	61.3

Glossary

Aggressive growth fund. A mutual fund that seeks maximum capital appreciation through the use of investment techniques involving greater than ordinary risk, such as investing borrowed money to provide leverage, short selling, hedging, and trading options and warrants.

Alpha rating. A measure of management efficiency that is a numerical statement of the difference between a fund's actual performance and its expected performance, given its volatility (beta).

Assets. The marketable securities, cash, and cash equivalents of a fund.

Balanced fund. A conservative fund that invests in bonds, preferred stocks, and common stocks in such proportions that risks in one or more areas are offset by stability and rewards in others.

Beta. A coefficient that measures a fund's volatility relative to the volatility of the total market. Market volatility is usually represented by the volatility of the S&P 500, which has a beta coefficient of 1.00. High beta funds typically have price fluctuations greater than low beta funds, and are riskier.

Bond fund. A mutual fund that invests in medium- to high-grade corporate bonds, convertible bonds, or combinations of bonds and preferred stocks. Its main investment objective is security of principal with as much income as possible.

Common stock fund. A mutual fund whose portfolio consists primarily of common stocks. Such a company may at times take defensive positions in cash, bonds, and other senior securities.

Convertible security. A bond or stock that may be exchanged for another issue, generally one of the same company.

Current yield. The payments to investors expressed as a percentage of current asset price. The payments usually are in the form of dividend or interest distribution.

Diversification. The method of spreading investments among many different securities to reduce certain risks inherent in investing.

Equity-income fund. A mutual fund which normally has 60 percent or more of its assets in equities (common stocks) and seeks an above-average yield.

Expense ratio. The proportion of a mutual fund's annual expenses to its average net assets for the year.

Gold fund. A mutual fund that invests primarily in shares of gold stocks.

Government National Mortgage Association (GNMA). A wholly government-owned corporation that facilitates the financing of certain types of mortgages that are, for all practical purposes, as safe as Treasury bonds.

Growth and income fund. A mutual fund that seeks both capital growth and current income. The assets of these funds may be balanced between equity and fixed-income securities or may consist of common stocks with high dividend yields.

Growth fund. A mutual fund for which the primary investment objective is long-term appreciation of invested capital. It invests principally in common stocks with growth potential.

High-yield bond fund. A fund that seeks high yield by investing in bonds that are rated below investment grade.

Income fund. A mutual fund for which the primary objective is current income rather than growth of capital. Investments usually are in bonds and stocks that pay high levels of interest and dividends.

Index fund. A mutual fund with an investment objective to match the investment performance of a large group of publicly traded common stocks, such as those represented by the S&P 500 Composite Stock Price Index.

Investment objective. The financial management goal of an individual or mutual fund.

Load. Sales charge or commissions assessed by a mutual fund.

Market timing. The active shifting of assets into or out of a mutual fund to maximize investment returns.

Money-market fund. A mutual fund that invests in short-term "money-market" securities, such as certificates of deposit, short-term government securities, bankers' acceptances, and so forth.

Moving average. A statistical device to smooth out data series to reveal trends.

Municipal bond fund. A mutual fund that invests in a broad range of tax-exempt bonds issued by states, cities, and other local governments. Interest obtained from these bonds is passed through to shareowners free of federal tax.

Mutual fund. A professionally managed investment company that pools the common financial interests of many investors (shareholders). Shares generally are offered on a continuous basis, which the fund stands ready to buy back (redeem) from shareholders on demand at the then-current share price (per-share net asset value).

No-load fund. A mutual fund that offers its shares to investors at the net asset value, without deducting a sales charge.

Performance. A percentage statement of changes in a fund's value per share, calculated for specified periods of time by comparing current net asset value plus dividends and capital gains with a particular previous equivalent value per share (usually a calendar year-end value).

Portfolio turnover. A measure of a mutual fund's annual purchase and sale activity of the securities it holds in its portfolio. It is calculated by dividing the lesser of the fund's annual purchases or sales (exclusive of purchases or sales of securities with maturities of less than one year) by the monthly average value of the securities owned by the fund during the year.

Preferred stock. A security, representing ownership in a corporation's assets, that has priority over common stocks in receiving a specified dividend or a proportion of assets in case of the corporation's liquidation.

R-squared. Known statistically as the coefficient of determination, an indication of the fund's diversification. A fund with an R-squared of 85 is 85 percent as diversified as the S&P 500 index.

Redemption fee. The charge levied by some mutual funds when shares are redeemed.

Return. *See Total return.*

Risk. The possibility of loss of future income. The level of uncertainty or degree of volatility involved in an investment decision.

Sales charge. A fee, paid to the dealer and underwriter, that is added to the net asset value per share of a mutual fund when a share in the fund is purchased.

Sector fund. A nondiversified, open-ended fund whose appeal lies in its concentration of assets in a particular industry.

Securities. Stocks (common and preferred) and bonds.

Specialty fund. An investment company with its holdings in specific industry groups (e.g., insurance, oil, computer stocks).

Standard & Poor's 500 Composite Stock Price Index. The weighted average of 500 stocks: 400 industrial, 40 financial, 40 utility, and 20 transportation stocks.

Standard deviation. A measure of a fund's total risk, reflecting dispersion of variability in the fund's monthly return.

Technology fund. A mutual fund holding the common stock of companies involved with, or developing products that require, a high level of scientific research. Examples of such firms are drug, electronic, computer, aerospace, defense, and communication companies.

Total return. A measure of performance that includes reinvested capital gains distributions and dividend payments. It is used to express a fund's investment performance over a stated period of time and can be compared to the total returns provided by other investments.

Turnover. *See Portfolio turnover.*

12b-1 plan. A plan authorized by the S.E.C. allowing a percentage of a fund's total assets to be used to cover sales and marketing costs.

Volatility. A measure of variability and risk that results from changes in the market, made by a comparison of a particular fund's performance with that of the entire market, as represented by a market index (usually the S&P 500 beta coefficient).

Yield. A measure of income for a specified period expressed as a percentage of the current price of a security or mutual fund.

Appendix: Advisors and Sources Addresses

The Donoghue Organization, Inc. (William Donoghue)
Box 540
Holliston, MA 01746

Equity Fund Outlook
Box 1040
Boston, MA 02117

Fundgraf Advisory
1012 Sitka Court
Loveland, CO 80538

Growth Fund Guide
Box 6600
Rapid City, SD 57709

Paul A. Merriman & Assoc., Inc. (Paul Merriman)
1200 Westlake Ave. N., Ste. 507
Seattle, WA 98109

The Mutual Fund Advantage (John McKeever)
Box 4130
Medford, OR 97501

Mutual Fund Chartist
Box 6600
Rapid City, SD 57709

Mutual Fund Letter (Gerald Perritt)
205 W. Wacker Drive
Chicago, IL 60606

Green Communications (Reg Green)
598 Fairhills Dr.
San Rafael, CA 94901

No-Load Fund Investor, Inc. (Sheldon Jacobs)
Box 283
Hastings on Hudson, NY 10706

DAL Investment Company (Burt Berry)
235 Montgomery St.
San Francisco, CA 94104

Personal Investing (John Waggoner)
Box 832
Boston, MA 02103

Sector Funds Newsletter (Cato Ohrn)
Box 1210
Escondedo, CA 92025

Telescan
11011 Richmond Ave.
Houston, TX 77042

ABOUT THE AUTHOR

Dr. Richard C. Dorf is a professor in the Graduate School of Management at The University of California, Davis. Professor Dorf has been a university administrator, teacher and industry consultant. His fields of interest are financial analysis, venture capital, new business ventures and investment analysis. Professor Dorf is the author of several books and his articles appear in leading investment, finance and business journals. His book *The New Mutual Fund Portfolio Planner* was published by Probus in 1986.

Mutual Fund Advisors, Inc.
Box 1975
Davis, CA 95617

Dr. Richard C. Dorf, President

Mutual Fund Advisors, Inc., offers *The New Mutual Fund Advisor Newsletter* with a focus on no-load funds and lower risk, higher return growth and income funds. (Trial issue: $5.00; annual subscription: $45.00 for 10 issues.)

It also offers a mutual fund asset allocation and portfolio management advisory service. This services uses no-load funds to achieve capital appreciation with attention to capital preservation during periods of market turmoil.